Springer Series in Language and Communication 8
Editor: W. J. M. Levelt

Springer Series in Language and Communication
Editor: W. J. M. Levelt

Volume 1 **Developing Grammars**
By W. Klein and N. Dittmar

Volume 2 **The Child's Conception of Language** 2nd Printing
Editors: A. Sinclair, R. J. Jarvella, and W. J. M. Levelt

Volume 3 **The Logic of Language Development in Early Childhood**
By M. Miller

Volume 4 **Inferring from Language**
By L. G. M. Noordman

Volume 5 **Retrieval from Semantic Memory**
By W. Noordman-Vonk

Volume 6 **Semantics from Different Points of View**
Editors: R. Bäuerle, U. Egli, A. von Stechow

Volume 7 **Lectures on Language Performance**
By Ch. E. Osgood

Volume 8 **Speech Act Classification**
By Th. Ballmer and W. Brennenstuhl

Volume 9 **The Development of Metalinguistic Abilities in Children**
By D. T. Hakes

Volume 10 **Modelling Language Behaviour**
By R. Narasimhan

Th. Ballmer · W. Brennenstuhl

Speech Act Classification

A Study in the Lexical Analysis of
English Speech Activity Verbs

With 4 Figures

Springer-Verlag Berlin Heidelberg New York 1981

Dr. Thomas T Ballmer
Dr. Waltraud Brennenstuhl

Ruhr-Universität Bochum
Sprachwissenschaftliches Institut, Universitätsstraße 150
D-4630 Bochum 1, Fed. Rep. of Germany

Series Editor:

Professor Dr. Willem J. M. Levelt

Max-Planck-Institut für Psycholinguistik, Berg en Dalseweg 79
6522 BC Nijmegen, The Netherlands

ISBN 3-540-10294-9 Springer-Verlag Berlin Heidelberg New York
ISBN 0-387-10294-9 Springer-Verlag New York Heidelberg Berlin

Library of Congress Cataloging in Publication Data. Ballmer, Thomas T, Speech act classification. (Springer series in language and communication; v. 8) Bibliography: p. Includes index. 1. Speech acts (Linguistics). 2. Lexicology. 3. English language – Verb. 4. English language – Semantics. I. Brennenstuhl, Waltraud, joint author. II. Title. III. Series. P95.55.B34 425 80-23840

This work is subject to copyright. All rights are reserved, whether the whole or part of the material is concerned, specifically those of translation, reprinting, reuse of illustrations, broadcasting, reproduction by photocopying machine or similar means, and storage in data banks. Under § 54 of the German Copyright Law where copies are made for other than private use, a fee is payable to the publisher, the amount of the fee to be determined by agreement with the publisher.

© by Springer-Verlag Berlin Heidelberg 1981
Printed in Germany

The use of registered names, trademarks, etc. in this publication does not imply, even in the absence of a specific statement, that such names are exempt from the relevant protective laws and regulations and therefore free for general use.

Offset printing and bookbinding: Brühlsche Universitätsdruckerei, Giessen
2153/3130-543210

Preface

This book presents a new *classification of speech acts.* It is an *alternative* to all previously published classifications of speech acts. The classification proposed here is based on *an extensive set of data*, namely on all the verbs designating *linguistic activities* and *aspects* thereof. A theoretically and methodologically justifiable method is used to proceed in a number of steps from these data to the classification. The classification is documented in *a lexicon* with two sections. The *first section* exhibits the classification in all its details. Each verb is listed according to its meaning at the appropriate place in the classification. The *second*, alphabetically ordered *section* enables one to locate the verbs classified in the first part.

The *speech act classification* as presented in this book has a number of consequences for linguistic theorizing: the book makes advances in three linguistically relevant fields — speech act theory, lexicology, and theory of meaning. In *speech act theory* firstly of course *a classification* is proposed which is theoretically justified and which is simultaneously based explicitly and systematically on linguistic data. Secondly, *a wider concept* of speech acts is introduced which proves its value by making possible a linguistically justified classification. Thirdly, the concept of *speech act sequence* (or more generally partial order) is brought into focus as a major organizational principle of the semantic relation between speech acts. Higher organizational units like models and model groups are found and put in relation to notions such as frames and scripts. In *lexicology, firstly* a synthesis between lexicology proper and lexicography is proposed and worked out in detail. *Secondly*, speech act classification is recognized as *a prototype analysis* which has a more general relevancy in relation to the lexical analysis of the entire verb thesaurus and even larger fragments of the lexical thesaurus. With respect to *a theory of meaning*, various *notions of meaning* are defined (heuristic meaning, explicatory meaning, justificatory meaning, theoretical meaning) which prove their validity with respect to *lexical analysis* and *speech act theory*. The *speech act classification* as presented in this book is to be seen in a larger *theoretical* context as well. It is considered to lay the foundations for a *sound theory* of *linguistic behavior* of human beings. The notions of meaning developed in this book go back in part to the view of the *Instrumental Character* of natural language which relies on the conception that linguistic expressions are instruments which aid the user *in changing the context* (affect the world) in a more or less *purposive* and *effective* manner. This view of *Instrumentalism* generalizes to what we call *Conceptual Behaviorism* which establishes a relation between *linguistic behavior* and some *more remote fields* like, for example, psychology and biology. On the level of *Instrumentalism* new light is shed on the relation between lexicon and grammar and likewise the relation between competence and performance. More traditional positions of logical language analysis are considered in this connection and compared to the *Logical Grammar* (Language Reconstruction Systems) of one of the authors.

The work on the German version began in 1972 when several students of linguistics gathered together in order to follow *Austin's* [1.1] program of investigating and classifying performative verbs. The members of the groups, the goals, and the ideas of the group changed several times until the group (Th. Ballmer, W. Brennenstuhl, K. Ehlich, J. Rehbein) was consolidated in the winter of 1974/1975 under the name of the Berlin Group and finished the classification of German speech acts in the summer of 1975 [1.10]. During their post-doctoral year at the University of California Berkeley (1975/1976) the authors (Th. Ballmer and W. Brennenstuhl) translated the German data into English and reworked and checked them with two students, J. Rosenberg and D. Clement. Afterwards the Authors generalized the methods of speech act classification to the entire German verb thesaurus, begun in 1976 and finished in 1978/1979, from which they gained a great deal of experience and theoretical insight which they could apply when they wrote the theoretical part of this book and when in that spirit they reorganized the speech act classification somewhat. In the meantime the German speech act classification *Sprachliches Handeln* underwent some revisons. We would have preferred to await the publication of the original German classification from which our English speech act classification derived, but feel now that we can no longer delay the publication of this book. The aims and the contents of the two books are in any case sufficiently different that neither of the two books will render the other superfluous. There are differences not only in language and classification, but also in focus, theoretical underpinning, elaborations of detail, and in the manner of presentation.

The authors would like to express their gratitude first and above all to Konrad Ehlich and Jochen Rehbein with whom they had the good fortune and the pleasure of developing the original German speech act classification. We owe a debt of gratitude also to Prof. Dr. H. Schnelle and to Prof. Dr. W.J.M. Levelt for their encouragement. Equally we would like to acknowledge the generous support from the Deutsche Forschungsgemeinschaft (DFG) and the Max Planck Gesellschaft (MPG) for the work leading to the present book. The authors have been very fortunate in having the assistance of the two English-speaking students J. Rosenberg and D. Clement from Berkeley and the student assistants J. Watson, S. Bramm, and K. Kuczera.

For discussion of various issues on speech act theory we would like to thank many colleagues and students, especially Ch. Fillmore, G. Grunst, G. Lakoff, W. Kummer, J.R. Searle, H. Singer, D. Vanderweken, I. Wegner, and D. Wunderlich.

In conclusion we would like to thank Mrs. Davidsohn for her efficient and careful typing of the manuscript.

Bochum, September 1980   Th. Ballmer
                                                                                  W. Brennenstuhl

Contents

Part I Classification

Chapter 1	Introduction	3
Chapter 2	Lexical Analysis: A New Approach	6
Chapter 3	Author's Motivation for a Speech Act Classification	13
Chapter 4	Description and Explanation of the Method	15
	4.1 Brief Statement of the Goal	15
	4.2 Selection of Verbs	15
	4.3 Formation of Categories	17
	4.4 Formation of Models	23
	4.5 The System of Models	30
Chapter 5	Survey of the Resulting Speech Act Classification	33
Chapter 6	Prospects and Limitations	39
	6.1 Relation to the Classification of the Entire Verb Thesaurus	39
	6.2 A General Theoretical Perspective	41
	6.3 Criticisms of Our Own Proposals	48
	6.4 Criticisms of Competing Proposals	53
	6.4.1 Remarks on Austin's Classification of Speech Acts	53
	6.4.2 Remarks on Searle's Classification of Speech Acts	55
	6.4.3 Remarks on the Notion of Meaning in Speech Act Theory	60
	6.5 Applications	61
Chapter 7	References	64
	Bibliography	67

Part II Lexicon Sections

        Directions for Using Lexicon Section I 70

Chapter 8 Lexicon Section I
        Semantic Classification of Speech Act Verbs 71

        8.1 EM Emotion Model 71
        8.2 EN Enaction Model 74
        8.3 KA Struggle Model 85
        8.4 NO Institutional Model 107
        8.5 W Valuation Models 118
        8.6 D Discourse Models 124
        8.7 X Text Models 134
        8.8 T Theme Models 155

        Directions for Using Lexicon Section II 168

Chapter 9 Lexicon Section II
        Alphabetic Index of Speech Act Verbs 169

Part I
Classification

Chapter 1 Introduction

The object of this book is to lay the foundations for a sound theory of linguistic behavior of human beings. In order to attain such a goal, the relevant aspects of linguistic behavior have to be taken into consideration. The criterion for what aspects of linguistic behavior are judged to be relevant is made dependent on the language itself and its speakers. In our case we have found that the lexicon of a language tells something about what is linguistically relevant for the speakers of that language: the verbs denoting speech acts, speech activities, or various aspects of linguistic behavior can be taken as an indication of what the speakers of a language regard as relevant in their linguistic behavior and many of its aspects. Starting from these verbs we would like to find out what the language tells us about the structure of linguistic behavior. How is this possible?

Our proposal is to start from the set of all those verbs which designate (aspects of) speech activities, list them, and categorize them according to a well-specified system which will be described below in sufficient detail. The basic idea guiding the categorization is to group verbs which are similar in meaning. The result will then be a structuring of a relevant part of the lexicon into semantical categories. These semantical categories reflect an ontological and a conceptual structuring of linguistic behavior in its various aspects.

The semantical verb categories we have found in this way tell us what semantical "junctions" are brought into focus by natural language. But they can tell us even more, because the semantical categories themselves can be grouped together in an additional step, according to their (semantical) similarity. By this procedure groups of categories result which we call models. Thus we arrive at a more complex hierarchical classification of speech act designating verbs[1] into categories and models and even groups of models.

---

[1] We shall call the verbs designating speech acts, speech activities, and any aspects of linguistic behavior *speech act designating verbs* or simply *speech act verbs*. We are

The next phase of our lexical analysis leads us yet a step further. The categories in a model and even the models themselves can be brought into a natural order, if one takes into account how such groups of verbs (categories or models) presuppose each other. The result of the whole procedure of categorization is a typology[2], a complex structure telling us about the relatedness of speech act designating verbs in two ways: with respect to similarity and with respect to presuppositional ancestry (or simply presupposition).

At this point we should glance back to earlier stages of the research in speech act classification. *Austin* [1.1] started out with the proposal to cover all performative verbs, which he estimated to be between 1000 and 9999. Without a precise criterion for delimiting what a performative verb is, this estimate cannot mean too much. But neither the method of determining this number nor the size of the number 1000 has as yet been challenged. (According to our findings the number of verbs determined by a linguistic method described in Sect. 4.2 [cf. (4.1)] is 4800.)

The specific classification proposal which *Austin* presented in his book was in any case a stimulating starting point. It evoked many criticisms and a series of amendments [1.2–7] and counterproposals [1.8–10]. Austin's classification of performative verbs was a mere subdivision into five classes [verdictives, exercitives, commissives, behabitives (a shocker this), expositives].

The classification was not based on external principles nor on theoretical criteria. The category names were just postulated and exemplified by a few illustrative verbs. This method made it extremely difficult or even impossible to extend the classification by adding to it verbs as yet unclassified.

---

aware of the fact that certain linguists and philosophers would like to restrict these terms to "performative verbs". Because there is no clear criterion for delimiting performative verbs in this narrow sense, as for instance by using verbs in the first person singular present indicative active in a performative utterance, we shall not make use of a narrower usage of "performative verb" (cf. Sects. 4.2 and 6.4).

[2] By typology we mean more than a classification. A classification of a given subject matter results in a partition of the objects into an exhaustive set of mutually exclusive classes. A typology — for instance the biological typology is, first, a classification, or even a hierarchical, i.e., iterated classification. But in addition its categories are endowed with an order, precedence, ancestry, or presupposition relation.

One of the best elaborations of Austin's primary proposal is *Searle*'s "Taxonomy of Illocutionary Acts" [1.2]. We present a detailed discussion of Austin's and Searle's classifications in Sect. 6.4.

A major result of the classification presented in this book is that there are 8 model groups, 24 models and typifications, 600 categories, and 4800 speech act verbs.

The book consists of two parts, a theoretical, basically lexicologically oriented part, and a data-providing, lexicographic part. The first part of the book begins with an introduction (Chap. 1) in which the background to the problem of speech act classification is briefly sketched. This chapter is followed by a new approach to lexical analysis (Chap. 2) which is considered in some more detail. Then the authors' motivation for classifying speech acts (Chap. 3) is expounded. Thereafter in the first of the three central theoretical chapters, the description and the explanation of the method is given (Chap. 4). After a brief statement of the goal, the selection of the verb material and the formation of the various classificatory units is explained. Chapter 5 then presents a survey of the resulting speech act classification. Chapter 6 is concerned with the prospect and limitations of our method and of our results. The relation to a classification of all verbs is discussed, theoretical considerations of more general character are undertaken, and criticisms of our own and competing proposals are given. The chapter concludes with the presentation of some applications of the speech act classification.

The second part of the book begins with the directions for using the lexicon and contains in addition the two portions of the lexicon. The first portion (Chap. 8) is a representation of the speech act classification by means of an explicit listing of the speech act designating verbs. It substantiates the survey of Chapter 5. The second portion (Chap. 9) is an alphabetical list of the categorized verbs with indications about the categories in which they occur and their corresponding page number of occurrence in Chapter 8.

Chapter 2 Lexical Analysis: A New Approach

In this chapter we would like to argue from a more general point of view for Lexical Analysis (LA). Under the term Lexical Analysis we would like to comprise two strands of the treatment of lexical expressions — lexicography and lexicology. In other words Lexical Analysis should comprise the more practical ways and the more theoretical ways of treating lexical material likewise. Traditionally the practically oriented lexicography and the theoretically conceived lexicology have been largely separated. Either lexical research was concentrated on establishing extensive collections of words or idiomatic phrases [2.1—4] or lexical research was directed towards theoretical questions such as investigating the structure of limited lexical domains [2.5—8] and considering which form a lexical entry should have [2.9—10]. An intermediate position is rarely taken. There are few research conceptions which attempted to conjoin the practical and theoretical work of lexicography and lexicology. One of them is the production of valency lexica and of the theoretical analyses accompanying this enterprise [2.11—13]. The advantages in conjoining lexicological and lexicographical approaches are manifold. It is therefore astonishing that a fusion on a systematic basis was not tried earlier. In the first place, the shortcomings of a restriction to either one of the approaches are obvious. A purely lexicographic account tends to degenerate into aimless collections of disconnected linguistic facts. Abstension from theoretical considerations allows short-sighted activities which lead to contradictions and circularities, phenomena which are not unknown to lexicography. A purely lexicological account also has its faults. The lack of constraints enforced by large data sets allows fanciful speculations with no empirical basis. The combination of the two, lexicography and lexicology, corrects the deficiencies of both in that a systematic and theoretically well-founded investigation of large corpora of well-chosen linguistic material can be conducted. The conception maintained in this book aims at realizing as far as possible this ideal combination. There are, however, neither lexicological nor grammatical approaches which recognized the fundamental position of the lexicon for a theory of language and which would therefore give the lexicon a place in a theory of language of equal importance to grammar.

The position we want to maintain is one in which the lexicon stands on a par with grammar, this is to say, that the irregular and idiosyncratic part of language is to be treated with as much care as the regular part. This conception implies that a theory of language is essentially more than a fabric of rules. The theory of language must deal with the regular and the irregular part, as well as with the links between the two. It is a simplification to identify irregularity with the lexicon and regularity with grammar; nevertheless it is a worthwhile simplification, and we follow *Bloomfield* [2.14] in adopting it.[1]

A sound conception of Lexical Analysis must therefore be clear about the connection between the lexicon and the grammar. As is readily seen most theories of grammar, however, give the lexicon a secondary place and do not consider it profitable to investigate its theoretical and practical roles. The lexicon is mostly used as a wastebasket in order to get rid of unpleasant problems not handleable by the grammar in question. Thus the lexicon of generative grammar or of many logical grammars is a list of disconnected lexical entries. A lexical entry may consist of a linguistic expression (a word), its grammatical category, markers, and distinguishers [2.9,15,16]. It may also contain information about frames and scripts [2.17,18].

But in most of these cases the lexicon is an accessory list, providing some auxiliary information in order to make the grammatical rules work. The body of the lexicon is not considered as an object in its own right, which would be the precondition for an equilibrated view as regards lexicon and grammar.

In these conceptions the lexicon mirrors essentially an alphabetical lexicon providing grammatical (phonological, morphological, syntactic, semantic, etc.) information about its entries. Accordingly we recognize that with respect to the semantic level of grammatical analysis this type of lexicon is semasiologic: it exhibits the various meanings of a given

---

[1] For reasons of convenience we may go so far as to declare the regular aspects of word formation and other "regular" parts of the "lexicon" as belonging to the realm of grammar, and on the other hand to declare the "irregular" parts of "syntax and semantics" as belonging to the lexicon. This way the lexicon is concerned by definition with the irregular parts of language, be it on the level of phonemes, morphemes, words, phrases, or even ritual speech. This seems theoretically a fruitful position. Grammar is then concerned by definition with the regular parts of language, again on whatever level.

expression. It is not onomasiologic in the sense that a certain meaning is given and the various ways of expressing it are assigned. The relevant interrelations between words (or more generally linguistic expressions) emerge, however, only from an onomasiologic point of view. For then the meaning of the expression is the starting point of analysis and is therefore in the foreground. A *semasiologic* point of view groups entries together which are alphabetically (or maybe syntactically) similar. The order which results from a semasiological lexicon is therefore trivial; it is the alphabetical order (or at best the "order" of grammatical categories) and hence not very informative about the internal semantic structure of the lexicon.

The optimal way of treating lexicon and grammar in a mutually fitting manner is to treat the lexicon both onomasiologically (in order to do justice to the intrinsic semantic lexicon structure) and semasiologically (in order to make the lexical information accessible to grammar).[2]

The reason why in the overwhelming number of cases the lexicon is treated in a semasiological manner and not onomasiologically is that the first poses much fewer theoretical problems. It simply starts from the linguistic expressions (words, phrases, etc.) which are phonologically or graphically represented. The onomasiological approach, which starts from the much less explicitly given meanings of linguistic expressions, is confronted with the problem of first determining what the relevant meanings are and then displaying those meanings in a representative way.

Making progress in Lexical Analysis requires therefore the solution of a theoretical and empirical problem: How can we find and display the meanings of linguistic expressions?

We shall give here a brief account of the procedure for arriving at the meanings of linguistic expressions and their mode of representation. Special attention is given to the optimal bootstrapping of this process, i.e., to the best way to start the process of meaning determination and to justify it. We distinguish various methodological stages of the

---

[2] An important task is also to base the (formalized) grammar on a footing such that the lexicon may provide its information on all relevant levels, i.e., on the phonologic, morphologic, word, phrase, clause, sentential, textual level. A proposal to accomplish this task is Language Reconstruction Systems [2.19,20]. These are grammatical systems which work essentially with one grammatical rule: the regular interpretation and production process of linguistic expressions with respect to their meanings. All specific and irregular, i.e., lexical information enters at the appropriate level of grammatic analysis and synthesis.

explication of linguistic meanings: a heuristic phase, an explicatory phase, a justificatory phase, and a theoretical phase.

The starting point for all the phases of meaning explication is to choose a set of linguistic expressions which are to be analyzed semantically. A good start is to choose an exhaustive collection of the words of a certain grammatical category. We shall present arguments elsewhere (cf. [2.21]) why it is best to start with the *verbs*, then to proceed to the adforms (adverbs and adjectives), and only then to continue the analysis with nouns.

Starting from this exhaustive collection we may find reasons for restricting our analysis to a reasonable subset. Thus for verbs we may restrict our attention in a first step only to standard verbs (excluding dialectal and technical language) and simple verbs (excluding composite verbs).

In the first, heuristic phase the analyst uses his maybe rather vague intuitions about the semantic content of expressions. His main task is to group those words which have the same semantic content, and to separate those which he takes to have a different semantic content. Let us call this gathering and separating task, based on the intuition of semantic content, procedure H. This gives rise to a first heuristic notion of meaning.

(2.1) *Heuristic* notion of *meaning*:
Two linguistic expressions mean
heuristically the same/a similar thing if
they belong to the same group
of linguistic expressions established
by procedure H.

In the second, explicatory phase the analyst uses a more rigorous method of collecting and separating linguistic expressions. The criterion whether two expressions belong to the same group or not is now based on a linguistic semantic relation, namely on meaning similarity (or meaning adjacency) between linguistic expressions. Together with additional conditions to be observed, when grouping linguistic expressions, this leads to a more rigorous procedure of grouping those meaning adjacent linguistic expressions, call it procedure E. This leads accordingly to a more rigorous notion of meaning, explicatory meaning, in analogy to (2.1).

The next stage, the justificatory phase, makes use of another semantic relation, the paraphrase relation. Meaning identity/similarity is then based on the existence of formally similar paraphrases. The justificatory phase is dependent on the previous, explicatory phase. It presupposes the groupings of the explicatory phase. Only with respect to groups pre-established in the explicatory phase does the paraphrase technique become effective.

The theoretical phase presupposing all the other phases leads to a cognitive and/or ontological underpinning of the thesaurus structure established by the previous stages. On this level it is focused upon the fact that the thesaurus structure reveals the frame analysis of concepts. But not only the contextual and the truth functional aspect of meaning becomes relevant. The very fundamental part of meaning based on context change is involved. Thesaurus structures and their cognitive and/or ontological counterpart serve as a cognitive (or ontological) guide, in other words, as a frame or script, for the (typical systematic) effects which the interpretation of linguistic expressions leads to.

The four phases of meaning explication will be touched upon at other points in the book (cf for instance Sect. 6.2). Here we simply stress the fact that the thesaurus structure resulting from the first three stages consists of a system of labelled groups of linguistic expressions which we call categories   These groups, homogeneous lexical fields, represent the (basic) meanings expressible by the class of investigated expressions.[3] The labels of the groups are the names of these meanings. The meanings themselves, established as entities in the fourth, theoretical phase, can be conceived as cognitive or ontological objects.

The procedures for arriving at the meaning-similar groups of linguistic expressions are not properly speaking onomasiological because they did not start from explicitly given meanings. The starting point was rather semantic relations like "meaning similarity", belonging to the repertoire of the abilities of human speakers. The result of the procedures is meanings and provides, therefore, a basis for further proper onomasiological procedures: namely what the various ways to express the same meaning are. A first result can be read off already, however, from the thesaurus structure. The categories tell us which different expressions express the same meaning. With respect to this result the

---

[3] One of the basic reasons to enter upon such a project of semantic classification is to determine explicitly what can be expressed by the linguistic expressions investigated. Once the entire thesaurus is thus studied the expressive power of the lexicon of the language is revealed and accessible to subsequent studies of the expressive power of complex expressions. Both the expressive power of the lexicon and the expressive power of combining simpler expressions to more complex ones are essential to delimit the overall expressive power of a language.

above-mentioned procedures of grouping linguistic expressions are in fact already onomasiological. They also provide much information about the semantic structure of the selected part of the thesaurus.

A remark is in order to clarify the methodological value of an enterprise such as our Lexical Analysis. A distinction drawn in scientific work is observation (passive perception of phenomena) and experimentation (interactive perception of phenomena). Observations are taken to be the starting point for (true) descriptions of the facts, experiments as the starting point for explanations (based on interactive predictions). A prerequisite for valuable observations is to have good sensory organs, a working brain, and a suitable body of notions. If some of these conditions, especially the existence of a suitable body of notions, are not met, observation may lead to true but certainly not to coherent descriptions, as is illustrated by the following characteristic example. (a) and (b) are both "true" descriptions of the "world" (c), the difference being that (a) is distorted in a way that (b) is not. We say that (a) uses a different parametrization to describe world (c) than (b) does. What is next to each other in the world is not necessarily next to each other in (a), whereas (b) preserves the "topology" of world (c). The parametrization (the conceptual grid, body of notions) can be judged to be better or worse depending on whether it represents the similarities, relatedness, adjacencies of the world more or less faithfully. A bad parametrization can be amended stepwise (e.g., by using evolution strategies) in order to make it more faithful in the way we just required. There are various

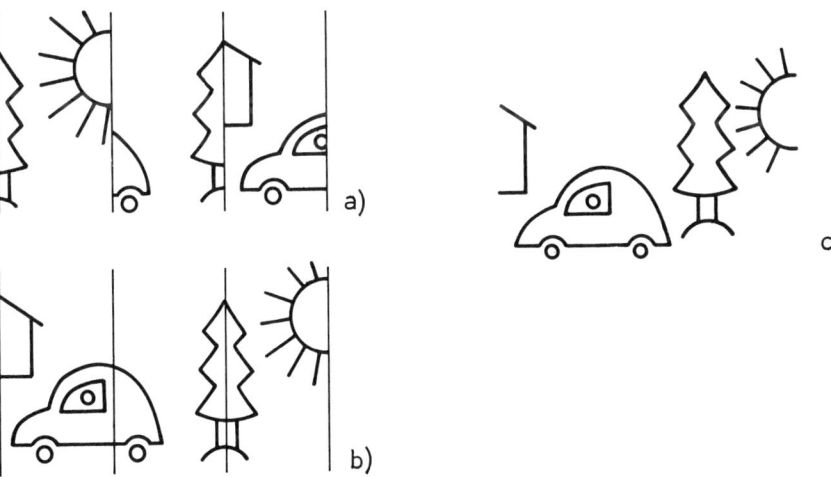

techniques to check whether a parametrization is good without making use of knowledge concerning what the world looks like (cf. [2.22]). Experimentation is needed essentially in order to accomplish this task.

Lexical Analysis is now just a method of providing the correct conceptual grid or parametrization (namely the categorization) in order to allow on its basis a faithful description of the semantic world. The categorization which we propose puts just those items together which are semantically related. We claim that only on the basis of the results of Lexical Analysis will it be possible to get at a nondistorted representation (i.e., description) and an adequate theory of linguistic phenomena. If we do not parametrize our way of looking at linguistic facts appropriately we may get true but totally disrupted and therefore useless descriptions of these facts. An experimentally substantiated explanation will not be obtainable at all. We think also that for an appropriate syntactic analysis of natural language a semantic parametrization is a necessary prerequisite. It cannot be hoped of course that syntactic patterns will fit the semantic categories in a one-to-one correspondence, but it turns out that there is an overall relation between syntactical patterns and semantic categories and models (cf [2.23]).

Chapter 3 Author's Motivation for a Speech Act Classification

One of the most basic motivations for starting out on a speech act classification is without doubt rooted in the aim of establishing a sound theory of language. The classification of speech acts, which afe basic units of linguistic behavior, seems to be a necessary precondition for a solid theory of language. A first approach to the problem is, as we know, *Austin*'s proposal brought forward in *How to do Things with Words* [1.1]. This proposal was criticized and extended on a theoretically more advanced level by *Searle* [1.2]. On closer inspection Searle's classification, which was at the time the most carefully elaborated one, turned out to be untenable. A criticism is given in Sect. 6.4. A fresh start was made by the Berlin Group [1.10]. In a very first step the Berlin Group tried to start out on the basis of Searle's speech act conditions. Every verb under consideration was analyzed in great detail in the manner of Searle's prototype analysis of promise. The hope was that the explicit representation of features exhibiting the speech act conditions of a verb in question would automatically lead to a classification. Our attempt to realize this hope showed it to be false. We recognized that every extension of the analysis to new verbs nearly always required the revision of the whole previous analysis. New relevant features were detected all through the analysis and made it necessary to reconsider everything which had been done before. No natural end of such revisions could be seen, even at an advanced stage of the investigation. On the contrary, there were good reasons to assume that such revisions could occur until the very last verb was analyzed. Because this would have rendered these investigations very time-consuming, they had to be broken off at a rather early stage.

This insight caused the Berlin Group to change its strategy of classification radically and to start with all relevant (speech act) verbs at once. They were considered on a par. We tried to approach the problem from a more holistic point of view and not to destroy the coherence of the body of verbs by disrupting them arbitrarily and by considering them one by one in an isolated way. We rather tried to use the speaker's ability to judge a verb as an unanalyzed entity in the context of other verbs. Thus the uncontrolled openness stemming from an undeterminable set of features was eliminated. This alternative approach guarantees an upper limit of revision from the outset, because the domain of investigation is determined explicitly from the beginning and is integrally available for the analysis.

The difficulty of Lexical Analysis lay in finding an intermediate register of inquiry between a totally holistic approach which does not allow any analysis whatsoever, strictly speaking, and an atomistic approach which is continually running in the wrong direction because of a lack of orientation. Our solution was guided in part by the theory of lexical fields (Wortfeldtheorie) [2.5,6] and by other sense semantic approaches to lexical meaning [3.1].

Based on a lexical analysis of German speech act verbs a classification of those verbs resulted which will be published as a book [1.10]. This classification, acceptable as it is, in the author's opinion required a more general theoretical basis: it became clear to the authors that the method has a more general relevance for the theory of language and especially for semantics. We therefore tried to extend the analysis to the whole verb lexicon and to investigate the impact of our method in this more general question [2.21,23].

The result was in fact that we succeeded in setting up a coherent program starting with a Lexical Analysis of elementary verbs designating states, processes, actions, and activities, then proceeding with speech act designating verbs, then with adforms (adverbs and adjectives), and then continuing with nouns. Later on, when simple expressions have been explored, Lexical Analysis is planned to be continued on the level of complex expressions like idiomatic expressions, coined expressions, metaphors, and even on the level of text patterns. The initial part of the program with elementary verbs, speech act designating verbs, and adforms has been brought to an end and/or is in the process of being finished [2.21,23].

Viewing the speech act classification which is presented in this book in the more general framework of an overall Lexical Analysis has important consequences. Not only is it possible to tighten up the theoretical foundations of the lexicographic and lexicological work, but there are also many practical applications of the large scale speech act classification (cf Sect. 6.5).

Chapter 4 Description and Explanation of the Method

4.1 Brief Statement of the Goal

The aim of this book as elaborated in preceding chapters is to classify speech acts by means of a classification of speech act verbs.[1] More precisely this means that we want to start from the set of all the verbs of a given language which designate (aspects of) speech activities, list them, and categorize them according to a well-specified system which we shall describe immediately. The resulting categorization will reflect the ontological and conceptual structuring of the linguistic behavior of the speakers of the language in its various facets.

4.2 Selection of Verbs

The method for arriving at this goal will now be described and explained. For many languages the material we can start with is dictionaries, or more or less complete word lists which carry grammatical information about parts of speech. Good examples of such dictionaries are the *Oxford English Dictionary* [4.1] and *Webster*'s [4.2] in English, and *Wahrig* [4.3] and *Duden* [4.4] in German. From such dictionaries more or less complete verb lists are easily extracted.[2] In

---

[1] In our conception we make in principle a working distinction between sentences (or expressions), sentences (or expressions) to describe events of some sort, sentences (or expressions) to perform linguistic activities, and the linguistic activities themselves. Thus we differentiate in typical cases between verb forms, verbs (in general), speech act verbs (used to describe linguistic activities, like *to lie, to discuss*) or "performative" verbs (used in sentences to perform linguistic acts (actions, activities) like *to order, to ask*), and speech acts.

[2] If no dictionary is available, verb lists have to be established from the outset. For this task (translations of) verb lists of other languages are helpful. They can guide the search for verbs in the target language in various ways: gathering verbs from texts and eliciting verbs from bilinguals and native speakers.

certain cases complete verb lists of a given language are already available, as is the case for German (*Mater* [4.5]).

In order to simplify the classification without real loss of generality the complete list of verbs is first cleared of dialectal variants and technical terms. A classification of those verbs can easily be regained afterwards by reference to a classification of standard expressions.

The first real problem for a classification of speech act verbs arises when we start to pick out the speech act verbs from a list of (standard) verbs. A viable test to separate speech act verbs — we use that term in the more general sense — from other verbs is to insert a verb (phrase) VP containing the verb in question in the following sentence frame:

(4.1) Someone VP-past "......".

If the frame makes sense when filled the verb (phrase) VP is to be taken as a speech act verb in our sense. The verb (phrase) VP can then be understood to specify the content or means of expression of the linguistic activity "......". The following examples may illustrate our test:

(4.2)   Alfonse declared "I am hungry".
Julia certified "Ruth is cute".
The officer instructed the soldiers "Go left".
The teeny adored her admirer "Oh".
The criminal blackmailed the director "If not, I'll kill you".
The teacher disapproved of his pupil "You will never succeed".

whereas:

*David kicked George "You asshole".
*The goalkeeper stopped the ball "What a marvellous reaction".
*The car driver transported the noodles "Here they are".

To be sure, our test does not and need not rely on the performative use of the verbs in question: we are not after the narrower set of performative verbs but rather after any kind of (aspect of) speech activity designating verb. We should stress the point that there are reasons to believe that the speech act verbs in our sense form a more relevant class of expressions with respect to linguistic behavior than the "performative" verbs. Many linguistic activities, like insincere speech activities (*to lie, to show off, to tease*), complex speech activities (*theologize, deliberate, chatter, joke*), special aspects of speech activities (*whisper, shout*), perlocutionary speech activities (*upset, tease, alarm, seduce*), interactive speech activities (*quarrel, discuss*), and so forth do not allow the performative formula, though they are of enormous relevancy for human linguistic behavior.

With respect to our test (4.1) there are of course some borderline cases. An interesting case of such a type is verbs of thinking.

(4.3) Harry pondered "If Susan gets a divorce the situation would not be better".
Charley calculated "Four and three makes ten".

The problem with these cases is that the sentence quoted can be read as an inner monologue. Then it is not a speech act of a usual sort, but something like a thought act. But because these cases are systematically ambiguous between such an inner monologue reading and a real speech activity reading (in a situation where the thoughts are said aloud), we have good reason to include these verbs in our list too.

Ideally the classification of speech act verbs should start afresh for every language investigated, i.e., on the basis of a complete verb list, clearing away all dialectal and technical words, separating out the speech act designating verbs, and so on. In our specific case of English speech act classification we did not do this, but used the German list of speech act verbs and the German classification as a starting point. For this reason we cannot be absolutely sure of having taken into account "all" English speech act verbs. In particular the method chosen is inapt to detect just those speech act verbs which are specific to English, i.e., have no equivalents in German. The German filter impoverishes our English data to a possibly relevant degree. The reason that we nevertheless chose this somewhat questionable method was that we, as nonnative English speakers, could prepare at least a provisional classification of English speech act verbs which could then be amended and made more specific by native informants. We preferred to take this imperfect approach.

4.3 Formation of Categories

We shall now give the reader a brief characterization of how speech act categories are formed. The entire set of speech act verbs is inspected and some semantic centers extracted. The meaning content of the verbs is taken as a guideline in this first heuristic phase to get groupings of verbs in areas around semantic centers. It was important to concentrate here on the main portion of the meaning content and not to get distracted by marginal features as had been done in previous attempts at classification. Some such semantic centers around which we found verbs grouped in areas were (for instance) the following:

(4.4) Expressing Emotion
Influencing Others (Enactions)
Verbal Struggle
Normative Behavior (Nouns)
Expressing Values
Complex Discourse Functions

The bulk of material made it more and more clear that the collected verbs got organized into structures around such centers. We shall illustrate how this happened by means of *verbs of verbal struggle*.

By the heuristic method sketched above we arrived at a list of verbs related in their major meaning component (with respect, of course, to their speech act reading) to *verbal struggle*. A selection of such verbs is given here in alphabetical order for illustrative reference.

(4.5)

affront	drop	refute
agree to	exact	reject
ally	fall out	relinquish
answer	feel sympathy with	renounce
approve of	fix up	reply
argue	fraternize	repudiate
ask	give up	require
assent to	haggle	resign
bargain	hammer at	retort
be fed up with	harmonize	sanction
bicker	insist on	scale down
blurt	insult	settle
break with s.o.	invalidate	shelve
capitulate	maintain	side with s.o.
cease	menace	split up
chat s.o. up	mistake s.o.	stick to
claim	misunderstand s.o.	struggle
come to terms	mock at	surrender
confute	offend	take to pieces
consent	object	threaten
content	persevere	trap
contest	persist in	turn down
decline	provoke	venture
defend o.s.	pursue	withdraw
desist from	quarrel	wrangle
disprove	rebut	

Starting from such a (not necessarily quite complete) list of verbs connected with verbal struggle we began to set up smaller groups of verbs which were semantically more homogeneous. After getting a rough grouping we tightened this procedure up by a sense semantical approach. Whereas in the first heuristic phase we used the denotation of the verbs to decide their rough grouping, we tried now to use a more rigorously linguistic method. In this second explicatory phase we made essential use of the semantical relation meaning similarity (or meaning adjacency) but also of the relations prototypicality and group-homogeneity.[3] These relations can be illustrated by the following group of verbs designating the activity of being in the middle of a verbal struggle:

(4.6) argue
       bargain
       bicker
       contend
       contest
       haggle
       quarrel
       struggle
       wrangle

As is seen, all the verbs occurring in the group are similar in meaning. This result is based on the ability of speakers of natural language to decide using their linguistic competence which two of three verbs are the most similar. Thus it is easy for a native speaker of English to judge that *quarrel* and *haggle* are the most alike pair with respect to the possible pairs which can be chosen from the three verbs

(4.7) agree
       haggle
       quarrel

The semantic relation of meaning similarity thus suffices to establish groups of verbs which are rather tightly connected in meaning, as the

---

[3] Deciding upon this relation of meaning similarity (meaning adjacency) is part of the repertoire of linguistic abilities of native speakers. In various situations (such as language learning, language teaching, finding stylistic variants, and so forth) this ability is practised and extended in multiple ways. It is one of the basic abilities of human speakers!

Another basic ability (entrenched by every occasion of language use) which is fundamentally used in the second explicatory stage is the ability to decide what is typical: namely what is a typical situation in which an expression is used and what is a typical meaning or effect such an expression has in such a typical situation (cf. *Rosch* [4.6].

A third (linguistic or metalinguistic) ability of speakers is to decide about the homogeneity of verb classes. Linguistic tests showed convincingly e.g. that a speaker is able to select inapt expressions from otherwise homogeneous verb-groups.

verb group (4.6) demonstrates. Sometimes it happens that a verb group of mutually similar verbs is nevertheless judged inhomogeneous. Take the following verb group which appears at first sight fairly homogeneous:

(4.8) defend o.s.
 object
 refute
 reject

In the process of adding more and more similar verbs an inhomogeneity appears.

(4.9) answer
 contest | newly added verbs
 defend o.s.
 object
 - - - - - - - - - - - - - -
 refute
 reject
 turn down   { newly added verb

The first part of the group consists of defense attempts, whereas the second part consists of successful repulsions. The dividing line goes right through the group which originally looked quite homogeneous. This process illustrates the gradual refinement of groups and the growth of their homogeneity. The ability which speakers of the language are able to rely on is to judge the semantic relation of homogeneity among the verbs occurring in a group.

A difficulty which has to be mastered frequently is selecting the typical meaning of a verb as opposed to a less typical and less adequate one. This typical meaning depends on various circumstances. It depends on our aim of classifying speech act verbs and not verbs in general, on the possible readings a verb has, and on the group in which the verb is to be filed.

Let us consider the example of the verb *contest*. For our studies the literal sense of struggle, i.e., with fists and weapons, is not relevant. Typicality for our purposes is restricted to speech act readings. But even with this restriction we have various choices: *contest* meaning deny, apply for, challenge, dispute a person's right and quarrel. The typical reading with respect to the verb group (4.6) is determined by the other verbs of the group "to quarrel". The notion of typicality (or proto-typicality) we make use of here is a *context susceptible* version of a notion of prototypicality in the vein of the Bay Area linguistics [4.6].

Accordingly this notion of typicality allows us to incorporate an idea of the German "Wortfeldtheorie" (theory of lexical fields), namely the idea that the typical meaning of a word is partly determined by its field neighbors.

In the process of grouping the verbs together the groups are given a name. The names chosen in the present classification are nouns which cover the meaning of all the verbs occurring in the group. They are predicates comprising the linguistic behavior designated by the verbs in the group. An is-a relation holds between the verbs and this predicate. These predicates found appropriate for the illustrative fragment of verbs of struggle are the following:

(4.10) Starting Situation
Making Claims
Dissent
Attack
Defense Attempt ⎫
Successful Repulsion ⎬ Tactical Phase
Reply to Defense
Involvement ⎭
Making a Coalition
Retreat
Victory ⎫
Defeat ⎬ Terminal Phase
Willingness to Cooperate ⎭

A verb group together with its title predicate is called a *category*. The categories resulting from the heuristic and explicatory phase of the classification procedure are represented below (4.11). But before this is done we would like to point out first a systematic ambiguity of which we make some use. The notion of verb and in parallel the notion of category and related notions (as for instance "model", introduced later on) may designate linguistic expressions or structured sets of expressions as well as their semantic counterparts. This semantic counterpart can be conceived moreover in various ways. For instance it could be taken as a physical activity or alternatively as mental concept related to these physical activities.

(4.11)
Starting Situation   *Making Claims*

agree to   ask
consent to   chat s.o. up
feel sympathy with   claim
side with s.o.   exact

Making Claims (continued)

request
require
trap
venture

Dissent

break with s.o.
fall out
mistake s.o.
misunderstand s.o.
split up

Attack

affront
insult
menace
mock at
offend
provoke
threaten

Tactical Phase

Defense Attempt

answer
contest
defend o.s.
object
reply
retort

Successful Repulsion

confute
decline
rebut
refute
reject
turn down

Tactical Phase (continued)

Reply to Defense

hammer at
insist on
maintain
persevere
persist in
pursue
stick to

Involvement

argue
bargain
bicker
contend
contest
haggle
quarrel
struggle
wrangle

Making a Coalition

ally
come to terms
fix up
fraternize
harmonize
settle

Retreat

be fed up with
cease
desist from
drop
give up

renounce
scale down
shelve

Retreat (continued)

surrender
withdraw

Victory/Defeat/Willingness to Cooperate

Victory

blurt
disprove
invalidate
repudiate
take to pieces

Victory/Defeat/Willingness to Cooperate

Defeat

capitulate
relinquish
renounce
resign

Willingness to Cooperate

agree to
approve of
assent to
come to terms
sanction

The entries of these categories are sometimes supplemented by phrases. The reasons for doing that were varied. First there were some phrases that we considered to fit the meaning demarcated by the category especially well, and hence taken to reinforce it. Secondly phrases were used for want of a verb equivalent when translating the verbs of the German classification used as a starting point for the English lexicon. It was not always possible to eliminate this latter sort of subsidiary phrases in the subsequent process of checking the data with native speakers.

4.4 Formation of Models

As the reader may have noticed, the example categories (4.11) of verbs of struggle are already endowed with a natural order. From a heuristic point of view the order of the categories displays the order of the main phases of a model struggle with verbal means: a Starting Situation (initial friendship, for example) is followed by an initiation of the struggle by Marking Claims and following Dissent. The real beginning of the struggle is then the Attack which is naturally followed by various Tactical Phases (Defense Attempt, Successful Repulsion, Reply to Defense, Involvement). Towards the end of the struggle Making Coalitions or Retreating takes place and the struggle results in a Victory for the one and the Defeat of the other opponent or in mutual Willingness to Cooperate.

Considering other semantic areas of speech act verbs we may observe a similar phenomenon. For instance for the verbs of enaction the main categories are ordered as follows:

(4.12) Volitions
   Putting into Focus

   Enactions $\begin{cases} \text{Call for Help} \\ \text{Commissioning} \\ \text{Pointing to a Norm or Danger} \\ \text{Demanding} \\ \text{Commanding} \\ \text{Influencing} \\ \text{Demanding Effectively} \end{cases}$

   Reactions to Enactions

The categories of this semantic area are ordered in a natural way. Looking more closely we see that the order is only partially temporally motivated. A model enaction starts with a Volition (*like, prefer, aspire to, desire, intend*) and continues with a Putting into Focus (*focus, point at, refer to*) which is followed by proper Enactions (*beg, plead; commission, order sth., reserve; exhort, warn threaten; ask, request, inquire; command, prescribe direct; entice, mislead, seduce; brainwash, annoy, scare*) and finally with Reactions to Enactions (*accept, answer, comply with, deny*). The four superordinated categories, Volitions, Putting into Focus, Enactions, and Reactions to Enactions, can be said to be temporally ordered. This is certainly not true for the subordinate categories of Enactions. These categories are rather ordered according to the rising degree of effectivity of enaction. The first categories are weaker attempts at getting the addressee to do something, whereas the later categories comprise more and more powerful, institutionally backed and efficient actions.[4]

The question is whether there is a common semantical relation underlying the various ordering relations of categories. Is there in other words a common relation underlying temporal ordering, effectivity ordering, ordering of the escalation of means, ordering of strength, ordering of the grade of interactivity, and so forth. We think that at a *very deep level* of theorizing such a relation may be found, namely the presupposition relation. That temporal order is reducible to a kind of pre-

---

[4] Because the possibilities of effectivity are multidimensional, a linear order as given in this book cannot be fully adequate of course. Further studies must elaborate these relations in detail.

supposition relation poses no serious problems, though not everything which precedes is presupposed. The cases which are relevant for our classification are however more favorable cases: we deal with a typical temporal order which is a kind of systematical or necessary temporal succession. It is not accidental; otherwise language would not make the effort of lexicalization. Thus preceding stages of the models are typically presupposed in order for later stages to occur.

Other kinds of ordering relations pose a more serious problem. For instance ordering by the strength of enaction (and other gradations) which is responsible for ordering (for example) Call for Help, Demanding, Commanding, Demanding Effectively in this succession is not easily reduced to presupposition, because Commanding does not (say) imply asking for, strictly speaking.

But we can save the position that a presupposition relation lies at the heart of all these ordering relations by analyzing these relations more rigorously. We shall illustrate the point with the relation between *command* and *ask for*. In one sense commanding is definitely not a kind of asking for. It is ruder, it is institutionally backed to a much higher degree by requiring, pretending, or establishing an authority relation between speaker and hearer. In another sense, however, commanding implies and even presupposes asking for. This is so because the hearer may abstract from the circumstantial accessories and take it that the speaker is using a stylistically somewhat *stronger* and *effective* means of getting the hearer to do something. In this sense commanding is a kind of asking for, and there is no commanding without simultaneously asking for in that sense.

To make an analogy we consider the case of a ten dollar bill. To have ten dollars implies having one dollar in one sense but not in another. If you want to operate a cigaret machine which requires a dollar coin the ten dollar bill is of no help to you. In this sense to have ten dollars does not imply having one dollar. In the usual sense the implication holds of course, because having ten dollars licenses one to get change for it with ease. In this latter sense we may then say that you cannot have ten dollars without having at the same time one dollar.

Thus the problem of the circumstances under which a presupposition (or implication) can be said to hold or not is of a general sort and is related to the problem of when to allow for certain abstractions and whether at a reasonably abstract level of abstraction most if not all ordering relations relevant for lexical classifications can be reduced to a kind of presupposition relation.

It becomes clear now that the heuristically proposed semantical areas get more and more structured. First there is the classificatory structure of their categories. Secondly there is the order relation between the categories which knits the categories together to a logically consolidated structure. The two semantical relations, meaning similarity and presupposition, are the *foundation* on which to establish this logically (semantically) based structure.

A semantical area structured by a set of categories connected by appropriate (partial) orderings is called a *model*. The speech act models we have found by applying the classification method described so far are the following:

(4.13)

Models	Labels
Emotion Model	$\underline{EM}$
Enaction Model	$\underline{EN}$
Struggle Model	$\underline{KA}$ (AV)
Institutional Model	$\underline{NO}$
Valuation Models	W: $\underline{WT}$, $\underline{WP}$, $\underline{WS}$, $\underline{WG}$
Discourse Models	D: $\underline{\underline{DI}}$, DT (IR), $\underline{\underline{TU}}$, DI/TU
Text Models	X: $\underline{\underline{ET}}$, ET/TE, $\underline{\underline{TE}}$, $\underline{\underline{IN}}$($\underline{VE}$), DE(VV)
Theme Models	T: $\underline{TO}$, $\underline{TV}$, $\underline{TP}$

(The underscored labels are labels of models, the doubly underscored labels are labels of models representing whole courses of speech activities. Nonunderscored labels are labels for less tightly structured semantic areas, which we have called typifications [Typisierungen]).

The labels used for the models stem from the original German version [1.10]. We did not want to change them, in order to make a comparison possible. The following list gives an overview of all labels used, their German signification, and an approximate English translation:

(4.14)

Label	German Signification	English Translation
EM	Emotionsmodell	Emotion Model
EN	Enaktionsmodell	Enaction Model
KA	Kampfmodell	Struggle Model
AV	Argumentationsverfahren	Arguing Devices
NO	Normmodel	Institutional Model (Norm Model)
W	–	Valuation Models
WT	Wertung einer Tat	Valuation of an Action
WP	Wertung einer Person	Valuation of a Person
WS	Selbstwertung	Valuation of Oneself
WG	Wertung von Gegenständen	Valuation of Objects
D	–	Discourse Models

(4.14) (continued)

Label	German Signification	English Translation
DI	Diskurs-Model	Discourse Model
DT	Diskurstypen	Discourse Types
IR	Ironie, Spaß und Spott	Irony, Joke, Ridicule
TU	Turn Modell	Turn Taking Model
DI/TU	Diskursleiter Tätigkeiten	Moderator Activities
X	–	Text Models
ET/TE	Vertextung	Making Texts
TE	Textmodell	Texting
IN	Informationsmodell	Information Model
VE	Verrat-Modell	Treason Model
DE	Denken	Thinking
VV	Vergleichsverfahren	Comparing Devices
T	–	Theme Models
TO	Themaorganisationsmodell	Theme Organization Model (Verbalization)
TV	Themaverlaufsmodell	Thematic Phases Model
TP	Themapräsentationsmodell	Topic Presentation

The term model is chosen mainly for the reason that these structured sets of categories model typical courses and modes of speech activities.[5] For those models which represent entire courses of speech activities (e.g., Enaction Model, Struggle Model, Institutional Model) a typical pattern obtains which is given a special name because of its prominence: *hat structure*. The reason for this somewhat peculiar name is that the intensity development of the process captured by the major categories in a model when graphically displayed looks as follows (as a hat):

(4.15)

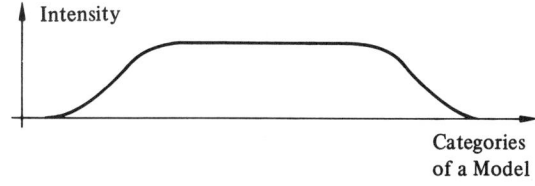

---

[5] Another reason for calling models by this name is to relate them to the logical and even the physical notion of model. In logic, models can be taken to be structured contexts relative to which meaning, truth, and effect of linguistic expressions are evaluated. In physics a model is an abstraction from reality which exhibits all relevant features in order to reconstruct formally the physical process under consideration.

The intensity in early phases of a model starts out low, gets gradually higher, and then cools off again. To express this more explicitly, in the initial phases of a model there are categories which designate quiet or "changeless" states, later on the categories designate busy activities, and towards the end of the model the designated activities calm down again. Let us consider some examples.

(4.16)

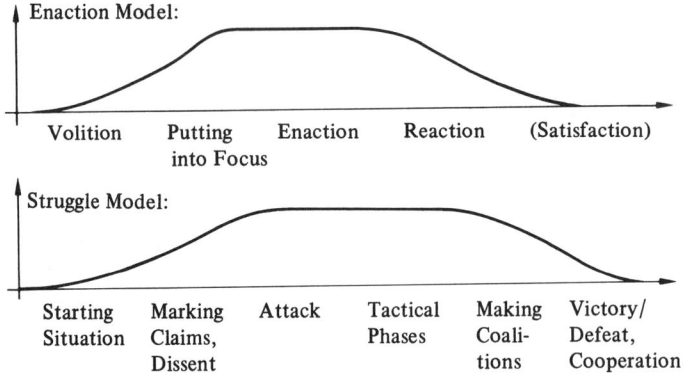

Enaction Model:

Volition   Putting   Enaction   Reaction   (Satisfaction)
            into Focus

Struggle Model:

Starting   Marking   Attack   Tactical   Making   Victory/
Situation   Claims,   Phases   Coali-   Defeat,
            Dissent   tions   Cooperation

Not all models capturing the temporal development of human speech activities have such a simple structure however. It may very well be that several "hats" are stacked together. A good example to demonstrate this is the Institutional Model (also called Norm Model). In this model during a Prephase certain agents are endowed with the right of establishing norms. This right is not attributed to them forever, but only for a limited time. The removal of that right is the Postphase. This gives rise to a first-level hat. The Imposing and later Cancelling of a Norm constitute a second-level hat. A possible Violation of a norm which is holding and its later Expiration constitute a third level, and the Detection of the violated norm, the following (official) Trial, Punishment and the final Acquittal constitute a fourth level.

It is important to note that the brim of the (lowest) hat is linguistically exceptional in many cases. The starting/final situation and the preconditions and result states of the ongoing activities are located there. Therefore we cannot normally expect simple speech act verbs to denote those phases, but rather verb phrases with copula plus adjective or noun phrase, sometimes state verbs, or the habitual readings of action verbs. Some examples from the most initial categories Friendship Status and Enemy Status of the Struggle Model may illustrate that fact (cf. 4.17).

(4.17)

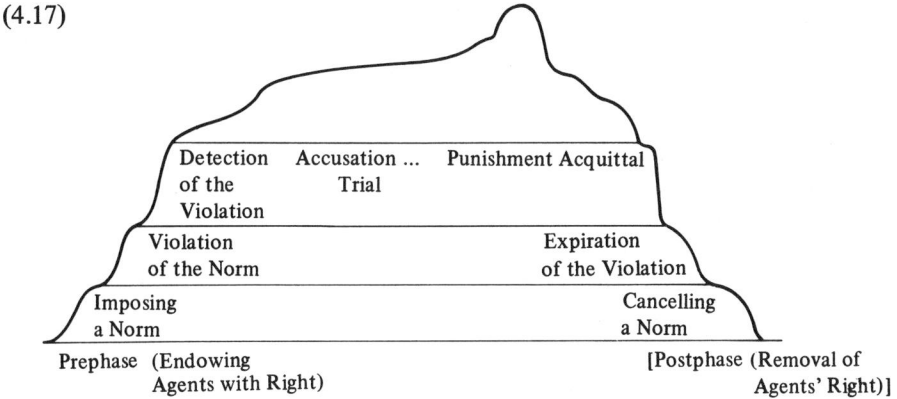

Prephase (Endowing Agents with Right) [Postphase (Removal of Agents' Right)]

(4.18) category: Friendship Status

    copula plus adjective
    or noun phrase constructions: be united
        be of one mind
        be in harmony

    state verbs: agree
        consent

    category: Enemy Status

    dispositional reading
    of action verbs: argue with s.o.
        combat
        dispute
        quarrel
        struggle

Some of these phrases do not really denote speech activities at all (like *be united, be in harmony*) but are included in order to complete the models from a systematic point of view (cf. 4.18)

The hat structures we discovered as a basic phenomenon for a certain class of models express an important grammatical phenomenon, namely aktionsarten.[6] The inchoative durative and terminative aktionsart are

---

[6] We make a distinction between Aspekt and Aktionsart which in the English literature (expect *Lyons* [4.7]) are both indiscriminately referred to as aspect. There are in fact two different ways to distinguish between Aspekt and Aktionsart, a morphosyntactic and a semantic one. The morphosyntactic distinction says that Aspekt is a syntactic phenomenon concerning the use of tense and aspect in texts, and that Aktionsart is a phenomenon of verb morphology especially in Slavic languages. The semantic distinction is the one we are interested in in this book. It says that Aspekt concerns the narrative perspective (like the complexive-cursive distinction of *Koschmieder* [4.8]), whereas Aktionsart concerns the phases of an ongoing process or activity denoted by a verb [4.9]. Because of the lack of a viable alternative we shall henceforth make use of these semantic notions in English, too.

the major ones. But there are others as well. In fact the (speech act) verb classification leads to a whole lot of different aktionsarten, e.g., preparative (*accuse, arrest*: for trial), "postparative" (= nachbereitend; *excuse, pardon*: for trial; *remedy, repair*: for struggle); intensifying (*agitate, intrigue, plot*: for struggle); cooling off (*neutralize, play down, trivialize*: for struggle); perseverative (*persevere, insist, urge*: for struggle), laissez-faire (*desist from, renounce, give in*: for struggle); decisive (*decide, continue*), accidental (*hesitate, stutter*); creative (*articulate, put into words, verbalize*), destructive (*eliminate, remove, skip*).

4.5 The System of Models

The models as they are displayed in (4.13) are not unrelated. The relation between them is displayed in the following graph:

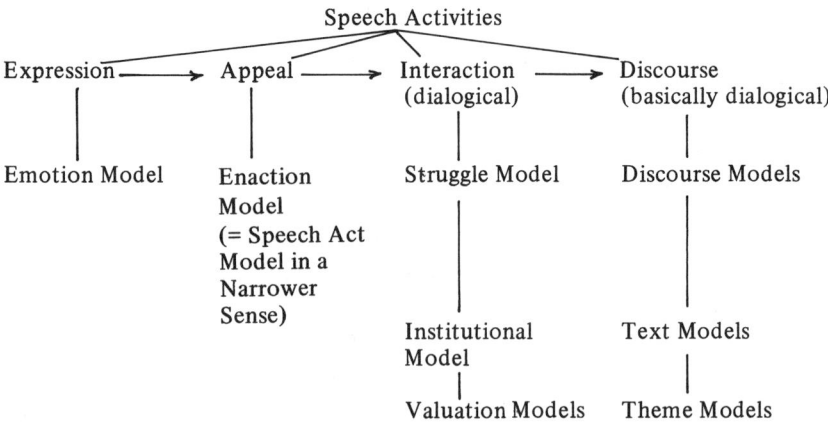

The topmost node in the graph, Speech Activities, characterizes the whole realm of classification treated in this book. There are four major model groups: Expression, Appeal, Interaction, and Discourse. These model groups represent four basic functions of language (and linguistic behavior). *Expression* is the least hearer-oriented and least extroverted function of the four. It is an often uncontrolled mirroring of emotional states of a human being. *Appeal* is a linguistic function clearly directed towards a hearer. It is, essentially, unidirectional from speaker to hearer. The speaker tries to get control over the hearer. *Interaction* then is the linguistic function involving speaker and hearer in mutual verbal actions. The hearer tries to get control over the speaker as well, which the speaker may try to avoid. Thus the basis for a (verbal) struggle is laid. After a possibly hot quarrel the mutual competition may go over into reciprocal cooperation. This is the basis for a better-behaved and more rigidly organized verbal interaction between speaker and hearer: the fourth function of linguistic behavior, *Discourse*, can become operative. The higher linguistic functions in typical cases imply (or even presuppose) the lower ones. That is, being a Discourse implies being (in part) also an Interaction, an Appeal, and an Expression, for example. More explicitly this means that being a discourse is being (an elaborated form of verbal) interaction, which means that many single mutual appeals occur and some kinds, if neutral, expressions of emotion. A noteworthy observation is that the four functions can be divided up into two unilateral (Expression, Enaction) and two bilateral or dialogical (Interaction, Discourse) functions. The first of every two functions (i.e., Expression, Interaction) can be said to be the more original and racy, whereas the second of every two functions (i.e., Enaction, Discourse) are the more institutionalized and controlled versions.

The four functions follow roughly the following cross classification which has the two dimensions of privacy (social entrenching) and discourse character (monologue-dialogue):

(4.20)

	private	socially entrenched
monological	Expression	Appeal
dialogial	Interaction	Discourse

The models and collections of models given in (4.13) fit into these four linguistic functions according to the graph (4.19), especially the Emotion Model, the Enaction Model, the Struggle Model and the Discourse Models. The rest of the models fit in indirectly, because they can be seen as special elaborations of the models (model collections) already filed.

It is interesting to compare these four functions extracted from our classification with *Bühler*'s (1934) three linguistic functions. His expression (Ausdruck), appeal (Appell), and representation (Darstellung) partially match our subdivisions.

(4.21) BÜHLER   BALLMER/BRENNENSTUHL
    Ausdruck $\cong$ Expression
    Appell $\cong$ Appeal
    Darstellung $\subset$ Discourse (esp. Text Models, ET)

We think that the classification of speech activities leads to a more adequate analysis than Bühler's. Because it is based on the classification of an exhaustive list of speech act designating verbs, it accounts fully for all the possibilities of linguistic behavior and does not neglect for instance interactions and a large part of discourse behavior. *Bühler*, by contrast to our proposal, neglects the linguistic behavior of dialogue in his sign model. The dialogic aspect of language becomes prominent in our two later model groups Interaction and Discourse. Bühler's representation (Darstellung) of objects and states of affairs used to inform a hearer belongs, on the basis of its dialogic intent, in our approach to the discourse function (text model groups, ET, DE, VV, ...). This demonstrates another difference of our conception with respect to more traditional ones, such as the conception adapted from classical logic (*Tarski* [4.10]) by *Bühler* [4.11] and *Searle* [1.2]. Representation is conceived dialogically from the outset. It is considered in the framework of communication, especially information, and not in the framework of abstract correspondence.

Chapter 5 Survey of the Resulting Speech Act Classification

In order to guide the reader through the semantically arranged lexicon and in order to substantiate our theoretical considerations with more illustrative material we shall present in this chapter a list of the models (and model groups) together with a short description of the semantic area they cover and the names of their main categories.

(5.1)

Models	Semantic Area Covered	Main Categories
EM *Emotion Model*	Linguistic expression of emotions with different grades of extrovertedness (hearer orientedness, appeal efficiency).	Processing Experiences – Indicators of Emotional States and Processes – Expression – Exothesis of Emotion – Exothesis of a Result of Processing an Emotion – Maledictions – Value Judgements – Attempt to Induce an Emotion – Addressee Oriented Expressive Speech Acts – Appeal.
EN *Enaction Model*	Speaker's more or less coercive attempts to get somebody to do something by expressing an idea, wish, intention, plan, goal, etc. including some standard reactions.	Volitions – Putting into/out of Focus – Call for/Offer Help – Commissioning – Pointing to a Norm or Danger – Demanding – Commanding – Influencing – Demanding Effectively – Reactions to Enactions.

(5.1) continued

Models	Semantic Area Covered	Main Categories
KA *Struggle Model* (Competition and Cooperation Model)	Verbal Struggle starting from making a claim and overtly attacking an addressee. The competitive verbal fight (e.g., argumentation) may result in the victory of one and the defeat of the other or in a compromise.	Starting Situation – Make Claims – Reasons for the Argument and Their Consequences – Attack – Tactical Phase (Attacking Moves, Opposing Moves, Replies to Defense, Involvement) – Making a Coalition – Retreat – Victory, Defeat, Willingness to Cooperate (Reconciliation, Compromise, Consensus).
AV *Arguing Devices*	Stages of Argumentation as part of a verbal struggle.	Argue – Explain – Validate – Exemplify – Criticize – Agree.
NO *Institutional Model* (Norm Model)	Establishment of a behavior in an institution, especially entering an institution and thereby adopting its norms, following its norms and rules, violating them, and being pursued by the upholders of the institution.	Prephase (Mandating, Making a Law) – Imposing a Norm on Someone (Putting Under a Norm, Allowing, Forbidding, Admitting in Institutions, Promoting, Dismissing, Entering a Contract (Committing) – Following a Norm – Abolishing a Norm – Violating a Norm – Detecting an Offense – Reporting – Summoning – Phases of the Institutional Quarrel (Accusing, Reaction to the Accusation, Examining, Testifying, Defending) – Judging – Punishing – Declaring the Judgement Void – Social Consequences of the Sentence.

(5.1) continued

Models	Semantic Area Covered	Main Categories
W *Valuation Models*	Positive and negative valuations of actions, persons, things, states of affairs, etc.; decisions and their aftereffects.	
WT Valuation of an Action		Exothesizing the Valuation of an Action — Blaming — Suggesting Promotion — Voting — Taking Good or Bad Reputation into Account — Prejudicing — Scolding — Correcting — Criticizing — Praising — Accepting — Rejecting — Aftereffects.
WP Valuation of a Person		Degrading a Person — Raising the Valuation of a Person.
WS Valuating Oneself		Self-degradation — Self-upgrading.
WG Valuation of Things, States of Affairs, etc.		Devaluing a State of Affairs — Recommending Consequences of the Valuation (Disregarding, Respecting).
D *Discourse Models*	Organization and Types of Discourse.	
DI Discourse Model	External Organization of Discourse.	Asking for Participation — Invite Discourse — Accept/Refuse/Cancel — Fixing Time — Entering Contact — Beginning the Discourse — Being in Discourse — Discourse Inconvenience — Reconciliation of Disturbances — Ending the Discourse.

(5.1) continued

Models	Semantic Area Covered	Main Categories
DT Discourse Types *plus* IR Irony, Joke, Ridicule	Types of Discourse.	Discourse Types with Several Speakers – Discourse Types with One Speaker – Special Types of Discourse.
TU Turn-Taking Model *plus* DI/TV Moderator Activities	Internal Organization of Discourse.	Intending Turn Taking – Permission to Speak – Beginning of the Turn – Having the Turn – Dragging out/Shortening – Turn – Turn Interruption – Continuing the Turn – Finishing the Turn.
X *Text Models*	Textual assimilation and processing of reality, especially producing, receiving, and manipulating texts (Experience and Text Model, Making Text, Texting) and data (Information Model).	
ET Experience and Text Model		Perceive Reality – Exotheticize Knowledge (Declare, Report, Utter, Communicate, Confirm, Swear; Inform; Reveal, Teach) – Perceive Knowledge (Understand, Learn).
ET/TE Making Texts		Making Texts (Producing Texts).
TE Texting		Promulgating Texts – Perceiving Texts (Deciphering, Read, Learning Texts, Interpret, Misinterpret) Exothesizing Text Knowledge (Reproduce, Fake and Parody, Reconstruct, Translate, Reformulate, Comment).

(5.1) continued

Models	Semantic Area Covered	Main Categories
IN Information Model		Systematically Searching for Data — Finding Data — Valuating/Sorting/Organizing Data — Retrieving Data — Distributing Data — Examining Data — Accept/Refuse Data — Denying/Testifying to Data.
VE Treason Model	A special case of the Information Model.	Hatch — Declaring as Secret — Entrusting — Keep Secret; Treason — Revealing Secrets.
DE Thinking	Thinking operations, a precondition for Text Models and Theme Models.	Reception and Understanding — Be Occupied with — Wondering — Thinking Over — Suppose — Thinking Procedures — Doubt — Planning/Deciding.
VV Comparing Devices	A special case of externalized Thinking Operations.	Categorize — Mark — Test — Compare — Differentiate — Comparative Designation — Value.
T *Theme Models*	Process of thematic structuring (Theme Organization) and its results (Thematic Phases, Topic Presentation).	
TO Theme Organization Model (Verbalization)		Think — Verbalize — Thematize (Leave Out, Include, Reorganize, Compress) — Structure — Connect — Relief (Focus, Defocussing, Accentuate, Weaken, Contrast).

(5.1) continued

Models	Semantic Area Covered	Main Categories
TV Thematic Phases Model		Clarifying Preliminarily — Announce — Sketching the Theme — Premising — Begin — Elaborating the Theme — Continuing the Topic — Anticipating and Delaying — Performing Successfully.
TP Topic Presentation		Evaluation of Presentation — Evaluation Presentation.

Chapter 6   Prospects and Limitations

6.1 Relation to the Classification of the Entire Verb Thesaurus

According to our conception of Lexical Analysis we had to find an intermediate register between a totally holistic approach and an atomistic approach. We saw that starting with the set of speech act verbs (in our sense) and proceeding according to the method displayed in this book were very profitable for the program of bootstrapping the program of lexical classification. The point was that we chose a semantically coherent and delimitable lexical area.

A natural way to continue this advance was to extend it to a larger area. What we did in the next step was to check and elaborate the methods — which at the beginning were not explicit in all respects and in every detail — using the larger corpus of all (German) verbs (cf [2.21, 23]). The results were manifold. It turned out that the sometimes implicit methods used by the Berlin Group were in principle feasible, but that there was justifiably a theoretical need for developing them further. Part of the results of such a development have been expounded already in some detail in the present book; part of them we shall mention later as far as they are relevant for the speech act classification.

A most interesting consequence of extending the classification method to a (considerably) larger set of material was noticing that the categories, and in general also the models of speech act verbs remained untouched and stable. They did not need to be revised much under the weight of the larger scale analysis. On the higher levels of the speech act classification, however, revision was unavoidable. Thus the Typology (4.19) is obtained only on the basis of an overall analysis of all verbs and deviates therefore from the original analysis of the Berlin Group. Before we explain this fact let us draw a conclusion about the general proceeding.

  The inclusion of larger portions of lexical and phrasal material does not (normally) affect lower levels of a categorization already established on the basis of meaning similarity and presupposition. What can be and normally is affected are higher levels of the classification. This confirms our method of starting at an intermediate register of semantically coherent and delimitable lexical material (like speech act verbs, verbs, adverbs, etc.) and continuing stepwise to larger, more and more comprehensive *registers* (including nouns, verb phrases, idiomatic expressions, and text patterns). The higher levels of the semantical organization of the lexicon (model groups, parts of speech, text types) exhibit their true shape only by sufficiently holistic approaches relying substantially on the lower levels. This is one of the leading lines of approaching our program of analyzing the "irregular" parts of language.

We now come back to the explanation of why Typology (4.19) gets its stable and justifiable form from the larger scale analysis of all verbs. For this reason we display here the model groups of the classification of the entire verb thesaurus.

(6.1) A) Models Concerning States of Affairs
 B) Models Concerning Processes
 C) Models Concerning the Existence of Individuals and Objects
 D) Models Presupposing the Existence of Individuals and Objects
 E) Movements of Objects in Space
 F) Experiences (influence of the environment on individuals and objects)
 G) Effecting (influence of individuals and objects on the environment)
 H) Controlled Interference (directed towards oneself, the environment, and others; Actions)
 I) Controlled Manipulation of Objects and Individuals (Grasping, Transport, and Work at)
 K) Controlled Production and Destruction of Objects and Environment
 L) Controlled Property Transactions (Property, Handing Over)
 M) Speech Activities
  a) Expression
  b) Appeal
  c) Interaction
  d) Discourse

The order of these model groups is legitimated by a presupposition relation (cf [2.21]). Later model groups presuppose earlier model groups in a specifiable way. As a result one can observe that the degree of involvement increases with the order of model groups. More precisely, the degree of control which the participants have over the process in which they are involved and which is denoted by the verbs of the (central categories of the models of the) model group increases with the ranking of the model groups.

If a process only happens to a person, without his being able to influence it, the degree of involvement is low, but if the process is brought about by an action and more so by an instrumental, or even by a socially interactive action, the degree is high. Speech activities, and also in a weak way Expressions, are typically instrumental (cf [6.1]) and interactive — i.e., addressed more or less directly towards somebody, or even dialogical. Speech activities presuppose in most typical cases, all the other activities of human beings captured by the Typology (6.1). They have in this sense the highest rank among the sociobiological achievements of human nature. This justifies their location at the upper end of the ranking of all the processes denoted by verbs. But the speech activity model groups are also ordered in our proposal according to the above-mentioned principles, principles the importance of which have been recognized only by studying the whole body of verbs.

6.2 A General Theoretical Perspective

As must have become clear, speech act classification is a field in its own right. But for many reasons we do not advocate an exclusively specialist point of view but would like to posit the field of speech act classification in a more general framework.

Our view is determined partly by the aims we are pursuing, partly by the traditions we find ourselves embedded in, and of course predominantly by the facts of natural language as we are bound to see them under the perspective of our preconceptions. For this reason we shall briefly display some of the general aims we have been pursuing for a long time, aims we think are getting recognized more and more by various groups of linguists and people related to linguistics.

According to this conception, the basic aim of linguistics is to describe and (formally) reconstruct human language in such a manner as to make human language amenable in a conscious and effective way to a full range of social uses.

Thus far we have expressed a general belief of many, if not all, linguists. The consequences of this conception may not be as uncontroversial, however, for it is clear that instrumentally and technologically facilitated applications have a leading function in making human language amenable to *social uses*. Briefly and somewhat pointedly, instrumental and technological advances pave the way for social improvement.[1,2]

Footnotes 1 and 2, see page 42

Technological objectives require a higher standard of precision on many levels of investigation: conceptual adequacy, formal rigor, empirical validity, and preciseness of data representation. A field like linguistics will profit in various ways from a strengthening of such a development. It will free itself from unprofitable ballast and grow towards a solid science. The pressure to head towards testable problems of application should not define linguistics as a mere servant to technology and social applications but should be seen as a valuable corrective for gaining worthwhile scientific knowledge.

For the linguist technologically facilitated applications create a coherent set of problems relative to a more or less well-defined set of means to solve these problems. From our point of view this fact has been operative since the early fifties but has not been appreciated well enough. The use and development of algebraic and logical formalisms in linguistics can only be understood on the basis of the increasing importance of computers in technology and society. Technological applications require a formal representation and even a formal reconstruction of the field in question. For linguistics a series of formal systems has proven its usefulness in the last two decades. Syntactically Chomsky's transformational grammars [2.15,6.4,5], *Montague* [2.16], *Lewis* [6.6], and *Cresswell* [6.7] grammars have found acceptance. These formal devices are rather abstract and cannot have direct practical applications. It is fair to mention, however, that this was not really the intention of the inventors of these formalisms. They all aimed at a structuralistic goal, namely at describing, categorizing, or explaining the underlying structure of linguistic expressions (their meaning) and language, and ignored or even discarded applications as being irrelevant for a theoretical approach to the field.

---

[1] We do not mean that technological advances necessarily imply social improvements in every respect. We mean rather that technological advances are vital to enable social progress. That technology may also lead to the opposite is demonstrated by many of its abuses and failures (cf. [6.1,2]).

[2] By technologically facilitated applications of linguistics we mean the use of mechanical, electronic, and maybe chemical devices for language processing in order to make conventional linguistic tasks more efficient, for instance data storage and retrieval; translation of words, phrases, and texts; composition of standardized texts; question-answering systems; computer-guided teaching; aids for linguistically and sensorily handicapped people; and many others.

Our view is quite different. A grammar ignoring application and performance is misdirected. It can at best serve as a preliminary clarification of some problems and their solutions. The empirical adequacy of such approaches can for obvious reasons never be tested. By their distance from application and performance they immunize themselves (cf [6.8]), against a valid test of facts about linguistic (and cognitive) abilities of human beings. This is of course not to say that experiments are not possible, but rather that the outcome of such experiments is not really telling with respect to the linguistic (and cognitive) abilities of human beings, only maybe with respect to linguistic behavior and abilities in experimentally artificial situations.

A much better position is held by Logical Grammar as devised by *Ballmer* [2.19,20] in that it is based on a tight interaction between linguistic abilities (competence) and performance. More precisely it is based on the Instrumental Character of Natural Language aiding the user of its expressions to *change the context* in a more or less purposive and efficient manner. Even linguistic abilities are thus open to perpetual revisions. Human beings may act and often do act on their linguistic abilities by linguistic performance.[3] Thus many grammatical, semantic and pragmatic rules are open to constant unrelated mutually independent change. Such changes are responsible for the enormous *irregularity* of natural language.[4]

Another criticism against many formal approaches concerns the lexicon, as has already been mentioned in Chap. 2. Except for Ballmer's

---

[3] Until proof is brought to the contrary we assume that linguistic competence, apart from some "trivial" preconditions, is genetically determined by genes controlling the *cognitive abilities*. We assume, in other words, apart from genes for the anatomy and physiology of (part of) the receptors and effectors of human beings, the existence of linguistic and cognitive "genes".

[4] Linguists of quite different shades are interested predominantly in the regular part of natural language. According to what we have come to know about language, it seems, however, that language is relatively simple as far as its regular aspects are concerned, but is complex and impenetrable with respect to its irregularities. The diversity and richness of languages have their sources in these irregularities. In order therefore to meet language on its own level, linguists should turn their attention more closely to the irregular parts of language. Methods have to be developed to cope with irregularities in a systematic way. In scientific terms, the problem of natural language is not so much to find the appropriate laws (differential equations, say) as to find a method to represent and analyze the border conditions. Maybe we shall turn our attention towards studying the border conditions of natural language in their full complexity and only after a longer period of having done that come back to looking for laws.

Logical Grammar which is based fundamentally on the lexicon, most formal approaches largely neglect it as a fundamental part of the grammar (cf Chap. 2). But even for Logical Grammar the lexicon is not elaborated in enough detail to render the grammar amenable to direct application and empirical testing.

The neglected lexica firstly contain too few lexical entries, which secondly are only superficially categorized with respect to their syntactic use, and which thirdly give barely any information about the lexical meaning content, especially about the relational meaning between lexical items, and hardly enough semantic information as is needed for determining the combination of lexical entries. As a result the output of a formal grammar is lexically impoverished, apt to be full of word-combination errors and not sufficiently semantically interpreted. That such outputs cannot be of practical use is obvious. Thus, one has to work on the lexicon of formal grammars in the first place, in order to bring these grammars closer to fruitful applicability and empirical testing.

A step towards amending these shortcomings is taken in the present book. But of course we are still far from a solution which could pass a technological applicability test. We think however that we are getting closer to the point of validating the empirical adequacy of our approach by psycholinguistic experiments.[5]

The intended goal of technologically facilitated socially relevant applications suggests another view, a view which we could capture in the following statement: linguistics is a *behavioral science*. As we shall immediately elaborate, linguistic semantics is to be revised. The traditional approaches of logical language analysis and speech act theory do not do justice to the dynamic aspects of language. A revision of the semantics of natural language will lead to a position we would call *Cognitive Behaviorism*. This is a variant of both behaviorism and mentalism. Interactive processes of a (possibly nondeterministic) stimulus-response type (and their structure) play a basic role. The stimulus-response relations are however not restricted to observable physical parameters but may include mental, conceptual, introspective, and theoretical dimensions. Especially we do not reject structural (nondynamic) properties

---

[5] We are planning to perform psycholinguistic and statistical experiments in the vein of *Rapoport* and *Fillenbaum* [6.9], *Coombs* [6.10], and *Kruskal* [6.11] in order to back our findings more thoroughly. The grouping of the verbs and the relationship between the categories will be the first object which deserves a more careful statistical consideration.

of language and communication; on the contrary we aim at relating the structural and the dynamic aspects of language in an intrinsic way.

This view implies in particular that linguistics is to be placed near scientific biology, especially ethology, and near psychology. Thus linguistics gets a more direct relation to (technologically facilitated) applications.

The notion of meaning, important for lexical and sentential linguistics, has been based until recently on the notion of correspondence to facts. Thus the logical and linguistic approaches were quite usually based on truth functional Tarskian [4.10] semantics. This is true for Montague, Lewis, and Cresswell grammars. But it is even true for the Katzian, originally not formally interpreted, marker semantics. The semantic markers are then reconstructed as predicates or even relations among objects. Meaning in speech act theory, as put forward by *Grice* [6.12], *Searle* [6.13] and *Schiffer* [6.14] is based on intentions. In a recent paper by *Searle* [6.15] we learn that speech act meaning should be based on representation, thus on correspondence to facts again. *Lewis* [6.6] provides with his performative analysis another proposal to base the semantics of nondeclaratives on correspondence theory of truth and meaning.

To base linguistic meaning on a mere correspondence to facts is not useful, however. As is argued elsewhere [2.19,20] the stative notion of correspondence to facts can be shown to be less adequate than a dynamic foundation of meaning. This dynamic foundation is (roughly) characterized by the following conception of (approximative) meaning:

(6.2) (Approximative) Theoretical notion of the meaning
of a linguistic expression:
The meaning of a linguistic expression is the
(typical) systematic effect it enforces on the
various aspects of the context when used by a
speaker in that context type.

This notion of meaning takes linguistic expressions as (see above) instruments which aid the user to change the context in a more or less purposive and efficient (systematic) manner. Relative to this notion of meaning, a notion which takes linguistic expressions to be stimuli for certain responses, linguistics comes near to behaviorism. But because we are liberal with respect to the various aspects of context and include besides physical parameters mental (conceptual) dimensions too, our conception is not strictly behavioristic, but rather behavioral. More details of *Cognitive Behaviorism* and of the corresponding behavioral conception of meaning can be found in [2.19,20,6.1].

This behavioral meaning is a real alternative to more traditional notions of meaning, and in particular to speech act theoretic kinds. First we take meaning to be modifiable by linguistic performance (in order to account for learning, altering, and forgetting meanings). Secondly we take meaning as a property of linguistic expressions (and the context) telling us what the typical (systematic) effect of the linguistic expressions is when used in a context by a user. Therefore meanings are related to performance in an additional way: they determine what the instrumental character of a specific linguistic expression (in a context) is. Thirdly, for the full-blown nonapproximative conception of meaning (see below for a definition) there is no difference between illocution and perlocution. There is simply meaning, namely meaning (determined by linguistic expression and context) determining the new context by its force of context change.

When we speak of the meaning of a linguistic expression (without mentioning a certain context) we mean an approximative kind of meaning capturing the typical systematic effect of that linguistic expression (especially lexical item or sentence) averaged over a certain set of typical contexts. When we speak of full-blown meaning we mean the meaning of a linguistic expression with respect to the specifically given context in which it is used.

Thus a full-blown notion of meaning is to be understood as follows:

(6.3) (Full-blown) Theoretical meaning of a linguistic
expression in a context:
The meaning of a linguistic expression in a context
is the effect on the (linguistic expression and)
context by the use of the linguistic expression
in the context.[6]

As a consequence of this conception of meaning we take a quite different stand on certain distinctions made in speech act theory, for instance on classifying various kinds of effects: from our point of view there is no strict binary distinction to be made between illocution and

---

[6] A performance-competence distinction (and quite similarly an illocutionary-perlocutionary or a direct-indirect distinction) only arises if the full-blown meaning is approximated in various possible ways. According to the kind and the degree of approximation different performance-competence distinctions could be drawn. Thus without a sound elaboration of a method of approximating meanings we should refrain from drawing such distinctions. A working approximation of a theory of meaning, however, presupposes a well-founded conception of structure of contexts, which we are just about to establish.

perlocution. This goes along with saying that there is no strict demarcation line between understanding and (re)acting, and hence between semantics and pragmatics.

The effect brought about by the use of a linguistic expression in a context may have different extents. (The following examples are ordered according to increasing extent). The effect may be restricted to the speaker himself (intended or not); it may reach the hearer acoustically; it may cause partial or full understanding of the hearer; it may lead the hearer to think about what he understood (to have been expressed); it may cause the hearer to plan and to take decisions (accepting, rejecting, delaying); it may cause him to perform linguistic actions, to perform bodily actions, cause him to pursue a whole program, to involve other persons, and to insist on doing these things in order to overcome inner or outer obstacles. It must be stressed that these cases exemplify our underlying (complex-structured) continuum of possible effects. No dichotomy like intention/convention, illocutionary force/ propositional content, or as we already mentioned illocution/perlocution is able to do justice to the differentiated possibilities of bringing about effects in the speaker, the hearer, and their environment.

To come back to the major question of this section, a behavioral notion of meaning links technological applicability and biopsychological background. For to conceive language, and especially its semantic component, dynamically puts language on the one hand in the neighborhood of machines, algorithms, and electronic devices (technology) and on the other hand in the neighborhood of organisms, especially information- and concept-processing organisms (biopsychology).

From the point of view of linguistic semantics the dynamical aspect of language becomes particularly relevant when sequences of linguistic actions are considered. Dynamical sequences of speech acts and more generally of actions and processes exhibit special structural patterns. We hit here a point where the dynamical and the structural aspects of language intertwine. The structural patterns are part of the context in which the dynamic processes go on. A simple example may illustrate this point. With respect to the structural pattern of (part of) the Institutional Model (Norm Model) the dynamics of speech act sequences (and more generally of action and process sequences) is so determined as to follow normally the paths (or the cognitive contextual structure) of the institutional events captured in our Institutional Model.

(6.4)

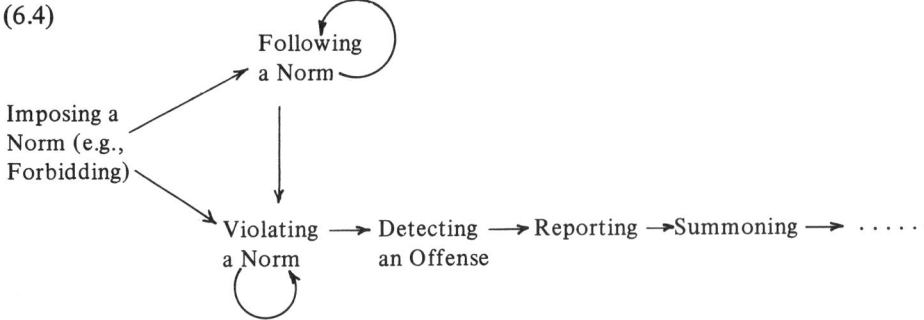

Thus our Lexical Analysis based essentially on the two semantic relations meaning similarity and presupposition leads to context structures guiding the dynamics of language based on the sequencing of speech acts (and more generally of acts and processes): (or *Cognitive Behaviorism* and *Structuralism* meet each other on the basis of Lexical Analysis.[7]

6.3 Criticisms of Our Own Proposals

In this section we shall present a list of more or less serious failures of our own proposals which we would like to criticize ourselves. Many of these failures could be eliminated. This would often take place at the cost of a considerable effort, however, because a total reworking of the semantic lexicon as well as the alphabetical list would be in order. For various reasons we are forced to refrain from doing this, one major reason being that every stage of amendment would allow us to come up with new criticisms which could then be removed in a further step, only to find new failures again and so on: in short, we would never be able to finish this work. Therefore we restrict ourselves to simply presenting a list of some inadequacies and, if necessary, some proposals on how to amend them.

---

[7] The idea of analyzing speech act sequences in an institution goes back to an early study by the Berlin Group. The various loops of differently stabilized paths of linguistic and other actions in a restaurant were investigated with the aim of exhibiting important dynamical recurrences within a social institution. A computer language *Actlan* was designed to formalize the dynamical processes and patterns. The notions pragmeme and hyperpragmeme used in these works can be seen as forerunners of the notions of frames, scripts, and schemata (cf. *Ehlich* and *Rehbein* [6.16]).

1) We started our English speech act classification by translating the verbs of the German classification and did not begin our analysis with the systematic collection of all English speech activity verbs. Therefore it may well be that some English words that have no German equivalents are missing. These should be looked for and added to the lexicon. It may even be that new categories not having an equivalent in German would arise through this procedure. This seems probable, because there were also some German categories for which we did not find corresponding verbs or even simple phrases (cf "empty" categories such as TU_7 Conflict of Turntaking and TU_{8b} Violent Turn Taking).

2) A minor point of criticism is that the lexicon lists do not generally give information about the case frames of the verbs occurring, only sometimes for reasons of disambiguation. It is worthwhile, however, to provide this information systematically. First this helps the user of the lexicon to employ the material readily. Secondly a systematic indication of the case frames has theoretical merits. Verbs together with their case frames, which we call verb schemata, allow the assessment of consequence and presupposition relations in relation to logical theory.

3) The names of the categories are not systematically chosen. Sometimes these names are verbs or verb phrases, sometimes they are nouns. Our analysis of the entire verb thesaurus has shown that it is preferable to select the most general verb of the semantically homogeneous verb group in question as category name.

4) Some of the labels are badly chosen. In rare cases it happens that a label is missing (e.g., TO_{5aa}, TO_{5ab}) or occurs doubly (e.g., NO_2). These cases have to be reconsidered and systematically amended. In the process of rearranging some categories and models, other changes of labels have to be carried out.

5) In the German classification of 1975 we had an appendix of verb lists (so-called typifications) which contained verbs difficult to include in the main body of the lexicon. We did not include the verbs in these lists in the English classification. In a newer version of the German classification these lists have been dissolved and incorporated in the major models of the classification. This should be done for the English classification too. Lists we excluded in this manner were for example speech rituals (e.g., *greet, congratulate*) speech acts in institutions (like *baptize, canonize*) and lies and deceptions (like *lie, deceive, defraud, swindle*).

6) In the present state some of the relations among models (e.g., DI, DT, IR, TU, DI/TU) of some model groups (e.g., D) are not specified

exactly enough. Especially the typifications (like DT, IR, DI/TU) should be comprised in an appropriate model, and some models and typifications should be arranged together (e.g., ET, [ET/TE] and TE) or divided up into different models (maybe the trial part of NO could be separated out). We cannot go into details here, because to find the reasons for regrouping typifications and models is a subtle and extensive task. In addition, thematically similar models could be unified (e.g., TO, TV, TP).

7) The speech act classification we present lacks, strictly speaking, the third phase, the justificatory phase. This phase would require us to provide paraphrases for each verb which justify the category, the verbs it contains, and the place of the category in a model by means of the form and structure of these paraphrases. In a further step the models and their places in the entire classification could also be justified by means of the form and structure of these paraphrases, and hence even the entire classification. This justificatory phase based on the paraphrases of the categories will work only after the criticisms we have been making are considered and some (minor) modifications of the classification made. After that, however, it will be rather a matter of routine because then the category name, the most general verb occurring in the category, will stand for the meaning content of the category, and the categories and models will be ordered perfectly with respect to presupposition. Thus it suffices to paraphrase only the category names. The paraphrases of the verbs in the category are obtained by modifying the category name by adverbs and adverbial, especially prepositional, noun phrases, [8] e.g.,

(6.5) KA_{1d} *Argue*   (old category name: Involvement)

argue	argue
bargain	argue about goods with the intention of buying or selling them
bicker	argue angrily
contend	argue with the intention of reaching an aim
contest	argue with the intention of reaching an aim
haggle	argue about goods with the intention of buying or selling them
quarrel	argue angrily
struggle	argue in order to get something
wrangle	argue grimly

---

[8] The use of adforms (adverbs, adverbial phrases, adjectives, and the like) in paraphrases is somewhat problematic, because these adforms could be used as a wastebasket for difficult cases. The only way to honestly prevent this is to classify ad-

The paraphrase(s) of the category name, e.g.,

(6.6) *argue* = *argue*
= *fight* verbally
= *interact* competitively in order to enlarge one's domain of control by verbal means

document by means of the verb nuclei occurring — *argue, fight,* or more abstractly *interact* — that the category belongs to the model of Verbal Struggle (= *arguing*), the more basic model of (nonverbal) Fighting, or to the model group of Interaction. Paraphrases of categories like

(6.7) *not yet* argue
prepare to argue
begin to argue
intensify arguing
argue
reduce arguing
cease to argue
no longer argue

determine by the aktionsarten (*not yet, prepare, begin, intensify, ..., reduce, calm down, cease, no longer*) the place of the categories in the model in question.

8) Starting from the paraphrases of the categories a set of elementary verbs could be found to which all the paraphrases can be reduced, thus barring lexical circularity. It could be suspected that we do not know anything about such a reduction to elementary verbs, because we did not list all the paraphrases of the speech act categories and reduce them explicitly to a definite set of verbs, which would be shown by this procedure to be the elementary verbs. This possible criticism is not quite correct however. For we did such an analysis for the entire German verb thesaurus (excluding the speech act readings of the verbs!) and came up with the following 11 good candidates for elementary verbs

(6.8) gelten   hold
      ablaufen   proceed
      geschehen   happen
      existieren   exist
      (als Teil) enthalten entail

---

forms with as much care as the verbs, and look for a **paraphrastic** reduction of these adforms as well. We have in fact begun this task (cf. [2.21]). A conclusive answer to whether systematic paraphrasing is possible for verbs and adforms together cannot, at the present state of our investigations, be given however.

(6.8) verursachen   cause
      wahrnehmen   perceive
      wollen   want
      versuchen   attempt
      berühren   touch
      benutzen   use

Because the speech act (readings of) verbs are often linguistically specialized versions of normal, nonlinguistic (readings of) verbs or can be related to such (readings of) verbs, we have good reason to assume that this set of (about) 10 elementary verbs will do the job for all verbs including the speech act verbs.

9) The method proposed in this book, based essentially on the semantic relations meaning similarity and presupposition, presents a real alternative to checklist theories and feature-based semantic categorizations (cf [2.17]). That is, the categorization judgments are based on the semantic intuition of speakers concerning the entire meaning of a lexical item and not on a possibly arbitrary focusing on a certain feature, meaning aspect, or similar abstraction.

To conclude this section of criticism of our own proposals we would like to summarize briefly the amendments which we added to the method of classifying verbs since the 1975 version of the German speech act classification. These amendments were developed in preparing and elaborating the *Structure of the German Verb Thesaurus* [2.23] and integrated therein. These amendments are also partly integrated in this book.

1) Systematic use of verb schemata.
2) No typifications, i.e., in other words no feature-checklist based sets of verbs.
3) Systematic and uniform choice of the category names.
4) Justification of categories and models by paraphrases.
5) Making explicit the onomasiological character of our classification based on semantic relations.
6) Making exclusive use of the presupposition relation for the ordering of categories in the models or for the ordering of the models themselves.
7) Making explicit the different kinds of aktionsarten.
8) A three-dimensional geometric display of models and the system of models.
9) Foundation of the lexicon on elementary verbs.
10) Preparation for a lexicon making use of formal logical entries [based on verb (and adverb) paraphrases].

11) Suggestions about relating lexicon and grammar especially thesaurus classification and logical grammar (language reconstruction systems).
12) Clarification of the four phases of setting up and justifying a thesaurus classification (heuristic phase, explicatory phase, justificatory phase, theoretical phase).
13) Clarification of what semantical relations and, more generally, linguistic abilities of the informants are needed for the classification.
14) Considerations about how to set up psycholinguistic tests.
15) More elaborate and specific ideas about the practical applicability of this type of lexicon.

6.4 Criticism of Competing Proposals

We shall now expose alternative proposals of classifying speech activities, mainly Austin's and Searle's, put forth some criticisms, and compare them to our own approach. The reason that we choose these two authors is that *Austin* seems to be the first to have noticed the importance of a program of speech act classification, and that *Searle* in relation to *Austin* seems to have worked out such a classification most explicitly and originally. Since *Austin* and *Searle* some further classifications of speech acts or speech act verbs have been developed. But because they are more or less along the lines of the two classifications of *Austin* and *Searle* and do not present radical alternatives — especially in method — we shall not enter on a discussion of these further approaches to speech act classification.

6.4.1 Remarks on Austin's Classification of Speech Acts

Austin attempted, as he says, to classify "more general families of related and overlapping speech acts [Ref. 1.1., p. 150]. He presents a brief sketch about ten pages long of a program which he himself considers to be merely preliminary. He distinguishes five general classes,

(6.9) Verdictives
Exercitives
Commissives
Behabitives
Expositives

Verdictives are "typified by the giving of a verdict, as the name implies, by a jury, arbitrator, or umpire". They "consist in the delivering of a finding, official or unofficial, upon evidence or reasons as to value or fact, so far as these are distinguishable". He gives 27 examples, among which there are *assess, value, analyze, grade, read it as, interpret as, estimate.* Exercitives are "the exercising of powers, rights or influence". An exercitive is the "giving of a decision in favour of or against a certain course of action, or advocacy of it. It is a decision that something is to be so, as distinct from a judgement that it is so". *Austin* gives 42 examples, among which are *offer, advise, press, enact, resign, pardon, annul, protest, withdraw.* Commissives "are typified by promising or otherwise undertaking; they *commit* you to doing something", "The whole point of a commissive is to commit the speaker to a certain course of action". Some of his 33 examples are *promise, undertake, vow, swear, consent.* Behabitives "have to do with attitudes and social behavior". They "include the notion of reaction to other people's behavior and fortunes and of attitudes and expressions of attitudes to someone else's past conduct or imminent conduct". *Austin* provides us with 33 examples, among which are *grumble about, applaud, resent, toast, welcome, congratulate, criticize, challenge.* Expositives "make plain how our utterances fit into the course of an argument or a conversation". They "are used in acts of exposition involving the expounding of views, the conducting of arguments and the clarifying of usages and of references". Among the 53 examples are *remark, correct, revise, mention, apprise.*

Austin posits his classification of speech acts on an analysis of verbs "using the simple test (with caution) of the first person singular present indicative active form, and going through the dictionary". This conception of using verbs extracted by a particular method from a dictionary and attempting to get a (language specific) classification of speech acts conforms very much to our view. One may discuss whether his method of selection is a very good one; we prefer ours (cf. Sect. 4.2). Nevertheless we are more in favor of Austin's rather wide conception of performative verb than of Searle's much narrower one. For example we include, contrary to Searle's opinion, *sympathize, regard as, mean to,* and *intend.* These verbs, in certain readings, can be used to denote speech activities. Especially we do not conform with *Searle* [1.2] that *intend* could not have the reading "expressing an intention".

Thus far we agree essentially with *Austin* [1.1]. There are some other points we cannot accept, however. First he does not provide a consistent principle of classification. As *Searle* also points out correctly "there is too much overlap of the categories, too much heterogeneity within the categories, [and] many of the verbs listed in the categories don't satisfy the definition given for the category". Relatively few verbs, namely 188, are given as examples. Thus neither the definitions nor the examples determine how Austin's classification can be enlarged and finally be completed. The examples in no way delimit the borderline cases of the classes. Austin's proposal is not therefore a real classification, which should provide a partition of the verbs: as he states himself, "it could well be said that *all* aspects are present in *all* my classes". This fact of course prevents any reasonable classification along Austin's lines.

Let us briefly mention some other criticisms. His numeric estimate of 1000 to 9999 performative verbs is very crude and demonstrates that he did not base his judgement on a careful study of the lexicon. His definitions of the classes are often circular, e.g., "The whole point of a commissive is to commit the speaker..", "Expositives are used in acts of exposition involving the expounding of views...". It is not clear what is gained by such definitions. Austin's classification has moreover definitely too few classes. The wealth of expressive power stored in the huge amount of performative verbs is in no way duly accounted for by putting these verbs into merely five classes (which because of the enormous overlaps condense in fact to one). Because the spirit behind Austin's and Searle's classifications is very similar and because Searle's classification can be seen as a specification and amendment in several (though not all respects), some of the criticisms directed against Searle's classification are also valid for Austin's and vice versa.

6.4.2 Remarks on Searle's Classification of Speech Acts

Searle [1.2] presents the same number of "basic categories of illocutionary acts" as Austin, i.e., five. He claims to have found a basis for the taxonomy, namely "the point or purpose of a type of illocution" which he calls its illocutionary point. There are some more "significant dimensions in which illocutionary acts differ from one another", for instance direction of fit between the word and the world, psychological state expressed, and nine further (for him less important) dimensions which are not used for the taxonomy into five classes, but only for determining the illocutionary force.

The five classes *Searle* comes up with are the following:

(6.10) Representatives
Directives
Commissives
Expressives
Declarations

Representatives: "The point ... is to *commit* the speaker to something being the case". "This class will contain most of *Austin*'s expositives and many of his verdictives" (*suggest, put forward as a hypothesis, insist, solemnly swear, flatly state*). Directives: "The illocutionary point of these consists in the fact that they are attempts by the speaker to get the hearer to do something". This class contains some of Austin's behabitives and many of Austin's exercitives. Examples: *order, command, request, invite, permit, advise.* Commissives: The "point is to commit the speaker to some future course of action". The class contains Austin's commissives except *shall, intend, favor.* Expressives: "The illocutionary point of this class is to express the psychological state specified in the sincerity condition about a state of affairs specified in the propositional content. Examples: *thank, congratulate, apologize, condole, deplore, welcome.* Declarations: "It is the defining characteristic of this class that the successful performance of one of its members brings about the correspondence between the propositional content and reality". Examples: *resign, fire somebody, excommunicate, christen, appoint somebody, declare war.*

Searle's five classes are briefly characterized by him as 1) "tell people how things are", 2) "try to get them to do things", 3) "commit ourselves to doing things", 4) "express our feelings and attitudes", 5) "bring about changes through our utterances". *Searle* thinks that "the most important conclusion to be drawn from this discussion" is that "there are not ... an infinite or indefinite number of language games or uses of language. Rather, the illusion of limitless uses of language is endangered by an enormous *unclarity* about what constitutes the criteria for delimiting one language game or use from another". We do not think, however, that *Searle* added much to the clarity about what constitutes such criteria of delimiting language games, as our criticisms will show.

First we have reason to believe that declarations do not constitute a proper class at all. For the defining feature of declarations, namely that they "bring about some alteration in the status or condition of the referred to object or objects solely in virtue of the fact that the declaration has been successfully performed", was the distinctive feature of the early distinction between performatives and constatives. With the collapse of this distinction in Austin's mature work it became a feature of all illocutionary acts. This proves our point that declarations do not constitute a proper class of speech acts. Accordingly acts of all four other classes can be stated in the manner of declarations. The inclusive nature of the category of declarations explains why it lends itself as a wastebasket for speech acts not falling easily into one of the first four classes.

This criticism leads to saying that *Searle*'s category of Declarations comprises all the other categories and serves as a buffer for difficult cases. Thus one way to remedy Searle's classification is to simply ignore the wastebasket category of Declarations. Because of the superficiality of the distinction between Directives and Commissives (only the addressee of the "order" is different) we are left with three categories: Expressives, Representative, and Directives. These are exactly *Bühler*'s three aspects of a linguistic sign (cf *Bühler* [4.11]). Thus Searle's purified classification can be conceived as an expression of an idea of *Bühler*. According to our findings it is questionable however whether a (disjoint and exhaustive) classification of speech acts can be built on Bühler's three aspects of signs. The analysis of the data rather suggests that it cannot (cf. 4.5).

Secondly, Searle's definition of his classes is not entirely flawless. For instance both representatives and commissives are characterized by the verb *commit* which demonstrates that the difference between the two classes cannot be very essential. A similar thing is true for directives and commissives, the difference being merely that in one case the hearer and in the other the speaker is led to do something. Moreover, as for *Austin*, some definitions are circular. Commissives are defined as making essential use of the verb *commit* and Expressives as making essential use of the verb *express*.

Thirdly, Searle's goal of classifying types of illocutionary acts is problematic from the outset. *Searle* maintains that *Austin* makes a "persistent confusion between verbs and acts". A similar reproach could be made to *Searle*: he uses verbs as examples for illocutionary acts without making precise the selection of those verbs which designate illocutionary acts (illocutionary verbs) from the set of all verbs or from the set of verbs designating a speech act. He also does not give a criterion to discriminate between illocutionary verbs and verbs designating the "style of performing the illocutionary act". We have strong reason to believe that this cannot be done.

Fourth, *Searle* who correctly attacks *Austin* for not providing a consistent principle of classification does not provide one either. He claims that it is sufficient to take "the illocutionary point, and its corollaries direction of fit and expressed sincerity conditions as the basis for constructing a classification". But it is by no means clear what the illocutionary point of a given illocutionary verb is. More precisely, how is the relation determined between a given verb and illocutionary point of the illocutionary act exemplified by that verb?

Fifth, *Searle* does not even give a definition of the notion essential for his classification, the notion of illocutionary point, except his very telling statement that "the point or purpose of a type of illocution I shall call its illocutionary point" (isn't that circular?) He relates his notion of illocutionary point, however, to another notion of his, illocutionary force, which hinges essentially on a clear possibility of separating off the propositional content of an utterance. There are reasons to believe that it is often not possible to draw the line between illocutionary force and propositional content unambiguously (cf [Ref. 6.1, p. 845]).

Sixth, *Searle*'s classification has extremely few examples, at most about 10 per class.

Seventh, as is argued in an article by one of the authors (*Ballmer* [6.3] Searle's "reasoned classification" is not a classification at all. Eleven properties which a classification should fulfill are given. Though respectable classifications such as the biological classification of animal and plant species fulfill many of the relevant requirements, it can be demonstrated that Searle's does not. Thus he did not really succeed in coming up with a classification.

As a reasonable condition for (principled) classifications it should be required that many, if not all, of the properties presented below should be fulfilled. It is shown that Searle's classification of speech acts does not fulfill this condition. For some of the properties it can easily be demonstrated that Searle's classification does not fulfill them; for others this is harder to show, partly because of the complexity of the subject matter of speech acts, partly because it is not yet absolutely settled what a speech act is, and partly also because Searle's classification is not yet formally precise enough.

We do not want to go into the details of that discussion but only list the properties a classification should fulfill.

Property 1
A classification is complete (exhaustive) iff all phenomena of a certain kind fit into the categories of the classification.

Property 2
A classification is saturated iff to every category of the classification there corresponds at least one actually retrieved phenomenon.

Property 3
A classification is disjoint iff a phenomenon falls at most into one category.

Property 4
A classification is distinctive iff different phenomena are classified differently, i.e., fall into different categories.

Property 5
A classification is homogeneous iff the depth of analysis is the same for all categories. This means especially that in a formal representation of the categories (essentially) the same kind of operators and predicates occur in all categories. In more colloquial terms, the different categories all have the same weight and importance.

Property 6
A classification is transparent iff the formal representation of a category exhibits the relation of that category to the other categories. Moreover, the form of the representation should allow one to read off the structure of the category.

Property 7
A classification is minimally redundant iff the representations of the categories are semantically and syntactically in their simplest form (expressions like $\ulcorner p \wedge p \urcorner, \ulcorner \neg \neg p \urcorner$ are not minimally redundant).

Property 8
A classification is notationally stable iff the categories are independent of their representation. A special case of notational instability occurs if different bracketing of the category representations induces a change of categories.

Property 9
A classification is logically transparent iff its categories can be characterized by a logical form.

Property 10
A classification is a weak classification iff not all phenomena are ranged into all categories of the classification in question. This is an extremely weak condition for classification. (It seems that a classification should at least fulfill the requirement of being a weak classification.)

Property 11
A classification is ontically principled iff the operators and predicates occurring in the representations of the categories belonging to the classification refer to a comprehensive and principled ontical system. (As the definition of this property of classification stands it is not extremely telling. We hope to find another more satisfying characterization of what we have in mind).

6.4.3 Remarks on the Notion of Meaning in Speech Act Theory

At this point we find it suitable to comment briefly on the notions of meaning pursued in speech act theory. Historically the trend in speech act theory seems to move gradually away from the originally maintained conception of meaning as use and to approach in various steps more and more the conception of a correspondence theory relying on a representation of facts. Thus it seems that the notion of meaning in speech act theory approaches more and more the view held in philosophical and mathematical logic (cf. [6.15]). As becomes clear from our book we cannot appreciate this development very much. From the biopsychological point of view of Cognitive Behaviorism it can be argued that a notion of meaning based on effects is more fundamental than a truth (or correspondence) based notion of meaning. Besides a bio-evolutional argument that the representation of facts is a late development coming long after mutual semiotic interaction of animals, there are many linguistic arguments why inducing effects is primary to the special situation of producing effects by linguistic means of representation. Thus greetings, swearing, warnings, and the like, having no "propositional content" (in other words not representing in an obvious way states of affairs) nevertheless have meaning, the meaning being their effect on the participants of the communication.[9,10] Intention, another notion to which meaning was attempted to be reduced, especially in speech act theory, cannot be fundamental either. For somebody to have an intention implies that he has an intention to produce a certain effect! Thus intending presupposes the notion of effect, or more precisely the notion of producing an effect. The basic (non-innate) intentions a living organism can conceive presuppose stable occurrences of

---

[9] The very basic meanings are — we repeat and illustratively expand what is contained in (6.3) — the historically unique full-fledged effects of the linguistic entities used in a historically unique full-fledged situation. Other meanings, the (average) meaning of a linguistic expression, the maybe misunderstood meaning of a certain use of a certain linguistic expression by a hearer, are secondary. A child builds his approximate meanings on his maybe partial understanding of the historically full-fledged meanings. The historically unique effects are the basic material on which ontogenetic and phylogenetic development builds.

[10] Mathematical and logical notions of meaning are based essentially on correspondence to states of affairs. Our view that effects are more basic than representations does not necessarily imply that mathematics and logic are not fundamental enough for scientific purposes, for in science description and descriptive reconstruction are what matters.

effects in a certain situation, the detection of such relations between occasions and effects, the means of interacting with courses of events which lead to the occasions in question, and the mental anticipation of these facts in order to get conscious control over the effects. The recognition of intentions of other organisms (when they are producing a specific effect) presupposes a notion of normal effects in a situation, a notion of violating these normal effects in that situation, and a notion of recognizing the focus of attention of other organisms: the recognition of an intention (when an organism produces a specific effect) is to recognize that the organism behaves in some special manner but with full awareness (focus of attention directed towards the effects in question). Intention is attributed especially to an organism if he makes provisions for attaining certain effects (preparation) and if he does not remove certain achieved effects (acceptance). To sum up, intention presupposes effects in a multiple way such that a notion of meaning based on intentions is automatically one based on effects. On the other hand there are "natural" notions of meaning not based on intention at all (cf *Grice*'s notion [6.12] of natural meaning, and *Strawson*'s conventional meaning [6.17]). Our view of meaning essentially based on an interactive notion is therefore adequately general. It lies at the base of the use of language in communication and is only secondarily related to representation and correspondence to facts and to intention.

6.5 Applications

Although our analysis of the structure of the English speech act verb thesaurus is in the first respect meant to be a piece of linguistic work, it is interesting for nonlinguists as well, because of its possible applications.

A practical application is the use as a dictionary of synonyms for looking up a suitable expression. We believe that our semantically motivated categorization facilitates the search for a suitable expression a great deal compared to other dictionaries which do not use such semantic criteria and list the meaning classes in part arbitrarily (e.g., [2.2, 6.18,19]).

Apart from this practical application there are possible applications for scholars in different fields.

A structured verb thesaurus is of interest to *sociologists* insofar as verb structures reflect socially relevant patterns of actions and processes. This holds in the first place for speech activity verbs.

Psychologists, especially cognitive psychologists, may be interested in the structured verb thesaurus as it can be a basis for psychological hypotheses. Its semantic structure reflects views of reality, i.e., cognitive structures. It can be assumed that results of reaction time tests, association tests, memory tests, and perhaps aphatic phenomena correspond to our category structure. In this sense our approach also includes an empirical claim, although no explicit empirical theory.

Artificial Intelligence, which is concerned with the computer simulation of cognitive processes, relates in part closely to cognitive psychology. Since in artificial intelligence one searches for knowledge and memory representation systems, direct use could be made of our lexicon structures, which represent nothing more than linguistically stored knowledge.

For *philosophers* our lexicon may have a number of interesting aspects. The philosopher of language can gain information about larger systems of meaning and about the relation between language and reality. The metaphysicist gains a linguistically based insight into the construction of reality.

Scholars in the theory of *literature* who are interested in text-linguistics can find in our verb classification building blocks for textual structures of different complexity. The structured verb thesaurus can function as a source for so-called microstructures as well as macrostructures. The model sequences allow the construction of simple texts. More complex texts can be produced by connecting several models in a suitable way.

Those working in *language acquisition*, for both first and second languages, can find rich material for vocabulary exercises in our lexicon. Thesauri can be taught and learned in a semantically systematic way with our lexicon, which promises an increase in learning speed. Since the meaning of a word can be read off from its position in the category system, the lexicon could be particularly useful for the acquisition of English as a foreign language. Without a teacher or bilingual dictionary the learner can grasp main aspects of the meaning of words.

Our structural verb thesaurus can help *language engineers* to detect systematic or accidental gaps in the vocabulary of an already existing language, to develop criteria on whether to fill them, and to eliminate gaps in a morphosyntactically adequate way. The structured verb thesaurus can also serve as a basis for the designing of an artificial natural language, which has morphosyntactically transparent expressions for the already more or less rudimentary given semantico-logical structures.

Finally, we want to make some suggestions about the relevance of our lexicon for linguists working on syntax. From the verb schemata, which are ordered by the categories, certain sentence patterns can be constructed. Syntax and semantics coincide only insofar as verb schemata of the same category often lead to the same sentence patterns. Where this is not the case one can find semantic reasons for the syntactic inhomogeneity. Looking at the matter in a simplified way one can establish a direct correlation between the semantically classified verb schemata and the syntactic sentence patterns. The syntax of complex sentences can be obtained recursively from such primary sentence patterns. What an appropriate formal grammar must look like for these matters can be learned from [2.19,20,6.20].

Chapter 7   References

1.1 J.L. Austin: *How to Do Things with Words* (Clarendon, Oxford 1962)
1.2 J.R.Searle: "A Taxonomy of Illocutionary Acts", in *Language, Mind and Knowledge*, ed. by K. Gunderson (University of Minnesota Press, Minneapolis 1975) pp. 334–369
1.3 B. Fraser: "Hedged Performativs", in *Syntax and Semantics*, ed. by P. Cole, J.L. Morgan (Academic Press, New York 1975) pp. 187–210
1.4 J. Petöfi, H. Kayser: „Sprechhandlungen und Semantische Interpretation", in *Sprechen–Handeln–Interaktion*, ed. by R. Meyer-Hermann (Niemeyer, Tübingen 1978) pp. 1–48
1.5 D. Wunderlich: *Studien zur Sprechakttheorie* (Suhrkamp, Frankfurt 1976)
1.6 F. Coulmas: *Rezeptives Sprachverhalten* (Buske, Hamburg 1977)
1.7 T. van Dijk: *Taal en Handelen* (Coutinho, Muiderberg 1978)
1.8 J. Allwood: *Linguistic Communication as Action and Cooperation: A Study in Pragmatics* (Dept. of Linguistics, Univ. of Göteborg, 1976)
1.9 J.L. Cohen: "Speech Acts", in *Current Trends in Linguistics*, Vol. XII, ed. by T. Sebeok (Mouton, Paris 1974) pp. 173–208
1.10 Th. Ballmer, W. Brennenstuhl, K. Ehlich, J. Rehbein(Berliner Gruppe):*Sprachliches Handeln (Listen, Kategorien, Modelle)* (Fink, Munich, forthcoming)
2.1 J. Grimm, W. Grimm: *Deutsches Wörterbuch* (Hirzel, Leipzig 1884)
2.2 P.M. Roget: *Roget's Thesaurus* (Longmans Green, London 1966)
2.3 *Langenscheidts Handwörterbuch*, Teil I, II (Langenscheidt, Berlin 1970)
2.4 *Cassell's German and English Dictionary* (Cassell, London 1957)
2.5 J. Trier: *Der Deutsche Wortschatz im Sinnbezirk des Verstandes* (Winter, Heidelberg 1931)
2.6 L. Weisgerber: *Grundzüge der Inhaltsbezogenen Grammatik* (Schwann, Düsseldorf 1962)
2.7 W. Porzig: *Das Wunder der Sprache* (Francke, Munich 1971)
2.8 E. Leisi: *Der Wortinhalt* (Quelle und Meyer, Heidelberg 1953)
2.9 J. Katz, P. Postal: *An Integrated Theory of Linguistic Description* (MIT Press, Cambridge, Mass. 1964)
2.10 Ch. Fillmore: "Types of Lexical Information", in *Studies in Syntax and Semantics*, ed. by F. Kiefer (Reidel, Dordrecht 1969) pp. 109–137
2.11 G. Helbig, W. Schenkel: *Wörterbuch zur Valenz und Distribution deutscher Verben* (VEB Enzyklopädie, Leipzig 1973)
2.12 H. Schuhmacher (ed.): *Untersuchungen zur Verbvalenz* (Gunther Narr, Tübingen 1976)

2.13 W. Busse, J.P. Dubost: *Französisches Verblexikon* (Klett-Cotta, Stuttgart 1977)
2.14 L. Bloomfield: *Language* (Holt, Rinehart & Winston, New York, and Allen & Unwin, London 1970)
2.15 N. Chomsky: *Aspects of the Theory of Syntax* (MIT Press, Cambridge, Mass. 1965)
2.16 R. Montague: *Formal Philosophy*, ed. by R. Thomason (Yale University Press, London 1974)
2.17 Ch. Fillmore: "An Alternative to Checklist Theories of Meaning", in *BLS 1* (Proceedings of the First Annual Meeting of the Berkeley Linguistics Society) (UCB, Berkeley 1975) pp. 123–131
2.18 M. Minsky: "A Framework for Representing Knowledge"; Artificial Intelligence Memo, No. 306, AI Lab, MIT (1975)
2.19 Th. Ballmer: *Logical Grammar* (with Special Consideration of Topics in Context Change) (North-Holland, Amsterdam 1978)
2.20 Th. Ballmer: "Context Change, Truth and Competence", in *Semantics from Different Points of View*, Springer Series in Language and Communication, Vol. 6, ed. by R. Bäuerle, U. Egli, A. von Stechow (Springer, Berlin, Heidelberg, New York 1979) pp. 21–31
2.21 Th. Ballmer, W. Brennenstuhl: Zum Verbwortschatz der deutschen Sprache. Ling. Ber. *55*, 18–37 (1978)
2.22 I. Rechenberg: *Optimierung technischer Systeme nach Prinzipien der biologischen Evolution* (Fromman-Holzboog, Stuttgart 1972)
2.23 Th. Ballmer, W. Brennenstuhl: *Die Struktur des Deutschen Verbwortschatzes* (Bochum, forthcoming)
3.1 J. Lyons: *Introduction to Theoretical Linguistics* (Cambridge University Press, Cambridge 1968)
4.1 *(The Shorter) Oxford English Dictionary* (2 Vols.) (Clarendon, Oxford 1977)
4.2 *Webster's Third New International Dictionary* (unabridged), ed. by P.B. Gove (G. & C. Merriam, Springfield, Mass. 1971)
4.3 G. Wahrig: *Deutsches Wörterbuch* (Bertelsmann Lexikon Verlag, Munich 1968)
4.4 *Das große Wörterbuch der Deutschen Sprache* (6 Vols.) (Bibliographisches Institut: Duden Verlag, Mannheim 1977)
4.5 E. Mater: *Deutsche Verben*, Bd. 1 (VEB Bibliographisches Institut, Leipzig 1966)
4.6 E. Rosch: Natural categories. Cog. Psychol. *4*, 328–350 (1973)
4.7 J. Lyons: *Semantics* (Vols. 1,2) (Cambridge University Press, Cambridge 1977)
4.8 E. Koschmieder: „Zur Bestimmung der Funktionen grammatischer Kategorien", in *Beiträge zur allgemeinen Syntax* (Winter, Heidelberg 1965) pp. 9–69
4.9 M. Deutschbein: „Die Einteilung der Aktionsarten", in *Englische Studien*, Vol. 54 (Reisland, Leipzig 1920) pp. 80–86
4.10 A. Tarski: „Der Wahrheitsbegriff in den formalisierten Sprachen", in *Stud. Philos. Comm. Soc. Phil. Pol.*, Vol. 1 (Leopoli, Lemberg 1935)
4.11 K. Bühler: *Sprachtheorie* (Fischer, Stuttgart 1934)
6.1 Th. Ballmer: "The Instrumental Character of Natural Language"; Habilitationsschrift, Ruhr University, Bochum (1977)

6.2 Th. Ballmer: „Perspektiven der Sprachwissenschaft", Inaugural Lecture at the Ruhr University of Bochum (1979)
6.3 Th. Ballmer: „Probleme der Klassifikation von Sprechakten", in *Sprechakttheorie und Semantik*, ed. by G. Grewendorf (Suhrkamp, Frankfurt 1979) pp. 247–274
6.4 N. Chomsky: *Reflections on Language* (Pantheon Books, New York 1975)
6.5 N. Chomsky: "Deep Structure, Surface Structure, and Semantic Interpretation", in *Semantics*, ed. by D.D. Steinberg, L.A. Jakobovits (Cambridge University Press, Cambridge 1969) pp. 183–216
6.6 D. Lewis: "General Semantics", in *Semantics of Natural Language*, ed. by D. Davidson, G. Harman (Reidel, Dordrecht 1972) pp. 169–218
6.7 M. Cresswell: *Logic and Languages* (Methuen, London 1973)
6.8 Th. Ballmer: „Inwiefern ist Linguistik empirisch ?", in *Wissenschaftstheorie der Linguistik*, ed. by D. Wunderlich (Athenäum, Kronberg 1976) pp. 6–53
6.9 A. Rapoport, S. Fillenbaum: "An Experimental Study of Semantic Structures", in *Multidimensional Scaling*, Vol. II, ed. by A. Kimball Romney (Seminar Press, New York 1972) pp. 93–131
6.10 C.H. Coombs: *A Theory of Data* (Wiley, New York 1964)
6.11 J.B. Kruskal: Multidimensional scaling: a numerical method. Psychometrika *29*, 1–27 (1964)
6.12 P. Grice: Meaning. Philos. Rev. *LXVI*, 377–388 (1957)
6.13 J.R. Searle: *Speech Acts: An Essay in the Philosophy of Language* (Cambridge University Press, Cambridge 1969)
6.14 St. Schiffer: *Meaning* (Clarendon, Oxford 1972)
6.15 J.R. Searle: "Meaning, Communication and Representation" (University of California, Berkeley 1976)
6.16 K. Ehlich, J. Rehbein: „Zur Konstitution pragmatischer Einheiten in einer Institution: Das Speiserestaurant", in *Linguistische Pragmatik*, ed. by D. Wunderlich (Athenäum, Frankfurt 1972) pp. 209–254
6.17 P.F. Strawson: Intention and convention in speech acts. Philos. Rev. *73*, 439–460 (1964)
6.18 F. Dornseiff: *Der Deutsche Wortschatz nach Sachgruppen* (de Gruyter, Berlin 1965)
6.19 H. Wehrle, H. Eggers: *Deutscher Wortschatz* (Klett, Stuttgart 1961)
6.20 Th. Ballmer: *Sprachrekonstruktionssysteme* (und einige ihrer Anwendungen in Satz- und Textlinguisitk) Scriptor, Kronberg 1975)

Bibliography

M. Black: Austin on performatives. Philosophy *38*, 217–226 (1963) ; reprinted in K.T. Fann (ed.): *Symposium on J.L. Austin* (Routledge & Kegan, London 1969) pp 401–411

W. Brennenstuhl: *Handlungstheorie und Handlungslogik* (Scriptor, Kronberg 1975)

B. Engelen: *Untersuchungen zu Satzbauplan und Wortfeld in der geschriebenen deutschen Sprache der Gegenwart* (Hueber, Munich 1975)

K.T. Fann (ed.): *Symposium on J.L. Austin* (Routledge & Kegan, London 1969)

M. Gross: *Méthodes en Syntaxe* (Hermann, Paris 1975)

J.S. Gruber: *Lexical Structures in Syntax and Semantics* (North-Holland, Amsterdam 1976)

J. Habermas:„Vorbereitende Bemerkungen zu einer Theorie der kommunikativen Kompetenz", in *Theorie der Gesellschaft oder Sozialtechnologie — Was leistet die Systemforschung*, ed. by J. Habermas, N. Luhmann (Suhrkamp, Frankfurt 1971) pp. 101–141

R. Harris: The descriptive interpretation of performative utterances. J. Ling. *14*, 129–375 (1978)

I. Hedenius: Performatives. Theoria *29*, 115–136 (1963)

F.W. Householder (ed.): *Problems in Lexicography* (Indiana University, Bloomington 1975)

R. Kempson: *Semantic Theory* (Cambridge University Press, Cambridge 1977)

A. Lehrer: *Semantic Fields and Lexical Structure* (North-Holland, Amsterdam 1974)

J. McCawley: "Lexical Insertion in a Transformational Grammar Without Deep Structure", in *CLS 4* (Proceedings of the Fourth Annual Meeting of the Chicago Linguistic Society) (University of Chicago, Chicago 1968)

E. Rosch, B. Lloyd (eds.): *Cognition and Categorization* (Lawrence Erlbaum, Hillsdale 1978)

R. Schank: *Conceptual Information Processing* (North-Holland, Amsterdam 1975)

A. Van der Ven: *Inleiding in de Schaaltheorie* (Van Loghum Slaterus, Deventer 1977)

Part II
Lexicon Sections

Directions for Using Lexicon Section I

Lexicon Section I contains the speech activity verbs and complex expressions listed in models and categories *according to their meaning*. The order of the models is the same as given in (4.14). The order of the categories of a model is made clear by their label, which precedes the category name. A complex label provides the following information:

e.g., TP_{2ab}

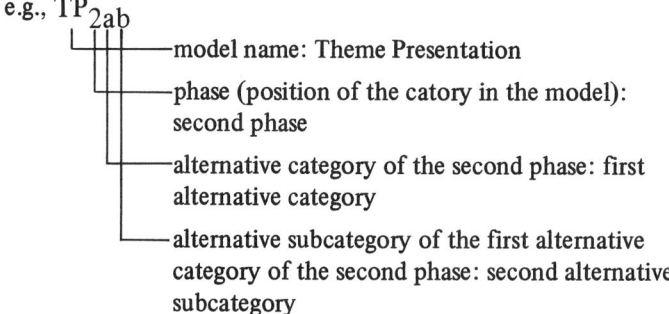

- model name: Theme Presentation
- phase (position of the catory in the model): second phase
- alternative category of the second phase: first alternative category
- alternative subcategory of the first alternative category of the second phase: second alternative subcategory

Categories are presented in the following way (an example for a category with a simple label):

e.g., $\underline{VE}_1$ ....

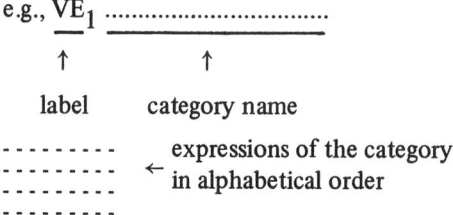

label   category name

expressions of the category ← in alphabetical order

Given an expression with a certain meaning, Lexicon Section I provides the following information

1) which expressions are approximatively synonymous;
   cf the other expressions in the same category
2) which kind of speech activity is expressed;
   cf the category name
3) which speech activities precede or follow;
   cf the neighbor phases
4) which alternative speech activities occur in the same phase;
   cf the neighbor categories of the same phase
5) which larger semantic field does the speech activity belong to;
   cf the model name

Chapter 8 Lexicon Section I

Semantic Classification of Speech Act Verbs
(List of Models, Categories and Verbs)

8.1 EM Emotion Model

EM$_1$ Processing Experiences

EM$_{2aa}$ Indicators of the Emotional Process

blush
chill suddenly
falter
get sad
give vent to (anger)
grow angry
hesitate
lower one's voice
raise one's voice
sob
stammer
stutter
turn pale
turn sad

EM$_{2ab}$ Indicators of States of Emotion

be angry
fidget
grimace
be nervous
have a red face
be sad
be shocked
tremble

EM$_{2b}$ Expression

blow up
boil over
burst out laughing
cry
explode
flare up
get into rage
moan
scream
shout
shout for joy
shriek
whimper

EM$_{2b'}$ Express the Suppression of Indicators

breathe heavily
hesitate
hold back
grin and bear it
grit one's teeth

EM$_{2ca}$ Exothesize Emotion, Processual

get angry
get furious
get vexed
gladden
have a falling out
take offense

EM$_{2ca}$* I-Exothesis, Processual

be pissed off ("I am pissed off")
get angry ("I am getting angry")
have had enough (I have had enough")

EM$_{2cb}$ Exothesize Emotion, Stative

be afraid
be angry
be disappointed
be grateful
hate
be in love
mourn
be sad
be sorry for
express sympathy
be uncomfortable
be worried

EM$_{2cb}$* I-Exothesis, Stative

admire ("I admire you")
be afraid ("I am afraid")
be angry ("I am angry")
be disappointed ("I am disappointed")
be glad ("I am glad")
hate ("I hate you")
love ("I love you")
be sad ("I am sad")
be sorry ("I am sorry")

EM$_{2d}$ Exothesis of a Recent Result of Processing an Emotion

burst out
get furious
start grumble about

EM$_{2e}$ Exothesis of a Short Lasting Result of Processing

cry
curse and swear

EM$_{2e}$ Exothesis of a Short Lasting Result of Processing (continued)

cuss
grumble about
grumble
shout
shout with joy
swear
rejoice
yell at a person

EM$_{2f}$ Exothesis of a Long Lasting Result of Processing

grieve
lament
moan
pout
quarrel
sulk
squabble
strive

EM$_{2ga}$ Utter Maledictions, in General

curse a person
cuss
damn (so.)
wish so. evil
swear

EM$_{2gb}$ Appeal to a Higher Authority

appeal to
(beg)
call down (blessings, curses) upon so.
implore
(imprecate)

EM$_{2h}$ Announce Value Judgments

applaud
bring out a toast

EM_{2h} Announce Value Judgments (countinued)

clap for so.
hail
make a toast
salute
curse so.
wish so. evil
boo so. off the stage
condemn by hissing/by booing
hiss off the stage
shout down
cheer loudly
be jubilant over
receive with exultation
rejoice at
shout to so.

EM_{2i} Show Emotion as an Attempt to Induce an Emotion

implore
be enthusiastic about
lament
rave

EM_{2j} Adressee-Oriented Expressive Speech Acts

adore so.
cheer so.
condemn so.
cuss at so.
curse so.
pity so.

EM_{2j} Adresse-Oriented Expressive Speech Acts (continued)

swear at so.
yell at so.

EM_{2k} Hidden Appeal

bitch at
carp about
dawdle
grumble
murmur
mutiny
nag
pout
rumble
sulk
whine
wrangle

EM_{2l} Open Appeal

address angrily
address imperiously
ask abruptly
give so. a severe scolding
growl at
scold
shout at
snap at
snarl at
sneer at
spit at
thunder at
heckle

8.2 EN Enaction Model

EN_0 Volitions

EN_{0a} Active Wishing

EN_{0aa} Wishing

dream of doing sth.
dream that sth. happens
like
love sth.
prefer
wish to do sth.
wish that sth. happens

EN_{0ab} Intending

aim at
aspire to
desire
endeavor to get
intend
like
ordain
plan to do sth.
strike for
want
want to have sth.
will to

EN_{0b} Passive Wishes

EN_{0ba} Waiting

desire
dream to get sth.
hope for
long for
wait
want to have
wish

EN_{0bb} Expecting

anticipate
attend to
await (with impatience)
expect
lurk for so.
wait for
watch for

EN_1 Taking into Focus/Taking out of Focus

EN_{1a} Taking into Focus

EN_{1aa} Wakening

awake so.
wake (up) so.
waken so.
rouse so.

EN_{1ab} Alerting

alert so.
call to so.

EN_{1ac} Pointing

call so.'s attention to sth.
draw so.'s attention to sth.
exhibit
focus
point at
point to sth.
show
show the way
allude to
indicate
hint at
refer to

EN₁ₐd Reminding

call to so.'s mind
refer back to
refresh so.'s memory
remind so.

EN₁ₐₑ Initiating

give rise to
initiate
incite
induce
motivate
stimulate
stir up
suggest

EN₁ᵦ Taking out of Focus

distract
dissuade
divert
divert a man's thoughts
turn away attention
make so. forget sth.
sidetrack

EN₂ Helping (Offer Help/Call for Help)

EN₂ₐ Offering

canvass
make propaganda for
offer sth.
offer to lend a hand
offer for sale
offer one's services
place at so.'s disposal
propagandize
propose
recommend

EN₂ᵦ Asking for

apologize for
appeal
apply to
approach with entreaties
ask advice for
ask in
ask out
aspire to
beg
beg (for)
beg forgiveness
beseech
bid
call on so.
entreat
implore
importune
invite
petition
plead
pray for sth.
prevail upon
request
require
solicit
strive after
summon
supplicate

EN₂ᵦ§ Asking Officially

apply for
file an application
move
petition
propose
propose (to a lady)
propose a motion for
request
make a formal request
sue (for)
solicit
woo

EN$_{2c}$ Advising

advise
advise against
commed
counsel
recommend
suggest

EN$_{2c\S}$ Proposing Officially

mandate
run for (presidency)
plead for

EN$_3$ Commissioning

EN$_{3a}$ Commissioning, in General

book (seats)
charge with
command
commission
countermand
cancel
direct
give an assignment
give a task, mission
order in advance
order so. to do sth.
order sth.
order subsequently
order a fresh supply
repeat an order
send for so.
subscribe to

EN$_{3aa}$ Ordering Messengers/Calling on for Change of Location

delegate
depute
direct
mandate
order so. to do sth.

EN$_{3aa}$ Ordering Messengers/Calling on for Change of Location (continued)

send so.
dispatch
giving directions
send

EN$_{3ab}$ Reserving

put on hold
put on layaway
put on reserve
reserve
reserve a seat
fix a date
make an appointment

EN$_{3b}$ Mandating

appoint
authorize
delegate
depute
empower
invest with full powers
license
mandate
nominate

EN$_{3c}$ Instructing (cf. ET$_{0da}$)

brief
direct
instruct
prepare so.
school
teach
train

EN$_{3d}$ Giving or Transferring Property/Expropriating

EN$_{3da}$ Giving or Transferring Property

EN₃da Giving or Transferring Property (continued)

assign to
bequeath
bestow
carry over
cede one's property
consecrate
consign a th. to so.
create a foundation
dedicate
donate
entrust a th. to so.
make a donation
give
grant
hand down
leave
present
present so. with a th.
refer one's money to so.
remit
sanctify
send one's money to so.
transfer

EN₃db Expropriating

annex
commandeer
confiscate
disinherit
dispossess
distrain
expropriate
seize
take in pledge

EN₄ Pointing at a Norm or Danger

EN₄a Admonishing

admonish
exhort

EN₄a Admonishing (continued)

remind
urge

EN₄b Warning

alarm
draw attention to a danger
caution
warn

EN₄c Threatening

admonish
make threatening gestures
menace (so. with sth.)
threaten (so. with sth.)

EN₅ Demanding

EN₅a Calling on

ask
call so.
call upon
challenge
invite
request
summon

EN₅b Demanding

ask
claim
demand
exact
insist on
make conditions
require
summon

EN₅c Asking Questions

EN$_{5ca}$ Making Guesses

estimate
guess
make guesses
(make out)
(solve)
(unravel)

EN$_{5cb}$ Inquiries

ask advice
ask around
ask for information
consult
gain information about
gather information
inquire
make inquiries

EN$_{5cc}$ Asking Questions, in General

ask
ask a question
consult
consult with so.
examine
inquire (into)
interrogate
probe with questions
put a question to so.
question
quiz

EN$_{5cd}$ Examine

ascertain by inquiring
bring out by questioning
examine
hear so.
hear a pupil's lesson
institute an inquiry
interview
investigate so.
put so. to a severe test

EN$_{5cd}$ Examine (continued)

test
try so.

EN$_6$ Commanding

EN$_{6a}$ Weak Commands

admonish
advise
allude to
exhort
inform
point out
point to

EN$_{6b}$ Commanding in the Proper Sense

bid
command
decree
dictate
direct
enact
give orders
ordain by decree
order
prescribe

EN$_{6c}$ Directing

act as chairman
browbeat
conduct
control
direct
govern
guide
instruct
introduce so. to sth.
lead
manipulate
manage
preside (over)

EN$_{6c}$ Directing (continued)

regulate
send so.
show
show the way
teach
train

EN$_{6d}$ Self-Commanding/Committing Oneself

accede to
acknowledge in writing
agree to
assent to
award
bind os. (to so.)
commit os.
confirm
declare
enter (into a treaty)
give bail
give one's word of honor
grant
guarantee
hold out a prospect of sth. to so.
join (a party)
pledge
promise
promise solemnly
sign (a contract)
take so.'s part
vouch
warrant

EN$_{6e}$ Cancelling Commands, Demands, Commissions

annul
cancel
countermand
declare void
disavow

EN$_{6e}$ Cancelling Commands, Demands, Commissions

quash
rescind
retract
revoke
suspend
withdraw

EN$_7$ Influencing

EN$_{7a}$ Seductions

EN$_{7aa}$ Making Compliments

adore
cajole
coax
compliment
court
fawn upon
flatter
flirt
make suggestions
pay compliments
say sweet nothings
wheedle

EN$_{7ab}$ Prepare Contact

buttonhole
come up to so.
walk up to so.

EN$_{7ac}$ Establishing Contact

accost
address os. to so.
approach
contact
start a conversation

EN$_{7ad}$ Acting Overfriendly

EN$_{7ad}$ Acting Overfriendly (continued)

behave in a familiar manner
captivate
charm
chum up with so.
fascinate
flatter
ingratiate os. with so.
make up to
making compliments
praise extravagantly

EN$_{7ae}$ Intruding os.

afflict so.
being obtrusive
talk too much
intrude os. upon so.
oppress so.
urge os.

EN$_{7af}$ Attracting/Seducing

allure
attract
bait
coax
decoy
delude
entice
induce
infatuate
influence by suggestion
lead astray
lure
mislead
seduce
tempt

EN$_{7ag}$ Persuading/Convincing

convert
convince

EN$_{7ag}$ Persuading/Convincing (continued)

fill with enthusiasm
influence
inspire
interest so.
make so. believe
persuade
talk so. into
talk over
wheedle so. out of sth.

EN$_{7b}$ Surprising

amaze
astonish
astound
bewilder
disconcert
flabbergast
shock
stagger
startle
strike
surprise

EN$_{7c}$ Stimulating and Calming

EN$_{7ca}$ Calming

allay
appease
assuage
calm
comfort
compose
commiserate
condole so.
console
hush up
lull (to sleep)
pacify
pity
quiet

EN$_{7ca}$ Calming (continued)

reassure
show sympathy
soften
solace
soothe
sympathize
still

EN$_{7cb}$ Encouraging

cheer so. up
comfort so.
confirm so.
corroborate so.
encourage so.
enliven
help so.
incite
inspire with courage
move so. to do sth.
rouse
spur (on)
stimulate
strengthen so.
support so.

EN$_{7cc}$ Stimulating

arouse
cheer up
excite
frame
goad on
incite
instigate
plot
prime
provoke
spur on
stimulate
stir up
urge

EN$_{7d}$ Arousing Disgust

arouse disgust
sicken

EN$_{7d'}$ Stirring up

afflict
depress
disquiet
distress
disturb
embarrass
grieve
move so.
touch so.
trouble
upset
worry

EN$_8$ Demanding Effectively

EN$_{8aa}$ Insisting

blackmail
bully sth. out of so.
coerce
compel
demand from
enforce
extort sth. from so.
force sth. from so.
force a thing upon so.
insist
intrude upon
obtain by begging
oppress
press
swindle so. out of a thing
thrust a thing upon so.
urge strongly upon so.

EN$_{8ab}$ Hindering Effectively

baffle
balk
debar
defeat a purpose
deter
frustrate
hinder
prevent
prohibit
restrain
thwart
ward off

EN$_{8b}$ Frightening away

chase away
eject
expel
frighten away
scare
send away
throw out

EN$_{8c}$ Teaching

brainwash
cram into
drum into
drum sth. into so.'s head
educate
impress sth. on so.
inculcate
school
teach
train

EN$_{8d}$ Frustrating

annoy
bother
daunt
demoralize
discourage

EN$_{8d}$ Frustrating (continued)

dishearten
frustrate
intimidate
irritate
put in a bad temper
scare
upset

EN$_9$ Reactions on Enactions

EN$_{9a}$ Reactions on Offering

(positive)
accept

(negative)
decline
pass up
refuse
reject
repulse

EN$_{9b}$ Reactions on Asking for Something

(positive)
comply with
fulfill
give a favorable hearing
grant
gratify

(negative)
deny
refuse
reject
repel
repulse

EN$_{9b\S}$ Reactions on Asking Officially

(positive)
accept
act favorably on
allow

EN9b§ Reactions on Asking Officially
(continued)

(positive)
approve
grant
pass a bill
permit

(negative)
answer in the negative
deny
react negatively
refuse
reject

EN9c Reactions on Advising

(positive)
accept
consider well
follow
heed
pay attention to
ponder
take to heart

(negative)
dismiss
disregard
ignore
pay no attention
pay no heed to
reject

EN9d Reactions on Commissioning

(positive)
carry out
execute
fulfill
obey

(negative)
disobey
disregard

EN9d Reactions on Commissioning
(continued)

(negative)
ignore
neglect
refuse
reject

EN9f Reactions on Expropriating

complain
mutiny
oppose
protest
resist
revolt

EN9g Reactions on Admonishing, Warning, Threatening

(positive)
act accordingly
consider well
heed
pay attention
pay heed to
ponder
take to heart

(negative)
disregard
ignore
neglect
pay no head to

EN9h Reactions on Demanding

(positive)
comply with
cooperate
fulfill
give in

(negative)
oppose

EN₉ₕ Reactions on Demanding (continued)

protest
rebel against
refuse
reject
repel
repulse
shake off

EN₉ₕ' Cancelling Request

cancel
disavow
disclaim
relinquish
renounce
waive

abandon

EN₉ᵢ Answering Questions

(answering in the positive)
accept
affirm
agree
answer in the affirmative
assent to
give consent to
give information

(answer in the negative)
contradict
deny
disavow

(reject the question)
disregard the question
evade the question
ignore the question
neglect
pass over
refuse to answer
reject
skip

EN₉ⱼ Reactions on Commanding

(positive)
carry out
execute
follow
fulfill
obey

(negative)
countermand
contravene
disobey
disregard
ignore
neglect
reject
violate

EN₉ₖ Reactions on Suggesting

(positive)
accept
agree to
consider
follow
heed
ponder
pay attention to
take to heart

(negative)
not agree to
not listen to
oppose
rebel against
refuse
reject

EN₉ₗ Reactions on Calming and Stimulating

calm down (intrans.)
cheer up (intrans.)
get excited
startle

EN₉' Fulfillment and Nonfulfillment of Volitions

EN₉'ₐ Fulfillment by Chance

sth. comes about
get
sth. happens
receive
turn out well

EN₉'ᵦ Doing it Oneself

act
bring about

EN₉'ᵦ Doing it Oneself (continued)

do
manage
succeed in

EN₉'ᵧ Reactions on Failure

accommodate os. to
be disappointed
resign
submit to

8.3. KA Struggle Model (Competition and Cooperation Model)

KA₋₃ Starting Situation

KA₋₃ₐ Unacquainted Status

be foreign
be strange
be unacquainted with a p.
be unknown
do not know each other
not to be known
not to be previously known

KA₋₃ᵦ Friendship Status

agree
be at one
be clearly aware of one another's view
be in harmony
be kindly disposed towards
be of importance to so.
be of one mind
be of the same opinion
be of value to so.
be united
be benevolent to so.

KA₋₃ᵦ Friendship Status (continued)

check
consent
correspond to
express sympathy with
feel sympathy with
get on well together
get on with one another
hit it off well
to mean sth. to so.
to share the opinion
side with so.
stand by
support
sympathize with
tally
understand one another
unify
unite

KA₋₃c Enemy Status

argue with so.
be at war with one another

KA₋₃c Enemy Status (continued)

be hostile to
be ill-feeling towards another
be implacable
be irreconcilable
be not at one
be not of one mind
bear ill to so.
combat
contest sth.
disagree
dispute
expostulate
fell enmity towards
feel hatred towards one another
have words with so.
not to come to terms
quarrel
struggle
wish to attack
wish to harm

KA₋₃ca Struggle

be at war with one another
be hostile to
be ill-feeling towards another
boycott
combat
compete
feel enmity towards
feel hatred towards one another
fight against
quarrel
refuse to have anything to do with
struggle
wish to attack
wish to harm

KA₋₃cb Semi-enmity Status

argue with so.
compete
debate

KA₋₃cb Semi-enmity Status (continued)

go into sth.
pretend to fight
simulate fighting
take part in a contest
discuss

KA₋₃cc Argumentation Status

argue
debate
discuss

KA₋₂ Make Claims

KA₋₂a Make Justifiable Claims on so.

ask
ask back
arrest
assert
bring to bear
call in
carry one's point
claim
confiscate
demand back
demand from a person
enforce
exact
have great pretensions
insist
lay claim to
reclaim
request
require
sequester
take possession of

KA₋₂b Make Negatively Viewed Claims

annex
approach
blackmail

KA$_{-2b}$ Make Negatively Viewed Claims (continued)

blandish
cajole
chat so. up
confiscate
court
demand sth. of so.
dissuade so. from sth.
ensnare
exact
extort
presume
requisition
set one's cap at
take the liberty
trap
try to get into so.'s favor
venture
wheedle

KA$_{-1}$ Reasons for the Argument and Their Consequences

KA$_{-1a}$ Agreement (cf. KA$_{4cc}$)

KA$_{-1c}$ Dissent

break with so.
fall out
fall out with so.
get in each other's hair
get so. wrong
have words with so.
make an enemy of so.
mistake so.
misunderstand so.
quarrel
split up
they are at loggerheads

KA$_{-1b}$ Reconciliation Attempts

appease
arrange
butt in
calm
calm so. down
come between
compose
counsel so.
deescalate
define one's position
depress
discuss
give advice
interfere
intervene
make clear
make one's position clear
make terms
make up
meddle with
mediate
negotiate
pacify
pass off
quieten
reconcile
see sth. in a different light
settle
silence
soften
soothe
supply
treat

KA$_{-1c}$ Incitement

agitate violently against
baffle
convince
exaggerate the importance
get so. set up

KA$_{-1c}$ Incitement (continued)

haul over the coals
incite
instigate
intrigue
kindle
make acrid
overemphazise
persuade so. of sth.
plot
put the skids on
rouse
set so. against so.
set so. off
sharpen
stir up
talk insistently
thwart

KA$_{-1d}$ Abstaining from an Attack ≅ KA$_{3b}$ Withdrawing One's Claims ≅ EN$_{9h}$, Cancelling One's Own Demands

abandon
abstain from
alter one's opinion partly
be inferior to
be second to
disclaim
dissociate os.
give in
give in partly
give up
give way
go back on
keep one's distance from
leave alone
leave it at that
let go
moderate
move away from
protude

KA$_{-1d}$ Abstaining from an Attack ≅ KA$_{3b}$ Withdrawing One's Claims ≅ EN$_{9h}$, Cancelling One's Own Demands (continued)

release
relinquish
renounce
resign
retreat
scale down
spare
stick out from
surrender
take back
waive
yield

KA$_0$ Attack

KA$_{0a}$ Undirected Aggression

attack without thinking
be furious
give vent to
go on the rampage
let loose
let sth. out on so.
lose one's head
rampage
react blindly
respond blindly

KA$_{0b}$ Unintentional Attack

be taken aback
be thunderstruck
bump into
cheat
crash into
dupe
offend unintentionally
tread on so.'s toes

KA_{0c} Concealed Attack

act subversively
agitate
baffle
carry a point
demoralize
devaluate
get one's own way
infiltrate
let so. know
rake
rummage
sabotage
sap
shoot down
spread the news
thwart
torpedo
turn up
undermine
upset
work on so.

KA_{0d} Indirect Attack

bicker
bother
employ good tactics
importune
intrigue
molest
nag
oppress
plot
press hard
pry
quarrel
skirmish
squabble
stir
wrangle

KA_{0e} Permanent Indirect Attack

be cross
be down
be sulky
bear a grudge
carp
find fault
grumble
keep on about
nag
poison the atmosphere

KA_{0f} Surprise Attacks

catch on the hop
surprise
take by surprise
take unawares

KA_{0g} Challenges

abuse
affront
backbite
be impudent
challenge
come too close
compromise
dare
declare war
deride
get into an argument with
have words with
insult
jeer at
jog
jolt
lose one's temper
make a fool of
make bold
menace
mock (at)
offend

KA$_{0g}$ Challenges (continued)

outrage
provoke
rebuff
revile
ridicule
shake
shoot at
show up
skirmish
slander
threaten
treat bluntly

KA$_{0g'}$ Protesting

give vent to
have a say in
lodge a protest
mutiny
not to stand for
oppose
protest against
put up with
rebel
refuse to tolerate
resist

KA$_{0g''}$ Enticing so. in

bring in
ensnare
entangle
entice
guide (in)
inveigle
involve (in)
lure (in)
seduce

KA$_{0h}$ Hostile Focusing

abuse
affront

KA$_{0h}$ Hostile Focusing (continued)

assail
attack
catch on the hop
fall upon
get into a discussion with
insult
lose one's temper
offend
oppose
set about
surprise
take by surprise
take unawares

KA$_{0i}$ Open Attack

abuse
affront
assail
attack
catch on the hop
fall upon
get into a discussion with
insult
lose one's temper
offend
oppose
set about
surprise
take by surprise
take unawares

KA$_{0j}$ Argumentative Attack in a Matter

affirm
assert
claim
claim one's rights
confront
maintain
object
oppose
play off against

KA$_1$ Tactical Phase

Ka$_{1a}$ Attacking Moves

KA$_{1aa}$ Permanently Recurring Attack

attack
bicker
bully
combat
deride
disconnect
dismantle
employ clever tactics
fight against
jeer at
keep (on) quarreling with
lower
play an unfair trick on
polemize
put the kibosh on
ruin
take apart
take to pieces
terrorize
thwart
upset
vex
wear down
wear out (with, by)
worry (s.o.)

KA$_{1ab}$ Intimidation

bewilder
bully
cause anxiety
command respect
confuse
demoralize
enervate
entangle
frighten
frustrate

KA$_{1ab}$ Intimidation (continued)

inspire with fear
intimidate
make s.o. afraid
paralyze
puzzle
scare (away)
swear at
terrorize
throw into confusion

KA$_{1b}$ Opposing Moves

KA$_{1ba}$ Prevention

ascertain
preclude
reassure (os.)
try to avoid risks

KA$_{1bb}$ Evasive Operations

KA$_{1bba}$ Evasive Maneuvres Without Loss for Defender

adjourn
apologize
avoid
camouflage
circumvent
conceal
contest
cover
delay
deny
devolve
dilly-dally
disagree with
disavow
disregard
dodge
elude
evade

Lexicon Section I

KA$_{1bba}$ Evasive Manoeuvres Without Loss for Defender (continued)

hide
hold up
keep out of
keep secret
leave out
mask
neglect
not fall in with
pass over
pass the buck
postpone
procrastinate
put off
retard
shift
shirk
sidestep
skip
spin out
vindicate
wrap up

KA$_{1bbb}$ Evasive Manoeuvres with Loss for Defender

abandon
abate
admit
agree to
allow
cease
concede
confess
diminish
fall back
give in
give up
give way
grant
have no pretensions to
own
relax

KA$_{1bbb}$ Evasive Manoeuvres with Loss for Defender (continued)

relent
renounce
resign
sacrifice
soften
yield

KA$_{1bbc}$ Neutralizing

defuse
deprecate
make (appear) banal
minimize
neutralize
play down
relativize
take the wind out of so.'s sails
trivialize

KA$_{1bc}$ Defense and Counterattacks

KA$_{1bca}$ Defense Attempt

answer
barricade os. behind
be contradictory
be face to face
come back
confront
contest
contradict os.
contrast
defend os.
dispute
encounter
face a thing
hold a view
impose a check on
invalidate
make objections
maintain

KA₁bca Defense Attempt (continued)

meet
object
obviate
oppose
put a stop to
put up a fight
put up against
raise
raise objections
refute
rejoin
retort
reply
requite
resist
return
set against
stand up for
take up a position
trump
vindicate

KA₁bcb Successful Checking of the Attack

block off
catch
check
decline
defuse
delay
demur to
deny
detain
deter
frustrate
hinder
hold off
hold one's ground
hold up
invalidate

KA₁bcb Successful Checking of the Attack (continued)

oppose
parry
prevent
refuse
reject
repel
repudiate
resist
restrain
restrict
retard
shake off
stop
suppress
thwart
turn down
ward off

KA₁bcc Successful Repulsion of the Attack

be quick-witted
clear
confute
debilitate
decline
disprove
disregard
enfeeble
give a ready answer
give the lie to
hold
invalidate
neglect
outdo
rebut
refuse
refute
regain
reject

KA₁bcc Successful Repulsion of the Attack (continued)

repair
repudiate
restore
slight
surpass
take in
trump
turn down
vindicate
win back

KA₁bcd Argumentative Defense with Foundation

base on
bring counterarguments
claim sth. for os.
confirm
confront
contradict
corroborate arguments
counter
decline
disprove
establish
formulate an objection
give reasons for
hold against
meet
negate
object
oppose (with)
plug at
refer (back) to
refuse
refute
reject
reply
repulse

KA₁bcd Argumentative Defense with Foundation (continued)

retort
set against
substantiate
support
throw out
turn down
undermine
verify an argument
weaken

KA₁c Replies to Defense

KA₁ca Reply to Evasive Move

KA₁caa Concealed Repetition of an Attack

bear ill-will towards
complain
criticize
find fault with
grouse
grumble
moan about
murmur
nag
whine

KA₁cab Pinning Down of Defender D. by Attacker A.

encircle
fix
force so. into a corner
force so. to show his true colors
let so. take up a position
pin down
tie down

KA_{1cb} Reply to Pinning Down

appease
be compliant
be open to
be yielding
console
get in under so.'s guard
jump from side to side
keep an escape route open
keep out of
leave (everything still) undecided
leave unsettled
make no decision
make no promises
make promises
put so. off with
stay flexible
take up a pluralistic position

KA_{1cc} Reply to Defense

KA_{1cca} Repetition of Attack

adhere to
claim
insist on
iterate
maintain
persevere
preach at
repeat
stick to
terrorize
urge

KA_{1ccb} (Neutrally Viewed) Insisting

be behind
bombard (with arguments)
bore after
charge sth. up to so.
consolidate (position)
continue in

KA_{1ccb} (Neutrally Viewed) Insisting (continued)

defend
fight for
hold (opinion)
persevere
persist in
press
pursue
stabilize (position)
stand up for
stick to
thrust

KA_{1ccc} (Negatively Viewed) Insisting

appear recalcitrant
be contentious
be obstinate about
bully
charge up to so.'s account (unjustifiably)
continue in (too forcibly)
fight for (too vehemently)
hammer at
insist on
keep on at
not come out with
persevere in (too penetratingly)
persist in
repeat (too often)
stand by (claim)
stay hard
stick to (too fiercely)

KA_{1d} Involvement

KA_{1da} Development of the Argument (no end yet in sight)

bicker
come to grips with
contend
dispute

KA₁da Development of the Argument (no end yet in sight) (continued)

employ tactics
expostulate
frighten
have words with
make an enemy of
quarrel
skirmish
struggle
talk at so.
wrangle

KA₁db Development of the Argument (end in sight)

argue
bargain
compete
contest
count up
deal with
decide
disagree
dispute
explain
fight out
fight through
go into
haggle
make a bargain
make a deal
reckon up
settle
settle one's differences
treat (with)
work out

KA₁dc Stabilization of the Argument

harden
persist in
secure (position)

KA₁dc Stabilization of the Argument (continued)

stabilize (position)
stick at

KA₂ Making a Coalition

KA₂a Initiating a Coalition

KA₂aa Coalition Attempts with Third Parties

accost
address
adulate
arrange
cajole
canvass
captivate
chum up with
contact
court
engage
enlist
ensnare
enter into relations
entrap
fascinate
feel the way
form an intimacy (with)
get round
grope towards
ingratiate os.
insinuate os. into
join up with
make overtures
pave the way (for)
prepare
recruit
scrape acquaintance
set one's cap at
sound out
speak to

KA$_{2aa}$ Coalition Attempts with Third Parties (continued)

take first soundings
wait in the antechambers
wheedle
worm one's way into
entice
involve
seduce

KA$_{2ab}$ Offer of Support from Third Parties

offer os.
offer one's services

KA$_{2b}$ Settlements

ally
arrange sth. with so.
ascertain
be in tune
come to terms
confer
decide
declare solidarity with
discuss
enter into a coalition
enter into an alliance
fix
fix up
fraternize
harmonize
make an agreement
make a pact
make certain
make sure (of)
safeguard
secure
settle
throw in one's lot with
work out

KA$_{2c}$ Assistance

KA$_{2ca}$ Assistance from Seconds

KA$_{2caa}$ Obtaining Assistance

be backed up by
give protection
gain support
obtain aid
obtain backing

KA$_{2cab}$ Giving Assistance

aid
animate
assist
cheer up
coax
comfort
confirm
consolidate
contribute
depend (on)
edify
embolden
encourage
enliven
fortify
goad
help
help out
hint
incite
persuade
point out
prompt
prop up
protest
put so. back on his feet
raise hopes
rely on

KA$_{2cab}$ Giving Assistance (continued)

step into the breach
stimulate
stir up
strengthen
support
tip off
urge

KA$_{2cb}$ Assistance from Supporters

act for
agree
answer for
assure
come to the help of
defend
guarantee
intercede for/on so.'s behalf
maintain
plead for
promise
put in a good word for
represent
side with
speak for
stand up for
step into the breach
take so.'s side
vindicate
vouch for

KA$_{2d}$ Dissolving the Coalition

abandon
brush off
cast off
cut os. loose
desert
disown
dissociate os. from
forsake

KA$_{2d}$ Dissolving the Coalition (continued)

give up
leave
leave in the lurch
part from so.
part with sth.
participate no longer
remove one's support
separate from
wash one's hands of
withdraw one's aid
write off
yield

KA$_3$ Retreat

KA$_{3a}$ Satiation

be fed up with
be tired of
cease
desist from
drop
forsake
give up
have enough of
leave off

KA$_{3b}$ Withdrawing the Claims
$\cong$ KA$_{-1b}$; $\cong$ EN$_{9h}$'

abandon
abstain from
come second to
curb
depart from
dissociate os.
drag one's feet
draw back
give in
give up
give way
hang back

KA$_{3b}$ Withdrawing the Claims
$\cong$ KA$_{-1b}$; $\cong$ EN$_{9h}$,(continued)

hold back
leave alone
leave at that
loosen
make concessions
moderate
move away from
put aside
put on one side
refrain from
relinquish
renounce
resign
restrain os.
scale down
shelve
spare
stand apart from
surrender
take back
tone down
undo
untie
withdraw

KA$_{3c}$ Losing Interest

be no longer interested in
desist from
have no longer an interest in
leave
leave alone
leave at that
leave in peace
let alone
let drop
let grass grow over
lose interest in
lose sight of
lose track of
push into the background

KA$_4$ Victory/Defeat/Willingness to Cooperate

KA$_{4a}$ Victory

KA$_{4aa}$ Successful Evasion of the Opponent

achieve one's aim
avoid (the issue)
carry one's point
circumvent
contrive
disregard
dodge
evade
gain one's end
get through
go through
ignore
manage
muddle one's way through
pass over
scrub round
shirk
succeed in
wangle

KA$_{4ab}$ Forcing a Concession from the Opponent

blackmail
dissuade
exact
extort
force
overrule
wrest

KA$_{4ac}$ Breaking Down the Resistance of the Opponent

accomplish
bar

KA₄ₐc Breaking Down the Resistance of the Opponent (continued)

bring so. to his knees
brush aside
carry through
checkmate
complete
crush
eliminate
exclude
exhaust
floor
gain
give the brush - off
go through
harass
humiliate
knock down
make so. feel small
make one's way
outdo
outshine
outsmart
overcome
overthrow
overturn
play a trick on
pull apart
put one over on
reduce to silence
send about one's business
settle
shut so.'s mouth
shut so. up
silence
squash
stop
subject
subjugate
succeed
supplant
suppress
sweep aside

KA₄ₐc Breaking Down the Resistance of the Opponent (continued)

take so. down a peg
take to pieces
teach so. his place
torment
trick
upset
wear out
win

KA₄ₐd Putting Someone to Flight

chase away
chase off
discharge
dismiss
drive away
drive back
force back
force out
frighten away
kick out
oust
put to flight
scare off
see off
send packing
squeeze out
throw out

KA₄ₐe Argumentative Victory in a Matter

blurt
bulldoze
confute
disable
disarm
disprove
get through
give the brush-off
invalidate
penetrate
rebut

KA₄ₐₑ Argumentative Victory in a Matter (continued)

refute
repudiate
ride roughshod over
send about one's business
take to pieces

KA₄ₐ' Triumph

be delighted
be glad
be joyful
be pleased
be triumphant
exult
give os. airs
gloat
rejoice
show malicious pleasure
strut
take pleasure in other's misfortune
triumph
turn up trumps

KA₄ᵦ Defeat

KA₄ᵦₐ Defeat in a Matter

KA₄ᵦₐₐ Losing the Fight

be at the end of one's tether
be checkmated
be defeated
be done for
be overthrown
be put on the shelf
be set aside
have done with
succumb

KA₄ᵦₐᵦ Refusing to Admit Defeat

be obstinate
be querulous

KA₄ᵦₐᵦ Refusing to Admit Defeat (continued)

be recalcitrant
be stubborn
brave
dare
defy
grumble
persevere
squirm
turn
twist

KA₄ᵦₐ꜀ Announcement and Admission of Defeat

abandon
announce one's resignation
back out
be overthrown
be taken down a peg
be upset
capitulate
chuck (up)
depart
draw in one's horns
entangle os. in contradictions
give in
give up
go
leave
quit
relinquish
renounce
resign
retire
secede
sing small
stand down
step back
step down
submit
surrender

KA₄bac Announcement and Admission of Defeat (continued)

throw in one's hand
vacate one's office
withdraw from

KA₄bad Establishing of the Defeat

be counted out (by referee)

KA₄bb Reaction to Defeat

KA₄bba Flight

break away
disengage os.
dodge
flee
prevaricate
take to flight
withdraw

KA₄bbb Changing Sides

change over to
change one's position
change sides
desert
go over to
turn one's coat

KA₄bc Giving Ground

admit (to)
give ground
relinquish
retire from
surrender

KA₄bd Conclusion of the Fight

KA₄bda Coming to Terms

accept
accomodate os. to

KA₄bda Coming to Terms (continued)

be resigned to
come to terms with
comply with
make the best of
put up with
resign os. to
resignate
submit to
swallow

KA₄bdb Revenge/Retaliation

bear a grudge
get even with
get one's own back
have it in for
pay back
play a trick on
put one over on
repay
requite
retaliate
revenge os. on
settle accounts with
take it out on
take revenge on

KA₄c Willingness to Cooperate

KA₄ca Reconciliation

KA₄caa Personal Reconciliation

agree
become reconciled
bury
bury the hatchet
calm down
compose one's mind
contact
file away
get in touch with
get on well

KA4caa Personal Reconciliation (continued)

hit it off well
let bygones be bygones
let sth. sink into oblivion
make a clean sweep of
make it up
make one's peace with
patch up a quarrel

KA4cab Expressing One's Opinion

discuss in full
exchange views
talk sth. through

KA4cac Reconciliation by a Third Party

act as go-between
advise
appease
arbitrate
arrange
bring to an agreement
bring together
calm
clarify
clear (up)
come between
compose
confer
counsel
cushion
deescalate
deliberate
determine
discuss
effect
force a consent
intercede
interfere
interpose
intervene

KA4cac Reconciliation by a Third Party (continued)

make a decision
make clear
make one's peace with
make up
meddle
mediate
negotiate
pacify
placate
put right
put straight
quieten
reach agreement
satisfy
set right
soften
soothe
straighten out
treat
unify
unite
work out

KA4cad Making Amends

adjust
atone for
balance out
compensate
equalize
iron out
make amends for
make good
pay off
put right
put straight
put to rights
redeem
redress
remedy
repair
righten

KA₄cad Making Amends (continued)

satisfy
set right again
settle
straighten out

KA₄cb Compromise

KA₄cba One-Sided Compromise

admit
agree
come round
concede
confess
consent to
fall in with
grant
humor
meet
meet halfway
own
relent
take back
withdraw

KA₄cbb Mutual Compromise/Establishing Assent

agree to
approve of
arrange
assent to
come to terms
consent to
cooperate with
sanction
see eye to eye
settle

KA₄cbc Provisos in the Compromise

accept in part
concede

KA₄cbc Provisos in the Compromise (continued)

confine
curtail
fall in with (partially)
give direction
grant
insist on
keep open
make a point of
make presuppositions
make reservations
make stipulations
presume
reserve
reserve the right to
restrict
state terms
stipulate
suppose
take for granted
work out

KA₄cbd Treaties

agree upon
ally os. with
arrange
come to an agreement
come to terms
concur
enter into an arrangement
form an alliance
league
make a compact
make a contract
make an agreement
make arrangements
make a settlement
ratify
settle

KA₄cc Consensus

KA₄cca Agreement ≅ KA₋₃b Friendship Status

agree
be at one with
be of importance (to)
be of one mind with
be of the same opinion
be united
be well-disposed towards
cohere
concur
feel kindly towards
get on well
get on with
hit it off (with)
mean sth. to
share the same opinion
side with
stick together
understand one another
unify
unite

KA₄ccb Pseudo-Agreement

harmonize

KA₄cd Accept and Respect the Consensus

KA₄cda Consequences of the Compromise

accept
accommodate os. to
acknowledge
admit
agree with
answer in the affirmative
appreciate
approve of

KA₄cda Consequences of the Compromise (continued)

be resigned to
come to accept
come to terms with
comply with
fall in with
make the best of
put up with
recognize
say yes to
submit to

KA₄cdb Respect

bring in
charge to so.'s account
comply with
consider
follow
have regard for
heed
include
keep
obey
observe
pay attention to
respect
take into consideration
take notice of
take seriously
take to heart
weigh

AV Arguing Devices

AV₁ Argue (General)

adduce (reasons)
advocate
argue
bombard with arguments
bring forward (arguments)

AV₁ Argue (General) (continued)

confront
confute
contradict
contrast with
demur to
disprove
enter a protest
negate
oppose
pursue an argument
put an antithesis
raise a protest
rebut
refute
remove objections
reply
retort
torpedo so. with arguments
undermine
wear away

AV₂ Explain

clarify
clear up
elucidate
explain
explicate
make clear
illuminate
illumine

AV₃ Validate

adduce reasons
base
be the devil's advocate
bring forward proof
build a foundation to
champion a topic
cite authorities
confirm
consolidate

AV₃ Validate (continued)

corroborate
deliver a validation
endow
establish
found
furnish a validation
give reasons for
lay a foundation
make good
manifest
point out
point to (an argument)
produce an argument
prove
quote authorities
refer to (an argument)
show
show proof of
substantiate support of an argument
supplement a validation
sustain an argument
underpin
validate

AV₄ Exemplify

adduce an example
exemplify
give an example
produce an example
refer to an example
refer a paradigm
set an example
use a paradigm

AV₅ Criticize

criticize
criticize adversely
find fault with
give deleterious critique

AV_6 Agree

agree to so.'s views
assent
be of the same opinion

AV_6 Agree (continued)

concur with
consent
support

8.4 NO Institutional Model (Norm Model)

NO_{-4} Giving S the Right of Control = EN_{3b} Mandating

appoint
authorize
delegate
depute
empower
invest with full powers
license
mandate
nominate

$NO_{-4§}$ Making a Law

enact
establish
institute
issue
issue a regulation
legislate
legalize
make a law
ordain
promulgate a law
put a law into effect
ratify
sign

NO_{-3} S Having a Right of Control = EN_{6c} Controlling Directing

act as chairman
act as guardian to

NO_{-3} S Having a Right of Control = EN_{6c} Controlling Directing (continued)

browbeat
command
conduct
control
direct
govern
guide
induce so. to do sth.
instruct
lead
lead so. like a child
manage
manipulate
preside over
regulate
send so. to
show
teach
train

NO_{-2} Claiming the Right of Control =: KA_{-2a}, Making (Neutral) Requests

claim
demand
confiscate
demand (payment)
lay claim to
make a claim
occupy

Lexicon Section I

NO$_{-2}$ Claiming the Right of Control =: KA$_{-2a}$, Marking (Neutral) Requests (continued)

require
seize

NO$_{-2\S}$ Asking Official Premission = EN$_{2b\S}$ Asking Officially

apply for
file an application
make a formal request
move
petition
propose
propose a motion for
solicit
sue (for)
woo

NO$_{-1}$ S Judging this Claim $\cong$ WT$_c$ Exothesizing the Valuation of an Action

estimate
give an opinion on
judge
pass judgment on
value

NO$_0$ Imposing a Norm on Someone

NO$_{0a}$ Putting Under a Norm

command
direct
give duties to
issue regulations
make so. promise
obligate
oblige
order
put under oath

NO$_{0a}$ Putting Under a Norm (continued)

swear in
give a task to

NO$_{0a\S}$ Proclaiming $\cong$ IN$_{6b}$, Distributing Public Data

advertise
decree
give notice
make know
notify
post
post bills
preach from the pulpit
proclaim
promulgate a law
publish

NO$_{0b}$ Allowing

accept
admit to
agree to
allow
approve to
authorize
concede
consent to
give leave of absence
give permission to
grant
let so. have his own way
permit
sanction
tolerate

NO$_{0b}$, Abandoning

abandon
cede
consign
give up

NO₀ᵦ' Abandoning (continued)

leave to
let have
surrender

NO₀ᵦ'' Distinguishing

award so.
distinguish so.
exclude so.
give a credential to
mark out so.
privilege
select so.
treat with distinction

NO₀c Forbidding

deny
forbid
limit
prevent
prohibit
refuse
restrict (rights)
taboo

NO₀da Admitting in Institutions (giving membership)

admit
adopt
appoint to an office
authorize
beatify
canonize
choose so.
christen
confer a degree
crown
declare so. of age
deputate
elect

NO₀da Admitting in Institutions (giving membership) (continued)

empower
engage
ennoble
enrol
entitle
hire
inaugurate
invest with
knight
mandate
marry (make husband and wife)
matriculate
nominate
ordain so. as a priest
recruit
swear in
take on (an employee)

NO₀db Leaving an Institution

abscond
desert
announce withdrawal
drop out
leave
quit
resign
retire from
secede from
step out
withdraw from

NO₀dc Promoting

advance
call away
give a degree
place above
promote
subordinate
upgrade

NO$_{0dd}$ Dismissing

banish
call away
cashier (an officer)
depose (a king)
disband (troops)
discard
discharge
dispel
dismiss
excommunicate
exempt
exile
expel
give leave of absence
give notice
give warning
grant
interdict
lock out
pension off
put under tutelage
relegate
remove
remove (from office)
rusticate (a student)
send down
suspend

NO$_{0de}$ Founding

constitute
establish
found

NO$_{0e}$ Putting Each Other Under an Obligation

make an agreement
make an alliance
make an appointment
draw up a confederation
enter a contract
engage

NO$_{0e}$ Putting Each Other Under an Obligation (continued)

marry
make a treaty

NO$_{0e\S}$ Entering a Contract

come to an agreement
come to an arrangement
countersign
enter an alliance
enter a contract
ratify
sign a contract
transact business

NO$_{0f}$ Putting Oneself Under an Obligation = EN$_{6d}$ Self-Commanding/Committing Oneself

accede to
agree to
assent to
award
bind os. (to so.)
commit os.
confirm in writing
declare
enter into a treaty
give bail
give one's word of honor
grant
guarantee
hold out a prospect of sth. to so.
join (a party)
pledge
promise
promise solemnly
vow
sign (a contract)
take so.'s part
vouch
warrant

NO_{0g} Fixing a Date

antedate
book
date
fix a date (time, term, day)
misdate
postdate
postpone to another day
set a limit

$NO_{0'}$ Being Under an Obligation

have a duty
be fit for so.
have to
be under an obligation to
to be obliged
should...
be suitable for so.

NO_1 Guaranteeing

assure of
bail
confirm in writing
ensure
give one's word of honor
guarantee
pledge one's word
promise
take responsibility for
vouch for
warrant

NO_{2a} Following a Norm

adhere to
bear in mind
comply with
consider well
follow
heed
keep (a promise)
live up to

NO_{2a} Following a Norm (continued)

obey
observe
pay attention to
respect
submit to
subordinate os. to
take to heart
take seriously

NO_{2ba} Joining = NO_{6f} = WT_2

confer together
confer with so.
deliberate
discuss
have a conference
have a meeting
have a session
hold a meeting
join
meet
meet for conference
take counsel together
talk over
unite

NO_{2bb} Conspiring

conspire
form a conspiracy
mutiny
plot sth.
protest
rebel
revolt

NO_{3ba} Withdrawing

give notice
give warning
retract
withdraw (from an engagement)

NO3bb Abolishing a Norm

abolish
abrogate
annul
cancel
declare an agreement null and void
declare void
do away with
dissolve partnership
divorce
invalidate
quash a judgment
repeal
revise a judgment
suspend
supersede (replace a law)

NO3bc Changing a Norm

amend
change the law
innovate
modify
reorganize

NO3bd Releasing from a Norm

absolve
acquit
discharge
dispense
exempt
exonerate
give leave of absence
liberate
release

NO2 Violating a Norm

be guilty of a misdemeanor
blaspheme
break the law
commit a crime
commit a fault

NO2 Violating a Norm (continued)

commit a misdeed
commit an offense
contravene
disobey
encroach (rights)
go astray
go wrong
infringe (laws)
insult
offend
offend against (tradition)
outrage
transgress against (law)
violate

NO2' Not Following a Convention

abuse
be blunt
be impolite
call so. names
(grieve)
have the impudence
(hurt so.'s feelings)
insult
(injure)
offend
provoke
(ridicule)
(vex)

NO2'' Not Paying Attention to a Norm

be obstinate
decline to do
not pay attention to
not pay heed to
refuse to do

NO3 Detecting an Offense

detect
discover

NO$_3$ Detecting an Offense (continued)

find
uncover

NO$_3$, Suspecting

be suspicious of
calumniate
cast suspicion on
defame
distrust
slander
suspect so. of
throw suspicion on

NO$_4$ Reporting

accuse (of)
betray
charge with
complain of a thing
denounce
denunciate
file a claim
inculpate (in)
inform against
make public
report
tell tales

NO$_4$, Instituting Legal Proceedings

bring an action against
carry on a lawsuit
go to a court
institute legal proceedings against so.
litigate
sue
sue so. for debt
take legal proceedings against

NO$_5$ Summoning

make so. appear in court
summon
take so. to task

NO$_5$, Arresting

arrest
apprehend
have so. seized
imprison
seize
take in charge
take into custody

NO$_6$ Phases of the Institutional Quarrel (Struggle)

NO$_{60}$ Procedures of Argumentation

adduce (proof)
appeal to so.
argue (for, against, about)
argue the point
bring forward
bring forward an argument
clinch an argument
combat
come to terms with so.
confirm
contest
deny
discuss
disprove
dispute
give reasons for
have an argument
leave a thing undecided
negotiate
object
offer an opinion on a subject
oppose
prove

NO_{60} Procedures of Argumentation (continued)

refer to
refute
reply
retort
settle a quarrel
show
take exception to
underpin
weaken an argument

NO_{6a} Accusing

accuse
blame so.
call so. to account
charge (with)
complain about so.
denounce
impute
indict
put the blame on so.
reproach so. with a th.

NO_{6a'} Accusing Oneself

admitting guilt
blame os.
confess
go to confession
make a confession

∝ NO_{6b} Reaction to the Accusation (by the Accused)

acknowledge
admit
apologize
answer for
account for
be frank
beg pardon
confess

NO_{6b} Reaction to the Accusation (by the Accused) (continued)

contradict
deny under oath
dispel doubts
exculpate so.
explain
give an account of
justify (os.)
own up (to)
plead guilty
put right
rectify
regret
show one's colors
show remorse
vindicate os.

NO_{6c} Examining

cross-examine
examine
hear
institute an inquiry
interrogate
pump
question
question closely

NO_{6c'} Proving the Guilt

prove guilty

✗ NO_{6da} Testifying

attest
attest upon oath
authenticate (by document)
bear witness to
certify
confirm by oath
declare
document
give evidence of

NO₆da Testifying (continued)

give testimony
manifest
prove
show proof
swear on oath
testify
verify

NO₆db Betraying

betray
disclose secrets
divulge a secret

NO₆e Defending

advocate
combat
contest
contradict
defend
deny
disprove
dispute
impugn
justify
object
oppose
plead for
refute
reply
side with
stand up for
vindicate

NO₆f Taking Counsel = NO₂ba Joining

confer with so.
confer together
deliberate
discuss
have a conference

NO₆f Taking Counsel = NO₂ba Joining (continued)

have a meeting
have a session
hold a meeting
join
meet
meet for conference
take counsel together
talk over
unite

⚘NO₇ Judging

convict
fine so.
give one's opinion
impose a fine
judge
pass judgment on so.
pass sentence on so.
pronounce a judgment
sentence

NO₇' Taking Extenuating Circumstances into Account vic. WT₃'

be forbearing with so.
let a person down gently over sth.
take a lenient view of sth.
value sth. highly
admit
alleviate
allow
concede
grant sth.
mitigate

NO₇a Making a Decision/Settle a Case

achieve a consensus
appease
arbitrate
clear up

NO₇ₐ Making a Decision/Settle a Case (continued)

decide
divorce
give judgment
make an arrangement
make up the quarrel
make an arbitration
make an award
make a decision
pass sentence
put under an obligation
reconcile conflicting ideas
release from an obligation
settle

NO₇ᵦ Declare Guilty

condemn
convict
sentence

NO₇ᴄ Acquitting

absolve
acquit
exculpate
excuse
exonerate (of a guilt)
relieve (of a guilt)

NO₈ₐ Punishing

admonish
ban
banish
brand
censure so.
deprive of citizenship
discipline
disqualify
dismiss
excommunicate
execute (a criminal)

NO₈ₐ Punishing (continued)

exile
expatriate
expel
extradite
fine
fire
impeach
impose sanctions
inflict a penalty
inflict a punishment
interdict
lock out (workmen)
outlaw
proscribe
punish
put under tutelage
put in the pillory
rebuke so.
remove from office
reprove so.
reprimand
requite
revenge
scold
suspend
stigmatize
transfer for disciplinary reasons

NO₈ₐ' Damning (Archaic)

curse so.
damn
excommunicate
execrate
maledict
wish sth. to happen to so.

NO₈ₐ'' Making Amends

admit guilt
apologize
atone for
do penance

NO$_{8a}$'' Making Amends (continued)

expiate
humiliate os.
make amends for

NO$_{9a}$ Attacking the Judgment

NO$_{9aa}$ Protest

appeal to a superior court
enter an appeal
enter a rehearing
protest against
resist the judgment

NO$_{9ab}$ Appealing for Mercy

appeal for mercy
beg for acquittal
beg for leniency
cry out for mercy
implore
intercede

NO$_{9b}$ Declaring the Judgment Void

NO$_{9ba}$ Revising the Judgment

annul
disclaim
quash a judgment
retract a judgement
revise

NO$_{9bb}$ Pardoning

absolve from
acquit

NO$_{9bb}$ Pardoning (continued)

amnesty
condone
excuse
exempt from
forgive
pardon
remove a guilt
remit a punishment
spare
take away (sins)

NO$_{9b}$' Reparation

beg forgiveness
clear up
compensate
make amends for
make good
pay off
set right
settle

NO$_{10}$ Social Consequences of the Sentence = WT$_{5a}$

abandon so.
be resentful of
bear a grudge against
brand so.
devalue so.'s reputation
label so.
make so. lose his status
pigeonhole so.
stereotype so.
take amiss

8.5 W Valuation Models

WT Valuation of an Action

WT_0 Exothesizing the Valuation of an Action = WT_3 Valuing/Judging = WG_0

appraise
appreciate
approve
ascribe
assess
attribute
be of opinion
be scandalized by
classify
consider (good/bad)
deem (good/bad)
depreciate
disapprove
esteem highly
estimate
evaluate
find (good/bad)
form an estimate of
form an opinion of
grade
hold as an opinion
judge
lay aside
give opinion on
pass expert judgment on
pass opinion on
rate
take offense at
value
value highly

WT_1 Blaming

accuse of
blame

WT_1 Blaming (continued)

charge with
complain
impute to
reproach so. with
throw sth. in so.'s face
(cf. NO_{6a})

WT_1, Suggesting Promotion

(in general)
advise sth. (for the selection etc.)
give advice
(recommending)
advocate
favor
nominate so.
plead for so.
propose so.
recommend
support
(resultative)
choose so.
elect so.
select so.
(negative)
advise so. against
disfavor
dissuade so. from

WT_2 Counseling = NO_{6f} = NO_{2ba}

advise
confer about a matter
confer together
counsel
deliberate
discuss
discuss in advance

WT_2 Counseling = NO_{6f} = NO_{2ba}
(continued)

have a conference
hold a meeting
meet for a conference
take counsel together
talk over

WT_2, Voting

elect so.
put sth. on the ballot
vote for so.

WT_3, Taking Good or Bad Reputation into Account

(negative)
charge with
show distrust
show doubts about so.
undervalue so.
(positive)
admit sth. to so.
allow sth. to so.
be forbearing with so.
concede sth. to so.
do not blame so.
grant sth. to so.
place one's trust in so.
rely on so.
take a lenient view of sth.
trust so.
value highly
(neutral)
bring up
judge so.'s merits
weigh the factors

WT_3,, Prejudicing

prejudice
prejudge
show bias
show prejudices

WT_3 Judging/Valuating = WT_0 = WG_0

WT_4 Consequences of Judging/Valuating

WT_{4a} Scolding

(in private)
abuse
admonish
blame
caution
degrade
discipline
find fault with
give a thorough scolding
give so. a lecture
inflict disciplinary punishment on
rebuke
reprove
reprimand
scold
take to task
upbraid
warn
(institutional punishment)
= NO_{8a}

WT_{4b} Correcting

clear up a point
correct so.
correct what so. has done
find mistakes
mark errors

WT_{4c} Criticizing

carp at
censure
condemn
contest
criticize
deplore
find fault with
find holes in
grouse
grumble
hiss at
object to

WT$_{4c}$ Criticizing (continued)

run down
shred to pieces
tear to pieces

WT$_{4e}$ Praising

applaud
award a prize to
celebrate so.
commend
decorate so.
exalt
extol
give praise to
glorify
laud
mention with praise
praise
rave about
recommend
speak in very high terms of so.

WT$_{4fa}$ Accepting

accept
acknowledge
admit
agree to
assent to
consent to
give consent
promise (= accept to do)
recognize

WT$_{4fb}$ Rejecting

decline
disagree
disavow
dismiss
do not share opinion
refuse
reject

WT$_{4fb}$ Rejecting (continued)

repudiate

WT$_{4f\S}$ Authenticating

authenticate (by documents)
attest
certify
confirm
document
give a receipt for
give an expert opinion
issue a certificate
pass expert judgment on
sign
validate
verify
vouch for
(cf. KA$_{4cda}$)

WT$_5$ After-Effects of Judging/Valuating

WT$_{5a}$ Stereotyping a Person = NO$_{10}$

abandon so.
be resentful of
bear a grudge against
brand so.
devalue so.'s reputation
label so.
make so. lose his status
pigeonhole so.
stereotype so.
take amiss

WT$_{5b}$ Congratulating

applaud
be jubilant over
cheer loudly
congratulate
exult at
propose a toast to so.
receive with exultation

WT₅ᵦ Congratulating (continued)

rejoice at
(cf. EM₂ₕ)

WT₅c Expressing Solidarity

fraternize
join a group
show goodwill towards so.
sympathize with so.
(cf. VE)

WT₅d Respecting

adore
appreciate so.
beatify
compliment so.
eulogize so.
esteem so.
glorify
honor
hold so. in high esteem
idolize
pay so. compliments
pay homage
pay one's respects
praise so. for sth.
respect
revere
sanctify
speak a memorial address
swear allegiance
worship

WP Valuation of a Person

WP₀ Valuating a Person

WP₀ₐ Degrading a Person

WP₀ₐₐ Disregarding

abandon
avoid so.

WP₀ₐₐ Disregarding (continued)

despise
discriminate
disclaim
disregard
disrespect
flee from so.
ignore
look down upon
neglect
reject so.
scorn
shun so.
take no notice of so.
treat so. with indifference
undervalue so.

WP₀ₐᵦ Public Degradation (Without an Opportunity for the Addressee to Resist)

abase
abuse
annoy
bring low
call so. names
compromise
heckle
humble
humiliate
insult
irritate
jeer at
laugh at so.
make fun of so.
mock
offend
outrage
put so. out of temper
revile
ridicule
scoff at
shock

WP$_{0ab}$ Public Degradation (Without an Opportunity for the Addressee to Resist) (continued)

unmask
vex
vilify

WP$_{0ac}$ Hidden Degradation

abase
attribute sth. to so.
bring discredit on so.
bring so. into discredit
calumniate
characterize so. as
defame
devalue so.
discriminate
disparage
give so. a bad name
gossip about so.
impute sth. to so.
intrigue
plot
slander
speak ill of so.
spread rumors about so.
spread stories about so.
(cf. Lying)

WP$_{0ad}$ Open Degradation

abase
address harshly
degradate
give a good scolding
hector
nag at
outlaw
reprimand sharply
scream at
upbraid
yell at

WP$_{0b}$ Raising the Valuation of a Person

WP$_{0ba}$ Praising = WT$_{4e}$

WP$_{0bb}$ Congratulating = WT$_{5b}$

WP$_{0bc}$ Expressing Solidarity = WT$_{5c}$

WS Valuating Oneself

WS$_a$ Self-degradation

WS$_{aa}$ Hidden Self-degradation

be overly modest
be self-effacing
hide one's light under a bushel
understate

WS$_{ab}$ Open Self-degradation

(unintentionally)
disgrace os.
expose os.
make a fool of os.
make os. ridiculous
(intentionally)
abase os.
accuse os.
be self-effacing
blame os.
humilate os.
speak ill of os.

WS$_b$ Self-Upgrading

WS$_{ba}$ Hidden Self-Upgrading

fraud
misrepresent os.
swindle

WS$_{bba}$ Very Indirect Self-Upgrading = EN$_{7aa}$ Making Compliments

adore
cajole
coax
compliment
court
flatter
fawn upon
flirt
pay compliments
say sweet nothings
wheedle

WS$_{bbb}$ Indirect Self-Upgrading (with hidden intention) = EN$_{7ad}$

behave in a familiar manner
capativate
charm
chum up with so.
ensnare
fascinate
flatter
ingratiate os. with so.
insinuate os. into
make up to
make compliments
praise extravagantly

WS$_{bc}$ Open Self-Upgrading

arrogate
be a snob
be loud
be overbearing
be overweening
be purse-proud
boast
brag
claim
exaggerate
give os.
make a parade of

WS$_{bc}$ Open Self-Upgrading (continued)

plume os.
presume
pretend to
put on airs
show off
swagger
talk big
usurp

WG Valuation of Things, States of Affairs, etc.

WG$_0$ Judging/Valuating of Things, States of Affairs, etc. = WT$_0$; WT$_3$

WG$_{0a}$ Devaluing a State of Affairs

depreciate
devalue
make banal
relativize

WG$_{0b}$ Recommending

advocate
endorse
recommend
support

WG$_1$ Consequences of the Valuation of a State of Affairs

WG$_{1a}$ Disregarding the Valuation

disregard
ignore
neglect
not accept
pay no heed to
reject

WG₁ᵦ Respecting the Valuation

take into account
take to heart

WG₁ᵦ Respecting the Valuation
(continued)

pay attention to
pay heed to
(cf. NO₂)

8.6 D Discourse Models

DI Discourse Model

DI₁ Asking for Participation

address
apply to so. (for particulars)
approach a person
ask for participation in
beg for participation
require participation
speak to so.
want to contribute
want to participate
urge participation
ask for participation
offer to participate
offer participation in

DI₁' Exploring Readiness of Discourse

explore readiness to converse
gain information about
feel one's way forward
feel one's way towards
get in communication with
get in contact with
make inquiries about
get in touch
put out feelers

DI₂ Show Readiness of Discourse

ascertain readiness
show interest

DI₂' Invite Discourse

DI₂'ₐ Invite

ask in
invite
request
summon

DI₂'ᵦ Convoke

appoint a time
arrange
bring about an arrangement
call together
convoke
fix a date
summon

DI₂'ᵧ Summon

summon

DI₃ Accept

accept
acknowledge
admit
assent to
appreciate
give consent to
recognize

DI_3' Refuse

decline
disown
negate
rebuff
refuse
reject

DI_3'' Cancel

annul
cancel
counteract
countermand
deny
disavow
draw back
invalidate
neutralize
recant
repeal
retract
revise
revoke
take back
withdraw
delay
suspend

DI_4 Fixing Time

arrange
change date
date
fix a date
make an appointment

DI_5 Entering Contact

accost
address
call to
challenge (military)
hail

DI_5 Entering Contact (continued)

make the first cut
speak to

DI_{5a} Meet

accept
come upon
encounter
join
meet
meet with
unite
accept invitation
follow an invitation

DI_6 Beginning the Discourse

begin
contrive
enter into a discussion
get involved in a discussion
initiate
introduce
open
preface
prelude
usher in
start

DI_7 Being in Discourse

DI_{7a} Several Speakers Collectively

argue with
confer (with)
consult
converse
contribute to a discussion
debate
deliberate
discuss
dispute
exchange opinion

DI₇ₐ Several Speakers Collectively (continued)

have a public debate/discussion
joke with
keep up (a correspondence)
participate at a discussion
speak together
take counsel together
talk over
telephone

DI₇ᵦ One Speaker

amuse
declare os.
deliver a speech
discourse (on)
entertain
express one's opinion
give a speech
lecture (on)
speak one's mind
teach

DI₇ᵦ' Talk Cleverly

talk brilliantly
talk cleverly
talk giftedly
talk masterfully
talk wittily

DI₈ Discourse Inconvenience

DI₈ₐ Internally

(people)
annoy
disturb
harrass
interfere
interrupt
jam
trouble

DI₈ₐ Internally (continued)

upset
(discourse)
be struck
break down (a speech)
come to a standstill
get bogged down
get stuck
run aground
stagnate
stand still
stop flowing
stop running

DI₈ᵦ Externally

(before)
inhibit
prohibit
(during)
break up (assembly)
drown out
howl down
shout down
stop

DI₈c Intervention

interfere
interpose
interrupt
intervene

DI₉ Reconciliation of Disturbances

bridge over
patch up
reconcile
settle (a difference)

DI₁₀ Ending the Discourse

adjourn
bring to an end

DI₁₀ Ending the Discourse (continued)

cease
close the session
come to a conclusion
conclude
conclude with a summary
desist from
discontinue
end
finish
leave off
prorogue (parliament)
put a stop to
terminate
terminate in
dismiss
say goodbye
take leave of
be over
die (discussion)
peter out

DI₁₀' Switching Discourse

change the subject
come around to a subject
switch the topic
turn from one topic to another
turn to

DI₁₀' Withdrawing from Discourse

drop out
retire
withdraw from

DI₁₀'' Dragging Out Discourse

chatter away
drag out
draw out
filibuster
pass time in chatting

DI₁₀'' Dragging Out Discourse (continued)

pass time in gossiping
prolong
protract
stretch out
talk longer than one wanted
waste time gossiping

DT Discourse Types

DT₁ Discourse Types with Several Speakers

DT₁ₐ Generally

confer with so.
converse with so.
discuss
exchange opinion
have a conference
have a public discussion
keep up a correspondence
speak together
talk
telephone

DT₁ᵦ Cooperatively

DT₁ᵦₐ Oriented Towards a Decision

counsel
debate
deliberate
discuss
discuss an acquisition
dispute
have a public debate
huckster
take counsel together
talk over
contribute to a discussion
participate in a discussion

DT$_{1bb}$ Discussing a Theme

argue about
debate
discuss
discuss preliminarily
dispute
exchange an opinion
talk over

DT$_{1bc}$ Maintaining Contact

confer with so.
converse with so.
exchange opinions
speak together
telephone
chatter
chatter away
pass time in chattering
pass time in gossiping
talk nonsense
babble
cackle
gabble
gaggle
prattle
quack

DT$_{1c}$ Erotically

charm
flirt
pay compliments
say sweet nothings
tease

DT$_{1d}$ Joke

be witty at another's expense
have fun with
jest
joke
make fun of
make a joke (of)

DT$_{1d}$ Joke (continued)

make witty remarks
mock something
play the fool
play the imbecile
poke fun (at)
ridicule sth./so.
talk wittily

DT$_{1e}$ Indecent

make smutty jokes
say obscenities
speak in a beastly way
talk bawdy
talk filthy
talk indecent
talk lewd
talk obscene
talk smut
talk smutty
tell dirty stories
use four-letter words

DT$_{1g}$ Talk Loudly

shout to each other
talk loudly
yell

DT$_{1h}$ Secret

brew
concoct
contrive
devise
hatch
plot

DT$_2$ Discourse Types with One Speaker

convey facts
comment
criticize

DT₂ Discourse Types with One Speaker (continued)

criticize adversely
declaim
delineate
deliver a speech
demonstrate
depict
describe
display
draw
exhibit
expound
give an account
give a monologue
give a lecture
give a speech
give a talk
gloss
indicate
inform
instruct
lecture
monologuize
moralize
narrate
paint (dialectical)
portray
preach
relate
repeat (what one has said)
report
report on
report upon a matter
sketch
soliloquize
speak of
teach
tell

DT₃ Special Types of Discourses

pettifog

DT₃ Special Types of Discourses (continued)

philosophize
split hairs
talk shop
theologize
theoretize

IR Irony, Joke, Ridicule

IR₁ Addressed/Not Addressed

IR₁ₐ With Respect to Hearer (present)

chaff
deride
dupe so.
expose to ridicule
fool
gibe at
have someone
hoax
jeer at
jibe at
laugh at
make a fool of
make an imbecile of
make fun of so.
make sport of
mock
pull so.'s leg
scoff at
sneer at
take in so.
taunt
tease so.
treat with scorn

IR₁ᵦ With Respect to a Nonpresent Third Person

caricature
deride

IR₁ᵦ With Respect to a Nonpresent Third Person (continued)

jeer at
lark about
make persiflage
mock
parody
pillory
ridicule
scoff at
travesty

IR₁c With no Respect to a Person

be absurd
be foolish
be silly
chaff
fool around
frolic
have fun with sth.
jest
joke
lark
laugh
make puns
make witty remarks
play the fool
play practical jokes
ridicule sth.
talk wittily

IR₂ Relative to Friend-Enemy Relation

IR₂ₐ Cooperative-Friendly (joke)

caricature
chaff
have fun with
have a pun
jest
joke
lark (about)
laugh (at)

IR₂ₐ Cooperative-Friendly (joke) (continued)

make fun of so.
make a joke (of)
play the fool
play practical jokes
poke fun (at)
tease

IR₂ᵦ Mimical (in play)

chaff
fool
have so.
hoax
hold to ridicule
jeer (at)
laugh (at)
make fun of
mock
mystify
parody
persiflage
ridicule
sneer (at)
take (so.) in
tease
travesty

IR₂c Inimical (Ridicule)

IR₂cₐ Weaker

chaff
deride
gibe
jeer
laugh at
make a fool of
mock
sneer
sneer at so.
taunt
tease

IR$_{2ca}$ Weaker (continued)

treat with irony

IR$_{2cb}$ Stronger

cast a slur on
deride
dupe so.
expose to ridicule
fool
give a bad name to
jeer (at)
jibe (at)
laugh (at)
laugh to scorn
make a fool of
make game of
mock
pillory
put in bad odor
put in ill repute
ridicule
scoff (at)
sneer (at)
treat with scorn

TU Turn-Taking Model

TU$_1$ Intending Turn-Taking

announce os.
announce one's wish to speak
ask leave to speak (parliament)
await one's turn
beg permission to speak
raise one's hand
have so. announced
send in one's name/card

TU$_1$' Suppressing Intention for Turn-Taking

be still
forego speaking

TU$_1$' Suppressing Intention for Turn-Taking (continued)

hold one's tongue
remain silent

TU$_2$ Give Permission to Speak

allow so. to speak
call on
give permission to speak
give so. a turn
let so. have his say
impart permission to speak
ask so. something
ask a question

TU$_2$' Refuse Permission to Speak

ignore
overlook
pass by
pass over
skip
not allow so. to get a word in edgewise
not give a chance to speak

TU$_2$'' Being One's Turn

claim one's turn
it's my turn
take one's turn

TU$_3$ Beginning of the Turn

begin to speak
commence to talk
rush ahead and start speaking
set about speaking

TU$_3$' Violent Turn-Taking

burst out with words
cut off so./a conversation
cut so. short
interpose

Lexicon Section I

TU$_3$, Violent Turn-Taking (continued)

interrupt so.
intervene
prevent from continuing
step in between
stop so. short
throttle

TU$_3$,, Renounce One's Turn

cancel one's turn
forego one's turn
give up
relinquish
renounce one's turn to speak
waive
withdraw one's turn

TU$_3$,,, Taking One's Turn

alternate
be at one's turn
filibuster
have the turn
relieve (another p.)
take one's turn

TU$_4$ Having the Turn (cf. DT$_2$)

bring forward
carry forward
convey facts
declaim
deliver a speech
demonstrate
depict
describe
display
exhibit
expound
express one's opinion
give an account
give a lecture
give a monologue

TU$_4$ Having the Turn (continued)

give a speech
give a talk
indicate
inform
lecture
monologuize
portray
read off
read out
recite
repeat (what one has said)
report
report on
report upon a matter
soliloquize
speak

TU$_5$ Dragging Turn

drag out
draw out
filibuster
prolong
protract
stretch out

TU$_5$, Short Turn

keep short
make a brief remark
speak concisely

TU$_6$ Interrupting the Turn by Others

break in
butt in
chime in
cut a conversation short
cut in
cut off so.
disrupt
heckle
horn in

TU$_6$ Interrupting the Turn by Others (continued)

interpose
interrupt
intervene
prevent from continuing
stop so. short
suspend
throttle

TU$_6$' Turn-Interruption by S

TU$_6$'a Intentionally

become silent
desist
grow dumb
leave off
pause
postpone
stop (intentionally)

TU$_6$'b Unintentionally

be stuck
be struck dumb
break down (in a speech)
come to a standstill
falter
get stuck
hesitate
stop

TU$_6$'' Omitting Interruption

let so. continue
let so. finish

TU$_7$ Conflict of Turn-Taking

cf. KA

TU$_{8a}$ Continuing the Turn

add (a remark)
carry on
continue
go on with
keep on with
pursue

TU$_{8a}$' Surrendering Turn

give up
surrender
pass

TU$_{8b}$ Violent Turn-Taking

= TU$_3$'

TU$_{9a}$ Finish the Turn

bring to an end
cease
close the session
come to a conclusion
conclude
conclude with a summary
desist from
discontinue
end
finish
leave off
make an end to
terminate
terminate in
say goodbye to
take leave of
adjourn
dismiss
prorogue (parliament)

TU$_{9b}$ Transferring the Turn

hand over (to)
transfer (to)

Lexicon Section I

133

DI/TU Moderator Activities

be chairman
moderate
preside over
introduce (the speaker)
open (session)
accept comments
allow so. to speak
call on
extend speaking time
give permission to speak
put on the list of speakers

DI/TU Moderator Activities (continued)

ignore so.
pass over so.
limit speaking time
lead (from one argument to another)
lead a discussion
summarize
enforce good order
come to a conclusion
conclude
leave off a subject (topic)

8.7 X Text Models

ET Experience and Text Model

ET$_{-1}$ Perceive Reality

ET$_{-1a}$ Perceive

notice
observe
perceive
take notice of
feel
hear
see
taste

ET*$_{-1a}$ Realize

apprehend
come to an understanding
perceive the reason
realize
feel
hear
see
taste

ET$_{-1b}$ Understand

comprehend
fathom
get to the bottom of
grasp
penetrate
see through (the trick)
understand

ET$_0$ Exotheticize Knowledge

ET$_{0a}$ Declare

affirm
announce
assert
call out
cry out
declare
ejaculate
exclaim
expound
maintain
proclaim

ET$_{0a}$ Declare (continued)

pronounce
say with conviction
set forth
state

ET$_{0a}$ Report

convey facts
depict
describe
give an account of
inform about
make acquainted with
notify
portray
relate
repeat (what one has heard)
repeat (what so. else has said)
report
report upon a matter
tell

ET$_{0a}$ Utter

advance an opinion
express
give voice to
insert an advertisement
manifest
mention
narrate (a story)
publish
remark
say (a remark)
utter

ET$_{0a}$ Communicate Verbally

cable
call
exchange information
talk with so.
telegraph

ET$_{0a}$ Communicate Verbally (continued)

telephone
transmit to so. in morse code (a message)
transmit to so. in morse code that
talk with so.

ET$_{0a}$ Confirm

confirm
corroborate
establish
substantiate
validate
verify

ET$_{0a}$ Oath

attest
give testimony to
swear
take an oath
testify

ET$_{0b}$ Inform

advertise (inform that it is for sale)
advertise (political matters)
announce
give information
give notice to
inform
make known
make public
notify
publicize
report
trade information

ET$_{0c}$ Reveal (antecedently hidden information)

disclose
expose
lay bare

ET$_{0c}$ Reveal (antecedently hidden information) (continued)

make known
make manifest
make overt
make out
make public
reveal
uncover
unveil

ET$_{0c}$ Reveal (general)

clarify
clear up
elucidate
explain
explicate
illuminate
illumine
make clear

ET$_{0d}$ Teach

ET$_{0da}$ Teach (general)

impart knowledge
introduce so. to a field
learn in: I'll learn you
teach

ET$_{0da}$ Lecture

give lecture
instruct so.
lecture
prepare so. for an exam
teach

ET$_{0da}$ Drill

brainwash
drill
drum sth. into so.'s head

ET$_{0da}$ Drill (continued)

force notice
impose (beliefs)
impress sth. upon so.
indoctrinate
iterate
prepare for an exam
reiterate
say over and over again

ET$_{0da}$ Practice

cram (last minute learning)
drill
exercise
learn
learn by heart
memorize
practice
say over and over again
train

ET$_{0da}$ Make Learning Easy

prepare an abstract
prepare a digest
show and tell
spoon-feed
sugar-coat

ET$_{0db}$ Ritualized Teaching

moralize
preach
sermonize
teach so. manners

ET$_{0db}$ Teaching by Demonstration

demonstrate
indicate
point out
present
show how to do

ET_{0dc} Teaching by Demonstration (orally and in writing)

count out to
pronounce for so.
sound out sth. for so.
spell out sth. for so.
write out sth. for so.

ET_{0dd} Elucidate

clarify
clear up
elucidate
explain
explicate
illuminate
illumine
make clear

ET_{0dd} Enlighten

cause so. to understand
enlighten
reveal sth. to so.
strike so.

ET_{0de} Present

depict
describe
display
exhibit
expound
give an exposition
present
set forth

ET_{0df} Explain

explain
give an explanation
give a justification
give a reason why

ET_{0dg} Help (on)

aid
give a hand
help
help on

ET_1 Perceive Knowledge

ET_{1a} Understand

ET_{1b} Learn

acquire
assimilate
catch on to sth.
imitate
learn
make progress
pick up (a word)

ET_{1c} Imitation

copy
do by rote
imitate
make a copy
mimic so.
model after
model on
repeat another's word
repeat mechanically
reproduce

ET_{1d} Learn Anew

change one's view
learn afresh
learn anew
learn new tricks
readjust one's ideas

ET/TE Making Texts

ET/TE_a Producing Texts (generally)

ET/TE$_{aa}$ Producing Texts (non-specifically)

author
compose (text)
draw up (documents)
formulate
produce (texts)
put into words
write (text)
write down
write out

ET/TE$_{ab}$ Record Texts

draw up
draw up the official report of
keep the minutes
keep a record of
note down
record
register
take down (a deposition)
take a note of
write down

ET/TE$_{ac}$ Compose Texts

author
coin (words)
compose
compose (as an author)
concoct
design
draft
draw up
make rhymes
outline
put into words
sketch
word
write
write poetry

ET/TE$_{ad}$ Produce Special Kinds of Text

couch in concise terms
draft a memorial address
draft a speech
eulogize
keep a diary
memorialize
write down experiences
write an essay, treatise

ET/TE$_b$ Produce Texts (fancy)

construe
dream
embellish
exaggerate
improvise
indulge in reveries, fancies
produce (science) fiction
spin yarns
talk idly
tell fish-stories (dial.)
tell tales
tell untruths
write purple prose
prophesy
read palms
read tarot cards
tell fortunes
tell fortunes in tea leaves

ET/TE$_b$ Incomprehensible, Unstructured

babble
be delirious
glossolalia
ramble (delirium)
rave
speak in tongues

ET/TE$_c$ Produce Texts (futuristic)

forecast (weather)

ET/TE$_c$ Produce Texts (futuristic)
(continued)

foretell
make prognoses
plan
predestinate so.
predestine so.
predetermine
predict
preplan
prognosticate
project
prophesy

ET/TE$_a$, Elaborating Texts

check
correct proofs
do proofreading
elaborate
go over
lengthen
look over
look through
make more popular
make worse
pad
polish
reorganize
retouch
review
revise
rework
rewrite
scrutinize
shorten
touch up
trim
amend
correct
dress up
embellish
improve

ET/TE$_a$, Elaborating Texts (continued)

perfect
rectify
repair a paper
restore
make worse
make worse instead of better
mess up

TE Texting

TE$_{-2}$ Promulgating Texts

TE$_{-2a}$ Promulgating Texts

circulate
diffuse
dispense
disseminate
distribute
make popular
popularize
promulgate ideas
propagate
spread
spread about

TE$_{-2a}$ Tradition of Text

hand down
mediate
pass on
tell the younger, others

TE$_{-2b}$ Publishing Texts

edit
make public by printing
publish
retail (texts)

TE$_{-1}$ Perceiving Texts

TE$_{-1a}$ Deciphering Texts

decipher
decode

TE$_{-1b}$ Read

peruse
read
read over
read through
check
examine
inspect
look through
ponder over old books
read through
review
scrutinize
study
test
browse
glance quickly over, into
run through
skim through

TE$_{-1b'}$ Working with Texts

adapt (from other languages)
condense
pull passages from
make excerpts from
recapitulate
summarize
sum up
write abstracts

TE$_{-1c}$ Achieving Text Knowledge

TE$_{-1ca}$ Learning Texts

impress
imprint
impress something upon one's memory
learn by heart

TE$_{-1cb}$ Interpret (with semantic adjustments)

conclude
explain
expound
gather
infer
interpret
learn
make an exegesis
take it to be
understand
understand from

TE$_{-1cc}$ Misinterpret

misinterpret
misjudge
misnomer
misread
misunderstand
(general)
err
fail
make a mistake

TE$_{-1cd}$ Changing Interpretation

give a new interpretation
give a new meaning
redefine
reinterpret

TE$_0$ Exothetizing (Exposing) Text Knowledge

TE$_{0a}$ Reproducing Texts

TE$_{0aa}$ Reproduce [say (orally) what you have read or heard]

act (a play)
cite
copy down
perform a play

TE_{0aa} Reproduce [say (orally) what you have read or heard] (continued)

read out
read a paper
recite
repeat (what one has heard before)
report (what one has heard)
reproduce
retell

TE_{0ab} Fake and Parody

counterfeit
falsify (a document)
forge
purport to be the original
disfigure
make something bad
murder the (Queen's, King's) English
speak distorted English
speak poor English
turn something into a bad text
make fun of
parody
satirize
travesty

TE_{0ac} Reconstruct

paraphrase
reconstruct
recreate
retell

TE_{0ad} Translate

adapt (from another language)
Anglicize
decipher
decode
encipher
encode
Germanize
interpret

TE_{0ad} Translate (continued)

transcribe
translate

TE_{0ae} Reformulate

Anglicize
Germanize
paraphrase
reshape
retranslate
translate back

TE_{0b} Expounding Texts

TE_{0ba} Exothetisize Interpretations

TE_{0bb} Comment

comment on
criticize
gloss
review
supply with (marginal) notes
(negative)
criticize
pick holes (in)
pull apart
pull into pieces
put down
rip apart
run down
tear apart
tear into pieces
(positive)
laud
praise
rave about

TE_{0bc} Exothetisizing of Reinterpretation

TE_1 Perceive Text Knowledge

TE$_2$ Reinterpretation of Texts

IN Information Model

IN$_{1a}$ Systematically Searching Data

IN$_{1aa}$ General

ascertain
determine
examine
examine thoroughly
explore
inquire after
investigate
look into
look up
search
search out
search through
sift through
trace
try to make out

IN$_{1ab}$ with Questions (cf. EN$_5$)

ask for information
ask for particulars
examine (so. in examinations)
inquire about, after
interrogate
make general inquiries
pump so.
query so.
question
quiz so.
sound out so. (as to his views)
test so. on

IN$_{1ab}$ Hypothesizing

conjecture
guess
hypothesize
surmise

IN$_{1ac}$ Special Kinds of Data Searching

confront witnesses
examine (in an examination)
hear case
hear a pupil's lesson
perform a psychoanalysis
question witnesses
take testimony

IN$_{1b}$ Perceiving and Observing of a Person

IN$_{2a}$ Finding Data

detect
discover
divine
elicit
get the meaning
grasp
guess
infer
penetrate

IN$_{2a*}$ Imply

convey information (indirectly)
extrude
express
insinuate
put information into

IN$_{2a'}$ Solving a Searching Problem

arrive at
clear up
decipher
decode
diagnose
disentangle
elucidate
find out
find one's way through
get to the bottom of sth.

$IN_{2a'}$ Solving a Searching Problem (continued)

get the truth out
make out
master (a problem)
solve (a riddle)
unravel

IN_{2b} Getting Answers

get an answer
get information
(cf. EN_{9i})

IN_{-1} Setting Up Lists, Tables, Categories

define a list
determine
fix
lay down
make up a list
set up a list

IN_{-1} Coining

abbreviate
coin
invent a name
make an abbreviation

IN_{3a} Sorting and Organizing Data

IN_{3aa} Organizing Data

arrange
classify
file
put in order
set in order
sort

IN_{3ab} Test = VV_c Test

IN_{3ac} Categorize

categorize
classify
compute
group
index
summarize

IN_{3b} Valuating and Sorting out Data

IN_{3ba} Comparing

(comparison)
compare
make a comparison
(selection)
choose
pick out
select
single out
sort out
(separation)
lay aside
separate
set aside
(identification)
equalize
identify
make equal
recognize identity

IN_{3bb} Evaluating

appraise
assess
estimate
evaluate
find bad
form an estimate of
find good
valuate (infrequent)
deprecate

IN$_{3bb}$ Evaluating (continued)

depreciate
impugn

IN$_{3c}$ Marking Data

label
mark
stamp

IN$_5$ Retrieving Data

IN$_{5aa}$ Searching

be aware of
be mindful of
take into account
associate to
associate sth. with sth.
recall
recall to memory
remember
think back (on)
think of
reflect on

IN$_{5ab}$ Searching in Vain

have forgotten
not remember

IN$_{5ac}$ Extracting Data

extract
pick out
pluck out
pull out

IN$_{5b}$ Finding Data in Long-Term Memory and Putting them in Short-Term Memory

call to mind
recall

IN$_{5b}$ Finding Data in Long-Term Memory and Putting them in Short-Term Memory (continued)

recollect
remember
occur to so.
strike one's mind

IN$_{6a}$ Distributing Data

IN$_{6aa}$ General

circulate
diffuse
disperse
disseminate
distribute
promulgate
propagate
spread
spread about
advertise
announce
convey facts
inform
publish
report
demonstrate
depict
describe
display
exhibit
expound
give an account
inform
indicate
post
repeat
report
report upon a matter
assert
say

IN₆ₐₐ General (continued)

telegraph
telephone
tell
transmit in morse code

IN₆ₐᵦ Distributing Texts (towards Hearer)

advertise
announce
deliver a message
impart information
instruct
proclaim
report so.

IN₆ₐc Distributing Texts (Speaker anonymous)

spread rumors
write anonymously
write under a pseudonym

IN₆ₐd Distributing Texts (regularly, towards Hearer)

give an orientation
inform regularly
orient so.
report to (regularly)

IN₆ᵦ Distributing Private Data Publicly

advertise
announce
announce removal
announce withdrawal
inform
insert an advertisement
make known
make public
notify

IN₆ᵦ Distributing Private Data Publicly (continued)

publish
register
report
report (one's arrival, one's departure) to the police
resign

IN₆ᵦ' Distributing Public Data

affix (at the bulletin board)
bring to light
call up (the reserve)
divulge
hang out (a shingle)
make known
notify
post
publish
proclaim
publish from the pulpit
stick bills on
stick upon (a bulletin board)
post bills

IN₆d Distributing Selected Data

bias
bowdlerize
censor
filter
fudge
screen
slant

IN₆c Distributing Data, guaranteed that they are true

acknowledge (sins, crime, truth)
admit
confess
give evidence (about)

IN$_{6c}$ Distributing Data, guaranteed that they are true (continued)

give a guarantee
give an oath
make an affidavit
make a deposition
own up to
plead guilty
swear
testify (to)
vouch (for)

IN$_7$ Examining and Questioning Distributed Data

IN$_{8a}$ Accept Distributed Data

accept
admit
acknowledge
appreciate
assent to
give consent to
recognize
share the same opinion

IN$_{8b}$ Refuse Distributed Data

challenge
combat
condemn
contest
decline
disallow
disavow
disown
dispute
excuse
negate
object
protest
refuse
reject
repudiate

IN$_{8b}$ Refuse Distributed Data (continued)

spurn
assail
attack

IN$_{9a}$ Denying (what has been stated before)

annul
cancel
contradict (explicitly)
countermand
deny
disavow
invalidate a contract
negate
neutralize
recant
repeal
retract
revise
revoke
suspend
take back
withdraw

IN$_{9b}$ Testify the Correctness of Distributed Data

acknowledge receipt of
acknowledge
acquit
affirm by oath
asseverate
assevere
assure (the truth)
attest
authenticate (by documents)
aver
certify
confirm by oath
convict
corroborate
demonstrate

IN9b Testify the Correctness of Distributed Data (continued)

document
endorse
ensure (the truth)
establish
establish firmly
guarantee
issue a certificate
make sure of (the truth)
prove
prove true
show
show proof of
swear to
validate
verify
vouch for

IN10 Refer to Reliable Data

appeal to
base sth. on
found sth. on
ground sth. on
refer to
rely on
rest on

VE Treason Model

VE$_{-2}$ Hatch

brew
concoct
contrive
devise
hatch
plot
plot secrets
plot treason

VE$_{-1}$ Declaring as Secret

classify
classify as secret
mark as secret
request to keep secret
stamp as secret

VE$_0$ Entrusting

confess
confide
confide in so.
communicate clandestinely
entrust to
go to confession
initiate so. into a field, society
place one's trust in
put in the know
put one's trust in
send a stiff
smuggle letters in prisoner's cell
take so. into one's confidence
unbosom
unbosom os. to so.

VE$_1$, Keep Secret

conceal
hide
keep one's mouth shut
keep a secret
keep sth. secret
keep secret
let the matter go no further
   (of a secret)
not break a word
not + (verb ϵ VE$_1$)

VE$_1$„ Treason

VE$_1$„$_a$ General

bug (the telephone, the wire)
catch (a word)

VE$_{1''a}$ General (continued)

eavesdrop
inform against/on
intercept (for letters, broadcasting)
keep your eyes and ears open
learn by eavesdropping
listen in on (conversations)
make inquiries
overhear
tap (the telephone, the wire)

VE$_{1''b}$ During Learning and Teaching

crib (school)
plagiarize
use a cribsheet
use a pony

VE$_1$ Revealing Secrets

betray (a secret)
betray a confidence
disclose
blow the lid off of
blab
divulge
inform against
let out (secrets)
reveal (secrets)
tell others
trumpet

VE*$_1$ Give Evidence of a Secret

manifest
give evidence of

VE$_{1a}$ Reveal Secrets to Another Person

disclose
expose
make known
reveal

VE$_{1a}$ Reveal Secrets to Another Person (continued)

uncover
unveil

VE$_{1a}$ Reveal Secrets to the Public

expose
make public
promulgate
publish
unearth
unmask

VE$_{1b}$ Give Evidence Before Court

give evidence
sing (like a canary)
make a sworn deposition
spill the beans
turn (Queen's, King's, State's) evidence

VE$_{1b,c,d}$ Bring Information to Authorities

blow the whistle on
bring a charge against
complain against
give information of
report
tip off the authorities

VE$_{1c}$ Denounce

denounce
inform against
tell on (American)
tell tales (in school, Eng.)

VE$_{1f}$ Forbidden Informing in School, etc.

whisper

VE$_{1g}$ Blab Secret Information

betray os.
blab
escape (one's lips)
give os. away
let the cat out of the bag
slip out from

DE Thinking

DE$_1$ Reception

absorb
assimilate
note
notice
perceive
receive
record
take notice of
take up
snatch up

DE$_1$ Understand

catch on
comprehend
conceive
grasp
snatch up
take up
understand

DE$_2$ Consider

bear in mind
consider
hold
pay attention to
picture sth. to os.
take into account
take into consideration
take notice of

DE$_3$ Wonder

be astonished
be surprised
hesitate
wonder (at)

DE$_4$ Thinking Over

brood (upon)
consider
consult with one's pillow
deliberate
meditate (on)
muse (on)
ponder sth.
rack one's brain about
think the matter over
think over carefully
weigh
be lost in thoughts
cogitate
concentrate upon
reflect (on)
sleep on sth.
think

DE$_5$ Suppose

assume
make the assumption
presume
presuppose
suggest
suppose
believe
be of the opinion
deem
fear
opine
suspect
think
conjecture
deduce

DE₅ Suppose (continued)

guess
hypothesize
postulate
speculate
suggest
surmise
attribute sth. to so.
comprise
imply
impute
insinuate

DE₆ Thinking Procedures

DE₆ₐ Gather

accumulate
amass
assemble
collect
compile
concentrate
gather
gather together

DE₆ᵦ Select

choose
file
pick out
rank
select
single out
sort out

DE₆ᵦ Separate

lay aside
separate
set aside
sort out

DE₆ᵦ Compare

compare
draw a comparison

DE₆ᵦ Identify

equalize
identify

DE₆c Analyze

abstract
analyze
arrange
articulate
classify
divide
divide up
fit in
generalize
make out
objectivize
qualify as
rationalize
reduce to
segment
subsume
trace back to

DE₆d Infer

abduce
conclude
deduce
derive
exclude
induce
infer
prove by exclusion
reduce to
work backwards

DE$_{6e}$ Differentiate

differentiate
discern
discriminate
distinguish
distinguish between
draw a distinction
keep apart
make a distinction

DE$_{6f}$ Construct

amalgamate
arrange
collate
combine
compose
concatenate
connect
construe
coordinate
design
form
form into files
form into ranks
invent
join
link
make up (a list)
organize
parallelize
place together
plan
project
put together
rank
summarize
systematize
synthesize

DE$_{6g}$ Compare

bring to bear upon
combine

DE$_{6g}$ Compare (continued)

compare
juxtapose

DE$_7$ Doubt

be suspicious of
call into question
doubt
question
suspect
throw suspicion upon

DE$_8$ Planning/Deciding

DE$_{8a}$ Hope

anticipate
desire
desire greatly
dream
expect
hope for
look for
long for
wait for
wish

DE$_{8b}$ Want

aim at + noun
aim to + verb
aspire to
be about to
endeavor to get sth.
have a mind to
have in view
intend
make an attempt to
mean to
strive for
try to get sth.
want

DE$_{8c}$ Ponder

balance
consider carefully
ponder
weigh

DE$_{8c}$ Prefer

(positive)
give preference to
place above
prefer
set over
(neutral)
choose
decide
determine
give judgment
judge
resolve (on)
(negative)
refuse
reject

DE$_{8d}$ Plan

brew
brood over
conceive
concoct
contrive
devise
dispose
hatch (out)
imagine
invent
plan
plot
scheme
set up a project
sketch
think out

DE$_{8e}$ Decide

(positive)
give preference to
place above
prefer
set over
superpose
(neutral)
choose
decide
decree
determine
give judgment
judge
resolve (on)
(negative)
refuse
reject
(cf. EN$_9$)

DE$_9$ Fancy

daydream
dream
gather wool
indulge in reveries, fancies
spin yarns

VV Comparing Devices

VV$_a$ Categorize

allot to
alphabetize
arrange
book
catalogue
categorize
chart
classify
count as
count up
define as

VV$_a$ Categorize (continued)

determine as
determine the position
enter on cards
enter in a list
enumerate
file
fit in
grade
identify
incorporate
inventory
lexicalize
list
locate
make a card index of
make a bibliography
make a list of
mark as
order
place on record
post (in a ledger)
record
register
rubrify
schedule
sift
sort
specify in a list
standardize
tabulate
take an inventory of
typify
adjoin
appoint to
associate with
attach to
coordinate

VV$_{a'}$ Categorize Oneself

pass os. off as so.
pass os. off (for a nobleman)
present os.

VV$_b$ Mark

VV$_{ba}$ Mark (General)

address sth.
affix a ticket to
baptize
brand
call
characterize
christen
denominate
designate
dub
give a heading, title
give a legend
give an inscription
give a name to
give a nickname
index
indicate
lable
make an inscription
mark
mark with a cross
mark with figures
name
number
number the pages
put a ticket on
sign
style
stamp
term

VV$_{bb}$ Change Marking

code
encipher
encode
rechristen
rename

VV$_{bc}$ Sign

affix a seal
countersign
give a receipt
mark off
put one's name to
put a signet
ratify
receipt (a bill)
seal
sign
sign (with a flourish)
sign provisionally
subscribe
undersign
underwrite

VV$_{bd}$ Date

antedate
backdate
date
misdate
postdate

VV$_c$ Test

ascertain
assay
assure
check
control
examine
falsify
look through
make sure
make sure of a thing
prove
put to the test
reassure
revise
scrutinize
see through

VV$_c$ Test (continued)

supervise
try
verify

VV$_d$ Compare

compare
estimate
evaluate
identify with

VV$_e$ Differentiate

differentiate
discriminate
discern
distinguish
distinguish between
keep apart
separate
tell apart

VV$_f$ Comparative Designation

call so./sth. as sth.
declare so./sth. as sth.
label so./sth. as sth.
qualify so./sth. as sth.
represent so./sth. as sth.
style (call) so./sth. as sth.

VV$_g$ Value

appraise
assess
be of the opinion
consider
consider carefully
contemplate
depreciate
eliminate
estimate
evaluate

VV_g Value (continued)

find good/bad
ponder
rate
regard
reject
select

VV_g Value (continued)

separate
single out
sort
take so. as
value
(cf. WP)

8.8 T Theme Models

TO Theme Organization Model (Verbalization)

TO₁ Think

cf. DE

TO₂ Verbalize

articulate
extemporize
improvise
put into words
tell sth. with the greatest of ease
verbalize

TO₂ Thematize

TO₂ₐ Marking Out

circumscribe
confine
define
delimit
delineate
demarcate
differentiate
enlarge
expand
extend
lay out

TO₂ₐ Marking Out (continued)

limit
mark off
mark out
outline
sketch in profile
stake out
trace
widen
sketch

TO₂ᵦ Thematize (narrower sense)

TO₂ᵦₐ Detailed (explicitly)

concern os. with
deal with
engage in
enter into
handle
occupy os. with
tackle
take as subject
treat
work at

TO₂ᵦᵦ Not So Detailed

have regard to
indicate

TO$_{2bb}$ Not So Detailed
(continued)

make comments
make notes
make remarks
make a statement
mark
notice
observe
perceive
point out
remark
state
take into account
take into consideration

TO$_{2bc}$ Incidentally

allude
graze
hint at
intimate
mention casually
note
notice
observe
perceive
put in a word
remark
suggest
touch lightly
touch on
touch upon
brush over
rush over

TO$_{2c}$ Leave Out

eliminate
except
exclude
exempt
reject
remove

TO$_{2c}$ Leave Out
(continued)

leave alone
leave out
let alone
neglect
omit

avoid
bypass
evade
jump over
pass over
skip

TO$_{2d}$ Include

add
comprise
embrace
enclose
fit in
imply
include
incorporate
insert
join
patch in
subsume

TO$_{2e}$ Reorganize

alter
amend
change
modify
rectify
remodel
reorganize
transform

TO$_{2f}$ Compress

abstract
compress

TO$_{2f}$ Compress
(continued)

concentrate
condense
consolidate
digest
solidify
summarize

TO$_{2g}$ Mention Unpleasant Topic

bring up an unpleasant subject
hit on a sore spot
touch on a sore spot

TO$_3$ Structure

TO$_{3a}$ Structure

arrange
articulate
bracket
classify
compose
construct
embed
entwine
form
form into files
form into ranks
interlard (with oaths)
interweave
make repetitive
mark out
organize
organize in paragraphs
pack together
partition
segment
select
splice
structure
subordinate
superordinate
systematize

TO$_{3a}$ Structure
(continued)

cut up
dissect
split up
subdivide

TO$_{3b}$ Restructuring

alter the succession
change the sequence
invert
place differently
rearrange
reorder
transpose

TO$_4$ Connect

amalgamate
attach to
bind together
chain together
combine
concatenate
conglomerate
connect
couple
entwine
interlace
interweave
join
juxtapose
knit together
link together
place together
put together
stick together
tie together
unite

count up
enumerate
make series

TO₅ Relief

TO₅ₐ Relief (General)

bring into prominence
bring to relief
call special attention to
display
highlight
make salient
place in the forefront
place in the foreground
put first
put into limelight
set off
spotlight
throw into relief

TO₅ₐ Focus

call attention to
call special attention
focus
follow with one's eyes
have one's eye on sth.
zoom in

TO₅ₐc Gradually Focusing

attract attention
call attention to
control the conversation upon a subject
direct the conversation upon a subject
guide the conversation upon a subject
steer the conversation upon a subject
turn the conversation upon a subject

TO₅ₐd Defocusing

bracket
insert in brackets
put in parentheses
screen

TO₅ₐb Accentuate

accent
accentuate
emphasize
lay stress on
stress

TO₅c Weaken

attenuate
be polite
diminish (the severity)
hedge
lessen
mitigate
moderate
play down
reduce (the severity)
scale down
soften
tone down
weaken

TO₅e Contrast

bring into relief
compare
confront
contrast
draw a comparison
make a comparison
oppose
set off

TV Thematic Phases Model

TV₁ Clarifying Preliminarily

approach (a task)
bring up
discuss preliminarily
present
set about (a task)
treat preliminarily
undertake (a task)

TV₂ Announce

announce a theme
give a heading
give a title to

TV₃ Sketching the Theme

circumscribe
confine
delimit
delineate
demarcate
design
draft
give an overview
outline
plan (theme)
sketch
sketch in profile

TV₄ Premising

introduce
make preliminary remarks
preface
prelude
premise
say in advance
say beforehand
say preliminarily

TV₅ Begin

air
begin
bring into play
bring up
call into notice
draw into
initiate
make mention
mention
open
start
usher in

TV₅ Begin (continued)

ventilate
note
raise a question

TV₅ Appeal

appeal to
apply os. (to)
approach
devote os. (to)
get to the subject
get to the theme
get to the topic
mention
raise (a problem)
touch upon

TV₆ Elaborating the Theme

TV₆ₐ General

amplify (a description)
broaden out
chew thoroughly
debate
develop
discuss
enlarge on (a description)
elaborate
extend
frame
run down the checklist
shape
spin out
stretch
work through
work out
treat

TV₆ᵦ Contribute

adduce (reasons)
be the devil's advocate
bring forward

TV$_{6b}$ Contribute (continued)

contribute to
contribute towards
defend (a position)
present (a subject)
support
support a view

TV$_6$' Interruption

TV$_6$'$_a$ of Other's Speech

break in
interfere
interject
interpose
interrupt
intervene
make an objection
raise an objection
take exception to

TV$_6$'$_b$ of Own Speech

(intentional)
deviate
digress
diverge
insert
make an excursion

(with specific intention)
glance back over
retrospect
review

(unintentional)
deviate
digress
diverge
go astray
jump from one thing to another
lose one's way
miss the point
not to come to grips with the matter
talk around the subject

TV$_6$''' Conflict of the Topic

(cf. KA)

TV$_6$''' Stagnate, Cause Stopping

get confused
get entangled in contradictions
get muddled
get tied up in one's own words
lose the thread
lose the track
run one's head against a brick wall
stagnate
stand still
stop flowing

TV$_7$ Continuing the Topic

TV$_{7a}$ Possibly After a Turn Change

add to
append
attach
catch on
join
recommence
reenter into
resume
still adhere to a viewpoint
still cling to sth.
still maintain (a claim)
supplement (previous remarks)
subjoin
take up

TV$_{7b}$ Comment

comment on
criticize
gloss
pick holes (in)
pluck into pieces
pull apart

TV$_{7b}$ Comment (continued)

pull into pieces
review
run down
supply with (marginal) notes

TV*$_{7b}$ Confirm

affirm
confirm
corroborate
establish
give reasons for
make good (an assertion)
prove
strengthen (the point)
substantiate

TV$_{7c}$ Improve

adjust
amend
clear up
complete
correct
deepen the point
elucidate
extend
improve
make actual
make more concrete
make more detailed
make more explicit
make more precise
perfect
put in order
put right
put straight
qualify
rectify
repair
revise
set right
sharpen

TV$_{7c}$ Improve (continued)

specify
standardize
tighten up
unify

TV$_{7d}$ Repeat

bring once more
bring up again
do again
repeat
repeat over and over
reiterate
say again

TV$_{7d}$ Perserverance

be obstinate
insist on/upon
persist
persevere
stick obstinately to a thing

TV$_{7e}$ Finish

complete
finish off
wind up
terminate

TV$_{7f}$ Summarize

condense
digest
make a digest
make a recapitulation
make a summary
make a synopsis
recapitulate
summarize
sum up

TV$_{7g}$ After an Intermediary Stop or Interruption

carry on
come back
continue
develop further
get on with
go ahead (with a topic)
go on with
keep on with
muddle on
pursue
proceed (with a topic)
progress (with a topic)
resume
return to the subject

TV$_{7h}$ After Longer Pause Within Discourse

add to
append
bridge over
form a transition
lead (from one argument to the other)
lead over
make an afterthought

TV$_{7i}$ After a Longer Time in a New Discourse

bring to light again
cite
refer to
report

(topic)
borrow from
bring up again
come back again
come to light again
derive from
reach back to
reappear

TV$_{7i}$ After a Longer Time in a New Discourse (continued)

recur
refer back to
renew (a dispute)
resume
return
return to
take up again

TV$_{7j}$ Memoratively

come back to
give an elegy
give a memorial address
look back
look behind
recall the past
recapitulate
reconstruct
reflect on the past
review the past
trace back

TV$_7$, Changing Topic

alter the topic
change the topic
vary the topic

TV$_8$ Anticipating and Delaying

TV$_{8a}$ Anticipate

anticipate
prejudge a matter
speak prematurely

TV$_{8b}$ Delay

adjourn
defer
delay
postpone

TV_{8b} Delay (continued)

procrastinate (rare)
prorogue
put off

TV_{8b} Leave Undecided

disregard
keep open
leave open
leave undecided
neglect

TV_9 Performing Successfully

agree upon a thing with so.
carry (a motion) with a majority
deal completely with
discuss thoroughly
exhaust a topic
talk out

TP Topic Presentation

TP_1 Evaluation of Presentation

TP_{1a} Reproductive Presentation

declaim
deliver in a monotonous, sing-song manner
rattle off
read off
recite
recite in a sing-song manner
reel of (a poem)
rehearse
repeat
repeat a formula
tell (one's beads)

greet
pray
say grace

TP_{1b} Babble (nongrammatical)

babble
speak in broken English
talk gibberish

TP_{1c} Exaggerate

brag
boast
draw the long boast
exaggerate
give os. airs
talk big

TP_{1d} Moralize

moralize
preach
sermonize

TP_{1e} Chatter

(empty talk)
chatter
prattle
jabber
gossip
gibber

(nonsense)
babble
prattle
prate
talk nonsense
talk bosh
talk twaddle
speak drivel
blabber
talk gibberish

TP_2 Evaluation Presentation

TP_{2a} Positive and Nonnegative Evaluation

TP$_{2aa}$ Presenting Adequately

convey facts
depict
describe
display
exhibit
give an account of sth.
inform so.
make acquainted with
notify
present
relate
portray
repeat (what one has heard os.)
repeat (what so. else has said)
report
report upon a matter
set forth

TP$_{2ab}$ Excellent Presentation

argue successfully/perfectly/soundly
be brilliant
be distinguished
be outstanding
make a moving speech
make a rousing speech
make a stirring speech
present sth. in a brilliant manner

TP$_{2ac}$ Elucidate

allegorize
analogize
be illustrative of
circumscribe
clarify
demonstrate
demystify
describe in outline
elaborate
elucidate
explain
illumine

TP$_{2ac}$ Elucidate (continued)

illuminate
illustrate
make clear
make more precise
metaphorize
outline
personify
reduce
show
simplify
sketch
symbolize
typify

TP$_{2ad}$ Tighten

economize words
formulate succinctly
use words sparingly
leave out (superfluous things)
lump together
omit (superfluous things)
stylize
tighten

TP$_{2ae}$ Embellish

adorn
deck out
decorate
embellish
lavish (words)
waste (words)

TP$_{2b}$ Negative Evaluation

be boring
be bookish
be farfetched
belabor a point
be too subtle
bore
flogging a dead horse
grasping at straws

TP$_{2b}$ Negative Evaluation (continued)

indulge in words
luxuriate in words
overburden with big words
overdo
overload with big words
put the audience to sleep
speak bombastically
speak pompously
speak pretentiously
split hairs
stretch a point

TP$_{2bb}$ Biased Presentation

TP$_{2bba}$ Blow up

blow up
boast
carry to excess
carry too far
complicate
exaggerate
inflate
play up
present expansively
puff up
overact
overdo
swell

TP$_{2bba}$ Upgrade

adore
be enthusiastic
dramatize
dream
estheticize
explain away
extenuate
glorify
gloss over
heroize
idealize

TP$_{2bba}$ Upgrade (continued)

idyllize
make bright
palliate
poeticize
produce euphemisms
put in a favorable light
rave about
romanicize
varnish over
smooth over
transfigure
upgrade

TP$_{2bba}$ Downgrade

put pessimistically

TP$_{2bbb}$ Trifle

banalize
belittle
depreciate
detract from
disparage
make a bagatell out of something
make shallow
make superficial
schematize
simplify
stereotype
trifle
trivialize
vulgarize

TP$_{2bbc}$ Moderate/Mitigate

attenuate
check
damp down
graduate
hedge
limit by provisos
mitigate

TP$_{2bbc}$ Moderate/Mitigate (continued)

moderate
relativize
shade
soften down
stifle
tint

TP$_{2bc}$ Disguised Presentation

allegorize
analogize
circumscribe
cloak
conceal
cover
disguise
envelop
hide
hoodwink
hush up
smooth over
metaphorize
muffle up
mystify
mythologize
palliate
put into metaphors
screen
symbolize
veil

TP$_{2bc}$ Suggest

allow to be noticed
give a hint
give so. to understand
intimate to somebody
put someting into

TP$_{2bd}$ Confused Presentation

blend
bring in confusion

TP$_{2bd}$ Confused Presentation (continued)

cloud
complicate
confound
confuse
disarrange
disorder
entangle
express os. in a blurred manner
express os. hazily
express os. indefinitely
express os. indistinctly
express os. vaguely
express os. in a woolly manner
get mixed up
jumble up
make intricate
make involved
mingle
mix
mystify
mix up
mix up with
obscure
tangle
throw together

TP$_{2be}$ Present Distortedly

adulterate
botch
bowdlerize
bungle
contort
counterfeit
deform
disfigure
distort
force
misrepresent
pervert
pull out of shape
put mechanical
put stereotyped

TP$_{2be}$ Present Distortedly (continued)

spoil
twist
murder the Queen's Engish
warp

TP$_{2be}$ Unimaginative Talk

use a hackneyed phrase
wear out an old horse

TP$_{2bf}$ Evasion

avoid
decline
digress
disregard
dodge
elude
evade
gloss over
ignore
manage to see over
pass over
shift
shirk
shun
talk round the subject
treat with ignorance
treat with indifference
transcend
varnish over

TP$_{2bg}$ Withhold

conceal
hide
intercept
keep back from so.
keep secret
pass over in silence
secrete
suppress
withhold

TP$_{2bh}$ Be Farfetched

be farfetched
grasp at straws
split hairs
take out of the context

TP$_{2bi}$ Insufficient Presentation

be cryptic
be fragmentary
be fragmented
be too spare with words
shorten too much
use words too sparingly

TP$_{2bi}$ Amending Bad Presentation

fix up
patch up
piece together

TP$_{2bj}$ Talk Nonsense

babble
be raving
blather
chat
chatter
crush
drivel on
flounder
gossip
jabber
prattle
rave
spin yarns
squash
talk balderdash
talk bosh
talk disconnectedly
talk nonsense
tell stories
talk stuff and nonsense
talk twaddle
tell untruths

Directions for Using Lexicon Section II

Lexicon Section II contains all speech activity verbs and complex expressions that can be found in Section I listed *in alphabetical order*. Complex expressions are listed under their first word and under a main noun or adverb. To the right of each expression are given the labels plus the page number on which the expression is to be found,

e.g.,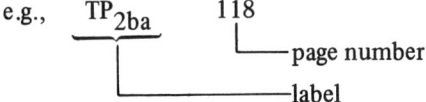

Given an expression, Lexicon Section II shows in which categories of which models it is listed and on which pages one can look it up.

Chapter 9   Lexicon Section II

Alphabetic Index of Speech Act Verbs

abandon
 $EN_{9h}.(84); KA_{-1d}(88);$
 $KA_{1bb}(92); KA_{2d}(98);$
 $KA_{3b}(98); KA_{4bac}(101);$
 $NO_{0b}.(108); NO_{10}(117);$
 $WP_{0aa}(121); WT_{5a}(120)$
abase
 $WP_{0ab}(121); WP_{0ac}(122);$
 $WP_{0ad}(122)$
abase os.
 $WS_{ab}(122)$
abate
 $KA_{1bb}(92)$
abbreviate
 $IN_{-1}(143)$
abbreviation, make an
 $IN_{-1}(143)$
abduce
 $DE_{6d}(150)$
abuse
 $KA_{0g}(89); KA_{0i}(90);$
 $KA_{0h}(90); WP_{0ab}(121)$
abolish
 $NO_{3bb}(112)$
about to
 $DE_{8b}(151)$
abrogate
 $NO_{3bb}(112)$

abruptly, ask
 $EM_{2l}(73)$
abscond
 $NO_{0db}(109)$
absende, give leave of
 $NO_{0dd}(110); NO_{0b}(108);$
 $NO_{3d}(112)$
absolve
 $NO_{4bd}(112); NO_{7c}(116)$
absolve from
 $NO_{9bb}(117)$
absorb
 $DE_1(149)$
abstain from
 $KA_{-1d}(88); KA_{3b}(98)$
abstract
 $DE_{6c}(105); TO_{2f}(156)$
abstract, prepare an
 $ET_{0da}(136)$
abstracts, write
 $TE_{-1b}(136)$
absurd, be
 $IR_{1c}(130)$
abuse
 $KA_{0h}(90); KA_{0i}(90);$
 $KA_{0g}(89); NO_2.(112);$
 $WP_{0ab}(121); WT_{4a}(119)$
accede to
 $EN_{6d}(79); NO_{0f}(110)$

accent
 $TO_{5ab}(158)$
accentuate
 $TO_{5ab}(158)$
accept
 $DI_3(124); DI_{5a}(125);$
 $EN_{9a}(82); EN_9(82);$
 $EN_{9i}(84); EN_{9k}(84);$
 $IN_{8a}(146); EN_{9c}(83);$
 $KA_{4bda}(102);$
 $KA_{4cda}(105);$
 $NO_{0b}(108); WT_{4fa}(120)$
accept, come to
 $KA_{4cda}(105)$
accept comments
 $DI/TU(134)$
accept in part
 $KA_{4cbc}(104)$
accept invitation
 $DI_{5a}(125)$
accept, not
 $WG_{1a}(123)$
accommodate os. to
 $EN_{9'c}(85); KA_{4bda}(102);$
 $KA_{4cda}(105)$
accomplish
 $KA_{4ac}(99)$
accost
 $DI_5(125); EN_{7ac}(79);$

accost (cont.)
  $KA_{2aa}(96)$
account for
  $NO_{6b}(114)$
account, call so. to
  $NO_{6da}(114)$
account, charge
  up to so.'s
  $KA_{4cdb}(105)$;
  $KA_{1ccc}(95)$
account, give an
  $TU_4(132); DT_2(128)$;
  $IN_{6aa}(144)$
account of, give an
  $NO_{6b}(114); ET_{0a}(135)$
account of sth., give an
  $TP_{2aa}(164)$
accounts with settle
  $KA_{4bdb}(102)$
account, take into
  $IN_{5aa}(144); TO_{2bb}(155)$;
  $WG_{1b}(124); DE_2(149)$
accumulate
  $DE_{6a}(150)$
accuse (of)
  $NO_4(113); WT_1(118)$
accuse
  $NO_{6a}(114)$
accuse os.
  $WS_{ab}(122)$
achieve a consensus
  $NO_{7a}(115)$
achieve one's aim
  $KA_{4aa}(99)$
acknowledge
  $DI_3(124); IN_{8a}(146)$;
  $IN_{9b}(146); KA_{4cda}(105)$;
  $NO_{6b}(114); WT_{4fa}(120)$
acknowledge in writing
  $EN_{6d}(79)$

acknowledge receipt of
  $IN_{9b}(146)$
acknowledge (sins,
  crime, truth)
  $IN_{6c}(145)$
acquaintance, scrape
  $KA_{2aa}(96)$
acquainted with, make
  $TP_{2aa}(164); ET_{0a}(135)$
acquire
  $ET_{1b}(137)$
acquisition, discuss an
  $DT_{1ba}(127)$
acquit
  $IN_{9b}(146); NO_{3bd}(112)$;
  $NO_{7c}(116); NO_{9bb}(117)$
acquittal, beg for
  $NO_{9ab}(117)$
acrid, make
  $KA_{-1c}(87)$
act
  $EN_{9'b}(85)$
act accordingly
  $EN_{9g}(83)$
act (a play)
  $TE_{0aa}(140)$
act as a go-between
  $KA_{4cac}(103)$
act as chairmann
  $EN_{6c}(78); NO_{-3}(107)$
act as guardian to
  $NO_{-3}(107)$
act favorably on
  $EN_{9b\S}(82)$
act for
  $KA_{2cb}(98)$
action against, bring an
  $NO_4.(113)$
act subversively
  $KA_{0c}(89)$

actual, make
  $TV_{7c}(161)$
adapt (from other
  languages)
  $TE_{-1b}(140); TE_{0ad}(141)$
add
  $TO_{2d}(156)$
add (a remark)
  $TU_{8a}(133)$
address
  $DI_1(124); DI_5(125)$;
  $KA_{2aa}(96)$
address angrily
  $EM_{2l}(73)$
address harshly
  $WP_{0ad}(122)$
address imperiously
  $EM_{2l}(73)$
address os. to so.
  $EN_{7ac}(79)$
address sth.
  $VV_{ba}(153)$
address, draft a memorial
  $ET/TE_{ad}(138)$
address, give a memorial
  $TV_{7j}(162)$
address, speak a memorial
  $WT_{5d}(121)$
add to
  $TV_{7a}(160); TV_{7h}(162)$
adduce an example
  $AV_4(106)$
adduce (proof)
  $NO_{60}(113)$
adduce reasons
  $AV_1(105); A_{1cca}(95)$;
  $TV_{6b}(159)$
adhere to
  $KA_{1cca}(95); NO_{2a}(111)$

(still) adhere to a viewpoint
$TV_{7a}(160)$
adjoin
$VV_a(153)$
adjourn
$DI_{10}(126); KA_{1bba}(91); TU_{9a}(133); TV_{8b}(162)$
adjust
$KA_{4cad}(103); TV_{7c}(161)$
admire
$EM_{2cb*}(72)$
admit
$DI_3(124); IN_{6c}(145); IN_{8a}(146); KA_{1bbb}(92); KA_{4cba}(104); KA_{4cda}(105); NO_{0da}(109); NO_{6b}(114); NO_7·(115); WT_{4fa}(120)$
admitting guilt
$NO_{6a}·(114); NO_{8a}··(116)$
admit sth. to so.
$WT_3·(119)$
admit (to)
$KA_{4bc}(102)$
admit to
$NO_{06}(108)$
admonish
$EN_{4a}(77); EN_{4c}(77); EN_{6a}(78); NO_{8a}(116); WT_{4a}(119)$
adopt
$NO_{0da}(109)$
adore
$EN_{7aa}(79); WS_{bba}(122); WT_{5d}(121); TP_{2bba}(165)$
adore a p.
$EM_{2j}(73)$
adorn
$TP_{2ae}(164)$

adulate
$KA_{2aa}(96)$
adulterate
$TP_{2be}(166)$
advance
$NO_{0dc}(109)$
advance an opinion
$ET_{0a}(135)$
advance, discuss in
$WT_2(118)$
advance, order in
$EN_{3a}(76)$
advance, say in
$TV_4(159)$
adversely, criticize
$AV_5(106); DT_2(128)$
advertise
$IN_{6aa}(144); IN_{6ab}(145); IN_{6b}(145)$
advertisement, insert an
$ET_{0a}(135); IN_{6b}(145)$
advertize
$NO_{0a§}(108)$
advertize (inform that it is for sale)
$ET_{0b}(135)$
advertize (political matters)
$ET_{0b}(135)$
advice, ask
$EN_{5cb}(78)$
advice for, ask
$EN_{2b}(75)$
advice, give
$WT_1(118); KA_{-1b}(87)$
advise
$EN_{2c}(76); EN_{6a}(78); KA_{4cac}(103); WT_2(118)$
advise so. against sth.
$EN_{2c}(76); WT_1(118)$

advise sth. (for the selection etc.)
$WT_1(118)$
advocate
$AV_1(105); NO_{6e}(115); WG_{0b}(123); WT_1(118)$
advocate, be the devil's
$AV_3(106); TV_{6b}(159)$
affirm
$ET_{0a}(134); EN_{9i}(84); KA_{0j}(90); TV*_{7b}(161)$
affirmative, answer in the
$EN_{9i}(84); KA_{4cda}(105)$
affirm by oath
$IN_{9b}(146)$
affix a seal
VV_{bc}
affix a ticket to
$VV_{ba}(154)$
affix (at the bulletin board)
$IN_{6b}·(145)$
afflict
$EN_{7d}·(81)$
afflict so.
$EN_{7ae}(80)$
afraid, be
$EM_{2cb}(72)$
affidavit, make an
$IN_{6c}(145)$
affront
$KA_{0g}(89); KA_{0h}(90); KA_{0i}(90)$
afraid, I am
$EM_{2cb*}(72)$
afraid, make so.
$KA_{1ab}(91)$
afresh, learn
$ET_{1d}(137)$
afterthought, make an
$TV_{7h}(162)$

171

again, do
 $TV_{7d}(161)$
age, declare so. of
 $NO_{0da}(109)$
agitate
 $KA_{0c}(89)$
agitate violently against
 $KA_{-1c}(87)$
agree
 $EN_{9i}(84); KA_{-3b}(85);$
 $KA_{2cb}(98); KA_{4caa}(102);$
 $KA_{4cba}(104);$
 $KA_{4cca}(105)$
agreement, bring to an
 $KA_{4cac}(103)$
agreement, come to an
 $KA_{-3b}(85); KA_{4cbd}(104);$
 $NO_{0e\S}(110)$
agreement, declare null & void an
 $NO_{3bb}(112)$
agreement, make an
 $KA_{4cab}(103); NO_{0e}(110);$
 $KA_{2b}(97)$
agreement, reach
 $KA_{4cac}(103)$
agree to
 $EN_{6d}(79); EN_{9k}(84);$
 $KA_{1bbb}(92);$
 $KA_{4cbb}(104);$
 $NO_{0b}(108); NO_{0f}(110);$
 $WT_{4fa}(120)$
agree to, not
 $EN_{9k}(84)$
agree to so.'s views
 $AV_6(107)$
agree upon
 $KA_{4cbd}(104)$
agree upon a thing with so.
 $TV_9(163)$

agree with
 $KA_{4cda}(105)$
ahead and start speaking, rush
 $TU_3(131)$
aid
 $ET_{0dg}(137); KA_{2cab}(97)$
aim at
 $EN_{0ab}(74)$
aim at + noun
 $DE_{8b}(151)$
aim at + verb
 $DE_{8b}(151)$
aid, obtain
 $KA_{2caa}(97)$
aid, withdraw one's
 $KA_{2d}(98)$
aim, achieve one's
 $KA_{4aa}(99)$
air
 $TV_5(159)$
airs, give os.
 $TP_{1c}(163); KA_{4a'}(101)$
airs, put on
 $WS_{bc}(123)$
alarm
 $EN_{4b}(77)$
alert so.
 $EN_{1ab}(74)$
allay
 $EN_{7ca}(80)$
allegiance, swear
 $WT_{5d}(121)$
allegorize
 $TP_{2ac}(164); TP_{2bc}(166)$
alleviate
 $NO_{7'}(115)$
alliance, enter into an
 $NO_{0e\S}(110); KA_{2b}(97)$

alliance, from an
 $KA_{4cbd}(104)$
alliance, make an
 $NO_{0e}(110)$
allot to
 $VV_a(152)$
allow
 $EN_{9b\S}(82); KA_{1bbb}(92);$
 $NO_{0b}(108); NO_{7'}(115)$
allow so. to get a word in edgewise, not
 $TU_{2'}(131)$
allow so. to speak
 $DI/TU(134); TU_2(131)$
allow sth. to so.
 $WT_{3'}(119)$
allow to be noticed
 $TP_{2bc}(166)$
allude
 $TO_{2bc}(156)$
allude to
 $EN_{1ac}(74); EN_{6a}(78)$
allure
 $EN_{7af}(80)$
ally
 $KA_{2b}(97)$
ally os. with
 $KA_{4cbd}(104)$
alphabetize
 $VV_a(152)$
alter
 $TO_{2e}(156)$
alter one's opinion partly
 $KA_{-1d}(88)$
alter the succession
 $TO_{3b}(157)$
alter the topic
 $TV_{7'}(162)$

alternate
 TU_3...(132)
amalgamate
 $DE_{6f}(151); TO_4(157)$
amass
 $DE_{6a}(150)$
amaze
 $EN_{7b}(80)$
amend
 ET/TE_a.(139);
 $NO_{3bc}(112); TO_{2e}(156);$
 $TV_{7c}(161)$
amends for, make
 NO_{9b}.(117); NO_{8a}...(116);
 $KA_{4cad}(103)$
(American) tell on
 $VE_{1c}(148)$
amiss, take
 $WT_{5a}(120)$
amnesty
 $NO_{9bb}(117)$
amplify (a description)
 $TV_{6a}(159)$
amuse
 $DI_{7b}(126)$
analogize
 $TP_{2ac}(164); TP_{2bc}(166)$
analyze
 $DE_{6c}(150)$
anew, learn
 $ET_{1d}(137)$
anger, give vent to
 $EM_{2aa}(71)$
anglicize
 $TE_{0ae}(141); TE_{0ad}(141)$
angrily, address
 $EM_{2e}(72)$
angry, be
 $EM_{2ab}(71); EM_{2cb}(72);$
 $EM_{2cb}*(72)$

angry, get
 $EM_{2ca}(71); EM_{2ca}*(72)$
angry, grow
 $EM_{2aa}(71)$
animate
 $KA_{2cab}(97)$
annex
 $EN_{3db}(77); KA_{-2b}(86)$
announce
 $ET_{0a}(134); ET_{0b}(135);$
 $IN_{6ab}(145); IN_{6b}(145)$
announce a theme
 $TV_2(159)$
announced, have so.
 $TU_1(131)$
announce removal
 $IN_{6b}(145)$
announce os.
 $TU_1(131)$
announce one's resignation
 $KA_{4bac}(101)$
announce one's wish to
 speak
 $TU_1(131)$
announce withdrawal
 $IN_{6b}(145); NO_{0db}(109)$
annoy
 $DI_{8a}(126); EN_{8d}(82);$
 $WP_{0ab}(121)$
annul
 DI_3...(125); $EN_{6e}(79);$
 $IN_{9a}(146); NO_{3bb}(112);$
 $NO_{9ba}(117)$
anonymously, write
 $IN_{6ac}(145)$
answer
 $KA_{1bca}(92)$
answer for
 $KA_{2cb}(98); NO_{6b}(114)$

answer, get an
 $IN_{2b}(143)$
answer, give a ready
 $KA_{1bcc}(93)$
answer in the affirmative
 $EN_{9i}(84); KA_{4cda}(105)$
answer in the negative
 $EN_{9bg}(83)$
answer, refuse to
 $EN_{9i}(84)$
antechambers, wait in the
 $KA_{2aa}(96)$
antedate
 $NO_{0g}(111); VV_{bd}(154)$
anticipate
 $DE_{8a}(151); EN_{0bb}(74);$
 $TV_{8a}(162)$
antithesis, put an
 $AV_1(105)$
anxiety, cause
 $KA_{1ab}(91)$
apologize
 $KA_{1bba}(91); NO_{6b}(114);$
 NO_{8a}...(116)
apologize for
 $EN_{2b}(75)$
appeal
 $EN_{2b}(75)$
appeal for mercy
 $NO_{9ab}(117)$
appeal to
 $EM_{2gb}(72); IN_{10}(147);$
 $TV_5(159)$
appeal to so.
 $NO_{6o}(113)$
appeal to a superior court
 $NO_{9aa}(117)$
appeal, enter an
 $NO_{9aa}(117)$

173

appear banal, make
  $KA_{1bbc}(92)$
appear in court, make so.
  $NO_5(113)$
appear recalcitrant
  $KA_{1ccc}(95)$
appease
  $EN_{7ca}(80); KA_{-1b}(87);$
  $KA_{1cb}(95); KA_{4cac}(103);$
  $NO_{7a}(115)$
append
  $TV_{7a}(106); TV_{7h}(162)$
applaud
  $EM_{2h}(72); WT_{4e}(120);$
  $WT_{5b}(120)$
application, file an
  $EN_{2b\S}(75); NO_{-2\S}(108)$
apply for
  $EN_{2b\S}(75); NO_{-2\S}(108)$
apply os. (to)
  $TV_5(159)$
apply to
  $EN_{2b}(75)$
apply to so. (for particulars)
  $DI_1(124)$
appoint
  $EN_{3b}(76); NO_{-4}(107)$
appoint a time
  $DI_{2'b}(124)$
appointment, make an
  $EN_{3ab}(76); NO_{0e}(110);$
  $DI_4(125)$
appoint to
  $VV_a(153)$
appoint to an office
  $NO_{0da}(109)$
appraise
  $IN_{3bb}(143); VV_g(154);$
  $WT_0(118)$

appreciate
  $DI_3(124); IN_{8a}(146);$
  $KA_{4cda}(105); WT_0(118)$
appreciate so.
  $WT_{5d}(121)$
apprehend
  $ET^*_{-1a}(134); NO_5.(113)$
approach
  $EN_{7ac}(79); KA_{-2b}(86);$
  $TV_5(159)$
approach so.
  $DI_1(124)$
approach a task
  $TV_1(158)$
approach with entreaties
  $EN_{2b}(75)$
approve
  $EN_{9b\S}(83); WT_0(118)$
approve of
  $KA_{4cbb}(104); KA_{4cda}(105)$
approve to
  $NO_{0b}(108)$
arbitrate
  $KA_{4cac}(103); NO_{7a}(115)$
arbitration, make an
  $NO_{7a}(115)$
argue
  $AV_1(105); KA_{-3cc}(86);$
  $KA_{1db}(96)$
argue about
  $DT_{1bb}(128)$
argue (for, against, about)
  $NO_{60}(113)$
argue successfully/perfectly/soundly
  $TP_{2ab}(164)$
argue the point
  $NO_{60}(113)$
argue with
  $DI_{7a}(125)$

argue with so.
  $KA_{-3c}(85); KA_{-3cb}(86)$
argument, clinch an
  $NO_{60}(113)$
argument, pursue an
  $KA_{1ccb}(95)$
argument, refer to an
  $AV_3(106)$
argument, point to an
  $AV_3(106)$
argument, produce an
  $AV_3(106)$
argument, substantiate an
  $AV_3(106)$
argument, support an
  $AV_3(106)$
argument, sustain an
  $AV_3(106)$
arguments, bombard with
  $AV_1(105); KA_{1ccb}(95)$
arguments, bring forward
  $NO_{60}(113); AV_1(105)$
arguments, corroborate
  $KA_{1bcd}(94)$
arguments, torpedo so. with
  $AV_1(105)$
argument to another, lead from an
  $DI/TU(134); TV_{7h}(162)$
argument, verify an
  $KA_{1bcd}(94)$
argument, weaken an
  $NO_{60}(113)$
argument with, get into an
  $KA_{0g}(89)$
arouse
  $EN_{7cc}(81)$
arouse disgust
  $EN_{7d}(81)$
arrange
  $DE_{6c}(150); DE_{6f}(151);$

arrange (cont.)
  $DI_{2'b}(124); DI_4(125);$
  $IN_{3aa}(143); KA_{-1b}(87);$
  $KA_{2aa}(96); KA_{4cac}(103);$
  $KA_{4cbb}(104);$
  $KA_{4cbd}(104); TO_{3a}(157);$
  $VV_a(152)$
arrangement, bring about an
  $DI_{2'b}(124)$
arrangement, come to an
  $NO_{0e\S}(110)$
arrangement, make an
  $NO_{7a}(115)$
arrangements, make
  $Ka_{4cbd}(104)$
arrangements, enter into an
  $KA_{4cbd}(104)$
arrange sth. with so.
  $KA_{2b}(97)$
arrest
  $KA_{-2a}(86); NO_{5'}(113)$
arrival to the police,
  repor one's
  $IN_{6b}(145)$
arrive at
  $IN_{2a'}(142)$
arrogate
  $WS_{bc}(123)$
articulate
  $DE_{6c}(150); TO_2(155);$
  $TO_{3a}(157)$
ascend to
  $DI_3(124)$
ascertain
  $IN_{1aa}(142); KA_{1ba}(91);$
  $KA_{2b}(97); VV_c(154)$
ascertain by inquiry
  $EN_{5cd}(78)$
ascertain readiness
  $DI_2(124)$

ascribe
  $WT_0(118)$
aside, set
  $DE_{6b}(150)$
ask
  $EN_{5a}(77); EN_{5b}(77);$
  $EN_{5cc}(78); KA_{-2a}(86)$
ask abruptly
  $EM_{2l}(73)$
ask advice
  $EN_{5cb}(78)$
ask a question
  $EN_{5cc}(78); TU_2(131)$
ask around
  $EN_{5cb}(78)$
ask back
  $KA_{-2a}(86)$
ask for information
  $EN_{5cb}(78); IN_{1ab}(142)$
ask for participation
  $DI_1(124)$
ask for participation in
  $DI_1(124)$
ask für particulars
  $IN_{1ab}(142)$
ask in
  $DI_{2'a}(142); EN_{2b}(75)$
ask leave to speak
  (parliament)
  $TU_1(131)$
ask out
  $EN_{2b}(75)$
ask so. sth.
  $TU_2(131)$
aspire to
  $DE_{8a}(151); EN_{0ab}(74);$
  $EN_{2b}(75)$
assail
  $KA_{0h}(90); KA_{0i}(90);$
  $IN_{8b}(146)$

assay
  $VV_c(154)$
assemble
  $DE_{6a}(150)$
assent
  $AV_6(107)$
assent to
  $EN_{6d}(79); EN_{9i}(84);$
  $IN_{8a}(146); KA_{4cbb}(104);$
  $NO_{0f}(110); WT_{4fa}(120)$
assert
  $ET_{0a}(134); IN_{6aa}(144);$
  $KA_{-2a}(86); KA_{0j}(90)$
assess
  $IN_{3bb}(143); WT_0(118);$
  $VV_g(154)$
asseverate
  $IN_{9b}(146)$
assevere
  $IN_{9b}(146)$
assignment, give an
  $EN_{3a}(76)$
assign to
  $EN_{3da}(77)$
assimilate
  $ET_{1b}(137); DE_1(149)$
assist
  $KA_{2cab}(97)$
associate to
  $IN_{5aa}(144)$
associate sth. with sth.
  $IN_{5aa}(144)$
associate with
  $VV_a(153)$
assuage
  $EN_{7ca}(80)$
assume
  $DE_5(149)$
assumption, make the
  $DE_5(149)$

assure
 $KA_{2cb}(98); VV_c(154)$
assure of
 $NO_1(111)$
assure (the truth)
 $IN_{9b}(146)$
astonish
 $EN_{7b}(80)$
astound
 $EN_{7b}(80)$
astray, go
 $NO_2(112); TV_{6'b}(160)$
astray, lead
 $EN_{7af}(80)$
atmosphere, poison the
 $KA_{0e}(89)$
atone for
 $KA_{4cad}(103); NO_{8a}"(116)$
attach
 $TV_{7a}(160)$
attach to
 $VV_a(153); TO_4(157)$
attack
 $KA_{0h}(90); KA_{0i}(90);$
 $KA_{1aa}(91); IN_{8b}(146)$
attack, wish to
 $KA_{-3c}(85); KA_{-3ca}(86)$
attack without thinking
 $KA_{0a}(88)$
attempt to, make an
 $DE_{8b}(151)$
attend to
 $EN_{0bb}(74)$
attention, attract
 $TO_{5ac}(158)$
attention, pay
 $EN_{9g}(83)$
attention, pay no
 $EN_{9c}(83)$

attention to a danger, draw
 $EN_{4b}(77)$
attention to, call
 $TO_{5a}(158); TO_{5ac}(158)$
attention to, call special
 $TO_{5a}(158)$
attention to, not pay
 $NO_2"(112)$
attention to, pay
 $EN_{9c}(83); KA_{4cdb}(105);$
 $EN_{9k}(84); WG_{1b}(124);$
 $NO_{2a}(111); DE_2(149)$
attention to sth.,
 call so.'s
 $EN_{1ac}(75)$
attention to sth., draw so.'s
 $EN_{1ac}(75)$
attention, turn away
 $EN_{1b}(75)$
attenuate
 $TO_{5c}(158); TP_{2bbc}(175)$
attest
 $ET_{0a}(135); IN_{9b}(146);$
 $NO_{6da}(114); WT_{4f§}(120)$
attest upon oath
 $NO_{6da}(114)$
attract
 $EN_{7af}(80)$
attract attention
 $TO_{5ac}(158)$
attribute
 $WT_0(118)$
attribute sth. to so.
 $WP_{0ac}(122); DE_5(150)$
audience to sleep put the
 $TP_{2b}(164)$
authenticate
 (by documents)
 $WT_{4f§}(120); NO_{6da}(114);$
 $IN_{9b}(146)$

author
 $ET/TE_{aa}(138);$
 $ET/TE_{ac}(138)$
authorities, cite
 $AV_3(106)$
authorities, quote
 $AV_3(106)$
authorities, tip off the
 $VE_{1b,c,d}(148)$
authorize
 $NO_{-4b}(107); NO_{0b}(108);$
 $NO_{0da}(109); EN_{3b}(76)$
aver
 $IN_{9b}(146)$
avoid
 $KA_{1bba}(91); TP_{2bf}(167);$
 $TO_{2c}(156)$
avoid so.
 $WP_{0aa}(121)$
avoid risks, try to
 $KA_{1ba}(91)$
avoid (the issue)
 $KA_{4aa}(99)$
await one's turn
 $TU_1(131)$
await (with impatience)
 $EN_{0bb}(74)$
awake so.
 $EN_{1aa}(74)$
award
 $EN_{6d}(79); NO_{0f}(110)$
award so.
 $NO_{0b}"(109)$
award a prize to
 $WT_{4e}(120)$
award, make an
 $NO_{7a}(115)$
aware of, be
 $IN_{5aa}(144)$

aware of one another's
view, be clearly
  $KA_{-3b}(85)$
away, call
  $NO_{0dc}(109)$
away, chatter
  DI_{10}"(127)

B
babble
  $DT_{1bc}(128); ET/TE_b(138);$
  $TP_{1b}(163); TP_{1e}(163);$
  $TP_{2bj}(167)$
babble (nonsense)
  $TP_{1c}(163)$
backbite
  $KA_{0g}(89)$
backdate
  $VV_{bd}(154)$
backed up by, be
  $KA_{2caa}(97)$
back, get one's own
  $KA_{4bdb}(102)$
background, push into the
  $KA_{3c}(99)$
backing, obtain
  $KA_{2aa}(97)$
back on his feet, put so.
  $KA_{2cab}(97)$
back out
  $KA_{4bac}(101)$
backwards, work
  $DE_{6d}(150)$
bad, deem
  $WT_0(118)$
bad, make sth.
  $TE_{0ab}(141)$
bad order, put in
  $IR_{2cb}(131)$

bad temper, put in a
  $EN_{8d}(82)$
bad text, turn sth. into a
  $TE_{0ab}(141)$
baffle
  $EN_{8ab}(82); KA_{-1c}(87); KA_{0c}(89)$
bagatelle out of sth., make a
  $TP_{2bbb}(165)$
bag, let the cat out of the
  $VE_{1g}(149)$
bail
  $NO_1(111)$
bail, give
  $EN_{6d}(79); NO_{0f}(110)$
bait
  $EN_{7af}(80)$
balance
  $DE_{8c}(152)$
balance out
  $KA_{4cad}(103)$
balk
  $EN_{8ab}(92)$
ballot, put sth. on the
  WT_2"(118)
ban
  $NO_{8a}(116)$
banalize
  $TP_{2bbb}(165)$
banal, make (appear)
  $KA_{1bbc}(92)$
banal make
  $WG_{0a}(123)$
banish
  $NO_{0dd}(110); NO_{8a}(116)$

baptize
  $VV_{ba}(153)$
bar
  $KA_{4ac}(103)$
bargain
  $KA_{1db}(96)$
bargain, make a
  $KA_{1db}(96)$
barricade so. behind
  $KA_{1bca}(92)$
base
  $AV_3(106)$
base on
  $KA_{1bcd}(94)$
base sth. on
  $IN_{10}(147)$
bawdy, talk
  $DT_{1e}(128)$
be about to
  $DE_{8b}(151)$
be absurd
  $IR_{1c}(130)$
beads, tell one's
  $TP_{1a}(163)$
be afraid
  $EM_{2cb}(72); EM_{2cb*}(72)$
be angry
  $EM_{2ab}(71); EM_{2cb}(72); EM_{2cb*}(72)$
beans, spill the
  $VE_{1b}(148)$
bear
  $NO_{6c}(114)$
bear a grudge
  $KA_{0e}(89); KA_{4bdb}(102)$
bear a grudge against
  $NO_{10}(117); WT_{5a}(120)$
bear ill-will to so.
  $KA_{-3c}(85)$

bear ill-will towards
$KA_{1caa}(94)$
bear in mind
$NO_{2a}(111); DE_2(149)$
bear it, grin and
EM_{2b}‘(71)
bear witness to
$NO_{6da}(114)$
be a snob
$WS_{bc}(123)$
beastly way, speak in a
$DE_{1e}(128)$
be astonished
$DE_3(149)$
beatify
$NO_{0da}(109); WT_{5d}(121)$
be at loggerheads
$KA_{-1c}(87)$
be at one
$KA_{-3b}(85)$
be at one with
$KA_{4cca}(105)$
be at the end of
  one's tether
$KA_{4baa}(101)$
be at war with
  one another
$KA_{-3c}(85); KA_{-3ca}(86)$
be aware of
$IN_{5aa}(144)$
be backed up by
$KA_{2caa}(97)$
be behind
$KA_{1ccb}(95)$
be benevolent to so.
$KA_{-3b}(85)$
be blunt
NO_2‘(112)
be bookish
$TP_{2b}(164)$

be boring
$TP_{2b}(164)$
be brilliant
$TP_{2ab}(164)$
be chairman
DI/TU(134)
be checkmated
$KA_{4baa}(101)$
be clearly aware of one
  another's view
$KA_{-3b}(85)$
become reconciled
$KA_{4caa}(102)$
become silent
TU_6'$_a(133)$
be compliant
$KA_{1cb}(95)$
be contentious
$KA_{1ccc}(95)$
be contradictory
$KA_{1bca}(92)$
be counted out
  (be referee)
$KA_{4bad}(102)$
be cross
$KA_{0e}(89)$
be cryptic
$TP_{2bi}(167)$
be defeated
$KA_{4baa}(101)$
be delighted
KA_{4a}‘(101)
be delirious
$ET/TE_b(138)$
be disappointed
EN_9‘$_c(85); EM_{2cb}(72); EM_{2cb}*(72)$
be distinguished
$TP_{2ab}(164)$

be done for
$KA_{4baa}(101)$
be down
$KA_{0e}(89)$
be enthuisiastic
$TP_{2bba}(165)$
be enthuisiastic about
$EM_{2i}(73)$
be face to face
$KA_{1bca}(92)$
be farfetched
$TP_{2b}(164); TP_{2bh}(167)$
be fed up with
$KA_{3a}(98)$
be fit for so.
NO_0‘(111)
be foolish
$IR_{1c}(130)$
be forbearing with so.
NO_7‘(115); WT_3‘(119)
beforehand, say
$TV_4(159)$
be foreign
$KA_{-3a}(85)$
be fragmentary
$TP_{2bi}(167)$
be fragmented
$TP_{2bi}(167)$
be frank
$NO_{6b}(114)$
be furious
$KA_{0a}(88)$
beg
$EN_{2b}(75); EM_{2gb}(72)$
beg (for)
$EN_{2b}(75)$
be for acquittal
$NO_{9ab}(117)$
be forgiveness
$EN_{2b}(75); NO_{9b}$‘(117)

beg for leniency
  $NO_{9ab}(117)$
begging, obtain by
  $EN_{8aa}(81)$
beg pardon
  $NO_{6b}(114)$
beg for participation
  $DI_1(124)$
beg permission to speak
  $TU_1(131)$
begin
  $DI_6(125); TV_5(159)$
begin to speak
  $TU_3(131)$
be glad
  $KA_{4a}\cdot(101); EM_{2cb}*(72)$
be grateful
  $EM_{2cb}(72)$
be guilty of a misdemeanor
  $NO_2(112)$
behave in a familiar manner
  $EN_{7ad}(80); WS_{bbb}(123)$
be hostile to
  $KA_{-3c}(86)$
be illustrative of
  $TP_{2ac}(164)$
be implacable
  $KA_{-3c}(86)$
be impolite
  $NO_2\cdot(112)$
be impudent
  $KA_{0g}(89)$
be inferior to
  $KA_{-1d}(88)$
being at one's turn
  $TU_3\text{'''}(132)$
behind, be
  $KA_{1ccb}(95)$

be in harmony
  $KA_{-3b}(85)$
be in love
  $EM_{2cb}(72)$
be in tune
  $KA_{2b}(97)$
be irreconcilable
  $KA_{-3c}(86)$
be joyful
  $KA_{4a}\cdot(101)$
be jubilant over
  $EM_{2h}(72); WT_{5b}(120)$
(be) kindly disposed towards
  $KA_{-3b}(85)$
be surprised
  $DE_3(149)$
belabor a point
  $TP_{2b}(164)$
beliefs, impose
  $ET_{0da}(136)$
believe
  $DE_5(149)$
belittle
  $TP_{2bbb}(165)$
be lost in thoughts
  $DE_4(149)$
be loud
  $WS_{bc}(123)$
be mindful of
  $IN_{5aa}(144)$
be nervous
  $EM_{2ab}(71)$
benevolent to, be
  $KA_{-3b}(85)$
be no longer interested in
  $KA_{3c}(99)$
be not at one
  $KA_{-3c}(86)$

be not of one mind
  $KA_{-3c}(86)$
be obliged
  $NO_0\cdot(111)$
be obstinate
  $TV_{7d}(161); NO_2\cdot(112); KA_{4bab}(101)$
be obstinate about
  $KA_{1ccc}(95)$
be obtrusive
  $EN_{7ae}(80)$
be of importance (to)
  $KA_{4cca}(105)$
be of importance to so.
  $KA_{-3b}(85)$
be of one mind
  $KA_{-3b}(85)$
be of one mind with
  $KA_{4cca}(105)$
be of opinion
  $WT_0(118)$
be of the opinion
  $DE_5(149); VV_g(154)$
be of the same opinion
  $AV_6(107); KA_{-3b}(85); KA_{4caa}(105)$
be of value to so.
  $KA_{-3a}(85)$
be open to
  $KA_{1cb}(95)$
be outstanding
  $TP_{2ab}(164)$
be over
  $DI_{10}(127)$
be overbearing
  $WS_{aa}(122)$
be overthrown
  $KA_{4baa}(101); KA_{4bac}(101)$
be overweening
  $WS_{bc}(123)$

be pissed off
  $EM_{2ca}*(72)$
be pleased
  $KA_{4a}\text{‘}(101)$
be polite
  $TO_{5c}(158)$
be purse-proud
  $WS_{bc}(123)$
be put on the self
  $KA_{4baa}(101)$
bequeath
  $EN_{3da}(77)$
be querulous
  $KA_{4bab}(101)$
be quick-witted
  $KA_{4baa}(101)$
be raving
  $TP_{2bj}(167)$
be recalcitrant
  $KA_{4bab}(101)$
be resentful of
  $NO_{10}(117); WT_{5a}(120)$
be resigned to
  $KA_{4bda}(102);$
  $KA_{4cda}(105)$
be sad
  $EM_{2ab}(71); EM_{2cb}(72);$
  $EM_{2cb}*(72)$
be scandalized by
  $WT_0(118)$
be second to
  $KA_{-1d}(88)$
beseech
  $EN_{2b}(75)$
be self-effacing
  $WS_{aa}(122); WS_{ab}(122)$
be set aside
  $KA_{4baa}(101)$
be shocked
  $EM_{2ab}(71)$

be silly
  $IR_{1c}(130)$
be sorry
  $EM_{2cb}*(72)$
be sorry for
  $EM_{2cb}(72)$
be still
  $TU_1\text{‘}(131)$
best of, make the
  $KA_{4cda}(105);$
  $KA_{4bda}(102)$
bestow
  $EN_{3da}(77)$
be strange
  $KA_{-3a}(85)$
be struck
  $DI_{8a}(126); TU_{6\text{‘}b}(133)$
be struck dumb
  $TU_{6\text{‘}b}(133)$
be stubborn
  $KA_{4bab}(101)$
be stuck
  $TU_{6\text{‘}b}(133)$

be suitable for so.
  $NO_0\text{‘}(111)$
be sulky
  $KA_{0e}(89)$
be suspicious of
  $DE_7(151); NO_3\text{‘}(113)$
be taken aback
  $KA_{0b}(88)$
be taken down a peg
  $KA_{4bac}(101)$
be the devil's advocate
  $AV_3(106); TV_{6b}(159)$
be thunderstruck
  $KA_{0b}(88)$
be tired of
  $KA_{3a}(98)$

be too spare with words
  $TP_{2bi}(167)$
be too subtle
  $TP_{2b}(164)$
betray
  $NO_4(113); NO_{6db}(115)$
betray a confidence
  $VE_1(148)$
betray (a secret)
  $VE_1(148)$
be triumphant
  $KA_{4a}\text{‘}(101)$
better, make worse instead of
  $ET/TE_a\text{‘}(139)$
be unacquainted with so.
  $KA_{-3a}(85)$
be uncomfortable
  $EM_{2cb}(72)$
be under an obligation to
  $NO_0\text{‘}(111)$
be united
  $KA_{-3b}(85); KA_{4cca}(105)$
be unknown
  $KA_{-3a}(85)$
be upset
  $KA_{4bac}(101)$
be well-disposed towards
  $KA_{4cca}(105)$
bewilder
  $EN_{7b}(80); KA_{1ab}(91)$
be witty at another's expense
  $DT_{1d}(128)$
be worried
  $EM_{2cb}(72)$
be yielding
  $KA_{1cb}(95)$
bias
  $IN_{6d}(145)$

bias, show
  WT_3"(119)
bibliography, make a
  VV_a(153)
bicker
  KA_{0d}(89); KA_{1aa}(91);
  KA_{1da}(85)
bid
  EN_{2b}(75); EN_{6b}(78)
big, talk
  WS_{bc}(123); TP_{1c}(163)
big words, overburden with
  TP_{2b}(164)
big words, overload with
  TP_{2b}(164)
bill, pass a
  EN_{9c}(83)
bill, receipt a
  VV_{bc}(154)
bills on, stick
  IN_{6b}'(145)
bills, post
  $NO_{0a\S}$(108); IN_{6b}'(145)
bind os. (to so.)
  EN_{6d}(79); NO_{0f}(110)
bind together
  TO_4(157)
bitch
  EM_{2k}(73)
blab
  VE_1(148); VE_{1g}(149)
blabber
  TP_{1e}(163)
blackmail
  EN_{8aa}(81); KA_{-2b}(86);
  KA_{4ab}(99)
blame
  WT_1(118); WT_{4a}(119)

blame os.
  NO_{6a}(114); WS_{ab}(122)
blame on so., put the
  NO_{6a}(114)
blame so.
  NO_{6a}(114)
blame so., do not
  WT_3'(119)
blandish
  KA_{-2b}(87)
blaspheme
  NO_2(112)
blather
  TP_{2bj}(167)
blend
  TP_{2bd}(166)
blessings and curses upon so., call down
  EM_{2gb}(72)
blindly, react
  KA_{0a}(88)
blindly, respond
  KA_{0a}(88)
block off
  KA_{1bcb}(93)
blow the lid off of
  VE_1(148)
blow the whistle on
  $VE_{1b,c,d}$(148)
blow up
  EM_{2b}(71); TP_{2bba}(165)
blunt, be
  NO_2'(112)
bluntly, treat
  KA_{0g}(89)
blurred manner, express os. in a
  TP_{2bd}(166)
blurt
  KA_{4ae}(100)

blush
  EM_{2aa}(71)
board, stick upon bulletin
  IN_{6b}'(145)
boast
  TP_{1b}(163); TP_{1c}(163);
  TP_{2bba}(165); WS_{bc}(123)
boast, draw the long
  TP_{1c}(163)
bogged, down get
  DI_{8a}(126)
boil over
  EM_{2b}(71)
bolderdash, talk
  TP_{2bj}(167)
bold, make
  KA_{0g}(89)
bombard (with arguments)
  AV_1(105); KA_{1ccb}(95)
bombastically, speak
  TP_{2b}(164)
booing, condemn by
  EM_{2h}(72)
book
  NO_{0g}(110); VV_a(152)
book (seats)
  EN_{3a}(76)
bookish, be
  TP_{2b}(164)
books, ponder over old
  TE_{-1b}(140)
boo so., off the stage
  EM_{2h}(72)
bore
  TP_{2b}(164)
bore after
  KA_{1ccb}(95)
boring, be
  TP_{2b}(164)

borrow from
  $TV_{7i}(162)$
bosh, talk
  $TP_{1c}(163); TP_{2bj}(167)$
botch
  $TP_{2be}(166)$
bother
  $EN_{8d}(82); KA_{0d}(89)$
bottom of, get to the
  $ET_{-1b}(134)$
bottom of sth., get to the
  $IN_{2a}‘(142)$
bowdlerize
  $IN_{6d}(145); TP_{2be}(166)$
boycott
  $KA_{-3ca}(86)$
bracket
  $TO_{3a}(157); TO_{5ad}(158)$
brackets, insert in
  $TO_{5ad}(158)$
brag
  $TP_{1c}(163); WS_{bc}(123)$
brain about, rack one's
  $DE_4(149)$
brainwash
  $EN_{8c}(82); ET_{0da}(136)$
brand
  $NO_{8a}(116); VV_{ba}(153)$
brand so.
  $NO_{10}(117); WT_{5a}(120)$
brave
  $KA_{4bab}(101)$
breach, step into the
  $KA_{2cab}(97); KA_{2cb}(98)$
break away
  $KA_{4bba}(102)$
break a word, not
  $VE_2‘(147)$
break down (a speech)
  $DI_{8a}(126); TU_{6‘b}(133)$

break in
  $TU_6(132); TV_{6‘a}(160)$
break the law
  $NO_2(112)$
break up (assembly)
  $DI_{8b}(126)$
break with so.
  $KA_{-1c}(87)$
breathe heavily
  $EM_{2b}‘(71)$
brew
  $DE_{8d}(152); DT_{1h}(128)$
  $VE_{-2}(147)$
brick wall, run one's
  head against a
  $TV_6‘‘‘(160)$
bridge over
  $DI_9(126); TV_{7h}(162)$
brief
  $EN_{3c}(76)$
brief remark, make a
  $TU_5‘(132)$
bright, make
  $TP_{2bba}(165)$
brilliant, be
  $TP_{2ab}(164)$
brilliant manner,
  present sth. in a
  $TP_{2ab}(164)$
brilliant, talk
  $DI_{7b}‘(126)$
bring about
  $EN_9‘_b(85)$
bring about an arrangement
  $DI_{2‘b}(124)$
bring a charge against
  $VE_{1b,c,d}(148)$
bring an action against
  $NO_4‘(113)$

bring so. into discredit
  $WP_{0ac}(122)$
bring counterarguments
  $KA_{1bcd}(94)$
bring discredit on so.
  $WP_{0ac}(122)$
bring forward
  $NO_{60}(113); TU_4(132);$
  $TV_{6b}(159)$
bring forward an argument
  $NO_{60}(113)$
bring forward arguments
  $AV_1(105)$
bring forward proof
  $AV_3(106)$
bring in
  $KA_{0g}(89); KA_{4cdb}(105);$
  $KA_{0g}(90)$
bring in confusion
  $TP_{2bd}(166)$
bring into play
  $TV_5(159)$
bring into prominence
  $TO_{5a}(158)$
bring into relief
  $TO_{5e}(158)$
bring low
  $WP_{0ab}(121)$
bring once more
  $TV_{7d}(161)$
bring out by questioning
  $EN_{5cd}(78)$
bring out a toast
  $EM_{2h}(72)$
bring so. to his knees
  $KA_{4aac}(100)$
bring to an agreement
  $KA_{4cac}(103)$
bring to an end
  $DI_{10}(126); TU_{9a}(133)$

bring to bear
  $KA_{-2a}(86)$
bring to bear upon
  $DE_{6g}(151)$
bring together
  $KA_{4cac}(103)$
bring to light
  $IN_{6b}\text{·}(145)$
bring to light again
  $TV_{7i}(162)$
bring to relief
  $TO_{5a}(158)$
bring up
  $TV_1(158); TV_5(159)$
  $WT_3\text{·}(119)$
bring up again
  $TV_{7d}(161); TV_{7i}(162)$
bring up an unpleasant
  subject
  $TO_{2g}(157)$
broadcasting, intercept for
  $VE_1\text{''}_a(147)$
broaden out
  $TV_{6a}(159)$
broken English, speak in
  $TP_{1b}(163)$
brood over
  $DE_{8d}(152)$
brook (upon)
  $DE_4(149)$
browbeat
  $EN_{6c}(78); NO_{-3}(107)$
browse
  $TE_{-1b}(140)$
brush aside
  $KA_{4ac}(103)$
brush off
  $KA_{2d}(98)$
brush-off, give the
  $KA_{4ac}(100); KA_{4ae}(100)$

brush over
  $TO_{2bc}(156)$
buck, pass the
  $KA_{1bba}(91)$
bug (the telephone,
  the wire)
  $VE_1\text{''}_a(147)$
build a foundation to
  $AV_3(106)$
bulldoze
  $KA_{4ae}(100)$
bulletin board, stick upon a
  $IN_{6b}\text{·}(145)$
bully
  $KA_{1aa}(91); KA_{1ab}(91);$
  $KA_{1ccc}(95)$
bully sth. out of so.
  $EN_{8aa}(81)$
bump into
  $KA_{0b}(88)$
bungle
  $TP_{2be}(166)$
burst out
  $EM_{2d}(72)$
burst out laughing
  $EM_{2b}(71)$
burst out with words
  $TU_3\text{·}(131)$
bury
  $KA_{4caa}(102)$
bury the hatchet
  $KA_{4caa}(102)$
bushel, hide one's
  light under a
  $WS_{aa}(122)$
business, send
  about one's
  $KA_{4ac}(100); KA_{4ae}(100)$
business, transact
  $NO_{0e§}(110)$

butt in
  $KA_{-1b}(87); TU_6(132)$
buttonhole
  $EN_{7ab}(79)$
bygones, let bygones be
  $KA_{4caa}(102)$
bypass
  $TO_{2c}(156)$

C

cable
  $ET_{0a}(135)$
cackle
  $DT_{1bc}(128)$
cajole
  $EN_{7aa}; KA_{-2b};$
  $KA_{2aa}; WS_{bba}$
call
  $ET_{0a}(135); NO_{0dc}(109);$
  $VV_{ba}(153)$
call so.
  $EN_{5a}(77)$
call so.'s attention to sth.
  $EN_{1ac}(75)$
call so. names
  $NO_2(112); WO_{0ab}(121)$
call so. to account
  $NO_{6a}(114)$
call attention to
  $TO_{5a}(158); TO_{5ac}(158)$
call away
  $NO_{0dd}(110)$
call down (blessings,
  curses) upon so.
  $EM_{2gb}(72)$
call in
  $KA_{-2a}(86)$
call into notice
  $TV_5(159)$

183

Lexicon Section II

call into question
  $DE_7(151)$
call on
  $DI/TU(134); TU_2(131)$
call on so.
  $EN_{2b}(75)$
call out
  $ET_{0a}(134)$
call special attention to
  $TO_{5a}(158)$
call so./ sth. as sth.
  $VV_f(154)$
call to
  $DI_5(125)$
call to so.'s. mind
  $EN_{1ad}(75)$
call together
  $DI_{2'b}(124)$
call to mind
  $IN_{5b}(144)$
call to so.
  $EN_{1ab}(74)$
call upon
  $EN_{5a}(77)$
call up (the reserves)
  $IN_{6b}\text{'}(145)$
calm
  $EN_{7ca}(80); KA_{-1b}(87);$
  $KA_{4cac}(103)$
calm down(intrans.)
  $EN_{9l}(89); KA_{4caa}(102)$
calumniate
  $NO_3\text{'}(113); WP_{0ac}(122)$
camouflage
  $KA_{1bba}(91)$
canary, sing like a
  $VE_{1b}(148)$
cancel
  $DI_3\text{''}(125); EN_{3a}(76);$
  $EN_{6e}(79); EN_{9h}\text{'}(84);$

cancel (cont.)
  $IN_{9a}(146); NO_{3bb}(112)$
cancel one's turn
  $TU_3\text{''}(132)$
canonize
  $NO_{0da}(109)$
canvass
  $EN_{2a}(75); KA_{2aa}(96)$
cap at, set one's
  $KA_{-2b}(87); KA_{2aa}(96)$
capitulate
  $KA_{4bac}(101)$
captivate
  $EN_{7ad}(80); KA_{2aa}(96);$
  $WS_{bbb}(123)$
card index of, make a
  $VV_a(153)$
card, send in one's
  $TU_1(131)$
cards, enter on
  $VV_a(153)$
cards, reading tarot
  $ET/TE_b(138)$
carefully, consider
  $DE_{8c}(152); VV_g(154)$
carefully, think over
  $DE_4(149)$
caricature
  $IR_{1b}(129); IR_{2a}(130)$
carp
  $KA_{0e}(89)$
carp about
  $EM_{2k}(73)$
carp at
  $WT_{4c}(119)$
carry a point
  $KA_{0c}(89)$
carry (a motion) with a majority
  $TV_9(163)$

carry forward
  $TU_4(132)$
carry on
  $TV_{7g}(162); TU_{8a}(133)$
carry on a lawsuit
  $NO_4\text{'}(113)$
carry one's point
  $KA_{-2a}(86); KA_{4aa}(99)$
carry out
  $EN_{9d}(83); EN_{9j}(84)$
carry over
  $EN_{3da}(77)$
carry through
  $KA_{4ac}(103)$
carry to excess
  $TP_{2bba}(165)$
carry too far
  $TP_{2bba}(165)$
case, hear
  $IN_{1ac}(142)$
cashier (an officer)
  $NO_{0dd}(110)$
cast a slur on
  $IR_{2ca}(130)$
cast off
  $KA_{2d}(98)$
cast suspicion on
  $NO_3\text{'}(113)$
casually, mention
  $TO_{2bc}(156)$
catalogue
  $VV_a(152)$
catch
  $KA_{1bcb}(93)$
catch (a word)
  $VE_1\text{''}_a(147)$
catch on
  $TV_{7a}(160); DE_1(149)$
catch on the hop
  $KA_{0f}(89); KA_{0h}(90);$

catch on the hop (cont.)
  $KA_{0i}(90)$
catch on to sth.
  $ET_{1b}(137)$
categorize
  $IN_{3ac}(143); VV_a(152)$
cat out of the bag,
let the
  $VE_{1g}(148)$
cause anxiety
  $KA_{1ab}(91)$
cause so. to understand
  $ET_{0dd}(137)$
caution
  $EN_{4b}(77); WT_{4a}(119)$
cease
  $DI_{10}(127); KA_{1bbb}(92);$
  $KA_{3a}(98); TU_{9a}(133)$
cede
  $NO_{0b}\text{'}(108)$
cede one's property
  $EN_{3da}(77)$
celebrate so.
  $WT_{4e}(120)$
cell, smuggle letters in
prisoner's
  $VE_0(147)$
censor
  $IN_{6d}(145)$
cencure
  $WT_{4c}(119)$
censure so.
  $NO_{8a}(116)$
certain, make
  $KA_{2b}(97)$
certificate, issue a
  $IN_{9b}(146); WT_{4f\S}(120)$
certify
  $IN_{9b}(146); NO_{6da}(114);$
  $WT_{4f\S}(120)$

chaff
  $IR_{1a}(129); IR_{1c}(130);$
  $IR_{2a}(130); IR_{2b}(130);$
  $IR_{2ca}(130)$
chain together
  $TO_4(157)$
chaimann, act as
  $EN_{6c}(78); NO_{-3}(107)$
chairman, be
  $DI/TU(134)$
challenge
  $EN_{5a}(77); IN_{8b}(146);$
  $KA_{0g}(89)$
challenge (military)
  $DI_5(125)$
chance to speak,
not to give a
  $TU_2\text{'}(131)$
change
  $TO_{2e}(156)$
change one's position
  $KA_{4bbb}(102)$
change one's view
  $ET_{1f}(137)$
change over to
  $KA_{4bbb}(102)$
change sides
  $KA_{4bbb}(102)$
change the law
  $NO_{3bc}(112)$
change the sequence
  $TO_{3b}(157)$
change the subject
  $DI_{10}\text{'}(127)$
change the topic
  $TV_7\text{'}(162)$
changing date
  $DI_4(125)$
characterize
  $VV_{ba}(153)$

characterize so. as
  $WP_{0ac}(122)$
charge against, bring a
  $VE_{1b,c,d}(148)$
charge sth. up to so.
  $KA_{1ccb}(95)$
charge, take in
  $NO_5\text{'}(113)$
charge to so.'s. account
  $KA_{4cdb}(105)$
charge up to so.'s.
account (unjustifiably)
  $KA_{1ccc}(95)$
charge with
  $EN_{3a}(76); NO_4(113);$
  $NO_{6a}(114); WT_1(118);$
  $WT_3\text{'}(119)$
charm
  $DT_{1c}(128); EN_{7ad}(80);$
  $WS_{bbb}(123)$
chart
  $VV_a(152)$
chase away
  $KA_{4ad}(100); EN_{8b}(82)$
chase off
  $KA_{4ad}(100)$
chat
  $TP_{2bj}(167)$
chat so. up
  $KA_{-2b}(87)$
chatter
  $DT_{1bc}(128); TP_{1e}(163);$
  $TP_{2bj}(167)$
chatter away
  $DI_{10}\text{''}(127); DT_{1bc}(128)$
chattering, pass time in
  $DT_{1bc}(128); DI_{10}\text{''}(127)$
cheat
  $KA_{0b}(88)$

check
  $KA_{-3b}(85)$;
  $ET/TE_a.(139)$;
  $KA_{1bcb}(93)$;
  $TE_{-1b}(140)$;
  $TP_{2bbc}(165)$
checklist, run down the
  $TV_{6a}(159)$
checkmate
  $KA_{4ac}(100)$
checkmated, be
  $KA_{4baa}(101)$
check one, impose a
  $KA_{1bca}(92)$
cheer so.
  $EM_{2j}(73)$
cheer so. up
  $EM_{7cb}(81)$
cheer loudly
  $WT_{5b}(120); EM_{2h}(72)$
cheer up
  $EN_{7cc}(81); KA_{2cab}(97)$
cheer up (intrans.)
  $EN_{91}(84)$
chew thoroughly
  $TV_{6a}(159)$
child, lead so. like a
  $NO_{-3}(107)$
chill suddenly
  $EM_{2aa}(71)$
chime in
  $TU_6(132)$
choose
  $DE_{6b}(150); DE_{8c}(152);$
  $DE_{8e}(152); IN_{3ba}(143)$
choose so.
  $NO_{0da}(109); WT_1(118)$
christen
  $NO_{0da}(109); VV_{ba}(153)$

chuck up
  $KA_{4bac}(101)$
chum up with
  $KA_{2aa}(46)$
chum up with so.
  $EN_{7ad}(80); WS_{bbb}(123)$
circulate
  $IN_{6aa}(144); TE_{-2a}(139)$
circumscribe
  $TO_{2a}(155); TP_{2ac}(164);$
  $TP_{2bc}(166); TV_3(159)$
circumvent
  $KA_{1bba}(91); KA_{4aa}(99)$
cite
  $TE_{0aa}(140); TV_{7i}(162)$
cite authorities
  $AV_3(106)$
citizenship, deprive of
  $NO_{8a}(116)$
claim
  $EN_{5b}(77); KA_{-2a}(86);$
  $KA_{0j}(90); KA_{1cca}(95);$
  $NO_{-2}(107); WS_{bc}(123)$
claim, file a
  $NO_4(113)$
claim, make a
  $NO_{-2}(107)$
claim one's rights
  $KA_{0j}(90)$
claim one's turn
  $TV_2.(131)$
claim sth. for os.
  $KA_{1bcd}(94)$
claim, stand by
  $KA_{1ccc}(95)$
claim, still maintain a
  $TV_{7a}(160)$
claim to, lay
  $KA_{-2a}(86); NO_{-2}(107)$

clandestinely, communicate
  $VE_0(147)$
clap for so.
  $EM_{2h}(73)$
clarify
  $AV_2(106); ET_{0c}(136);$
  $ET_{0dd}(137);$
  $KA_{4cac}(103);$
  $TP_{2ac}(164)$
classify
  $DE_{6c}(150); TO_{3a}(157);$
  $VE_{-1}(147); WT_0(118);$
  $VV_a(152); IN_{3aa}(143);$
  $IN_{3ac}(143)$
classify as secret
  $VE_{-1}(147)$
clean sweep of, make a
  $KA_{4caa}(102)$
clear
  $KA_{1bcc}(93)$
clear, make
  $KA_{-1b}(87); AV_2(106);$
  $TP_{2ac}(164); ET_{0dd}(137);$
  $ET_{0c}(136); KA_{4cac}(103)$
clear, make one's
  position
  $KA_{-1b}(87)$
clear up
  $AV_2(106); ET_{0c}(136);$
  $ET_{0dd}(137); IN_{2a}.(142);$
  $KA_{4cac}(103); NO_{7a}(115);$
  $NO_{9b}.(117); TV_{7c}(161)$
clear up a point
  $WT_{4b}(119)$
clearly aware of one
  another's view, be
  $KA_{-3b}(85)$
cleverly, talk
  $DI_{7b}.(126)$

clever tactics, employ
  $KA_{1aa}(91)$
clinch an argument
  $NO_{60}(113)$
cling to sth. (still)
  $TV_{7a}(160)$
cloak
  $TP_{2bc}(166)$
close, come too
  $KA_{0g}(89)$
closely, question
  $NO_{6c}(114)$
close the session
  $DI_{10}(127); TU_{9a}(133)$
cloud
  $TP_{2bd}(166)$
coalition, enter into a
  $KA_{2b}(97)$
coals, haul over the
  $KA_{-1c}(87)$
coat, turn one's
  $KA_{4bbb}(102)$
coax
  $EN_{7aa}(79); EN_{7af}(80);$
  $KA_{2cab}(97);$
  $WS_{bba}(122)$
code
  $VV_{bb}(153)$
coerce
  $EN_{8aa}(81)$
cogitate
  $DE_4(149)$
cohere
  $KA_{4cca}(105)$
coin
  $IN_{-1}(143)$
coin (words)
  $ET/TE_{ac}(138)$
collate
  $DE_{6f}(151)$

collect
  $DE_{6a}(150)$
colors, force so. to show his true
  $KA_{1cab}(103)$
colors, show one's
  $NO_{6b}(114)$
combat
  $IN_{8b}(146); KA_{-3c}(85);$
  $KA_{-3ca}(86); KA_{1aa}(91);$
  $NO_{6e}(115); NO_{60}(113)$
combine
  $DE_{6f}(151); DE_{6g}(151);$
  $TO_4(157)$
come about
  $EN_{9'a}(85)$
come around to a subject
  $DI_{10'}(127)$
come back
  $KA_{1bca}(92); TV_{7g}(162)$
come back again
  $TV_{7i}(162)$
come back to
  $TV_{7j}(162)$
come between
  $KA_{-1b}(87); KA_{4cac}(103)$
come out with
  $KA_{1ccc}(95)$
come round
  $KA_{4cba}(104)$
come second to
  $KA_{3b}(98)$
come to accept
  $KA_{4cda}(105)$
come to a conclusion
  $DI_{10}(127); DI/TU(134);$
  $TU_{9a}(133)$
come to an agreement
  $KA_{4cbd}(104); NO_{0e§}(110)$

come to an arrangement
  $NO_{0e§}(110)$
come to an understanding
  $ET*_{-1a}(134)$
come to a stand still
  $DI_{8a}(126); TU_{6'b}(133)$
come to grips, not to
  $TV_{6'b}(160)$
come to grips with
  $KA_{1da}(95)$
come to light again
  $TV_{7i}(162)$
come too close
  $KA_{0g}(89)$
come to terms
  $KA_{2b}(97); KA_{4cbb}(104);$
  $KA_{4cbd}(104)$
come to terms, not to
  $KA_{-3c}(86)$
come to terms with
  $KA_{4bda}(102); KA_{4cda}(105);$
  $NO_{60}(113)$
come to the help of
  $KA_{2cb}(98)$
come upon
  $DI_{5a}(125)$
come up to so.
  $EN_{7ab}(79)$
comfort
  $EN_{7ca}(80); KA_{2cab}(97)$
comfort so.
  $EN_{7cb}(81)$
command
  $EN_{3a}(76); EN_{6b}(78);$
  $NO_{-3}(107); NO_{0a}(108)$
commandeer
  $EN_{3db}(77)$
command respect
  $KA_{1ab}(91)$

Lexicon Section II

commence to talk
  $TU_3(131)$
commend
  $EN_{2c}(76); WT_{4e}(120)$
comment
  $DT_2(128)$
comment on
  $TE_{0bb}(141); TV_{7b}(160)$
comments, accept
  $DI/TU(134)$
comments, make
  $TO_{2bb}(156)$
commiserate
  $EN_{7ca}(80)$
commission
  $EN_{3a}(76)$
commit a crime
  $NO_2(112)$
commit a fault
  $NO_2(112)$
commit a misdeed
  $NO_2(112)$
commit an offense
  $NO_2(112)$
commit os.
  $EN_{6d}(79); NO_{0f}(110)$
communicate clandestinely
  $VE_0(147)$
communication with, get in
  $DI_1.(124)$
compact, make a
  $KA_{4cbd}(104)$
compare
  $DE_{6b}(150); DE_{6g}(151);$
  $IN_{3ba}(143); TO_{5e}(158);$
  $VV_d(154)$
comparison, draw a
  $DE_{6b}(150); TO_{5e}(158)$
comparison, make a
  $IN_{3ba}(143)$

compel
  $EN_{8aa}(81)$
compensate
  $KA_{4cad}(103); NO_{9b}$.
  (117)
compete
  $KA_{-3ca}(86); KA_{-3cb}(86);$
  $KA_{1db}(96)$
compile
  $DE_{6a}(150)$
complain
  $EN_{9f}(83); KA_{1caa}(94);$
  $WT_1(118)$
complain about so.
  $NO_{6a}(114)$
complain against
  $VE_{1b,c,d}(148)$
complain of a thing
  $NO_4(113)$
complete
  $KA_{4ac}(100); TV_{7c}(161);$
  $TV_{7e}(161)$
completely with, deal
  $TV_9(163)$
compliant, be
  $KA_{1cb}(95)$
complicate
  $TP_{2bba}(165); TP_{2bd}(166)$
compliment
  $EN_{7aa}(79); WS_{bba}(123)$
compliment so.
  $WT_{5d}(121)$
compliments, make
  $EN_{7ad}(80); WS_{bbb}(123)$
compliments, pay
  $EN_{7aa}(79); WS_{bba}(123);$
  $DT_{1c}(128); WT_{5d}(121)$
comply with
  $EN_{9b}(82); EN_{9h}(83);$

comply with (cont.)
  $KA_{4bda}(102); KA_{4cda}(105$
  $KA_{4cdb}(105); NO_{2a}(111)$
compose
  $DE_{6f}(151); EN_{7ca}(80);$
  $ET/TE_{ac}(138); KA_{-1b}(87);$
  $KA_{4cac}(103); TO_{3a}(157)$
compose (as an author)
  $ET/TE_{ac}(138)$
compose one's mind
  $KA_{4caa}(102)$
compose (text)
  $ET/TE_{aa}(138)$
comprehend
  $ET_{-1b}(134); DE_1(149)$
compress
  $TO_{2f}(156)$
comprise
  $TO_{2d}(156); DE_5(150)$
compromise
  $KA_{0g}(89); WP_{0ab}(121)$
compute
  $IN_{3ac}(143)$
concatenate
  $DE_{6f}(151); TO_4(157)$
conceal
  $KA_{1bba}(91); TP_{2bc}(166);$
  $TP_{2bg}(167); VE_1.(148)$
concede
  $KA_{1bbb}(92); KA_{4cba}(104)$
  $KA_{cbc}(104); NO_{0b}(108);$
  $NO_7.(115)$
concede sth. to so.
  $WT_3.(119)$
conceive
  $DE_{8d}(152); DE_1(149)$
concentrate
  $DE_{6a}(150); TO_{2f}(157)$
concentrate upon
  $DE_4(149)$

concern os. with
  $TO_{2ba}(155)$
concessions, make
  $KA_{3b}(98)$
concisely, speak
  $TU_5(132)$
conclude
  $DE_{6d}(150); DI/TU(134);$
  $DI_{10}(127); TE_{-1cb}(140);$
  $TU_{9a}(133)$
conclude with a summary
  $DI_{10}(127); TU_{9a}(133)$
conclusion, come to a
  $DI_{10}(127); DI/TU(134);$
  $TU_{9a}(133)$
concoct
  $DE_{8d}(152); DT_{1h}(128);$
  $ET/TE_{ac}(138); VE_{-2}(147)$
concrete, making more
  $TV_{7c}(161)$
concur
  $KA_{4cbd}(104); KA_{4cca}(105)$
concur with
  $AV_6(107)$
condemn
  $IN_{8b}(146); NO_{7b}(116);$
  $WT_{4c}(119)$
condemn so.
  $EM_{2j}(73)$
condemn by hissing/booing
  $EM_{2h}(73)$
condense
  $TE_{-1b}(140); TO_{2f}(157);$
  $TV_{7f}(161)$
conditions, make
  $EN_{5b}(77)$
condole so.
  $EN_{7ca}(80)$
condone
  $NO_{9bb}(117)$

conduct
  $EN_{6c}(78); NO_{-3}(107)$
confederation, draw up a
  $NO_{0e}(110)$
confer
  $KA_{2b}(97); KA_{4cac}(103)$
confer about a matter
  $WT_2(118)$
confer a degree
  $NO_{0da}(109)$
conference, have a
  $WT_2(118); NO_{2ba}(111);$
  $NO_{6f}(115); DT_{1a}(127)$
conference, meet for
  $NO_{2ba}(111); NO_{6f}(115);$
  $WT_2(118)$
confer together
  $NO_{2ba}(111); NO_{6f}(115);$
  $WT_2(118)$
confer with so.
  $DT_{1a}(127); NO_{2ba}(111);$
  $NO_{6f}(115)$
confer with so.
  $DT_{1bc}(128)$
confer (with)
  $DI_{7a}(125)$
confess
  $IN_{6c}(145); KA_{1bbb}(92);$
  $KA_{4cba}(104); NO_{6a}(114);$
  $NO_{6b}(114); VE_0(147)$
confession, go to
  $NO_{6a}(114); VE_0(147)$
confession, make a
  $NO_{6a}(114)$
confide
  $VE_0(147)$
confide in so.
  $VE_0(147)$

confidence, betray a
  $VE_1(148)$
confidence, take so. into one's
  $VE_0(147)$
confine
  $KA_{4cbc}(104); TO_{2a}(155);$
  $TV_3(159)$
confirm
  $AV_3(106); EN_{6d}(79);$
  $ET_{0a}(135); KA_{1bcd}(94);$
  $KA_{2cab}(97); NO_{60}(113)$
confirm so.
  $EN_{7cb}(81); TV*_{7b}(161);$
  $WT_{4f\S}(120)$
confirm by oath
  $IN_{9b}(146); NO_{6da}(114)$
confirm in writing
  $NO_{0f}(110); NO_1(111)$
confiscate
  $EN_{3db}(77); KA_{-2a}(86);$
  $KA_{-2b}(87); NO_{-2}(107)$
conflicting ideas, reconcile
  $NO_{7a}(115)$
confound
  $TP_{2bd}(166)$
confront
  $AV_1(106); KA_{0j}(90);$
  $KA_{1bcd}(94); TO_{5e}(158);$
  $KA_{1bca}(92)$
confront witness
  $IN_{1ac}(142)$
confuse
  $KA_{1ab}(91); TP_{2bd}(166)$
confused, get
  $TV_6(160)$
confusion, bring in
  $TP_{2bd}(166)$
confusion, throw into
  $KA_{1ab}(91)$

confute
  $AV_1(106); KA_{1bcc}(93);$
  $KA_{4ae}(100)$
conglomerate
  $TO_4(157)$
congratulate
  $WT_{5b}(120)$
conjecture
  $DE_5(149); IN_{1ab}(142)$
connect
  $DE_{6f}(131); TO_4(157)$
consecrate
  $EN_{3da}(77)$
consensus, achieve a
  $NO_{7a}(115)$
consent
  $AV_6(107); KA_{-3b}(85);$
  $WT_{4fa}(120)$
consent, force a
  $KA_{4cac}(103)$
consent to
  $KA_{3cba}(104);$
  $KA_{4cbb}(104);$
  $NO_{0b}(108); WT_{4fa}$
consent to, give
  $DI_3(124); IN_{8a}(146);$
  $EN_{9i}(84); WT_{4fa}(120)$
consider
  $DE_4(149); EN_{9k}(84);$
  $KA_{4cdb}(105); VV_g(154);$
  $DE_2(149)$
consideration, take into
  $KA_{4cdb}(105); TO_{2bb}(155);$
  $DE_2(149)$
consider (good/bad)
  $WT_0(118)$
consider carefully
  $DE_{8c}(152); VV_g(154)$
consider well
  $EN_{9c}(83); EN_{9g}(83);$

consider well (cont.)
  $NO_{2a}(111)$
consign
  $NO_{0b}(104)$
consign a th. to so.
  $EN_{3da}(77)$
console
  $EN_{7ca}(80); KA_{1cb}(95)$
consolidate (position)
  $AV_3(106); KA_{1ccb}(95);$
  $KA_{2cab}(97); TO_{2f}(157)$
conspiracy, form a
  $NO_{2bb}(111)$
conspire
  $NO_{2bb}(111)$
constitute
  $NO_{0de}(110)$
construct
  $TO_{3a}(157)$
construe
  $DE_{6f}(151); ET/TE_b(138)$
consult
  $DI_{7a}(125); EN_{5cb}(78);$
  $EN_{5cc}(78)$
consult with so.
  $EN_{5cc}(78)$
consult with one's pillow
  $DE_4(149)$
contact
  $EN_{7ac}(79); KA_{2aa}(96);$
  $KA_{4caa}(102)$
contact with, get in
  $DI_1.(124)$
contemplate
  $VV_g(154)$
contend
  $KA_{1da}(95)$
contentious, be
  $KA_{1ccc}(95)$

contest sth.
  $KA_{-3c}(86); KA_{1bba}(91);$
  $KA_{1bca}(92); KA_{1db}(96);$
  $NO_{6e}(115); NO_6(113);$
  $WT_{4c}(119)$
contest, take part in a
  $KA_{-3cb}(86)$
contest
  $IN_{8b}(146)$
context, take out of
  $TP_{2bh}(167)$
continue
  $TU_{8a}(133); TV_{7g}(162)$
continue in
  $KA_{1ccb}(95)$
continue in (too forcibly)
  $KA_{1ccc}(95)$
continue, let so.
  $TU_6..(133)$
continuing, prevent from
  $TU_3.(131); TU_6(132)$
contort
  $TP_{2be}(166)$
contract, enter a
  $NO_{0e}(110); NO_{0e§}(110)$
contract, invalidate a
  $IN_{9a}(146)$
contract, make a
  $KA_{4cbd}(104)$
contract, sign a
  $EN_{6d}(79); NO_{0e}(110);$
  $NO_{0e§}(110)$
contradict (explicitly)
  $AV_1(106); EN_{9i}(84);$
  $IN_{9a}(146); KA_{1bcd}(94);$
  $NO_{6b}(114); NO_{6e}(115)$
contradict os.
  $KA_{1bca}(92)$

contradictions, entangle
os. in
    $KA_{4bac}(101)$
contradictory, be
    $KA_{1bca}(92)$
contrast
    $TO_{5e}(158); KA_{1bca}(92)$
contrast with
    $AV_1(106)$
contravene
    $EN_{9j}(84); NO_2(112)$
contribute
    $KA_{2cab}(97)$
contribute to
    $TV_{6b}(159)$
contribute to a discussion
    $DT_{1ba}(127); DI_{7a}(125)$
contribute towards
    $TV_{6b}(159)$
contribute, want to
    $DI_1(124)$
contrive
    $DT_{1h}(128); DI_6(125);$
    $DE_{8d}(152); KA_{4aa}(99);$
    $VE_{-2}(147)$
control
    $EN_{6c}(78); NO_{-3}(107);$
    $VV_c(154)$
control the conversation upon a subject
    $TO_{5ac}(158)$
conversation, cut off so.'s/a
    $TU_3.(131)$
conversation, listen in on a
    $VE_{1"a}(147)$
conversation short, cut a
    $TU_3.(131)$
conversation, start a
    $EN_{7ac}(79)$

conversations upon a subject, control the
    $TO_{5ac}(158)$
conversation upon a subject, guide a
    $TO_{5ac}(158)$
conversation upon a subject, steer the
    $TO_{5ac}(158)$
conversation upon a subject, turn the
    $TO_{5ac}(158)$
conversation upon, direct the
    $TO_{5ac}(158)$
converse
    $DI_{7a}(125)$
converse, explore readiness to
    $DI_1.(124)$
converse with so.
    $DT_{1a}(127); DT_{1bc}(128)$
convert
    $EN_{7ag}(80)$
convey facts
    $TP_{2aa}(164); TU_4(132);$
    $DT_2(128); IN_{6aa}(144);$
    $ET_{0a}(135)$
convey information (indirectly)
    $IN_{2a*}(142)$
convict
    $NO_7(115); NO_{7b}(116);$
    $IN_{9b}(146)$
conviction, say with
    $ET_{0a}(135)$
convince
    $EN_{7ag}(80); KA_{-1c}(87)$
convoke
    $DI_{2`b}(124)$

coordinate
    $DE_{6f}(151); VV_a(153)$
cooperate
    $EN_{9a}(82)$
cooperate with
    $KA_{4cbb}(104)$
copy
    $ET_{1c}(137)$
copy down
    $TE_{0aa}(140)$
copy, make a
    $ET_{1c}(137)$
corner, force so. into a
    $KA_{1cab}(94)$
correct
    $TV_{7c}(161); ET/TE_a.(139)$
correct so.
    $WT_{4b}(119)$
correct proofs
    $ET/TE_a.(139)$
correct what so. has done
    $WT_{4b}(119)$
correspondence, keep up
    $DI_{7a}(125); DT_{1a}(127)$
correspond to
    $KA_{-3b}(85);$
corroborate
    $AV_3(106); TV*_{7b}(161);$
    $IN_{9b}(146); ET_{0a}(135)$
corroborate so.
    $EN_{7cb}(81)$
corroborate arguments
    $KA_{1bcd}(94)$
couch in concise terms
    $ET/TE_{ad}(138)$
counsel
    $WT_2(118); KA_{4cac}(103);$
    $DT_{1ba}(127); EN_{2c}(76)$

counsel so.
  $KA_{-1b}(87)$
counsel together, take
  $DT_{1ba}(127); DI_{7a}(125);$
  $NO_{2ba}(111); WT_2(118);$
  $NO_{6f}(115)$
count as
  $VV_a(152)$
counted out (by referee), be
  $KA_{4bad}(102)$
counter
  $KA_{1bcd}(94)$
counteract
  $DI_3"(125)$
counterargument, bring
  $KA_{1bcd}(94)$
counterfeit
  $TE_{0ab}(141); TP_{2be}(166)$
countermand
  $EN_{9j}(84); EN_{6e}(79);$
  $EN_{3a}(76); DI_3"(125);$
  $IN_{9a}(146)$
countersign
  $NO_{0e}\S(110); VV_{bc}(154)$
count out to
  $ET_{0dc}(137)$
count up
  $KA_{1db}(96); VV_a(152);$
  $TO_4(157)$
couple
  $TO_4(157)$
courage, inspire with
  $EN_{7cb}(81)$
court
  $EN_{7aa}(79); KA_{-2b}(87);$
  $KA_{2aa}(96); WS_{bba}(123)$
court, appeal to a superior
  $NO_{9aa}(117)$

court, go to a
  $NO_4.(113)$
court, make so appear in
  $NO_5(113)$
cover
  $KA_{1bba}(91); TP_{2bc}(166)$
cram (last minute learning)
  $ET_{0da}(136)$
cram into
  $EN_{8c}(82)$
crash into
  $KA_{0b}(88)$
create a foundation
  $EN_{3da}(77)$
credential to, give a
  $NO_{0b}"(109)$
crib (school)
  $VE_1"_b(148)$
cribshead, use a
  $AV_5(106)$
crime, commit a
  $NO_2(112)$
criminal, execute a
  $NO_{8a}(116)$
criticize
  $AV_5(106); DT_2(128);$
  $KA_{1caa}(94); TE_{0bb}(141);$
  $TV_{7b}(160); WT_{4c}(119)$
criticize adversely
  $AV_5(106); DT_2(129)$
critique, give deleterious
  $AV_5(106)$
cross, be
  $KA_{0e}(89)$
cross-examine
  $NO_{6c}(114)$
cross, mark with a
  $VV_{ba}(153)$

crown
  $NO_{0da}(109)$
crush
  $KA_{4ac}(100); TP_{2bj}(167)$
cry
  $EM_{2b}(71); EM_{2e}(72)$
cry out
  $ET_{0a}(134)$
cry out for mercy
  $NO_{9ab}(117)$
cryptic, be
  $TP_{2bi}(167)$
pull passages from
  $TE_{-1b}.(140)$
curb
  $KA_{3b}(98)$
curse so.
  $EM_{2ga}(72); EM_{2h}(72);$
  $EM_{2j}(73); NO_{8a}.(116)$
curse and swear
  $EM_{2e}(72)$
curses upon so., call down blessings and
  $EM_{2gb}(72)$
curtail
  $KA_{4cbc}(104)$
cushion
  $KA_{4cac}(103)$
cuss
  $EM_{2e}(72); EM_{2ga}(72)$
cuss at so.
  $EM_{2j}(73)$
custody, take into
  $NO_5.(113)$
cut a conversation short
  $TU_6(132)$
cut so. short
  $TU_3.(131)$
cut in
  $TU_6(132)$

cut, make the first
  $DI_5(125)$
cut off so./a conversation
  $TU_3.(131)$
cut off so.
  $TU_6(132)$
cut os. loose
  $KA_{2d}(98)$
cut up
  $TO_{3a}(157)$

D
damm
  $NO_{8a}.(116)$
damn so.
  $EM_{2ga}(72)$
damp down
  $TP_{2bbc}(165)$
danger, draw attention to a
  $EN_{4b}(77)$
dare
  $KA_{0g}(89); KA_{4bab}(101)$
date
  $DI_4(125); NO_{0g}(111); VV_{bd}(154)$
date, change
  $DI_4(125)$
date, fix a
  $DI_4(125); DI_{2'b}(124)$
date (time, term, day) fix a
  $NO_{0g}(111)$
daunt
  $EN_{8d}(82)$
dawdle
  $EM_{2k}(73)$
daydream
  $DE_9(152)$

day, postpone to another
  $NO_{0g}(111)$
dead horse, flog a
  $TP_{2b}(164)$
deal completely with
  $TV_g(163)$
deal, make a
  $KA_{1db}(96)$
deal with
  $KA_{1db}(96); TO_{2ba}(155)$
debar
  $EN_{8ab}(82)$
debate
  $DT_{1ba}(127); DT_{1bb}(128); DI_{7a}(125); Ka_{-3cb}(86); KA_{-3cc}(86); TV_{6a}(159)$
debate, have a public
  $DT_{1ba}(127)$
debilitate
  $KA_{1bcc}(73)$
debt, sue so. for
  $NO_4.(113)$
decide
  $DE_{8c}(152); DE_{8e}(152); KA_{1db}(96); KA_{2b}(97); NO_{7a}(116)$
decipher
  $IN_{2a}.(142); TE_{-1a}(140); TE_{0ad}(141)$
decision, make a
  $NO_{7a}(116); KA_{4cac}(103)$
decision, make no
  $KA_{1cb}(95)$
deck out
  $TP_{2ae}(164)$
declaim
  $DT_2(129); TP_{1a}(163); TU_4(132)$

declare
  $EN_{6d}(79); ET_{0a}(134); NO_{0f}(110); NO_{6da}(114)$
declare an agreement null and void
  $NO_{3bb}(112)$
declare so. of age
  $NO_{0da}(109)$
declare os.
  $DI_{7b}(126)$
declare solidarity with
  $KA_{2b}(97)$
declare so. sth. as sth.
  $VV_f(154)$
declare void
  $EN_{6e}(79); NO_{3bb}(112)$
declare war
  $KA_{0g}(89)$
decline
  $DI_3.(125); EN_{8a}(81); IN_{8b}(146); KA_{1bcb}(93); KA_{1bcc}(93); KA_{1bcd}(94); TP_{2bf}(167); WT_{4fb}(120)$
decline to do
  $NO_2..(112)$
decode
  $IN_{2a}.(142); TE_{-1a}(140); TE_{0ad}(141)$
decorate
  $TP_{2ae}(164)$
decorate so.
  $WT_{4e}(120)$
decoy
  $EN_{7af}(80)$
decree
  $DE_{8e}(152); EN_{6b}(78); NO_{0a§}(108)$

decree, ordain by
  $EN_{6b}(78)$
dedicate
  $EN_{3da}(77)$
deduce
  $DE_5(149); DE_{6d}(150)$
deem
  $DE_5(149)$
deem (good/bad)
  $WT_0(118)$
deepen the point
  $TV_{7c}(161)$
deescalate
  $KA_{-1b}(87); KA_{4cac}(103)$
defame
  $WP_{0ac}(122)$
defame
  $NO_3.(113)$
defeat a purpose
  $EN_{8ab}(82)$
defeated, be
  $KA_{4baa}(101)$
defend
  $KA_{1ccb}(95); KA_{2cb}(98); NO_{6e}(115)$
defend os.
  $KA_{1bca}(92)$
defend (a position)
  $TV_{6b}(160)$
defer
  $TV_{8b}(162)$
define
  $TO_{2a}(155)$
define as
  $VV_a(152)$
define a list
  $IN_{-1}(143)$
define one's position
  $KA_{-1b}(87)$

deform
  $TP_{2be}(166)$
defuse
  $KA_{1bbc}(92); KA_{1bcb}(93)$
defy
  $KA_{4bab}(101)$
degradate
  $WP_{0ad}(122)$
degrade
  $WT_{4a}(119)$
degree, confer a
  $NO_{0da}(109)$
degree, give a
  $NO_{0dc}(109)$
delay
  $DI_3.(125); KA_{1bba}(91); KA_{1bcb}(93); TV_{8b}(162)$
delegate
  $EN_{3aa}(76); EN_{3b}(76); NO_{-4}(107)$
deleterious critique, give
  $AV_5(106)$
deliberate
  $DE_4(149); DI_{7a}(125); DT_{1ba}(127); KA_{4cac}(103); NO_{2ba}(111); NO_{6f}(115) WT_2(118)$
delighted, be
  $KA_{4a}.(101)$
delimit
  $TO_{2a}(155); TV_3(159)$
delineate
  $DT_2(129); TO_{2a}(155); TV_3(159)$
delirious, be
  $ET/TE_b(138)$
(delirium), ramble
  $ET/TE_b(138)$

deliver a message
  $IN_{6ab}(145)$
deliver a speech
  $DI_{7b}(126); DT_2(129); TU_4(132)$
deliver a validation
  $AV_3(106)$
deliver in a monotonous sing-song manner
  $TP_{1a}(163)$
delude
  $EN_{7af}(80)$
demand
  $NO_{-2}(108); EN_{5b}(77)$
demand back
  $KA_{-2a}(86)$
demand from
  $EN_{8aa}(81)$
demand from so.
  $KA_{-2a}(86)$
demand (payment)
  $NO_{-2}(108)$
demand sth. of so.
  $KA_{-2b}(87)$
demarcate
  $TO_{2a}(155); TV_3(159)$
demonstrate
  $DT_2(129); ET_{0db}(136); IN_{6aa}(144); IN_{9b}(147); TP_{2ac}(164); TU_4(132)$
demoralize
  $EN_{8d}(82); KA_{0c}(89); KA_{1ab}(91)$
demur to
  $AV_1(106); KA_{1bcb}(93)$
demystify
  $TP_{2ac}(164)$
denominate
  $VV_{ba}(153)$

denounce
  $NO_4(113); NO_{6a}(114);$
  $VE_{1c}(148)$
denunciate
  $NO_4(113)$
deny
  $DI_{3'i}(125); EN_{9b}(82);$
  $EN_{9b\S}(83); EN_{9i}(84);$
  $IN_{9a}(146); KA_{1bba}(91);$
  $KA_{1bcb}(93); NO_{0c}(109);$
  $NO_{6e}(115); NO_{60}(113)$
deny under oath
  $NO_{6b}(114)$
depart
  $KA_{4bac}(101)$
depart from
  $KA_{3b}(98)$
departure to the police, report one's
  $IN_{6b}(145)$
depend (on)
  $KA_{2cab}(97)$
depict
  $DT_2(129); ET_{0a}(135);$
  $ET_{0de}(137); IN_{6aa}(144);$
  $TP_{2aa}(164); TU_4(132)$
deplore
  $WT_{4c}(119)$
depose (a king)
  $NO_{0dd}(110)$
deposition, make a
  $IN_{6c}(145)$
deposition, make a sworn
  $VE_{1b}(148)$
deposition, take down a
  $ET/TE_{ab}(138)$
deprecate
  $IN_{3bb}(143); KA_{1bbc}(92)$

depreciate
  $TP_{2bbb}(165); VV_g(154);$
  $WT_0(118); WG_{0a}(123);$
  $IN_{3bb}(144)$
depress
  $EN_{7d'}(81); KA_{-1b}(87)$
deprive of citizenship
  $NO_{8a}(116)$
deputate
  $NO_{0da}(109)$
depute
  $EN_{3aa}(76); EN_{3b}(76);$
  $NO_{-4}(107)$
deride
  $IR_{1a}(129); IR_{2ca}(130);$
  $IR_{2cb}(131); KA_{0g}(89);$
  $KA_{1aa}(91); IR_{1b}(129)$
derive
  $DE_{6d}(159);$
derive from
  $TV_{7i}(162)$
describe
  $DT_2(129); ET_{0a}(135);$
  $ET_{0de}(137); IN_{6aa}(144);$
  $TP_{2aa}(164); TU_4(132)$
describe in outline
  $TP_{2ac}(164)$
description, enlarge on a
  $TV_{6a}(159)$
desert
  $KA_{2d}(98); KA_{4bbb}(102);$
  $NO_{0db}(109)$
design
  $DE_{6f}(151); ET/TE_{ac}(138);$
  $TV_3(159)$
designate
  $VV_{ba}(153)$
desire
  $DE_{8a}(151); EN_{0ab}(74);$
  $EN_{0ba}(74)$

desire greatly
  $DE_{8a}(151)$
desist
  $TU_{6'a}(133)$
desist from
  $DI_{10}(127); KA_{3a}(98);$
  $KA_{3c}(99); TU_{9a}(133)$
despise
  $WP_{0aa}(121)$
detailed, making more
  $TV_{7c}(161)$
detain
  $KA_{1bcb}(93)$
detect
  $IN_{2a}(142); NO_3(112)$
deter
  $EN_{8ab}(82); KA_{1bcb}(93);$
determine
  $DE_{8c}(152); DE_{8e}(152);$
  $IN_{-1}(143); IN_{1aa}(142);$
  $KA_{4cac}(103)$
determine as
  $VV_a(152)$
determine the position
  $VV_a(152)$
detract from
  $TP_{2bbb}(165)$
devaluate
  $KA_{0c}(89)$
devalue
  $WG_{0a}(123)$
devalue so.
  $WP_{0ac}(122)$
devalue so.'s reputation
  $NO_{10}(117); WT_{5a}(120)$
develop
  $TV_{6a}(159)$
develop further
  $TV_{7g}(162)$
deviate
  $TV_{6'b}(160)$

Lexicon Section II

devil's advocate, be the
  $AV_3(106); TV_{6b}(159)$
devise
  $DE_{8d}(152); DT_{1h}(128);$
  $VE_{-2}(147)$
devolve
  $KA_{1bba}(91)$
devote os. (to)
  $TV_5(159)$
diagnose
  $IN_{2a}\cdot(142)$
(dialectical), paint
  $DT_2(129)$
diary, keep a
  $ET/TE_{ad}(138)$
dictate
  $EN_{6b}(78)$
die (discussion)
  $DI_{10}(127)$
difference, settle a
  $DI_9(126)$
differences, settle one's
  $KA_{1db}(96)$
differentiate
  $DE_{6e}(151); TO_{2a}(155);$
  $VV_e(154)$
different light, see sth. in a
  $KA_{-1b}(87)$
differently, place
  $TO_{3b}(157)$
diffuse
  $IN_{6aa}(144); TE_{-2a}(139)$
digest
  $TO_{2f}(157); TV_{7f}(161)$
digest, make a
  $TV_{7f}(161)$
digest, prepare a
  $ET_{0da}(136)$
digress
  $TP_{2bf}(167); TV_{6'b}(160)$

dilly-dally
  $KA_{1bba}(91)$
diminish
  $KA_{1bbb}(92)$
diminish (the severity)
  $TO_{5c}(158)$
direct
  $EN_{3a}(76); EN_{3aa}(76);$
  $EN_{3c}(76); EN_{6b}(78);$
  $EN_{6c}(78); NO_{-3}(107);$
  $NO_{0a}(108)$
direction, give
  $KA_{4cbc}(104)$
directions, giving
  $EN_{3aa}(76)$
direct the conversation
upon a subject
  $TO_{5ac}(158)$
dirty stories, tell
  $DT_{1e}(128)$
disable
  $KA_{4ae}(100);$
disagree
  $KA_{-3c}(86); KA_{1db}(96);$
  $WT_{4fb}(120)$
disagree with
  $KA_{1bba}(91)$
disallow
  $IN_{8b}(146)$
disappointed, be
  $EM_{2cb}(72); EN_{9'c}(85)$
disappointed, I am
  $EM_{2cb}*(72)$
disapprove
  $WT_0(118)$
disarm
  $KA_{4ae}(100)$
disarrange
  $TP_{2bd}(166)$

disavow
  $DI_3\cdot(125); EN_{6e}(79);$
  $EN_{9h}\cdot(83); EN_{9i}(84);$
  $IN_{8b}(146); IN_{9a}(146)$
  $KA_{1bba}(91); WP_{4fb}(120)$
disband (troops)
  $NO_{0dd}(110)$
discard
  $NO_{0dd}(110)$
discern
  $DE_{6e}(151); VV_e(154)$
discharge
  $NO_{0dd}(110); NO_{3bd}(112);$
  $KA_{4ad}(100)$
disciplinary punishment
on, inflict
  $WT_{4a}(119)$
disciplinary reasons,
transfer for
  $NO_{8a}(116)$
discipline
  $NO_{8a}(116); WT_{4a}(119)$
disclaim
  $EN_{9h}\cdot(84); KA_{-1d}(88);$
  $NO_{9ba}(117); WP_{0aa}(121)$
disclose
  $ET_{0c}(135); VE_1(148);$
  $VE_{1a}(148)$
disclose secrets
  $NO_{6db}(115)$
disconcert
  $EN_{7b}(80)$
disconnect
  $KA_{1aa}(91)$
disconnectedly, talk
  $TP_{2bj}(167)$
discontinue
  $DI_{10}(127); TU_{9a}(133)$

discourse (on)
  $DI_{7b}(126)$
discover
  $IN_{2a}(142); NO_3(112)$
discourage
  $EN_{8d}(82)$
discredit, bring so. into
  $WP_{0ac}(122)$
discriminate
  $DE_{6e}(151); VV_e(154);$
  $WP_{0aa}(121); WP_{0ac}(122)$
discuss
  $DT_{1a}(127); DT_{1bb}(128);$
  $DT_{1ba}(127); DI_{7a}(125);$
  $KA_{-3cb}(86); KA_{-3cc}(86);$
  $KA_{-1b}(87); KA_{2b}(97);$
  $KA_{4cac}(103); NO_{2ba}(111);$
  $NO_{6f}(115); NO_{60}(113);$
  $TV_{6a}(159); WT_2(118)$
discuss an acquisition
  $DT_{1ba}(127)$
discuss in advance
  $WT_2(118)$
discuss in full
  $KA_{4cab}(103)$
discussion, contribute to a
  $DT_{1ba}(127); DI_{7a}(125)$
(discussion), die
  $DI_{10}(127)$
discussion, enter into a
  $DI_6(125)$
discussion, get involved in a
  $DI_6(125)$
discussion, have a public
  $DT_{1ba}(127)$
discussion, lead a
  $DI/TU(134)$
discussion, participate at a
  $DI_{7a}(125); DT_{1ba}(127)$

discussion with,
  get into a
  $KA_{0h}(90); KA_{0i}(90)$
disengage os.
  $KA_{4bba}(102)$
disentangle
  $IN_{2a'}(142)$
disfavor
  $WT_1(118)$
disfigure
  $TE_{0ab}(141); TP_{2be}(166)$
disgrace os.
  $WS_{ab}(122)$
disguise
  $TP_{2bc}(166)$
dishearten
  $EN_{8d}(82)$
disinherit
  $EN_{3db}(77)$
dismantle
  $KA_{1aa}(91)$
dismiss
  $DI_{10}(127); EN_{9c}(83);$
  $KA_{4ad}(100); NO_{0dd}(110);$
  $NO_{8a}(116); TU_{9a}(133);$
  $WT_{4fb}(120)$
disobey
  $EN_{9d}(83); EN_{9j}(84);$
  $NO_2(112)$
disorder
  $TP_{2bd}(166)$
disown
  $DI_{3'}(125); IN_{8b}(146);$
  $KA_{2d}(98)$
disparage
  $WP_{0ac}(122); TP_{2bbb}(165)$
dispatch
  $EN_{3aa}(76)$
dispel
  $NO_{0dd}(110)$

dispel doubts
  $NO_{6b}(114)$
disposal, place at so.'s
  $EN_{2a}(75)$
dispose
  $DE_{8d}(152)$
disposed towards,
  be kindly
  $KA_{-3b}(85)$
dispossess
  $EN_{3db}(77)$
disprove
  $NO_{60}(113); NO_{6e}(115);$
  $AV_1(105); KA_{1bcc}(93);$
  $KA_{1bcd}(94); KA_{4ae}(100)$
dispute
  $IN_{8b}(146); DI_{7a}(125);$
  $DT_{1ba}(127); KA_{-3c}(86);$
  $KA_{1bca}(92); KA_{1da}(95);$
  $KA_{1db}(96); NO_{60}(113);$
  $NO_{6e}(115)$
dispute, renew a
  $TV_{7i}(162)$
display
  $IN_{6aa}(144); DT_2(129);$
  $TU_4(132); TO_{5a}(158);$
  $TP_{2aa}(164); ET_{0de}(137)$
dispense
  $TE_{-2a}(139); NO_{3bd}(112)$
disperse
  $IN_{6aa}(144)$
disqualify
  $NO_{8a}(116)$
disquiet
  $EN_{7d'}(81)$
disregard
  $TV_{8b}(163); TP_{2bf}(167);$
  $KA_{1bba}(91); KA_{1bcc}(93);$
  $KA_{4aa}(99); EN_{9c}(83);$
  $EN_{9d}(83); EN_{9g}(83);$

disregard (cont.)
  $EN_{9j}(84); WP_{0aa}(121);$
  $WG_{1a}(123)$
disregard the question
  $EN_{9i}(84)$
disrespect
  $WP_{0aa}(121)$
disrupt
  $TU_6(132)$
dissect
  $TO_{3a}(157)$
disseminate
  $TE_{-2a}(139); IN_{6aa}(144)$
dissociate os.
  $KA_{-1d}(88); KA_{3b}(98)$
disscociate os. from
  $KA_{2d}(98)$
dissolve partnership
  $NO_{3bb}(112)$
dissuade
  $KA_{4ab}(99); EN_{1b}(75)$
dissuade so. from
  $WT_1(118)$
dissuade so. from sth.
  $KA_{-2b}(87)$
distance from, keep one's
  $KA_{-1d}(88)$
distinction, draw a
  $DE_{6e}(151)$
distinction, make a
  $DE_{6e}(151)$
distinction, treat with
  $NO_{0b}\text{``}(109)$
distinguish
  $DE_{6e}(151); VV_e(154)$
distinguish between
  $DE_{6e}(151); VV_e(154)$
distinguished, be
  $TP_{2ab}(164)$
distinguish so.
  $NO_{0b}\text{``}(109)$

distort
  $TP_{2be}(166)$
distorted English, speak
  $TE_{0ab}(141)$
distract
  $EN_{1b}(75)$
distrain
  $EN_{3db}(77)$
distress
  $EN_{7d}\text{`}(81)$
distribute
  $IN_{6aa}(144); TE_{-2a}(139)$
distrust
  $NO_3\text{`}(113)$
distrust, show
  $WT_3\text{`}(119)$
disturb
  $DI_{8a}(126); EN_{7d}\text{`}(81)$
diverge
  $TV_6\text{`}b(160)$
divert
  $EN_{1b}(75)$
divert a man's thoughts
  $EN_{1b}(75)$
divide
  $DE_{6c}(150)$
divide up
  $DE_{6c}(150)$
divine
  $IN_{2a}(142)$
divorce
  $NO_{3bb}(112); NO_{7a}(116)$
divulge
  $IN_{6b}\text{`}(145); VE_1(148)$
divulge a secret
  $NO_{6db}(115)$
do
  $EN_9\text{`}b(85)$
do again
  $TV_{7d}(161)$

do away with
  $NO_{3bb}(112)$
do by rote
  $ET_{1c}(137)$
do, decline to
  $NO_2\text{``}(112)$
do penance
  $NO_{8a}\text{``}(117)$
do proofreading
  $ET/TE_a\text{`}(139)$
document
  $IN_{9b}(147); NO_{6da}(114);$
  $WT_{4f\S}(120)$
documents, draw up
  $ET/TE_{aa}(138)$
document, falsify a
  $TE_{0ab}(141)$
dodge
  $KA_{1bba}(91); KA_{4aa}(99):$
  $KA_{4bba}(102); TP_{2bf}(167)$
donate
  $EN_{3da}(77)$
donation, make a
  $EN_{3da}(77)$
done for, be
  $KA_{4baa}(101)$
done with, have
  $KA_{4baa}(101)$
(do) not blame so.
  $WT_3\text{`}(119)$
(do) not know each other
  $KA_{-3a}(85)$
(do) not share opinion
  $WT_{4fb}(120)$
do, refuse to
  $NO_2\text{``}(112)$
do, show how to
  $ET_{0b}(135)$
do. sth., induce so. to
  $NO_{-3}(107)$

do sth., move so. to
  $EN_{7cb}(81)$
doubt
  $DE_7(151)$
doubts, dispel
  $NO_{6b}(114)$
doubts about so., show
  $WT_3.(119)$
down, be
  $KA_{0e}(89)$
down gently over sth., let so.
  $NO_7.(115)$
draft
  $ET/TE_{ac}(138)$
draft
  $TV_3(159)$
draft a memorial address
  $ET/TE_{ad}(138)$
draft a speech
  $ET/TE_{ad}(138)$
drag one's feet
  $KA_{3b}(98)$
drag out
  $DI_{10"}(127); TU_5(132)$
dramatize
  $TP_{2bba}(165)$
draw
  $DT_2(129)$
draw a comparison
  $DE_{6b}(150); TO_{5e}(158)$
draw a distinction
  $DE_{6e}(151)$
draw so.'s attention to sth.
  $EN_{1ac}(74)$
draw attention to a danger
  $EN_{4b}(77)$
draw back
  $DI_3"·(125); KA_{3b}(98)$
draw in one's horns
  $KA_{4bac}(101)$
draw into
  $TV_5(159)$
draw the long boast
  $TP_{1c}(163)$
draw out
  $DI_{10"·}(127); TU_5(132)$
draw up
  $ET/TE_{ab}(138); ET/TE_{ac}(138)$
draw up a confederation
  $NO_{0e}(110)$
draw up documents
  $ET/TE_{aa}(138)$
draw up the official report of
  $ET/TE_{ab}(138)$
dream
  $TP_{2bba}(165); DE_{8a}(151);$
  $DE_9(152); ET/TE_b(138)$
dream of doing sth.
  $EN_{0aa}(74)$
dream to get sth.
  $EN_{0ba}(74)$
dream that sth. happens
  $EN_{0aa}(74)$
dress up
  $ET/TE_a.(139)$
drill
  $ET_{0da}(136)$
drive away
  $KA_{4ad}(100)$
drive back
  $KA_{4ad}(100)$
drivel on
  $TP_{2bj}(167)$
drivel, speak
  $TP_{1e}(163)$
drop
  $KA_{3a}(98)$
drop out
  $DI_{10·}(127); NO_{0db}(109)$
drown out
  $DI_{8b}(126)$
drum into
  $EN_{8c}(82);$
drum sth. into so's head
  $EN_{8c}(82); ET_{0da}(136)$
dub
  $VV_{ba}(153)$
dumb, be struck
  $TU_{6'b}(133)$
dumb, grow
  $TU_{6'a}(133)$
dupe
  $KA_{0b}(88)$
dupe so.
  $IR_{1a}(129); IR_{2cb}(131)$
duties to, give
  $NO_{0a}(108)$
duty, have a
  $NO_{0·}(111)$

E

ears open, keep your eyes and
  $VE_{1"a}(147)$
ease, tell sth. with the greatest of
  $TO_2(155)$
eavesdrop
  $VE_{1"a}(147)$
eavesdropping, learn by
  $VE_{1"a}(147)$
economize words
  $TP_{2ad}(164)$

edgewise, not allow so. to get a word in
TU_2.(131)
edify
$KA_{2cab}(97)$
edit
$TE_{-2b}(139)$
educate
$EN_{8c}(82)$
effect
$KA_{4cac}(103)$
effect, put a law into
$NO_{-4\S}(107)$
ejaculate
$ET_{0a}(134)$
eject
$EN_{8b}(82)$
elaborate
ET/TE_a.(139); $TP_{2ac}(164)$; $TV_{6a}(159)$
elect
$NO_{0da}(109)$
elect so.
$WT_1(118); WT_2$.(119)
elegy, give an
$TV_{7j}(162)$
elicit
$IN_{2a}(142)$
eliminate
$KA_{4ac}(100); TO_{2c}(156); VV_g(154)$
elucidate
$AV_2(106); ET_{0c}(136); ET_{0dd}(137); IN_{2a}$.(142); $TP_{2ac}(164); TV_{7c}(161)$
elude
$KA_{1bba}(91); TP_{2bf}(167)$
embarrass
EN_{7d}.(81)

embed
$TO_{3a}(157)$
embellish
ET/TE_a.(139); $ET/TE_b(138); TP_{2ae}(164)$
embolden
$KA_{2cab}(97)$
embrace
$TO_{2d}(156)$
emphasize
$TO_{5ab}(158)$
employ clever tactics
$KA_{1aa}(91)$
employee, take on an
$NO_{0da}(109)$
employ good tactics
$KA_{0d}(89)$
employ tactic
$KA_{1da}(95)$
empower
$EN_{3b}(76); NO_{0da}(109); NO_{-4}(107)$
enact
$EN_{6b}(78); NO_{-4\S}(107)$
encipher
$TE_{0ad}(141); VV_{bb}(153)$
encircle
$KA_{1cab}(94)$
enclose
$TO_{2d}(156)$
encode
$TE_{0ad}(141); VV_{bb}(153)$
encounter
$DI_{5a}(125); KA_{1bca}(92)$
encourage so.
$EN_{7cb}(81); KA_{2cab}(97)$
encroach on (rights)
$NO_2(112)$
end
$DI_{10}(127); TU_{9a}(133)$

end, bring to an
$DI_{10}(127); TU_{9a}(133)$
endeavor to get
$EN_{0ab}(74)$
endeavor to get something
$DE_{8b}(151)$
end, gain one's
$KA_{4aa}(99)$
end of one's thether, be at the
$KA_{4baa}(101)$
endorse
$IN_{9b}(147); WG_{0b}(123)$
endow
$AV_3(106)$
end to, make an
$TU_{9a}(133)$
enemy of, make an
$KA_{1da}(96); KA_{-1c}(87)$
enervate
$KA_{1ab}(91)$
enfeeble
$KA_{1bcc}(93)$
enforce
$EN_{8aa}(81); KA_{-2a}(86)$
enforce good order
$DI/TU(134)$
engage (in)
$KA_{2aa}(96); NO_{0da}(109); NO_{0e}(110); TO_{2ba}(155)$
engagement, withdraw from an
$NO_{3ba}(111)$
English, speak distorted
$TE_{0ab}(141)$
English, speak in broken
$TP_{1b}(163)$
English, speak poor
$TE_{0ab}(141)$

enlarge
  $TO_{2a}(155)$
enlarge on (a description)
  $TV_{6a}(159)$
enlighten
  $ET_{0dd}(137)$
enlist
  $KA_{2aa}(96)$
enliven
  $EN_{7cb}(81); KA_{2cab}(97)$
enmity towards, feel
  $KA_{-3ca}(86); KA_{-3c}(86)$
ennoble
  $NO_{0da}(109)$
enough, have had
  $EM_{2ca^*}(72)$
enough of, have
  $KA_{3a}(98)$
enrole
  $NO_{0da}(109)$
ensnare
  $KA_{-2b}(87); KA_{0g\cdot\cdot}(90);$
  $KA_{2aa}(96); WS_{bbb}(123)$
ensure
  $NO_1(111)$
ensure (the truth)
  $IN_{9b}(147)$
entangle
  $KA_{0g\cdot\cdot}(90); KA_{1ab}(91);$
  $TP_{2bd}(166)$
entangled in contradictions, get
  $TV_{6\cdot\cdot\cdot}(160)$
entangle os. in contradiction
  $KA_{4bac}(101)$
enter a contract
  $NO_{0e}(110); NO_{0e\S}(110)$
enter an alliance
  $NO_{0e\S}(110)$

enter an appeal
  $NO_{9aa}(117)$
enter a protest
  $AV_1(106)$
enter a rehearing
  $NO_{9aa}(117)$
enter in a list
  $VV_a(153)$
enter into
  $TO_{2ba}(155)$
enter into a coalition
  $KA_{2b}(97)$
enter a discussion
  $DI_6(125)$
enter into an alliance
  $KA_{2b}(97)$
enter into an arrangement
  $KA_{4cbd}(104)$
enter (into a treaty)
  $EN_{6d}(79)$
enter into a treaty
  $NO_{0f}(110)$
enter into relations
  $KA_{2aa}(96)$
enter on cards
  $VV_a(153)$
entertain
  $DI_{7b}(126)$
enthusiasm, fill with
  $EN_{7ag}(80)$
enthusiastic, be
  $TP_{2bba}(165)$
enthusiastic about, be
  $EM_{2i}(73)$
entice
  $EN_{7af}(80); KA_{0g\cdot\cdot}(90);$
  $KA_{2aa}(96)$
entitle
  $NO_{0da}(109)$

entrap
  $KA_{2aa}(96)$
entreat
  $EN_{2b}(75)$
entreaties, approach with
  $EN_{2b}(75)$
entrust a th. to so.
  $EN_{3da}(77)$
entrust to
  $VE_0(147)$
entwine
  $TO_{3a}(157); TO_4(157)$
enumerate
  $TO_4(157); VV_a(153)$
envelop
  $TP_{2bc}(166)$
equalize
  $DE_{6b}(150); IN_{3ba}(143);$
  $KA_{4cad}(103)$
equal, make
  $IN_{3ba}(143)$
err
  $TE_{-1cc}(140)$
errors, mark
  $WT_{4b}(119)$
escape (one's lips)
  $VE_{1g}(149)$
escape route open, keep an
  $KA_{1cb}(95)$
essay, write an
  $ET/TE_{ad}(138)$
establish
  $AV_3(106); ET_{0a}(135);$
  $IN_{9b}(147); KA_{1bcd}(94);$
  $NO_{0de}(110); NO_{-4\S}(107);$
  $TV^*_{7b}(161)$
establish firmly
  $IN_{9b}(147)$

esteem so.
  $WT_{5d}(121)$
esteem highly
  $WT_0(118)$
esteem, hold so. in high
  $WT_{5d}(121)$
estheticize
  $TP_{2bba}(165)$
estimate
  $EN_{5ca}(78); IN_{3bb}(143);$
  $NO_{-1}(108); VV_d(154);$
  $VV_g(154); VV_g(154);$
  $WT_0(118)$
estimate of, form an
  $IN_{3bb}(143); WT_0(118)$
eulogize
  $ET/TE_{ad}(138); WT_{5d}(121)$
eulogize so.
  $WT_{5d}(121)$
euphemisms, produce
  $TP_{2bba}(165)$
evade
  $KA_{1bba}(91); KA_{4aa}(99);$
  $TO_{2c}(156); TP_{2bf}(167)$
evade the question
  $EN_{9i}(84)$
evaluate
  $IN_{3bb}(143); VV_d(154);$
  $VV_g(154); WT_0(118)$
even with, get
  $KA_{bdb}(102)$
evidence (about), give
  $IN_{6c}(145)$
evidence, give
  $VE_{1b}(148)$
evidence of, give
  $NO_{6da}(114); VE^*_1(148)$
evidence, turn (Queen's, King's, State's)
  $VE_{1b}(148)$

evil, wish so.
  $EM_{2ga}(72); EM_{2h}(73)$
exact
  $EN_{5b}(77); KA_{-2a}(86);$
  $KA_{-2b}(87); KA_{4ab}(99)$
exaggerate
  $ET/TE_b(138); TP_{1c}(163);$
  $TP_{1c}(163); TP_{2bba}(165);$
  $WS_{bc}(123)$
exaggerate the importance
  $KA_{-1c}(87)$
exalt
  $WT_{4e}(120)$
examine
  $EN_{5cc}(78); EN_{5cd}(78);$
  $IN_{1aa}(142); NO_{6c}(114);$
  $TE_{-1b}(140); VV_c(154)$
examine (in an examination)
  $IN_{1ac}(142)$
examine (so. in examinations)
  $IN_{1ab}(142)$
examine thoroughly
  $IN_{1aa}(142)$
example, aduce an
  $AV_4(106)$
example, give an
  $AV_4(106)$
example, produce an
  $AV_4(106)$
example, refer to an
  $AV_4(106)$
example, set an
  $AV_4(106)$
exam, prepare for an
  $ET_{0da}(136)$
exam, prepare so. for an
  $ET_{0da}(136)$

except
  $TO_{2c}(156)$
exception to, take
  $TV_6{}^\prime a(106); NO_{6O}(113)$
excerpts from, make
  $TE_{-1b'}(140)$
excess, carry to
  $TP_{2bba}(165)$
exchange information
  $ET_{0a}(135)$
exchange opinion
  $DI_{7a}(125); DT_{1a}(127);$
  $DT_{1bb}(128); DT_{1bc}(128)$
exchange views
  $KA_{4cab}(103)$
excite
  $EN_{7cc}(81)$
excited, get
  $EN_{9I}(84)$
exclaim
  $ET_{0a}(134)$
exclude
  $DE_{6d}(150); KA_{4ac}(100);$
  $TO_{2c}(156); NO_{0b'}(109)$
exclusion, prove by
  $DE_{6d}(150)$
excommunicate
  $NO_{0dd}(110); NO_{8a}(116);$
  $NO_{8a'}(116)$
exculpate (so.)
  $NO_{6b}(114); NO_{7c}(116)$
excursion, making an
  $TV_6{}^\prime b(160)$
excuse
  $IN_{8b}(146); NO_{7c}(116);$
  $NO_{9bb}(117)$
execrate
  $NO_{8a'}(116)$
execute
  $EN_{9d}(83); EN_{9j}(84)$

execute (a criminal)
  $NO_{8a}(116)$
exegesis, make an
  $TE_{-1cb}(140)$
exemplify
  $AV_4(106)$
exempt
  $NO_{0dd}(110);NO_{3bd}(112);$
  $TO_{2c}(156)$
exempt from
  $NO_{9bb}(117)$
exercise
  $ET_{0da}(136)$
exhaust
  $KA_{4ac}(100)$
exhaust a topic
  $TV_9(163)$
exhibit
  $DT_2(129);ET_{0de}(137);$
  $EN_{1ac}(94);IN_{6aa}(144);$
  $TP_{2aa}(164);TU_4(132)$
exhort
  $EN_{4a}(77);EN_{6a}(78)$
exile
  $NO_{0dd}(110);NO_{8a}(116)$
exonerate
  $NO_{3bd}(112)$
exonerate (of a guilt)
  $NO_{7c}(116)$
expand
  $TO_{2a}(155)$
expansively, present
  $TP_{2bba}(165)$
expatriate
  $NO_{8a}(116)$
expect
  $DE_{8a}(151);EN_{0bb}(74)$
expel
  $EN_{8b}(82);NO_{0dd}(110);$
  $NO_{8a}(116)$

expense, be witty at
  another's
  $DT_{1d}(128)$
experiences, write down
  $ET/TE_{ad}(138)$
expert judgement on,
  pass
  $WT_{4f\S}(120);WT_0(118)$
expert opinion, give an
  $WT_{4f\S}(120)$
expiate
  $NO_{8a}(117)$
explain
  $AV_2(106);ET_{0c}(136);$
  $ET_{0dd}(137);ET_{0df}(137);$
  $KA_{1db}(96);NO_{6b}(114);$
  $TE_{-1cb}(140);TP_{2ac}(164)$
explain away
  $TP_{2bba}(165)$
explanation, give an
  $ET_{0de}(137)$
explicate
  $AV_2(106);ET_{0c}(136);$
  $ET_{0dd}(137)$
explicit, make more
  $TV_{7c}(161)$
explode
  $EM_{2b}(71)$
explore
  $IN_{1aa}(142)$
explore readiness to
  converse
  $DI_1(124)$
expose
  $ET_{0c}(135);VE_{1a}(148)$
expose os.
  $WS_{ab}(122)$
expose to ridicule
  $IR_{1a}(129);IR_{2cb}(131)$

exposition, give an
  $ET_{0de}(137)$
expostulate
  $KA_{-3a}(86);KA_{1da}(96)$
expound
  $DT_2(129);ET_{0a}(134);$
  $ET_{0de}(137);IN_{6aa}(144);$
  $TE_{-1cb}(140);TU_4(132)$
express
  $ET_{0a}(135);IN_{2a*}(142)$
express os. hazily
  $TP_{2bd}(166)$
express os. in a blurred
  manner
  $TP_{2bd}(166)$
express os. in a woolly
  manner
  $TP_{2bd}(166)$
express os. indefinitely
  $TP_{2bd}(166)$
express os. indistinctly
  $TP_{2bd}(166)$
express os. vaguely
  $TP_{2bd}(166)$
express one's opinion
  $DI_{7b}(126);TU_4(132)$
express sympathy
  $EM_{2cb}(72)$
express sympathy with
  $KA_{-3b}(85)$
expropriate
  $EN_{3db}(77)$
extemporize
  $TO_2(155)$
extenuate
  $TP_{2bba}(165)$
extend
  $TO_{2a}(155);TV_{6a}(159);$
  $TV_{7c}(161)$

extend speaking time
  DI/TU(134)
extol
  $WT_{4e}(120)$
extort
  $KA_{-2b}(87); KA_{4ab}(99)$
extort sth. from so.
  $EN_{8aa}(81)$
extract
  $IN_{5ac}(144)$
extradite
  $NO_{8a}(116)$
extravagantly, praise
  $EN_{7ad}(80); WS_{bbb}(123)$
extrude
  $IN_{2a*}(142)$
exult
  $KA_{4a}.(101)$
exult at
  $WT_{5b}(120)$
exultation, receive with
  $WT_{5b}(120); EM_{2h}(73)$
eye on sth., have one's
  $TO_{5a}(158)$
eyes and ears open, keep your
  $VE_{1"a}(148)$
eyes, follow with one's
  $TO_{5a}(158)$
eye to eye, see
  $KA_{4cbb}(104)$

F
face a thing
  $KA_{1bca}(92)$
face, have a red
  $EM_{2ab}(71)$
face to face, be
  $KA_{1bca}(92)$
factors, weigh the
  $WT_3.(119)$

facts, convey
  $TP_{2aa}(164); TU_4(132);$
  $DT_2(129); IN_{6aa}(144);$
  $ET_{0a}(135)$
fail
  $TE_{-1cc}(140)$
fall back
  $KA_{1bbb}(92)$
falling out, have a
  $EM_{2ca}(71)$
fall in with
  $KA_{4cba}(104); KA_{4cda}(105)$
fall in with, not
  $KA_{1bba}(91)$
fall in with (partially)
  $KA_{4cbc}(104)$
fall out
  $KA_{-1c}(87)$
fall out with so.
  $KA_{-1c}(87)$
fall upon
  $KA_{0i}(90); KA_{0h}(90)$
falsify
  $VV_c(154)$
falsify (a document)
  $TE_{0ab}(141)$
falter
  $TU_6.(133); EM_{2aa}(71)$
familiar manner, behave in a
  $EN_{7ad}(80); WS_{bbb}(123)$
fancies, indulge in
  $DE_9(152); ET/TE_b(138)$
far, carry too
  $TP_{2bba}(165)$
farfetched, be
  $TP_{2b}(164); TP_{2bh}$

fascinate
  $WS_{bbb}(123); EN_{7ad}(80);$
  $KA_{2aa}(96)$
fathom
  $ET_{-1b}(134)$
fault, commit a
  $NO_2(112)$
fault, find
  $KA_{0e}(89)$
fault with, find
  $AV_5(106); WT_{4c}(119);$
  $WT_{4a}(119); KA_{1caa}(94)$
favor
  $WT_1(118)$
favorably, act on
  $EN_{9b\S}(82)$
favorable hearing, give a
  $EN_{9b}(82)$
favorable light, put in a
  $TP_{2bba}(165)$
favor, try to get into so.'s
  $KA_{-2b}(87)$
fawn upon
  $WS_{bba}(123); EN_{7aa}(79)$
fear
  $DE_5(149)$
fear, inspire with
  $KA_{1ab}(91)$
fed up with, be
  $KA_{3a}(98)$
feel
  $ET_{-1a}(134); ET^*_{-1a}(134)$
feel enmity towards
  $KA_{-3ca}(86); KA_{-3c}(86)$
feelers, put out
  $DI_1.(124)$
(feel) hatred toward one another
  $KA_{-3c}(86); KA_{-3ca}(86)$

feelings, hurt so.'s
  NO_2.(112)
feel kindly towards
  KA_{4cca}(105)
feel one's way forwards
  DI_1.(124)
feel one's way towards
  DI_1.(124)
feel small, make so.
  KA_{4ac}(100)
feel sympathy with
  KA_{-3b}(85)
feel the way
  KA_{2aa}(96)
feet, drag one's
  KA_{3b}(98)
feet, put so. back on his
  KA_{2cab}(97)
fiction, produce (science)
  ET/TE_b(138)
fidget
  EM_{2ab}(71)
field, initiate so. into a
  VE_0(147)
field, introduce so. to a
  ET_{0da}(136)
fiercely, stick to too
  KA_{1ccc}(95)
fight against
  KA_{1aa}(91); KA_{-3ca}(86)
fight for
  KA_{1ccb}(95)
fight for (too vehemently)
  KA_{1ccc}(95)
fighting, simulate
  KA_{-3cb}(86)
fight out
  KA_{1db}(96)
fight, pretend to
  KA_{-3cb}(86)

fight, put to
  KA_{4ad}(100)
fight, put up a
  KA_{1bca}(92)
fight through
  KA_{1db}(96)
figures, mark with
  VV_{ba}(153)
file
  VV_a(153); IN_{3aa}(143); DE_{6b}(150)
file a claim
  NO_4(113)
file an application
  $EN_{2b\S}$(75); $NO_{-2\S}$(108)
file away
  KA_{4caa}(102)
files, form into
  DE_{6f}(151); TO_{3a}(157)
filibuster
  TU_5(132); TU_3"'(132); DI_{10}"'(127)
fill with enthusiasm
  EN_{7ag}(80)
filter
  IN_{6d}(145)
filthy, talk
  DT_{1e}(128)
find
  NO_3(113)
find bad
  IN_{3bb}(143)
find fault
  KA_{0e}(89)
find fault with
  AV_5(106); WT_{4c}(119); WT_{4a}(119); KA_{1caa}(95)
find good
  IN_{3bb}(143)

find good/bad
  VV_g(155); WT_0(118)
find holes in
  WT_{4c}(119)
find mistakes
  WT_{4b}(119)
find one's way through
  IN_{2a}.(142)
find out
  IN_{2a}.(142)
find so.
  NO_7(115)
fine
  NO_{8a}(116)
fine, impose a
  NO_7(115)
finish
  DI_{10}(127); TU_{9a}(133)
finish, let so.
  TU_6"(133)
finish off
  TV_{7e}(161)
fire
  NO_{8a}(116)
firmly, establish
  IN_{9b}(147)
first cut, make the
  DI_5(125)
first soundings, take
  KA_{2aa}(96)
fish-stories, tell
  ET/TE_b(138)
fit for so., be
  NO_0.(111)
fit in
  TO_{2d}(156); VV_a(153); DE_{6c}(150)
fix
  KA_{2b}(97); KA_{1cab}(94); IN_{-1}(143)

fixe a date
　$DI_4(125); DI_{2'b}(124)$
fix a date (time, term, day)
　$NO_{0g}(111)$
fix up
　$KA_{2b}(97); TP_{2bi}(167)$
flabbergast
　$EN_{7b}(80)$
flare up
　$EM_{2b}(71)$
flatter
　$WS_{bbb}(123); WS_{bba}(123);$
　$EN_{7ad}(80); EN_{7aa}(79)$
flee from so.
　$WP_{0aa}(121)$
flee
　$KA_{4bba}(102)$
flexible, stay
　$KA_{1cb}(95)$
flight, take to
　$KA_{4bba}(102)$
flirt
　$WS_{bba}(123); EN_{7aa}(79);$
　$DT_{1c}(128)$
flog a dead horse
　$TP_{2b}(164)$
floor
　$KA_{4ac}(100)$
flounder
　$TP_{2bj}(167)$
flourish, sign with a
　$VV_{bc}(154)$
flowing, stop
　$DI_{8a}(126); TV_{6'''}(160)$
focus
　$EN_{1ac}(74); TO_{5a}(158)$
follow
　$KA_{4cdb}(105); EN_{9c}(83);$
　$EN_{9k}(84); EN_{9j}(84);$
　$NO_{2a}(111)$

follow an invitation
　$DI_{5a}(125)$
follow with one's eyes
　$TO_{5a}(158)$
fool
　$IR_{2cb}(131); IR_{2b}(130);$
　$IR_{1a}(129)$
fool around
　$IR_{1c}(130)$
foolish, be
　$IR_{1c}(130)$
fool of, make a
　$KA_{0g}(89); IR_{2cb}(131);$
　$IR_{2ca}(130); IR_{1a}(129)$
fool of os., make a
　$WS_{ab}(122)$
fool, play the
　$IR_{1c}(130); IR_{2a}(130)$
forbearing with so., be
　$NO_{7'}(115); WT_{3'}(119)$
force
　$KA_{4ab}(99); TP_{2be}(167)$
force a consent
　$KA_{4cac}(103)$
force a thing upon so.
　$EN_{8aa}(81)$
force back
　$KA_{4ad}(100)$
force notice
　$ET_{0da}(136)$
force out
　$KA_{4ad}(100)$
force so. into
　a corner
　$KA_{1cab}(94)$
force so. to show
　his true colors
　$KA_{1cab}(94)$
force sth. from so.
　$EN_{8aa}(81)$

forbid
　$NO_{0c}(109)$
forcibly, continue in too
　$KA_{1ccc}(95)$
forecast (weather)
　$ET/TE_c(138)$
forefront, place in the
　$TO_{5a}(158)$
forego one's turn
　$TU_{3'''}(132)$
forego speaking
　$TV_1(158)$
foreground, place in the
　$TO_{5a}(158)$
foreign, be
　$KA_{-3a}(85)$
foretell
　$ET/TE_c(139)$
forge
　$TE_{0ab}(141)$
forget sth., make so.
　$EN_{1b}(75)$
forgive
　$NO_{9bb}(117)$
forgiveness, beg
　$EN_{2b}(75); NO_{9b'}(117)$
forgotten, have
　$IN_{5ab}(144)$
form
　$DE_{6f}(151); TO_{3a}(157)$
form a conspiracy
　$NO_{2bb}(111)$
formal request, make a
　$EN_{2b§}(75); NO_{-2§}(108)$
form an alliance
　$KA_{4cbd}(104)$
form an estimate of
　$IN_{3bb}(143); WT_0(118)$
form an intimacy (with)
　$KA_{2aa}(96)$

form an opinion of
  $WT_0(118)$
form a transition
  $TV_{7h}(162)$
form into files
  $DE_{6f}(151); TO_{3a}(157)$
form into ranks
  $DE_{6f}(151); TO_{3a}(157)$
formula, repeating a
  $TP_{1a}(163)$
formulate
  $ET/TE_{aa}(138)$
formulate an objection
  $KA_{1bcd}(94)$
formulate succinctly
  $TP_{2ad}(164)$
forsake
  $KA_{3a}(98); KA_{2d}(98)$
fortify
  $KA_{2cab}(97)$
fortunes in tea leaves, tell
  $ET/TE_b(138)$
fortunes, tell
  $ET/TE_b(138)$
forward, bring
  $NO_{6o}(113); TU_4(132);$
  $TV_{6b}(160)$
found
  $NO_{0de}(110); AV_3(106)$
foundation, create a
  $EN_{3da}(77)$
foundation, lay a
  $AV_3(106)$
foundation to, build a
  $AV_3(106)$
found sth. on
  $IN_{10}(147)$
four-letter words, use
  $DT_{1e}(128)$

fragmentary, be
  $TP_{2bi}(167)$
fragmented, be
  $TP_{2bi}(167)$
frame
  $TV_{6a}(159); EN_{7cc}(81)$
frank, be
  $NO_{6b}(114)$
fraternize
  $WT_{5c}(121); KA_{2b}(97)$
fraud
  $WS_{ba}(122)$
frighten
  $KA_{1ab}(91)$
frighten
  $KA_{1da}(96)$
frighten away
  $EN_{8b}(82); KA_{4ad}(100)$
frolic
  $IR_{1c}(130)$
frustrate
  $EN_{8ab}(82); EN_{8d}(82);$
  $KA_{1bcb}(93); KA_{1ab}(91)$
fudge
  $IN_{6d}(145)$
fulfill
  $EN_{9j}(84); EN_{9h}(83);$
  $EN_{9d}(83); EN_{9b}(82)$
full, discuss in
  $KA_{4cab}(103)$
full powers, invest with
  $EN_{3b}(76); NO_4(113)$
fun (at), poke
  $IR_{2a}(130); OT_{1d}(128)$
fun of, make
  $IR_{2b}(130); TE_{0ab}(141)$
fun of so., make
  $WP_{0ab}(121); IR_{2a}(130);$
  $IR_{1a}(129)$

fun with, have
  $DT_{1d}(128); IR_{2a}(130)$
fun with sth., have
  $IR_{1c}(130)$
furios, be
  $KA_{0a}(88)$
furious, get
  $EM_{2ca}(71); EM_{2d}(72)$
furnish a validation
  $AV_3(106)$
further develop
  $TV_{7g}(162)$
further (of a secret),
  let the matter go no
  $VE_1(147)$

G
gabble
  $DT_{1bc}(128)$
gaggle
  $DT_{1bc}(128)$
gain
  $KA_{4ac}(100)$
gain information about
  $DI_1(124); EN_{5cb}(78)$
gain one's end
  $KA_{4aa}(99)$
gain support
  $KA_{2caa}(97)$
game of, make
  $IR_{2cb}(131)$
gather
  $DE_{6a}(150); TE_{-1cb}(140)$
gather information
  $EN_{5cb}(78)$
gather together
  $DE_{6a}(150)$
gather wool
  $DE_9(152)$

Germanize
   $TE_{0ae}(141); TE_{0ad}(141)$
general inquiries, make
   $IN_{1ab}(142)$
generalize
   $DE_{6c}(150)$
general, utter maledictions in
   $EM_{2ga}(72)$
gently over sth., let so. down
   $NO_7.(115)$
gestures, make threatening
   $EN_{4c}(77)$
get
   $EN_{9a}(82)$
get an answer
   $IN_{2b}(143)$
get angry
   $EM_{2ca}(71); EM_{2ca}*(72)$
get a word in edgewise, not allow so. to
   $TU_2.(131)$
get bogged down
   $DI_{8a}(126)$
get confused
   TV_6...(160)
get, endeavor to
   $EN_{0ab}(74)$
get entangled in contradiction
   TV_6...(160)
get even with
   $KA_{4bdb}(102)$
get excited
   $EN_{9l}(84)$
get furious
   $EM_{2ca}(71); EM_{2d}(72)$
get in communication with
   $DI_1.(124)$
get in contact with
   $DI_1.(124)$
get in each other's hair
   $KA_{-1c}(87)$
get information
   $IN_{2b}(143)$
get into a discussion with
   $KA_{0h}(90); KA_{0i}(90)$
get into an argument with
   $KA_{0g}(89)$
get into rage
   $EM_{2b}(71)$
get into so.'s favor, try to
   $KA_{-2b}(87)$
get in touch
   $DI_1.(124)$
get in touch with
   $KA_{4caa}(102)$
get under so.'s guard
   $KA_{1cb}(95)$
get involved in a discussion
   $DI_6(125)$
get mixed up
   $TP_{2bd}(166)$
get muddled
   TV_6...(160)
get on well
   $KA_{4cca}(105); KA_{4caa}(102)$
get on well together
   $KA_{-3b}(85)$
get on with
   $TV_{7g}(162); KA_{4cca}(105)$
get on with one another
   $KA_{-3b}(85)$
get one's own back
   $KA_{4bdb}(102)$
get one's own way
   $KA_{0c}(89)$
get round
   $KA_{2aa}(96)$
get sad
   $EM_{2aa}(71)$
get so. set up
   $KA_{-1c}(87)$
get so. wrong
   $KA_{-1c}(87)$
get sth., endeavor to
   $DE_{8b}(151)$
get sth., try to
   $DE_{8b}(151)$
get stuck
   $DI_{8a}(126); TU_6\text{'}_b(133)$
get the meaning
   $IN_{2a}(142)$
get the truth out
   $IN_{2a}.(143)$
get through
   $KA_{4aa}(99); KA_{4ae}(100)$
get tied up in one's own words
   TV_6...(160)
get to the bottom of
   $ET_{-1b}(134)$
get to the bottom of sth.
   $IN_{2a}.(142)$
get to the subject
   $TV_5(159)$
get to the theme
   $TV_5(159)$
get to the topic
   $TV_5(159)$
get vexed
   $EM_{2ca}(71)$
gibber
   $TP_{1e}(163)$

gibberish, talk
  $TP_{1e}(163); TP_{1b}(163)$
gibe
  $IR_{2ca}(130)$
gibe at
  $IR_{1a}(129)$
giftedly, talk
  $DI_{7b}.(126)$
give
  $EN_{3da}(77)$
give a bad name to
  $IR_{2cb}(131)$
give a chance to speak, not to
  $TU_2.(131)$
give a credential to
  $NO_{0b}..(109)$
give a degree
  $NO_{0dc}(109)$
give advice
  $WT_1(118); KA_{-1b}(87)$
give a favorable hearing
  $EN_{0b}(82)$
give a good scolding
  $WP_{0ad}(122)$
give a guarantee
  $IN_{6c}(146)$
give a hand
  $ET_{0dg}(137)$
give a heading
  $TV_2(159)$
give a heading, title
  $VV_{ba}(153)$
give a hint
  $TP_{2bc}(166)$
give a justification
  $ET_{0df}(137)$
give a lecture
  $DT_2(129); TU_4(132)$
give a legend
  $VV_{ba}(153)$

give a memorial address
  $TV_{7j}(162)$
give a monologue
  $TU_4(132); DT_2(129)$
give a name to
  $VV_{ba}(153)$
give a new interpretation
  $TE_{-1cd}(140)$
give a new meaning
  $TE_{-1cd}(140)$
give a nickname
  $VV_{ba}(153)$
give so. a bad name
  $WP_{0ac}(122)$
give so. a lecture
  $WT_{4a}(119)$
give so. a severe scolding
  $EM_{2l}(73)$
give a ready answer
  $KA_{1bcc}(93)$
give a reason why
  $ET_{0df}(137)$
give a receipt
  $VV_{bc}(154)$
give a receipt for
  $WT_{4f\S}(120)$
give a speech
  $DI_{7b}(126); DT_2(129);$
  $TU_4(132)$
give a talk
  $TU_4(132); DT_2(129)$
give a task, mission
  $EN_{3a}(76)$
give a task to
  $NO_{0a}(108)$
give a title to
  $TV_2(159)$
give a thorough scolding
  $WT_{4a}(119)$

give an account
  $TU_4(132); DT_2(129);$
  $IN_{6aa}(144)$
give an account of
  $NO_{6b}(114); ET_{0a}(135)$
give an account of sth.
  TP_{2aa}
give an assignment
  $EN_{3a}(76)$
give an elegy
  TV_{7j}
give an overview
  $TV_3(159)$
give an example
  $AV_4(106)$
give an expert opinion
  $WT_{4f\S}(120)$
give an explanation
  $ET_{0df}(137)$
give an exposition
  $ET_{0de}(137)$
give an inscription
  $VV_{ba}(153)$
give an oath
  $IN_{6c}(146)$
give an opinion on
  $NO_{-1}(108)$
give an orientation
  $IN_{6ad}(145)$
give bail
  $EN_{6d}; NO_{0f}$
give consent to
  $DI_3(129); IN_{8a}(146);$
  $EN_{9i}(84); WT_{4fa}(120)$
give deleterious critique
  $AV_5(106)$
give direction
  $KA_{4cbc}(104)$
give duties to
  $NO_{0a}(108)$

give evidence
  $VE_{1b}(148)$
give evidence (about)
  $IN_{6c}(145)$
give evidence of
  $NO_{6da}(114); VE*_1(148)$
give ground
  $KA_{4bc}(102)$
give in
  $KA_{1bbb}(92); KA_{3b}(98);$
  $KA_{4bac}(101); EN_{9h}(83);$
  $KA_{-1d}(88)$
give information
  $ET_{0b}(135); EN_{9i}(84)$
give information of
  $VE_{1b,c,d}(148)$
give in partly
  $KA_{-1d}(88)$
give judgement
  $DE_{8c}(152); DE_{8e}(152);$
  $NO_{7a}(116)$
give leave of absence
  $NO_{0dd}(110); NO_{0b}(108);$
  $NO_{3bd}(112)$
give lecture
  $ET_{0da}(136)$
give notice
  $NO_{0a\S}(108); NO_{0dd}(110);$
  $NO_{3ba}(111)$
give notice to
  $ET_{0b}(135)$
give one's opinion
  $NO_7(115)$
give one's word of honor
  $NO_1(111); NO_{0f}(110);$
  $EN_{6d}(79)$
give os.
  $WS_{bc}(123)$
give o.s. airs
  $TP_{1c}(163); KA_{4a'}(101)$

give o.s. away
  $VE_{1g}(149)$
give opinion on
  $WT_0(118)$
give orders
  $EN_{6b}(78)$
give permission to
  $NO_{0b}(108)$
give permission to speak
  $TU_2(131); DI/TU(134)$
give praise to
  $WT_{4e}(120)$
give preference to
  $DE_{8c}(152); DE_{8e}(152)$
give protection
  $KA_{2caa}(97)$
give reasons for
  $KA_{1bcd}(94); AV_3(106);$
  $NO_{60}(113); TV*_{7b}(161)$
give rise to
  $EN_{1ae}(75)$
give so. a turn
  $TU_2(131)$
give so. to understand
  $TP_{2bc}(166)$
give testimony to
  $ET_{0a}(135); NO_{6da}(115)$
give the brush-off
  $KA_{4ac}(100); KA_{4ae}(100)$
give the lie to
  $KA_{1bcc}(93)$
give up
  $KA_{1bbb}(92); KA_{3a}(98);$
  $KA_{2d}(98); KA_{3b}(98);$
  $KA_{4bac}(101); NO_{0b'}(109);$
  $TU_{3''}(132); TU_{8a'}(133);$
  $KA_{-1d}(88)$
give vent to
  $KA_{0a}(88); KA_{0g'}(90)$

give vent to (anger)
  $EM_{2aa}(71)$
give voice to
  $ET_{0a}(135)$
give warning
  $NO_{0dd}(110); NO_{3ba}(111)$
give way
  $KA_{1bbb}(92); KA_{3b}(98);$
  $KA_{-1d}(88)$
giving directions
  $EN_{3aa}(76)$
glad, be
  $KA_{4a'}(101)$
gladden
  $EM_{2ca}(71)$
glance back over
  $TV_{6'b}(160)$
glance quickly over, into
  $TE_{-1b}(140)$
gloat
  $KA_{4a'}(101)$
glorify
  $TP_{2bba}(165); WT_{4e}(120);$
  $WT_{5d}(121)$
gloss
  $TE_{0bb}(141); DT_2(129);$
  $TV_{7b}(160)$
gloss over
  $TP_{2bf}(167); TP_{2bba}(165)$
glossolalia
  $ET/TE_b(138)$
go
  $KA_{4bac}(101)$
go ahead (with a topic)
  $TV_{7g}(162)$
go astray
  $NO_2(112); TV_{6'b}(160)$
goad
  $KA_{2cab}(97)$

goad on
$EN_{7cc}(81)$
go back on
$KA_{-1d}(88)$
go into
$KA_{1db}(96)$
go into sth.
$KA_{-3cb}(86)$
good (an assertion), make
$TV^*_{7b}(161)$
good/bad, find
$VV_g(155); WT_0(118)$
goodbye, say
$DI_{10}(127)$
goodbye to, say
$TU_{9a}(133)$
good, consider
$WT_0(118)$
good, deem
$WT_0(118)$
good, find
$IN_{3bb}(143)$
good, make
$NO_{9b}(117); AV_3(106); KA_{4cad}(103)$
good order, enforce
$DI/TU(134)$
good scolding, give a
$WP_{0ad}(122)$
good tactics, employ
$KA_{0d}(89)$
goodwill towards so., show
$WT_{5c}(121)$
good word for, put in a
$KA_{2cb}(98)$
go on the rampage
$KA_{0a}(88)$
go on with
$TV_{7g}(162); TU_{8a}(133)$

gossip
$TP_{1e}(163); TP_{2bj}(167)$
gossip about so.
$WP_{0ac}(122)$
gossiping, pass time in
$DT_{1bc}(128); DI_{10"}(127)$
gossiping, waste time
$DI_{10"}(127)$
go through
$KA_{4ac}(100); KA_{4aa}(99)$
go to confession
$NO_{6a"}(114); VE_0(147)$
go to a court
$NO_4.(113)$
govern
$EN_{6c}(78); NO_{-3}(107)$
go over to
$KA_{4bbb}(102)$
go over
$ET/TE_a.(134)$
go wrong
$NO_2(112)$
grace, say
$TP_{1a}(163)$
grade
$VV_a(153); WT_0(118)$
graduate
$TP_{2bbc}(135)$
grant
$KA_{4cba}(104); KA_{1bbb}(92); KA_{4cbc}(104); EN_{6d}(79); EN_{9b}(82); EN_{9b\S}(83); NO_{0b}(108); NO_{0dd}(110); NO_{0f}(110); EN_{3da}(77)$
grant a thing
$NO_7.(115)$
granted, take for
$KA_{4cbc}(104)$
grant sth. to so.
$WT_3.(110)$

grasp
$ET_{-1b}(134); IN_{2a}(143); DE_1(149)$
grasp at straws
$TP_{2b}(164); TP_{2bb}(167)$
grass grow over, let
$KA_{3c}(99)$
grateful, be
$EM_{2cb}(72)$
gratify
$ET_{gb}(82)$
graze
$TO_{2bc}(156)$
greatest of ease, tell sth. with the
$TO_2(155)$
greatly, desire
$DE_{8a}(151)$
great pretensions, have
$KA_{-2a}(86)$
greet
$TP_{1a}(163)$
grieve
$EM_{2f}(72); EN_{7d}.(81); NO_2.(112)$
grimace
$EM_{2ab}(71)$
grin and bear it
$EM_{2b}.(71)$
grips with, come to
$KA_{1da}(96)$
grips with the matter, not to come to
$TV_{6'b}(160)$
grit one's teeth
$EM_{2b}.(71)$
grope towards
$KA_{2aa}(96)$
ground, give
$KA_{4bc}(102)$

ground, hold one's
  $KA_{1bcb}(93)$
ground sth. on
  $IN_{10}(147)$
group
  $IN_{3ac}(143)$
group, join a
  $WT_{5c}(121)$
grouse
  $KA_{1caa}(94); WT_{4c}(119)$
grow angry
  $EM_{2aa}(71)$
grow dump
  $TU_{6'a}(133)$
growl at
  $EM_{2l}(73)$
grow over, let grass
  $KA_{3c}(99)$
grudge against, bear a
  $NO_{10}(117); WT_{5a}(120)$
grudge, bear a
  $KA_{0e}(89); KA_{4bdb}(102)$
grumble
  $KA_{1caa}(94); KA_{4bab}(101);$
  $EM_{2e}(72); EM_{2k}(73);$
  $WT_{4c}(119); KA_{0e}(89)$
grumble about
  $EM_{2e}(72)$
grumble about, start to
  $EM_{2d}(72)$
guarantee
  $KA_{2cb}(98); IN_{9b}(147);$
  $EN_{6d}(79); NO_{0f}(110);$
  $NO_{1}(111)$
guarantee, give a
  $IN_{6c}(146)$
guard, get in under so.'s
  $KA_{1cb}(95)$

guess
  $DE_{5}(150); IN_{1ab}(142);$
  $EN_{5ca}(78); IN_{2a}(142)$
guesses, make
  $EN_{5ca}(78)$
guide
  $EN_{6c}(78); NO_{-3}(107)$
guide (in)
  $KA_{0g''}(90)$
guide the conversation
  upon a subject
  $TO_{5ac}(158)$
guild, exonerate of a
  $NO_{7c}(116)$
guild, relieve of a
  $NO_{7c}(116)$
guilt, remove a
  $NO_{9bb}(117)$
guilty of a
  misdemeanor, be
  $NO_{2}(112)$
guilty, prove
  $NO_{6c}(114)$

H
hackneyed phrase,
  use a
  $TP_{2be}(167)$
haggle
  $KA_{1db}(96)$
hail
  $EM_{2h}(73); DI_{5}(125)$
hair, get in each other's
  $KA_{-1c}(87)$
hairs, split
  $DT_{3}(129); TP_{2b}(164);$
  $TP_{2bh}(167)$
halfway, meet
  $KA_{4cba}(104)$

hammer at
  $KA_{1ccc}(95)$
hand down
  $EN_{3da}(77)$
hand, give a
  $ET_{0da}(137)$
hand, offer to lend a
  $EN_{2a}(75)$
hand over (to)
  $TU_{9b}(133)$
hand, raise one's
  $TU_{1}(131)$
hands of, wash one's
  $KA_{2d}(98)$
hand, throw in one's
  $KA_{4bac}(101)$
handle
  $TO_{2ba}(155)$
hang back
  $KA_{3b}(98)$
hang out (a shingle)
  $IN_{6b'}(145)$
happen
  $EN_{g'a}(85)$
happens, dream that sth.
  $EN_{0aa}(74)$
happens, wish that sth.
  $EN_{0aa}(74)$
happen to so.,
  wish sth.
  $NO_{8a}(116)$
harass
  $DI_{8a}(126); KA_{4ac}(100)$
hard, press
  $KA_{0d}(89)$
hard, stay
  $KA_{1ccc}(95)$
harden
  $KA_{1dc}(96)$

harmonize
  $KA_{2b}(97); KA_{4ccb}(105)$
harmony, be in
  $KA_{-3b}(85)$
harm, wish to
  $KA_{-3c}(86); KA_{-3ca}(86)$
harshly, address
  $WP_{0ad}(122)$
hatch
  $DT_{1h}(128); VE_{-2}(147)$
hatch (out)
  $DE_{8d}(152)$
hatchet, bury the
  $KA_{4caa}(102)$
hate
  $EM_{2cb}(72); EM_{2cb}*(72)$
I hate you
  $EM_{2cb}*(72)$
hatred toward
  one another, feel
  $KA_{-3c}(86); KA_{-3ca}(86)$
haul over the coals
  $KA_{-1c}(87)$
have a conference
  $WT_2(118); NO_{2ba}(111); NO_{6f}(110); DT_{1a}(127)$
have a duty
  $NO_0·(111)$
have a falling out
  $EM_{2ca}(71)$
have a meeting
  $NO_{6f}(115); NO_{2ba}(111)$
have a mind to
  $DE_{8b}(151)$
have an argument
  $NO_{6o}(113)$
have anything to
  do with, refuse to
  $KA_{-3ca}(86)$

have a person
  $IR_{2b}(130)$
have a public debate
  $DT_{1ba}(127)$
have a public discussion
  $DT_{1ba}(127)$
have a public
  debate/discussion
  $DI_{7a}(126)$
have a pun
  $IR_{2a}(130)$
have a red face
  $EM_{2ab}(71)$
have a say in
  $KA_{0g}·(90)$
have a session
  $NO_{2ba}(111); NO_{0f}(110)$
have done with
  $KA_{4baa}(101)$
have enough of
  $KA_{3a}(98)$
have forgotten
  $IN_{5ab}(144)$
have fun with
  $DT_{1d}(128); IR_{2a}(130)$
have fun with sth.
  $IR_{1c}(130)$
have great pretensions
  $KA_{-2a}(86)$
have had enough
  $EM_{2ca}*(72)$
have his own way, let so.
  $NO_{0b}(108)$
have his say, let so.
  $TU_2(131)$
have in view
  $DE_{8b}(151)$
have it in for
  $KA_{4bdb}(102)$

have, let
  $NO_{0b}·(109)$
have no longer an
  interest in
  $KA_{3c}(99)$
have no pretensions to
  $KA_{1bbb}(92)$
have one's eye on sth.
  $TO_{5a}(158)$
have regard for
  $KA_{4cdb}(105)$
have regard to
  $TO_{2bb}(155)$
have so. seized
  $NO_5·(113)$
have someone
  $IR_{1a}(129)$
have so. announced
  $TU_1(131)$
have sth., want to
  $EN_{0ab}(74)$
have the impudence
  $NO_2·(112)$
have to
  $NO_0·(111)$
have, want to
  $EN_{0ab}(74)$
have words with
  $KA_{1da}(95); KA_{0g}(89)$
have words with so.
  $KA_{-1c}(87); KA_{-3c}(86)$
have the turn
  $TU_3···(132)$
hazily, express os.
  $TP_{2bd}(166)$
head against a
  brick wall, run one's
  $TV_6···(160)$

head, drum sth. into so.'s.
  $EN_{8c}(82); ET_{0da}(136)$
heading, give a
  $TV_2(159)$
heading title, give a
  $VV_{ba}(153)$
head, lose one's
  $KA_{0a}(88)$
hear
  $ET_{-1a}(134); ET^*_{-1a}(134);$
  $NO_{6c}(114)$
hear so.
  $EN_{5cd}(78)$
hear a pupil's lesson
  $EN_{5cd}(78); IN_{1ac}(142)$
hear case
  $IN_{1ac}(142)$
hearing, give a favorable
  $EN_{9b}(82)$
heart, learn by
  $TE_{-1ca}(140); ET_{0da}(136)$
heart, take to
  $NO_{2a}(111); KA_{4cdb}(105);$
  $EN_{9g}(83); EN_{9k}(84);$
  $EN_{9c}(83); WG_{1b}(124)$
heavily, breathe
  $EM_{2b'}(71)$
heckle
  $EM_{2l}(73); TU_6(132);$
  $WP_{0ab}(121)$
hector
  $WP_{0ad}(122)$
hedge
  $TP_{2bbc}(165); TO_{5c}(158)$
heed
  $KA_{4cdb}(105); EN_{9c}(83);$
  $EN_{9g}(83); EN_{9k}(84);$
  $NO_{2a}(111); DE_2(149)$
heed to, not pay
  $NO_{2''}(112)$

heed to, pay
  $EN_{9g}(83); WG_{1b}(124)$
heed to, pay no
  $EN_{9c}(83); WG_{1a}(123)$
help
  $KA_{2cab}(97); ET_{0dg}(137)$
help so.
  $EN_{7cb}(81)$
help on
  $ET_{0dg}(137)$
help out
  $KA_{2cab}(97)$
help, come to the ... of
  $KA_{2cb}(98)$
herorize
  $TP_{2bba}(165)$
hesitate
  $EM_{2aa}(71); EM_{2b'}(71);$
  $TU_{6''b}(133); DE_3(149)$
het up, get so.
  $KA_{-1c}(88)$
hide
  $KA_{1bba}(92); VE_1(147);$
  $TP_{2bg}(167); TP_{2bc}(166)$
hide one's light under
  a bushel
  $WS_{aa}(122)$
high esteem, hold so. in
  $WT_{5d}(121)$
highlight
  $TO_{5a}(158)$
highly, esteem
  $WT_0(118)$
highly, value
  $WT_0(118); WT_{3'}(119)$
highly, value sth.
  $NO_{7'}(115)$
high terms of so.,
  speak in very
  $WT_{4e}(120)$

hinder
  $KA_{1bcb}(93); EN_{8ab}(82)$
hint
  $KA_{2cab}(97)$
hint at
  $EN_{1ac}(74); TO_{2bc}(156)$
hint, give a
  $TP_{2bc}(166)$
hire
  $NO_{0da}(109)$
hiss at
  $WT_{4c}(119)$
hissing, condemn by
  $EM_{2h}(73)$
hiss off the stage
  $EM_{2h}(73)$
hit it off well
  $KA_{4caa}(103); KA_{-3b}(85)$
hit it off (with)
  $KA_{4cca}(105)$
hit on the sore spot
  $TO_{2g}(157)$
hoax
  $IR_{1a}(129); IR_{2b}(130)$
hold
  $KA_{1bcc}(93)$
hold against
  $KA_{1bcd}(94)$
hold a meeting
  $WT_2(118); NO_{2ba}(111);$
  $NO_{6f}(115)$
hold so. in high esteem
  $WT_{5d}(121)$
hold as an opinion
  $WT_0(118)$
hold a view
  $KA_{1bca}(92)$
hold back
  $EM_{2b'}(71); KA_{3b}(99)$

hold off
  $KA_{1bcb}(93)$
hold one's ground
  $KA_{1bcb}(93)$
hold one's tongue
  $TU_1.(131)$
hold (opinion)
  $KA_{1ccb}(95)$
hold out a prospect of sth. to so.
  $NO_{0f}(110); EN_{6d}(79)$
hold, put on
  $EN_{3ab}(76)$
hold to ridicule
  $IR_{2b}(130)$
hold up
  $KA_{1bcb}(93); KA_{1bba}(92)$
holes in, find
  $WT_{4c}(119)$
holes (in), pick
  $TV_{7b}(160); TE_{0bb}(141)$
homage, pay
  $WT_{5d}(121)$
honor
  $WT_{5d}(121)$
honor, give one's word of
  $NO_1(111); NO_{0f}(110); EN_{6d}(79)$
hoodwink
  $TP_{2bc}(166)$
hop, catch on the
  $KA_{0f}(89); KA_{0h}(90); KA_{0i}(90)$
hopes, raise
  $KA_{2cab}(97)$
hope for
  $DE_{8a}(151); EN_{0ba}(74)$
horn in
  $TU_6(132)$

horns, draw in one's
  $KA_{4bac}(101)$
horse, flog a dead
  $TP_{2b}(164)$
horse, wear out an old
  $TP_{2be}(167)$
hostile to, be
  $KA_{-3c}(86); KA_{-3ca}(86)$
howl down
  $DI_{8b}(126)$
how to do, show
  $ET_{0b}(135)$
huckster
  $DT_{1ba}(127)$
humble
  $WP_{0ab}(121)$
humiliate
  $KA_{4ac}(100); WP_{0ab}(121)$
humiliate os.
  $NO_{8a}.(117); WS_{ab}(122)$
humor
  $KA_{4cba}(104)$
(hurt so.'s feelings)
  $NO_2.(112)$
hush up
  $TP_{2bc}(166); EN_{7ca}(80)$
hypothesize
  $IN_{1ab}(142); DE_5(150)$

I
I admire you
  $EM_{2cb}*(72)$
I am afraid
  $EM_{2cb}*(72)$
I am angry
  $EM_{2cb}*(72)$
I am disappointed
  $EM_{2cb}*(72)$
I am getting angry
  $EM_{2ca}*(72)$

I am glad
  $EM_{2cb}*(72)$
I am pissed off
  $EM_{2ca}*(72)$
I am sad
  $EM_{2cb}*(72)$
I am sorry
  $EM_{2cb}*(72)$
idealize
  $TP_{2bba}(165)$
ideas, promulgate
  $TE_{-2a}(139)$
ideas, readjust one's
  $ET_{1d}(137)$
ideas, reconcile conflicting
  $NO_{7a}(116)$
identify
  $DE_{6b}(150); IN_{3ba}(143); VV_a(153)$
identify with
  $VV_d(154)$
identity, recognize
  $IN_{3ba}(143)$
idly, talk
  $ET/TE_b(138)$
idolize
  $WT_{5d}(121)$
idyllize
  $TP_{2bba}(165)$
ignorance, treat with
  $TP_{2bf}(167)$
ignore
  $EN_{9c}(83); EN_{9d}(83); EN_{9g}(83); EN_{9j}(84); KA_{4aa}(99); TP_{2bf}(167); TU_2.(131); WG_{1a}(123); WP_{0aa}(121)$
ignore so.
  $DI/TU(134)$

Lexicon Section II

ignore the question
  $EN_{9i}(84)$
I hate you
  $EM_{2cb*}(72)$
I have had enough
  $EM_{2ca*}(72)$
ill-feeling towards one
  another, be
  $KA_{-3c}(86); KA_{-3ca}(86)$
ill of so., speak
  $WP_{0ac}(122)$
ill of os., speak
  $WS_{ab}(122)$
ill repute, put in
  $IR_{2cb}(131)$
ill-will to so., bear
  $KA_{-3c}(85)$
ill-will towards, bear
  $KA_{1caa}(94)$
illuminate
  $AV_2(106); ET_{0c}(136);$
  $ET_{0dd}(132); TP_{2ac}(164)$
illumine
  $AV_2(106); ET_{0c}(136);$
  $ET_{0dd}(137); TP_{2ac}(164)$
illustrate
  $TP_{2ac}(164)$
illustrative of, be
  $TP_{2ac}(164)$
I love you
  $EM_{2cb*}(72)$
imagine
  $DE_{8d}(152)$
imbecile of, make an
  $IR_{1a}(129)$
imbecile, play the
  $IR_{2a}(130)$
imitate
  $ET_{1b}(137); ET_{1c}(137)$

impart information
  $IN_{6ab}(145)$
impart knowledge
  $ET_{0da}(136)$
impart permission
  to speak
  $TU_2(131)$
impeach
  $NO_{8a}(116)$
imperiously, address
  $EM_{2l}(73)$
I'm pissed off
  $EM_{2ca*}(72)$
implacable, be
  $KA_{-3c}(86)$
implore
  $EM_{2gb}(72); EM_{2i}(73);$
  $EN_{2b}(75); NO_{9ab}(117)$
imply
  $TO_{2d}(156); DE_5(150)$
impolite, be
  $NO_2.(112)$
importance to, be of
  $KA_{4cca}(105)$
importance to so., be of
  $KA_{-3b}(85)$
importance,
  exaggerate the
  $KA_{-1c}(88)$
importune
  $EN_{2b}(75); KA_{0d}(89)$
impose (beliefs)
  $ET_{0da}(136)$
impose a check on
  $KA_{1bca}(92)$
impose a fine
  $NO_7(115)$
impose sanctions
  $NO_{8a}(116)$

(imprecate)
  $EM_{2gb}(72)$
impress
  $TE_{-1ca}(140)$
impress sth. on so.
  $EN_{8c}(82)$
impress sth. upon so.
  $ET_{0da}(136)$
impress sth. upon
  one's memory
  $TE_{-1ca}(140)$
imprint
  $TE_{-1ca}(140)$
imprison
  $NO_5.(113)$
improve
  $ET/TE_a.(139); TV_{7c}(161)$
improvise
  $ET/TE_b(138); TO_2(155)$
impudence, have the
  $NO_2.(112)$
impudent, be
  $KA_{0g}(89)$
impugn
  $IN_{3bb}(144); NO_{6e}(115)$
impute
  $NO_{6a}(114); DE_5(150)$
impute sth. to so.
  $WP_{0ac}(122)$
impute to
  $WT_1(118)$
inaugurate
  $NO_{0da}(109)$
incite
  $EN_{1ae}(75); EN_{7cb}(81);$
  $EN_{7cc}(81); KA_{-1c}(87);$
  $KA_{2cab}(97)$
include
  $KA_{4cdb}(105); TO_{2d}(156)$

incorporate
  $TO_{2d}(156); VV_a(153)$
inculcate
  $EN_{8c}(82)$
inculpate (in)
  $NO_4(113)$
indecent, talk
  $DT_{1e}(128)$
indefinitely, express os.
  $TP_{2bd}(166)$
index
  $IN_{3ac}(143); VV_{ba}(153)$
index of, make a card
  $VV_a(153)$
inidicate
  $DT_2(129); EN_{1ac}(74); ET_{0db}(136); IN_{6aa}(144); TO_{2bb}(155); TU_4(132); VV_{ba}(153)$
indict
  $NO_{6a}(114)$
indifference, treat so. with
  $WP_{0aa}(121)$
indifference, treat with
  $TP_{2bf}(167)$
indirectly, convey information
  $IN_{2a*}(142)$
indistinctly, express os.
  $TP_{2bd}(166)$
indoctrinate
  $ET_{0da}(136)$
induce
  $DE_{6d}(150); EN_{1ae}(75); EN_{7af}(80)$
induce so. to do sth.
  $NO_{-3}(107)$

indulge in reveries, francis
  $DE_9(152); ET/TE_b(138)$
indulge in words
  $TP_{2b}(164)$
infatuate
  $EN_{7af}(80)$
infer
  $DE_{6d}(150); IN_{2a}(142); TE_{-1cb}(140)$
inferior to, be
  $KA_{-1d}(88)$
infiltrate
  $KA_{0cc}(89)$
inflate
  $TP_{2bba}(165)$
inflict a penalty
  $NO_{8a}(116)$
inflict a punishment
  $NO_{8a}(116)$
inflict disciplinary punishment on
  $WT_{4a}(119)$
influence
  $EN_{7ag}(80)$
influence by suggestion
  $EN_{7af}(80)$
inform
  $DT_2(129); EN_{6a}(78); ET_{0b}(135); IN_{6aa}(144); IN_{6b}(145); TU_4(132)$
inform about
  $ET_{0a}(135)$
inform against
  $NO_4(113); VE_1(148); VE_{1c}(148)$
inform against/on
  $VE_{1a}(148)$
inform regularly
  $IN_{6ad}(145)$

inform so.
  $TP_{2aa}(164)$
information about, gain
  $DI_1(124); EN_{5cb}(78)$
information, ask for
  $EN_{5cb}(78)$
information, convey (indirectly)
  $IN_{2a*}(142)$
information, exchange
  $ET_{0a}(135)$
information, gather
  $EN_{5cb}(78)$
information, get
  $IN_{2b}(143)$
information give
  $ET_{0b}(135); EN_{9i}(84)$
information, impart
  $IN_{6ab}(145)$
information of, give
  $VE_{1b,c,d}(148)$
information to, put
  $IN_{2a*}(142)$
information, trade
  $ET_{0b}(135)$
infringe (laws)
  $NO_2(112)$
ingratiate os.
  $KA_{2aa}(96)$
ingratiate os. with so.
  $EN_{7ad}(80); WS_{bbb}(123)$
inhibit
  $DI_{8b}(126)$
initiate
  $EN_{1ae}(75); TV_5(159); DI_6(125)$
initiate so. into a field, society
  $VE_0(147)$

(injure)
NO_2.(112)
innovate
NO_{3bc}(112)
inquire
EN_{5cb}(78)
inquire about, after
IN_{1ab}(142)
inquire after
IN_{1aa}(142)
inquire (into)
EN_{5cc}(78)
inquiries about, make
DI_1.(124)
inquiries, make
EN_{5cb}(78); $VE_{1"a}$(148)
inquiry, ascertain by
EN_{5cd}(78)
inquiry, institute an
EN_{5cd}(78); NO_{6c}(114)
inscription, give an
VV_{ba}(153)
inscription, make an
VV_{ba}(153)
insert
TO_{2d}(156); $TV_{6'b}$(160)
insert an advertisement
ET_{0a}(135); IN_{6b}(145)
insert in brackets
TO_{5ad}(158)
insinuate
IN_{2a}*(142); DE_5(150)
insinuate os. into
KA_{2aa}(96); WS_{bbb}(123)
insist
EN_{8aa}(81); KA_{-2a}(86)
insistently, talk
KA_{-1c}(87)
insist on/upon
TV_{7d}(161)

insist on
EN_{5b}(77); KA_{1cca}(95); KA_{1ccc}(95); KA_{4cbc}(104)
inspect
TE_{-1b}(140)
inspire
EN_{7ag}(80)
inspire with courage
EN_{7cb}(81)
inspire with fear
KA_{1ab}(91)
instead of better, make worse
ET/TE_a.(139)
instigate
EN_{7cc}(81); KA_{-1c}(88)
institute
NO_{-4g}(107)
institute an inquiry
EN_{5cd}(78); NO_{6c}(114)
institute legal proceedings against so.
NO_4.(113)
instruct
DT_2(129); EN_{3c}(76); EN_{6c}(78); IN_{6ab}(145); NO_{-3}(107)
instruct so.
ET_{0da}(136)
insult
KA_{0g}(89); KA_{0h}(90); KA_{0i}(90); NO_2(112); NO_2.(112); WP_{0ab}(121)
intend
DE_{8b}(151); EN_{0ab}(74)
intentionally, stop
$TU_{6'a}$(133)
intercede
KA_{4cac}(103); NO_{9ab}(117)

intercede for/on so.'s behalf
KA_{2cb}(98)
intercept
TP_{2bg}(167)
intercept (for letters, boadcasting)
$VE_{1"a}$(148)
interdict
NO_{0dd}(110); NO_{8a}(116)
interest so.
EN_{7ag}(80)
interes in, be no longer
KA_{3c}(99)
interested in, have no longer an
KA_{3c}(99)
interest in, lose
KA_{3c}(99)
interest, show
DI_2(124)
interfere
DI_{8a}(126); DI_{8c}(126); KA_{-1b}(87); KA_{4cac}(103); $TV_{6'a}$(160)
interject
$TV_{6'a}$(160)
interlace
TO_4(157)
interlard (with oaths)
TO_{3a}(157)
interpose
DI_{8c}(126); KA_{4cac}(103); TU_6(133); TU_3.(131); $TV_{6'a}$(160)
interpret
TE_{0d}(141); TE_{-1cb}(140)
interpretation, give a new
TE_{-1cd}(140)

interrogate
$EN_{5cc}(78); IN_{1ab}(142); NO_{6c}(114)$
interrupt
$DI_{8a}(126); DI_{8c}(126); TU_6(133); TV_{6'a}(160)$
interrupt so.
$TU_{3'}(132)$
intervene
$DI_{8c}(126); KA_{-1b}(87); KA_{4cac}(103); TU_{3'}(132); TU_6(133); TV_{6'a}(160)$
interview
$EN_{5cd}(78)$
interweave
$TO_{3a}(157); TO_4(157)$
intimacy with, form an
$KA_{2aa}(96)$
intimate
$TO_{2bc}(156)$
intimate to so.
$TP_{2bc}(166)$
intimidate
$EN_{8d}(82); KA_{1ab}(91)$
intricate, make
$TP_{2bd}(166)$
intrigue
$KA_{-1c}(87); KA_{0d}(89); WP_{0ac}(122)$
introduce
$DI_6(125); TV_4(159)$
introduce so. to sth.
$EN_{6c}(78)$
introduce so. to a field
$ET_{0da}(136)$
introduce (the speaker)
$DI/TU_{Anhang}(134)$
intrude os. upon so.
$EN_{7ae}(80)$

intrude upon
$EN_{8aa}(81)$
intrust sth. to so.
$EN_{3da}(77)$
invalidate
$DI_{3''}(125); KA_{1bca}(92); KA_{1bcb}(93); KA_{1bcc}(93); KA_{4ae}(100); NO_{3bb}(112)$
invalidate a contract
$IN_{9a}(146)$
inveigle
$KA_{0g''}(90)$
invent
$DE_{6f}(151); DE_{8d}(152)$
invent a name
$IN_{-1}(143)$
inventory
$VV_a(153)$
inventory of, take an
$VV_a(153)$
invert
$TO_{3b}(157)$
invest with
$NO_{0da}(109)$
invest with full powers
$EN_{3b}(76); NO_{-4}(107)$
investigate
$IN_{1aa}(142)$
investigate so.
$EN_{5cd}(78)$
invitation, accept
$DI_{5a}(125)$
invitation, follow
$DI_{5a}(125)$
invite
$DI_{2'a}(124); EN_{2b}(75); EN_{5a}(77)$
involve (in)
$KA_{0g''}(90)$

involve
$KA_{2aa}(96)$
involved in a discussion, get
$DI_6(125)$
involved, make
$TP_{2bd}(166)$
iron out
$KA_{4cad}(103)$
irony, treat with
$IR_{2ca}(130)$
irreconcilable, be
$KA_{-3c}(86)$
irritate
$EN_{8d}(82); WP_{0ab}(121)$
issue
$NO_{-4§}(107)$
issue a certificate
$IN_{9b}(147); WT_{4f§}(120)$
issue regulations
$NO_{0a}(108); NO_{-4§}(107)$
issue, avoid the
$KA_{4aa}(99)$
iterate
$ET_{0da}(136); KA_{1cca}(95)$
it's my turn
$TU_{2''}$
it up, make
$KA_{4caa}(103)$
I've had enough
$EM_{2ca*}(72)$

J

jabber
$TP_{2bj}(167); TP_{1e}(163)$
jam
$DI_{8a}(126)$
jeer
$IR_{2ca}(130)$

jeer at
$IR_{1b}(130); IR_{1a}(129);$
$IR_{2b}(130); IR_{2cb}(131);$
$WP_{0ab}(121); KA_{0g}(89);$
$KA_{1aa}(91)$
jest
$IR_{2a}(130); IR_{1c}(130);$
$DT_{1d}(128)$
jibe (at)
$IR_{2cb}(131)$
jibe at
$IR_{1a}(129)$
jog
$KA_{0g}(89)$
join
$DI_{5a}(125); DE_{6f}(151);$
$NO_{6f}(115); NO_{2ba}(111);$
$TO_{2d}(156); TO_4(157);$
$TV_{7a}(160)$
join a group
$WT_{5c}(121)$
join (a party)
$NO_{0f}(110); EN_{6d}(79)$
join up with
$KA_{2aa}(96)$
joke
$IR_{2a}(130); IR_{1c}(130);$
$DT_{1d}(128)$
joke of, make a
$IR_{2a}(130); DT_{1d}(128)$
jokes, make smutty
$DT_{1e}(128)$
jokes, play practical
$IR_{2a}(130); IR_{1c}(130)$
joke with
$DI_{7a}(125)$
jolt
$KA_{0g}(89)$

joy, shout for/with
$EM_{2b}(71); EM_{2e}(72)$
joyful, be
$KA_{4a}(101)$
jubilant over, be
$EM_{2h}(73); WT_{5b}(120)$
judge
$DE_{8e}(152); DE_{8c}(152);$
$NO_{-1}(108); NO_7(115);$
$WT_0(118)$
judgement, give
$DE_{8c}(152); DE_{8e}(152);$
$NO_{7a}(116)$
judgement on, pass
$NO_{-1}(108)$
judgement on,
  pass expert
$WT_{4f\S}(120); WT_0(118)$
judgement on so., pass
$NO_7(115)$
judgement, pronounce a
$NO_7(115)$
judgement, quash a
$NO_{9ba}(117); NO_{3bb}(112)$
judgement, resist the
$NO_{9aa}(117)$
judgement, retract a
$NO_{9ba}(117)$
judgement, revise a
$NO_{3bb}(112)$
judge so.'s merits
$WT_3.(119)$
jumble up
$TP_{2bd}(166)$
jump from one thing to
  other
$TV_{6'b}(160)$
jump from side to side
$KA_{1cb}(96)$

jump over
$TO_{2c}(156)$
justification, give a
$ET_{0df}(137)$
justify
$NO_{6e}(115)$
justify (os.)
$NO_{6b}(114)$
juxtapose
$TO_4(157); DE_{6g}(151)$

K
keep
$KA_{4cdb}(105)$
keep a diary
$ET/TE_{ad}(138)$
keep an escape route
  open
$KA_{1cb}(95)$
keep apart
$VV_e(154); DE_{6e}(151)$
keep (a promise)
$NO_{2a}(111)$
keep a record of
$ET/TE_{ab}(138)$
keep a secret
$VE_1.(147)$
keep a secret, request to
$VE_{-1}(147)$
keep back from so.
$TP_{2bg}(167)$
keep on about
$KA_{0e}(89)$
keep on at
$KA_{1ccc}(95)$
keep one's distance from
$KA_{-1d}(88)$
keep one's mouth shut
$VE_1.(147)$

keep (on) quarreling with
   $KA_{1aa}(91)$
keep on with
   $TU_{8a}(133); TV_{7g}(162)$
keep open
   $TV_{8b}; KA_{4cbc}$
keep out of
   $KA_{1bba}; KA_{1cb}$
keep secrets
   $VE_1\text{'}; TP_{2bg}$;
   KA_{1bba}
keep short
   $TU_5\text{'}$
keep sth. secret
   $VE_1\text{'}$
keep the minutes
   $ET/TE_{ab}(138)$
keep up a coorespondence
   $DI_{7a}(126); DT_{1a}(127)$
keep your eyes and ears open
   $VE_1\text{"}_a(148)$
kibosh out, put the
   $KA_{1aa}(91)$
kick out
   $KA_{4ad}(100)$
kindle
   $KA_{-1c}(88)$
kindly disposed towards, be
   $KA_{-3b}(85)$
kindly towards, feel
   $KA_{4cca}(105)$
king, depose a
   $NO_{0dd}(110)$
knees, bring so. to his
   $KA_{4ac}(100)$
knight
   $NO_{0da}(109)$

knit together
   $TO_4(157)$
knock down
   $KA_{4ac}(100)$
know each other, (do) not
   $KA_{-3a}(85)$
knowledge, impart
   $ET_{0da}(136)$
know, let so.
   $KA_{0c}(89)$
known, make
   $VE_{1a}(148); NO_{0a}\S(108)$;
   $IN_{ab}(145); ET_{0c}(136)$;
   $ET_{0b}(135); IN_{6b}\text{'}(145)$
known, not to be
   $KA_{-3a}(85)$
known, not to be previously
   $KA_{-3a}(85)$
known, put in the
   $VE_0(147)$

L
label
   $VV_{ba}(153); IN_{3c}(144)$
label so.
   $NO_{10}(117); WT_{5a}(120)$
label so. sth. as sth.
   $VV_f(154)$
lady, propose to a
   $EN_{2b}\S(75)$
lament
   $EM_{2f}(72); EM_{2i}(73)$
lark
   $IR_{1c}(130)$
lark about
   $IR_{1b}(130); IR_{2a}(130)$
laud
   $TE_{0bb}(141); WT_{4e}(120)$

laugh
   $IR_{1c}(130)$
laugh (at)
   $IR_{2b}(130); IR_{2ca}(130)$;
   $IR_{2cb}(131); IR_{1a}(129)$;
   $IR_{2a}(130)$
laugh at so.
   $WP_{0ab}(121)$
laughing, burst out
   $EM_{2b}(71)$
laugh to scorn
   $IR_{2cb}(131)$
lavish (words)
   $TP_{2ae}(164)$
law, break the
   $NO_2(112)$
law, change the
   $NO_{3bc}(112)$
law into effect, put a
   $NO_{-4}\S(107)$
law, make a
   $NO_{-4}\S(107)$
law, promulgate a
   $NO_{-4}\S(107); NO_{0a}\S(108)$
laws, infringe
   $NO_2(112)$
lawsuit, carry on a
   $NO_4\text{'}(113)$
law, supersede (replace) a
   $NO_{3bb}(112)$
law, transgress against
   $NO_2(112)$
lay a foundation
   $AV_3(106)$
lay aside
   $WT_0(118); IN_{3ba}(143)$;
   $DE_{6b}(150)$
layaway, put on
   $EN_{3ab}(76)$

lay bare
 $ET_{0c}(136)$
lay claim to
 $KA_{-2a}(86); NO_{-2}(108)$
lay down
 $IN_{-1}(143)$
lay out
 $TO_{2a}(155)$
lay stress on
 $TO_{5ab}(158)$
lead
 $NO_{-3}(107); EN_{6c}(78)$
lead a discussion
 $DI/TU(134)$
lead so. like a child
 $NO_{-3}(107)$
lead astray
 $EN_{7af}(80)$
lead (from one argument to another)
 $DI/TU(134); TV_{7h}(162)$
lead over
 $TV_{7h}(162)$
league
 $KA_{4cbd}(104)$
learn
 $TE_{-1cb}(140); ET_{1b}(137); ET_{0da}(136)$
learn afresh
 $ET_{1d}(137)$
learn anew
 $ET_{1d}(137)$
learn by heart
 $TE_{-1ca}(140); ET_{0da}(136)$
learn by eavesdropping
 $VE_{1"a}(148)$
learning, cram last minute
 $ET_{0da}(136)$
learn in: I'll learn you
 $ET_{0da}(136)$

learn new tricks
 $ET_{1d}(137)$
leave
 $NO_{0db}(109); KA_{4bac}(101);$
 $KA_{3c}(99); KA_{2d}(98);$
 $EN_{3da}(77)$
leave alone
 $KA_{-1d}(88); TO_{2c}(156);$
 $KA_{3c}(99); KA_{3b}(99)$
leave a thing undecided
 $NO_{60}(113)$
leave at that
 $KA_{3c}(99); KA_{3b}(98)$
leave (everything still) undecided
 $KA_{1cb}(95)$
leave in peace
 $KA_{3c}(99)$
leave in the lurch
 $KA_{2d}(98)$
leave it at that
 $KA_{-1d}(88)$
leave of absence, give
 $NO_{0dd}(110); NO_{0b}(108);$
 $NO_{3bd}(112)$
leave off
 $TU_{9a}(133); TU_{6'a}(133);$
 $DI_{10}(127); KA_{3a}(98)$
leave off a subject (topic)
 $DI/TU(134)$
leave of, take
 $DI_{10}(127); TU_{9a}(133)$
leave open
 $TV_{8b}(163)$
leave out
 $TO_{2c}(156); KA_{1bba}(92)$
leave out (superfluous things)
 $TP_{2ad}(164)$
leave to
 $NO_{0b'}(109)$

leave undecided
 $TV_{8b}(163)$
leave unsettled
 $KA_{1cb}(95)$
lecture
 $TU_4(132); ET_{0da}(136);$
 $DT_2(129)$
lecture, give
 $ET_{0da}(136)$
lecture, give a
 $DT_2(129); TU_4(132)$
lecture, give so. a
 $WT_{4a}(119)$
lecture (on)
 $DI_{7b}(126)$
legalize
 $NO_{-4§}(107)$
legal proceedings against so., institute
 $NO_4.(113)$
legal proceedings against, take
 $NO_4.(113)$
legend, give a
 $VV_{ba}(153)$
legislate
 $NO_{-4§}(107)$
leg, pull so.'s
 $IR_{1a}(129)$
lend a hand, offer to
 $EN_{2a}(75)$
lengthen
 $ET/TE_a.(139)$
leniency, beg for
 $NO_{9ab}(117)$
lenient view of sth., take a
 $WT_3.(119); NO_7.(115)$
lessen
 $TO_{5c}(158)$

lesson, hear a pupil's
 $EN_{5cd}(78); IN_{1ac}(142)$
let alone
 $TO_{2c}(156); KA_{3c}(99)$
let so. down gently
 over a thing
 $NO_7.(115)$
let so. have his own way
 $NO_{0b}(108)$
let bygones be bygones
 $KA_{4caa}(103)$
let drop
 $KA_{3c}(99)$
let go
 $KA_{-1d}(88)$
let grass grow over
 $KA_{3c}(99)$
let have
 $NO_{0b}.(109)$
let loose
 $KA_{0a}(88)$
let somebody continue
 $TU_6".(133)$
let somebody finish
 $TU_6".(133)$
let so. have his say
 $TU_2(131)$
let so. know
 $KA_{0c}(89)$
let so. take up a position
 $KA_{1cab}(94)$
let sth. out on so.
 $KA_{0a}(88)$
let sth. sink into
 oblivion
 $KA_{4caa}(103)$
letters in prisoner's
 cell, smuggle
 $VE_0(147)$

letters, intercept for
 $VE_1"_a(148)$
let the cat out of the
 bag
 $VE_{1g}(149)$
let the matter go no
 further (of a secret)
 $VE_1.(147)$
let out (secret)
 $VE_1(148)$
lewd, talk
 $DT_{1e}(128)$
lexicalize
 $VV_a(153)$
liberate
 $NO_{3bd}(112)$
liberty, take the
 $KA_{-2b}(87)$
license
 $EN_{3b}(76); NO_{-4}(107)$
lid off of, blow the
 $VE_1(148)$
lie to, give the
 $KA_{1bcc}(92)$
light again, bring
 $TV_{7i}(162)$
light again, come to
 $TV_{7i}(162)$
light, bring to
 $IN_{6b}.(145)$
lightly, touch
 $TO_{2bc}(156)$
light, put in a favorable
 $TP_{2bba}(165)$
light, see sth. in a
 different
 $KA_{-1b}(87)$
light under a bushel,
 hide one's
 $WS_{aa}(122)$

like
 $EN_{0aa}(74); EN_{0ab}(74)$
like a child, lead so.
 $NO_{-3}(107)$
limelight, put in
 $TO_{5a}(158)$
limit
 $TO_{2a}(155); NO_{0c}(109)$
limit by provisos
 $TP_{2bbc}(165)$
limit, set a
 $NO_{0g}(111)$
limit speaking time
 $DI/TU(134)$
link
 $DE_{6f}(151)$
link together
 $TO_4(157)$
lips, escape one's
 $VE_{1g}(148)$
list
 $VV_a(153)$
listen in on
 (a conversation)
 $VE_1"_a(148)$
list, define a
 $IN_{-1}(143)$
list, enter in a
 $VV_a(153)$
listen to, not
 $EN_{9k}(84)$
list, make up a
 $DE_{6f}(151); IN_{-1}(143)$
list of, make a
 $VV_a(153)$
list of speakers,
 put on the
 $DI/TU(134)$
list, set up a
 $IN_{-1}(143)$

list, specify a
  $VV_a(153)$
litigate
  $NO_4.(113)$
live up to
  $NO_{2a}(111)$
locate
  $VV_a(153)$
lock out (workmen)
  $NO_{8a}(116)$
lock out
  $NO_{0dd}(110)$
lodge a protest
  $KA_{0g}.(90)$
loggerheads, be at
  $KA_{-1c}(87)$
loggerheads, they are at
  $KA_{-1c}(87)$
longer an interest in, have no
  $KA_{3c}(99)$
longer interested in, be no
  $KA_{3c}(99)$
longer, participate no
  $KA_{2d}(98)$
longer than one wanted, talk
  $DI_{10}".(127)$
long for
  $EN_{0ba}(74); DE_{8a}(151)$
look back
  $TV_{7j}(162)$
look behind
  $TV_{7j}(162)$
look down upon
  $WP_{0aa}(121)$
look for
  $DE_{8a}(151)$
look into
  $IN_{1aa}(142)$

look over
  $ET/TE_a.(139)$
look through
  $VV_c(154); TE_{-1b}(140); ET/TE_a.(139)$
look up
  $IN_{1aa}(142)$
loose, cut os.
  $KA_{2d}(98)$
loose, let
  $KA_{0a}(88)$
loosen
  $KA_{3b}(99)$
lose his status, make so.
  $WT_{5a}(120); NO_{10}(117)$
lose one's head
  $KA_{0a}(88)$
lose one's temper
  $KA_{0g}(89); KA_{0i}(90); KA_{0h}(90); KA_{0g}(89)$
lose one's way
  $TV_{6'b}(160)$
lose sight of
  $KA_{3c}(99)$
lose the thread
  $TV_6"'.(160)$
lose the track
  $TV_6"'.(160)$
lose track of
  $KA_{3c}(99)$
lose interest in
  $KA_{3c}(99)$
lost in thoughts, be
  $DE_4(149)$
lot with, throw in one's
  $KA_{2b}(97)$
loud, be
  $WS_{bc}(123)$
loudly, cheer
  $WT_{5b}; EM_{2h}$

loudly, talk
  $DT_{1g}(128)$
love sth.
  $EN_{0aa}(74)$
love, (be in)
  $EM_{2cb}(72); EM_{2cb}*(72)$
low, bring
  $WP_{0ab}(121)$
lower
  $KA_{1aa}(91)$
lower one's voice
  $EM_{2aa}(71)$
lull (to sleep)
  $EN_{7ca}(80)$
lump together
  $TP_{2ad}(164)$
lurch, leave in the
  $KA_{2d}(98)$
lure
  $EN_{7af}(80)$
lure (in)
  $KA_{0g}".(90)$
lurk for so.
  $EN_{0bb}(74)$
luxuriate in words
  $TP_{2b}(165)$

M

maintain
  $KA_{2cb}(98); ET_{0a}(134); KA_{0j}(90); KA_{1bca}(93); KA_{1cca}(95)$
maintain (a claim), still
  $TV_{7a}(160)$
majority, carry (a motion) with a
  $TV_9(163)$
make a bagatelle out of sth.
  TP_{2bbb}

make a bargain
  $KA_{1db}(96)$
make a bibliography
  $VV_a(153)$
make a brief remark
  $TU_5(132)$
make a card index of
  $VV_a(153)$
make a claim
  $NO_{-2}(108)$
make a clean sweep of
  $KA_{4caa}(103)$
make a compact
  $KA_{4cbd}(104)$
make a comparison
  $IN_{3ba}(143); TO_{5e}(158)$
make a confession
  $NO_{6a}(114)$
make a contract
  $KA_{4cbd}(104)$
make a copy
  $ET_{1c}(137)$
make acquainted with
  $TP_{2aa}(164); ET_{0a}(135)$
make acrid
  $KA_{-1c}(87)$
make actual
  $TV_{7c}(161)$
make a deal
  $KA_{1db}(96)$
make a decision
  $NO_{7a}(116); KA_{4cac}(103)$
make a deposition
  $IN_{6c}(146)$
make a digest
  $TV_{7f}(161)$
make a distinction
  $DE_{6e}(151)$
make a donation
  $EN_{3da}(77)$
make a fool of
  $KA_{0g}(89); IR_{2cb}(131);$
  $IR_{2ca}(130); IR_{1a}(129)$
make a fool of os.
  $WS_{ab}(122)$
make a formal request
  $EN_{2b\S}(75); NO_{-2\S}(108)$
make a joke (of)
  $IR_{2a}(130); DT_{1d}(128)$
make a law
  $NO_{-4\S}(107)$
make a list of
  $VV_a(153)$
make amends for
  $NO_{9b'}(117); NO_{8a''}(117);$
  $KA_{4cad}(103)$
make a mistake
  $TE_{-1cc}(140)$
make a moving speech
  $TP_{2ab}(164)$
make an abbreviation
  $IN_{-1}(143)$
make an afterthought
  $TV_{7h}(162)$
make an affidavit
  $IN_{6c}(146)$
make an agreement
  $KA_{3cbd}(104); NO_{0e}(110);$
  $KA_{2b}(97)$
make an alliance
  $NO_{0e}(110)$
make an appointment
  $EN_{3ab}(76); NO_{0e}(110);$
  $DI_4(125)$
make an arbitration
  $NO_{7a}(116)$
make an arrangement
  $NO_{7a}(116)$
make an attempt to
  $DE_{8b}(151)$
make an award
  $NO_{7a}(116)$
make an end to
  $TU_{9a}(133)$
make an enemy of
  $KA_{1da}(96); KA_{-1c}(87)$
make an excursion
  $TV_{6'b}(160)$
make an exegesis
  $TE_{-1cb}(140)$
make an imbecile of
  $IR_{1a}(129)$
make an inscription
  $VV_{ba}(153)$
make an objection
  $TV_{6'a}(160)$
make a pact
  $KA_{2b}(97)$
make a parade of
  $WS_{bc}(123)$
make a point of
  $KA_{4cbc}(104)$
make a rousing speech
  $TP_{2ab}(164)$
make arrangements
  $KA_{4cbd}(104)$
make a settlement
  $KA_{4cbd}(104)$
make a statement
  $TO_{2bb}(156)$
make a stirring speech
  $TP_{2ab}(164)$
make a summary
  $TV_{7f}(161)$
make a sworn deposition
  $VE_{1b}(148)$
make a synopsis
  $TV_{7f}(161)$
make a toast
  $EM_{2h}(73)$

make a treaty
  $NO_{0e}(110)$
make (appear) banal
  $KA_{1bbc}(92)$
make a recapitulation
  TV_{7f}
make banal
  $WG_{0a}(123)$
make bold
  $KA_{0g}(89)$
make bright
  TP_{2bba}
make certain
  $KA_{2b}(97)$
make clear
  $KA_{-1b}(87); AV_2(106);$
  $TP_{2ac}(164); ET_{0dd}(137);$
  $ET_{0c}(136); KA_{4cac}(103)$
make comments
  $TO_{2bb}(156)$
make compliments
  $EN_{7ad}(80); WS_{bbb}(123)$
make concessions
  $KA_{3b}(99)$
make conditions
  $EN_{5b}(77)$
make equal
  $IN_{3ba}(143)$
make excerpts from
  $TE_{1b}\cdot(140)$
make fun of
  $IR_{2b}(130); TE_{0ab}(141);$
  $DT_{1d}(128)$
make fun of so.
  $WP_{0ab}(121); IR_{2a}(130);$
  $IR_{1a}(129)$
make game of
  $IR_{2cb}(131)$
make general inquiries
  $IN_{1ab}(142)$

make guesses
  $EN_{5ca}(78)$
make good
  $NO_{9b}\cdot(117); AV_3(106);$
  $KA_{4cad}(103)$
make good (an assertion)
  $TV^*_{7b}(161)$
make inquiries
  $EN_{5cb}(78); VE_1\text{``}_a(148)$
make inquiries about
  $DI_1\cdot(124)$
make intricate
  $TP_{2bd}(166)$
make involved
  $TP_{2bd}(166)$
make it up
  $KA_{4caa}(103)$
make known
  $VE_{1a}(148); NO_{0a\S}(108);$
  $IN_{6b}(145); ET_{0c}(136);$
  $ET_{0b}(135); IN_{6b}\cdot(145)$
make manifest
  $ET_{0c}(136)$
make mention
  $TV_5(159)$
make more concrete
  $TV_{7c}(161)$
make more detailed
  $TV_{7c}(161)$
make more explicit
  $TV_{7c}(161)$
make more popular
  $ET/TE_a\cdot(139)$
make more precise
  $TP_{2ac}(164); TV_{7c}(161)$
make no decision
  $KA_{1cb}(95)$
make no promises
  $KA_{1cb}(95)$

make notes
  $TO_{2bb}(156)$
make objections
  $KA_{1bca}(93)$
make one's peace with
  $KA_{4cac}(103);$
  $KA_{4caa}(103)$
make one's position clear
  $KA_{-1b}(87)$
make one's way
  $KA_{4ac}(100)$
make os. ridiculous
  $WS_{ab}(122)$
make out
  $IN_{2a}\cdot(143); EN_{5ca}(78);$
  $DE_{6c}(150); ET_{0c}(136)$
make out, try to
  $IN_{1aa}(142)$
make overt
  $ET_{0c}(136)$
make overtures
  $KA_{2aa}(96)$
make persiflage
  IR_{1b}
make popular
  $TE_{-2a}(139)$
make preliminary
  remarks
  $TV_4(159)$
make presuppositions
  $KA_{4cbc}(104)$
make progress
  $ET_{1b}(137)$
make prognoses
  $ET/TE_c(139)$
make promises
  $KA_{1cb}(95)$
make propaganda for
  $EN_{2a}(75)$

make public
    $NO_4(113); VE_{1a}(148);$
    $IN_{6b}(145); ET_{0c}(136);$
    $ET_{0b}(135)$
make public by printing
    $TE_{-2b}(139)$
make puns
    $IR_{1c}(130)$
make remarks
    $TO_{2bb}(156)$
make repetitive
    $TO_{3a}(157)$
make reservations
    $KA_{4cbc}(104)$
make rhymes
    $ET/TE_{ac}(138)$
make salient
    $TO_{5a}(158)$
make so. appear in court
    $NO_5(113)$
make so. believe
    $EN_{7ag}(80)$
make so. promise
    $NO_{0a}(108)$
make shallow
    TP_{2bbb}
make smutty jokes
    $DT_{1e}(128)$
make series
    $TO_4(157)$
make so. afraid
    $KA_{1ab}(91)$
make so. feel small
    $KA_{4ac}(100)$
make so. forget sth.
    $EN_{1b}(75)$
make so. lose his status
    $WT_{5a}(120); NO_{10}(117)$

make sth. bad
    $TE_{0ab}(141)$
make sport of
    $IR_{1a}(129)$
make stipulations
    $KA_{4cbc}(104)$
make suggestions
    $EN_{7aa}(79)$
make superficial
    TP_{2bbb}
make sure (of)
    $VV_c(154); KA_{2b}(97)$
make sure of sth.
    $VV_c(154)$
make sure of (the truth)
    $IN_{9b}(147)$
make terms
    $KA_{-1b}(87)$
make the assumption
    $DE_5(149)$
make the best of
    $KA_{4cda}(105); KA_{4bda}(102)$
make the first cut
    $DI_5(125)$
make threatening gestures
    $EN_{4c}(77)$
make up
    $KA_{-1b}(87); KA_{4cac}(103)$
make up (a list)
    $DE_{6f}(151); IN_{-1}(143)$
make up the quarrel
    $NO_{7a}(116)$
make up to
    $EN_{7ad}(80); WS_{bbb}(123)$
make witty remarks
    $IR_{1c}(130); DT_{1d}(128)$
make worse
    $ET/TE_{a'}(139)$

make worse instead of better
    $ET/TE_{a'}(139)$
maledict
    $NO_{8a'}(116)$
maledictions in general, utter
    $EM_{2ga}(72)$
malicious pleasure, show
    $KA_{4a'}(101)$
manage
    $KA_{4aa}(99); EN_{6c}(78);$
    $EN_{9'b}(85); NO_{-3}(107)$
manage to see over
    $TP_{2bf}(167)$
mandate
    $EN_{2c\S}(76); NO_{-4}(107);$
    $NO_{0da}(109); EN_{3aa}(76);$
    $EN_{3b}(76)$
manifest
    $ET_{0a}(135); VE^*_1(148);$
    $AV_3(106); NO_{6da}(115)$
manifest, make
    $ET_{0c}(136)$
manipulate
    $EN_{6c}(78); NO_{-3}(107)$
manner, behave in a familiar
    $EN_{7ad}(80); WS_{bbb}(123)$
manner, deliver in a monotonous sing-song
    $TP_{1a}(163)$
manner, express os. in a blurred
    $TP_{2bd}(166)$
manner, express os. in a woolly
    $TP_{2bd}(166)$

manner, present sth. in
 a brilliant
 $TP_{2ab}(164)$
manners, teach so.
 $ET_{0da}(136)$
man's thoughts, divert a
 $EN_{1b}(75)$
marginal notes, supply
 with
 $TE_{0bb}(141); TV_{7b}(161)$
mark
 $VV_{ba}(153); IN_{3c}(144);$
 TO_{2bb}
mark as
 $VV_a(153)$
mark as secret
 $VE_{-1}(147)$
mark errors
 $WT_{4b}(119)$
mark off
 $TO_{2a}(155); VV_{bc}(154)$
mark out
 $TO_{3a}(157); TO_{2a}(155)$
mark out so.
 $NO_{0b}.(109)$
mark with a cross
 $VV_{ba}(153)$
mark with figures
 $VV_{ba}(153)$
marry
 $NO_{0e}(110)$
marry (make husband
 and wife)
 $NO_{0da}(109)$
mask
 $KA_{1bba}(92)$
master (a problem)
 $IN_{2a}.(143)$
masterfully, talk
 $DI_{7b}.(126)$

matriculate
 $NO_{0da}(109)$
matter, confer about a
 $WT_2(118)$
matter go no further
 (of a secret), let the
 $VE_1.(147)$
matter, not to come to
 grips with the
 $TV_{6'b}(160)$
matter, prejudge a
 $TV_{8a}(162)$
matter, report upon a
 $TU_4(132); DT_2(129);$
 $ET_{0a}(135); TP_{2aa}(164);$
 $IN_{6aa}(144)$
meaning, get the
 $IN_{2a}(142)$
meaning, give a new
 $TE_{-1cd}(140)$
mean to
 $DE_{8b}(151)$
mean sth. to
 $KA_{4cca}(105)$
mean sth. to so.
 $KA_{-3b}(85)$
mechanically, repeat
 $ET_{1c}(137)$
mechanical, put
 $TP_{2be}(166)$
meddle (with)
 $KA_{-1b}(87); KA_{4cac}(103)$
mediate
 $KA_{4cac}(103); TE_{-2a}(139);$
 $KA_{-1b}(87);$
meditate (on)
 $DE_4(149)$
meet
 $KA_{1bcd}(94); KA_{1bca}(93);$
 $KA_{4cba}(104); DI_{5a}(125);$

meet (cont.)
 $NO_{6f}(115); NO_{2ba}(111)$
meet for conference
 $NO_{2ba}(111); NO_{6f}(115);$
 $WT_2(118)$
meet halfway
 $KA_{4cba}(104)$
meeting, have a
 $NO_{6f}(115); NO_{2ba}(111)$
meeting, hold a
 $WT_2(118); NO_{2ba}(111);$
 $NO_{6f}(115)$
meet with
 $DI_{5a}(125)$
memorialize
 $ET/TE_{ad}(138)$
memorial address,
 draft a
 $ET/TE_{ad}(138)$
memorial address,
 give a
 $TV_{7j}(162)$
memorial address,
 speak a
 $WT_{5d}(121)$
memorize
 $ET_{0da}(136)$
memory, recall to
 $IN_{5aa}(144)$
memory, refresh so.'s
 $EN_{1ad}(75)$
menace
 $KA_{0g}(89)$
menace (so. with sth.)
 $EN_{4c}(77)$
mention
 $TV_5(159); ET_{0a}(135)$
mention casually
 $TO_{2bc}(156)$

mention, make
  $TV_5(159)$
mention with praise
  $WT_{4e}(120)$
merits, judge so.'s
  $WT_3.(119)$
mercy, cry out for
  $NO_{9ab}(117)$
message, deliver a
  $IN_{6ab}(145)$
message, transmit to so. in morse code a
  $ET_{0a}(135)$
mess up
  $ET/TE_a.(139)$
metaphorize
  $TP_{2ac}(164); TP_{2bc}(166)$
metaphors, put into
  $TP_{2bc}(166)$
mimic so.
  $ET_{1c}(137)$
mind, bear in
  $NO_{2a}(111); DE_2(149)$
mind, be not of one
  $KA_{-3c}(86)$
mind, call to
  $IN_{5b}(144)$
mind, call to so.'s
  $EN_{1ad}(75)$
mind, compose one's
  $KA_{4caa}(102)$
mindful of, be
  $IN_{5aa}(144)$
mind, speak one's
  $DI_{7b}(126)$
mind, strike one's
  $IN_{5b}(144)$
mind to, have a
  $DE_{8b}(151)$

mingle
  $TP_{2bd}(166)$
minimize
  $KA_{1bbc}(92)$
minutes, keep the
  $ET/TE_{ab}(138)$
misdate
  $NO_{0g}(111); VV_{bd}(154)$
misdeed, commit a
  $NO_2(112)$
misdemeanor, be guilty of a
  $NO_2(112)$
misfortune, take pleasure in other's
  $KA_{4a}.(101)$
misinterpret
  $TE_{-1cc}(140)$
misjudge
  $TE_{-1cc}(140)$
mislead
  $EN_{7af}(80)$
misnomer
  $TE_{-1cc}(140)$
misrepresent
  $TP_{2be}(166)$
misrepresent os.
  $WS_{ba}(122)$
misread
  $TE_{-1cc}(140)$
miss the point
  $TV_{6'b}(160)$
mistakes, find
  $WT_{4b}(119)$
mistake so.
  $KA_{-1c}(87)$
mission, give a
  $EN_{3a}(76)$
mistake, make a
  $TE_{-1cc}(140)$

misunderstand
  $TE_{-1cc}(140)$
misunderstand so.
  $KA_{-1c}(87)$
mitigate
  $TP_{2bbc}(165); NO_7.(115); TO_{5c}(158)$
mix
  $TP_{2bd}(166)$
mixed up, get
  $TP_{2bd}(166)$
mix up
  $TP_{2bd}(166)$
mix up with
  $TP_{2bd}(166)$
moan
  $EM_{2b}(71); EM_{2f}(72)$
moan about
  $KA_{1caa}(94)$
mock
  $IR_{1a}(129); IR_{1b}(130); IR_{2b}(130); IR_{2ca}(130); IR_{2cb}(131); WP_{0ab}(121)$
mock (at)
  $KA_{0g}(89)$
mock sth.
  $DT_{1d}(128)$
model after
  $ET_{1c}(137)$
model on
  $ET_{1c}(137)$
moderate
  $KA_{3b}(99); TP_{2bbc}(166); DI/TU(134); KA_{-1d}(88); TO_{5c}(158)$
modest, be overly
  $WS_{aa}(122)$
modify
  $NO_{3bc}(112); TO_{2e}(156)$

molest
  $KA_{0d}(89)$
money to so., refer one's
  $EN_{3da}(77)$
money ro so., send one's
  $EN_{3da}(77)$
monologue, give a
  $TU_4(132); DT_2(129)$
monologuize
  $DT_2(129); TU_4(132)$
monotonous sing-song
  manner, deliver in a
  $TP_{1a}(163)$
moralize
  $ET_{0da}(136); TP_{1d}(163);$
  $DT_2(129)$
more concrete, make
  $TV_{7c}(161)$
more detailed, make
  $TV_{7c}(161)$
more explicit, make
  $TV_{7c}(161)$
more popular, make
  $ET/TE_a \cdot (139)$
more precise, make
  $TP_{2ac}(164); TV_{7c}(161)$
morse code (a message).
  transmit to so. in
  $ET_{0a}(135)$
morse code that,
  transmit to so. in
  $ET_{0a}(135)$
morse code,
  transmit in
  $IN_{6aa}(145)$
motion for, propose a
  $NO_{-2\S}(108)$

motion with a
  majority, carry a
  $TV_9(163)$
motivate
  $EN_{1ae}(75)$
mourn
  $EM_{2cb}(72)$
mouth shut, keep one's
  $VE_1 \cdot (147)$
mouth, shut so.'s
  $KA_{4ac}(100)$
move
  $EN_{2b\S}(75); NO_{-2\S}(108)$
move so. to do sth.
  $EN_{7cb}(81)$
move so.
  $EN_{7d} \cdot (81)$
move away from
  $KA_{3b}(99); KA_{-1d}(88)$
moving speech, make a
  $TP_{2ab}(164)$
much, talk too
  $EN_{7ae}(80)$
muddled, get
  $TV_{6}\text{'''}(160)$
muddle on
  $TV_{7g}(162)$
muddle one's way
  through
  $KA_{4aa}(99)$
muffle up
  $TP_{2bc}(166)$
murder the Queen's,
  King's English
  $TP_{2be}(166); TE_{0ab}(141)$
murmur
  $KA_{1caa}(94); EM_{2k}(73)$
muse (on)
  $DE_4(149)$

mutiny
  $KA_{0g} \cdot (90); EM_{2k}(73);$
  $EN_{9f}(83); NO_{2bb}(111)$
mystify
  $IR_{2b}(130); TP_{2bd}(166);$
  $TP_{2bc}(166)$

N
nag
  $KA_{0d}(89); KA_{0e}(89);$
  $EM_{2k}(73); KA_{1caa}(94)$
nag at
  $WP_{0ad}(122)$
name
  $VV_{ba}(153)$
name, give so. a bad
  $WP_{0ac}(122)$
name, invent a
  $IN_{-1}(143)$
name send in one's
  $TU_1(131)$
names, call so.
  $NO_2 \cdot (112); WP_{0ab}(121)$
name to, give a
  $VV_{ba}(153)$
name to, give a bad
  $IR_{2cb}(131)$
name to, put one's
  $VV_{bc}(154)$
narrate
  $DT_2(129)$
narrate (a story)
  $ET_{0a}(135)$
negate
  $AV_1(106); IN_{9a}(146);$
  $IN_{8b}(146); DI_3 \cdot (125);$
  $KA_{1bcd}(94)$
negative, answer in the
  $EN_{9\S}(83)$

negatively, react
 $EN_{9b\S}(83)$
neglect
 $KA_{1bba}(92); WG_{1a}(123);$
 $WP_{0aa}(121); TO_{2c}(156);$
 $EN_{9j}(83); EN_{9i}(84);$
 $EN_{9g}(83); EN_{9d}(83);$
 $TV_{8b}(163); KA_{1bcc}(93)$
negotiate
 $KA_{-1b}(87); NO_{60}(113);$
 $KA_{4cac}(103)$
nervous, be
 $EM_{2ab}(71)$
neutralize
 $IN_{9a}(146); DI_{3}\cdot\cdot(125);$
 $KA_{1bbc}(92)$
new interpretations, give a
 $TE_{-1cd}(140)$
new meaning, give a
 $TE_{-1cd}(140)$
news, spread the
 $KA_{0c}(89)$
nickname, give a
 $VV_{ba}(153)$
nobleman, pass os.
 off for a
 $VV_{a}\cdot(153)$
no decision, make
 $KA_{1cb}(95)$
no longer interested
 in, be
 $KA_{3c}(99)$
no longer, participate
 $KA_{2d}(98)$
nominate
 $EN_{3b}(76); NO_{0da}(109);$
 $NO_{-4}(107)$
nominate so.
 $WT_{1}(118)$

nonsense, talk
 $DT_{1bc}(128); TP_{1e}(163);$
 $TP_{2bj}(167)$
nonsense, talk stuff and
 $TP_{2bj}(167)$
no promises, make
 $KA_{1cb}(95)$
not + (Verb ε VE_1)
 $VE_{1}\cdot(147)$
not accept
 $WG_{1a}(123)$
not agree to
 $EN_{9k}(84)$
not allow so. to get
 a word in edgewise
 $TU_{2}\cdot(131)$
not at one, be
 $KA_{-3c}(86)$
(do) not blame so.
 $WT_{3}\cdot(119)$
not break a word
 $VE_{1}\cdot(147)$
not come out with
 $KA_{1ccc}(95)$
note
 $TV_{5}(159); TO_{2bc}(156);$
 $DE_{1}(149)$
note down
 $ET/TE_{ab}(138)$
note of, take a
 $ET/TE_{ab}(138)$
notes, make
 $TO_{2bb}(156)$
notes, supply
 with (marginal)
 $TE_{0bb}(141); TV_{7b}(161)$
not fall in with
 $KA_{1bba}(92)$

nothings, say sweet
 $DT_{2c}(128); EN_{7aa}(79);$
 $WS_{bba}(123)$
notice
 $TO_{2bb}(156); TO_{2bc}(156);$
 $ET_{-1a}(134); DE_{1}(149)$
notice call into
 $TV_{5}(159)$
notice, force
 $ET_{0da}(136)$
notice, give
 $NO_{0a\S}(108),$
 $NO_{0dd}(110);$
 $NO_{3bd}(112)$
notice of, take
 $KA_{4cbd}(104);$
 $ET_{-1a}(134);$
 $DE_{1}(149); DE_{2}(149)$
notice to, give
 $ET_{0b}(135)$
notice of so., take no
 $WP_{0aa}(121)$
notify
 $NO_{0a\S}(108);$
 $TP_{2aa}(164);$
 $IN_{6b}\cdot(145); IN_{6b}(145);$
 $ET_{0b}(135); ET_{0a}(135)$
(do) not know each other
 $KA_{-3a}(85)$
not listen to
 $EN_{9k}(84)$
not of one mind, be
 $KA_{-3c}(86)$
not pay attention to
 $NO_{2}\cdot\cdot(112)$
not pay heed to
 $NO_{2}\cdot\cdot(112)$
not remember
 $IN_{5ab}(144)$

(do) not share opinion
  $WT_{4fb}(120)$
not to be known
  $KA_{-3a}(85)$
not to be previously
  known
  $KA_{-3a}(85)$
not to come to grips
  with the matter
  $TV_{6'b}(160)$
not to come
  to terms
  $KA_{-3c}(86)$
not to give a
  chance to speak
  $TU_{2'}(131)$
not to stand for
  $KA_{0g'}(90)$
null and void, declare
  an agreement
  $NO_{3bb}(112)$
number
  $VV_{ba}(153)$
number the pages
  $VV_{ba}(153)$

O

oath, affirm by
  $IN_{9b}(146)$
oath, attest upon
  $NO_{6da}(114)$
oath, confirm by
  $IN_{9b}(146)$
oath, deny under
  $NO_{6b}(114)$
oath, give an
  $IN_{6c}(146)$
oath, put under
  $NO_{0a}(108)$

oaths, interlard with
  $TO_{3a}(157)$
oath, swear on
  $NO_{6da}(115)$
oath, take an
  $ET_{0a}(135)$
obey
  $NO_{2a}(111); EN_{9j}(84);$
  $EN_{9d}(83); KA_{4cdb}(105)$
object
  $NO_{6e}(115); NO_{60}(113);$
  $IN_{8b}(146); KA_{1bcd}(94);$
  $KA_{1bca}(93); KA_{0j}(90)$
objection, formulate an
  $KA_{1bcd}(94)$
objection, make an
  $TV_{6'a}(160)$
objection, raise an
  $TV_{6'a}(160)$
objections, make
  $KA_{1bca}(93)$
objections, raise
  $KA_{1bca}(93)$
objections, remove
  $AV_1(106)$
objectivize
  $DE_{6c}(150)$
object to
  $WT_{4c}(119)$
obligate
  $NO_{0a}(108)$
obligate, put under an
  $NO_{7a}(116)$
obligation, release
  from an
  $NO_{7a}(116)$
obligation to,
  be under an
  $NO_{0'}(111)$

oblige
  $NO_{0a}(108)$
obliged, be
  $NO_{0'}(111)$
oblivion, let sth. sink into
  $KA_{4caa}(103)$
obscene, talk
  $DT_{1e}(128)$
obscenities, say
  $DT_{1e}(128)$
obscure
  $TP_{2bd}(166)$
observe
  $TO_{2bc}(156); TO_{2bb}(156);$
  $NO_{2a}(111); ET_{-1a}(134);$
  $KA_{4cdb}(105)$
obstinate about, be
  $KA_{1ccc}(95)$
obstinate, be
  $TV_{7d}(161); NO_{2''}(112);$
  $KA_{4bab}(101)$
obstinately to sth., stick
  $TV_{7d}(161)$
obtain aid
  $KA_{2caa}(97)$
obtain backing
  $KA_{2caa}(97)$
obtain by begging
  $EN_{8aa}(81)$
obtrusive, be
  $EN_{7ae}(80)$
obviate
  $KA_{1bca}(93)$
occupy
  $NO_{-2}(108)$
occupy os. with
  $TO_{2ba}(155)$
occur to so.
  $IN_{5b}(144)$

offend
  $KA_{0h}(90); KA_{0g}(89);$
  $KA_{0i}(90); NO_2(112);$
  $NO_2·(112); WP_{0ab}(121)$
offend against (tradition)
  $NO_2(112)$
offend unintentionally
  $KA_{0b}(88)$
offense at, take
  $WT_0(118)$
offense, commit an
  $NO_2(112)$
offense, take
  $EM_{2ca}(71)$
offer an opinion
  on a subject
  $NO_{60}(113)$
offer for sale
  $EN_{2a}(75)$
offer os.
  KA_{2ab}
offer one's services
  $KA_{2ab}(97); EN_{2a}(75)$
offer participation in
  $DI_1(124)$
offer sth.
  $EN_{2a}(75)$
offer to lend a hand
  $EN_{2a}(75)$
offer to participate
  $DI_1(124)$
office, appoint to an
  $NO_{0da}(109)$
officer, cashier an
  $NO_{0dd}(110)$
office, remove from
  $NO_{0dd}(110). NO_{8a}(116)$
office, vacate one's
  $KA_{4bac}(102)$

official report of,
  draw up the
  $ET/TE_{ab}(138)$
often, repeat too
  $KA_{1ccc}(95)$
old books, ponder over
  $TE_{-1b}(140)$
old horse, wear out an
  $TP_{2be}(167)$
omit
  $TO_{2c}(156)$
omit (superfluous
  things)
  $TP_{2ad}(164)$
once more, bring
  $TV_{7d}(161)$
one another, get on with
  $KA_{-3b}(85)$
one, be at
  $KA_{-3b}(85)$
one with, be at
  $KA_{4cca}(105)$
open
  $DI_6(125); TV_5(159)$
open (session)
  $DI/TU\ (134)$
open to, be
  $KA_{1cb}(95)$
opine
  $DE_5(149)$
opinion, partly alter one's
  $KA_{-1d}(88)$
opinion, advance an
  $ET_{0a}(135)$
opinion, be of
  $WT_0(118)$
opinion, be of the
  $DE_5(149); VV_g(154)$

opinion, be of the same
  $AV_6(107); KA_{-3b}(85);$
  $KA_{4cca}(105)$
opinion, do not share
  $WT_{4fb}(120)$
opinion, exchange
  $DI_{7a}(125); DT_{1a}(127);$
  $DT_{1bb}(128); DT_{1bc}(128)$
opinion, express one's
  $TU_4(132)$
opinion, give an expert
  $WT_{4f§}(120)$
opinion, give one's
  $NO_7(115)$
opinion, hold
  $KA_{1ccb}(95)$
opinion, hold as an
  $WT_0(118)$
opinion of, form an
  $WT_0(118)$
opinion on a subject,
  offer an
  $NO_{60}(113)$
opinion on, give
  $WT_0(118)$
opinion on, give an
  $NO_{-1}(108)$
opinion on, pass
  $WT_0(118)$
opinion, share
  $KA_{-3b}(85)$
opinion, share the same
  $IN_{8a}(146);$
  $KA_{4cca}(105)$
oppose
  $EN_{9f}(83); EN_{9h}(83);$
  $NO_{60}(113); EN_{9k}(84);$
  $NO_{6e}(115); TO_{5e}(158);$

oppose (cont.)
  $KA_{1bcb}(93); AV_1(106);$
  $KA_{0g}(90); KA_{0h}(90);$
  $KA_{0i}(90); KA_{0j}(90);$
  $KA_{1bca}(93)$
oppose (with)
  $KA_{1bcd}(94)$
oppress
  $KA_{0d}(89); EN_{8aa}(81)$
opress so.
  $EN_{7ae}(80)$
ordain
  $NO_{-4g}(107);$
  $EN_{0ab}(74)$
ordain by decree
  $EN_{6b}(78)$
ordain so. as a priest
  $NO_{0da}(109)$
order
  $VV_a(153); NO_{0a}(108);$
  $EN_{6b}(78)$
order a fresh supply
  $EN_{3a}(76)$
order, enforce good
  $DI/TU (134)$
order in advance
  $EN_{3a}(76)$
order, put in
  $TV_{7c}(161); IN_{3aa}(143)$
order, put in bad
  $IR_{2cb}(131)$
order, repeat an
  $EN_{3a}(76)$
orders, give
  $EN_{6b}(78)$
order so. to do sth.
  $EN_{3a}(76); EN_{3aa}(76)$
order sth.
  $EN_{3a}(76)$

order subsequently
  $EN_{3a}(76)$
order, set in
  $IN_{3aa}(143)$
organize
  $TO_{3a}(157); DE_{6f}(151)$
organize in paragraphs
  $TO_{3a}(157)$
orientation, give an
  $IN_{6ad}(145)$
orient so.
  $IN_{6ad}(145)$
original, purport to be the
  $TE_{0ab}(141)$
others, tell the
  $TE_{-1a}(140)$
oust
  $KA_{4ad}(100)$
outdo
  $KA_{4ac}(100); KA_{1bcc}(93)$
outlaw
  $NO_{8a}(116); WP_{0ad}(122)$
outline
  $ET/TE_{ac}(138);$
  $TP_{2ac}(164); TO_{2a}(155);$
  $TV_3(159)$
outline, describe in
  $TP_{2ac}(164)$
outrage
  $KA_{0g}(90); NO_2(112);$
  $WP_{0ab}(121)$
outshine
  $KA_{4ac}(100)$
outsmart
  $KA_{4ac}(100)$
outstanding, be
  $TP_{2ab}(164)$
overact
  $TP_{2bba}(165)$

over an over, repeat
  $TV_{7d}(161)$
over, boil
  $EM_{2b}(71)$
over, be
  $DI_{10}(127)$
over and over again, say
  $ET_{0da}(136)$
overbearing, be
  $WS_{bc}(123)$
overburden with big words
  $TP_{2b}(165)$
overcome
  $KA_{4ac}(100)$
overdo
  $TP_{2b}(165); TP_{2bba}(165)$
overemphasize
  $KA_{-1c}(88)$
overhear
  $VE_{1"a}(148)$
overload with big words
  $TP_{2b}(165)$
overlook
  $TU_2.(131)$
overly modest, be
  $WS_{aa}(122)$
overrule
  $KA_{4ab}(99)$
overthrow
  $KA_{4ac}(100)$
overthrown, be
  $KA_{4baa}(101); KA_{4bac}(101)$
overt, make
  $ET_{0c}(136)$
overtures, make
  $KA_{2aa}(96)$
overturn
  $KA_{4ac}(100)$

overview, give an
  $TV_3(159)$
overweering, be
  $WS_{bc}(123)$
own
  $KA_{4cba}(104); KA_{1bbb}(92)$
own up (to)
  $NO_{6b}(114); IN_{6c}(146)$

P

pacify
  $EN_{7ca}(80); KA_{4cac}(103); KA_{-1b}(87)$
packing, send
  $KA_{4ad}(100)$
pack together
  $TO_{3a}(157)$
pact, make a
  $KA_{2b}(97)$
pad
  $ET/TE_{a}\cdot(139)$
pages, number the
  $VV_{ba}(153)$
paint (dialectical)
  $DT_2(129)$
pale, turn
  $EM_{2aa}(71)$
palliate
  $TP_{2bba}(165); TP_{2bc}(166)$
paper, read a
  $TE_{0aa}(141)$
paper, repair a
  $ET/TE_{a}\cdot(139)$
parade of, make a
  $WS_{bc}(123)$
paradigma, refer a
  $AV_4(106)$
paradigma, use a
  $AV_4(106)$

paragraphs, organize in
  $TO_{3a}(157)$
parallelize
  $DE_{6f}(151)$
paralyze
  $KA_{1ab}(91)$
paraphrase
  $TE_{0ac}(141); TE_{0ae}(141)$
pardon
  $NO_{9bb}(117)$
pardon, beg
  $NO_{6b}(114)$
parentheses, put in
  $TO_{5ad}(158)$
parry
  $KA_{1bcb}(93)$
part from so.
  $KA_{2d}(98)$
partially, fall in with
  $KA_{4cbc}(104)$
participate at
  a discussion
  $DI_{7a}(126); DT_{1ba}(127)$
participate no longer
  $KA_{2d}(98)$
participate, offer to
  $DI_1(124)$
participate, want to
  $DI_1(124)$
participation, beg for
  $DI_1(124)$
participation in, offer
  $DI_1(124)$
participation, requiring
  DI_1
participation, urge
  $DI_1(124)$
partition
  $TO_{3a}(157)$

part in a contest, take
  $KA_{-3cb}(86)$
partly, give in
  $KA_{-1d}(88)$
partnership, dissolve
  $NO_{3bb}(112)$
part, take so.'s
  $NO_{0f}(110); EN_{6d}(79)$
part with sth.
  $KA_{2d}(98)$
party, join a
  $NO_{0f}(110); EN_{6d}(79)$
pass
  $TU_{8a}\cdot(133)$
pass a bill
  $EN_{9b\S}(83)$
passages from, pull
  $TE_{-1b}\cdot(140)$
pass by
  $TU_2\cdot(131)$
pass expert
  judgement on
  $WT_{4f\S}(120); WT_0(118)$
pass judgement on
  $NO_{-1}(108)$
pass judgement on so.
  $NO_7(115)$
pass off
  $KA_{-1b}(87)$
pass on
  $TE_{-2a}(139)$
pass os. off
  (for a nobleman)
  $VV_a\cdot(153)$
pass os. off as so.
  $VV_a\cdot(153)$
pass opinion on
  $WT_0(118)$

pass over
 $EN_{9i}(84); KA_{4aa}(99);$
 $KA_{1bba}(92); TO_{2c}(156);$
 $TP_{2bf}(167); TU_{2}.(131)$
pass over in silence
 $TP_{2bg}(167)$
pass over so.
 DI/TU (134)
pass sentence
 $NO_{7a}(116)$
pass sentence on so.
 $NO_{7}(115)$
pass the buck
 $KA_{1bba}(92)$
pass time in chattering
 $DT_{1bc}(128); DI_{10}.(127)$
pass time in gossiping
 $DT_{1bc}(128); DI_{10}.(127)$
pass up
 $EN_{9a}(82)$
past, recall the
 $TV_{7j}(162)$
past, reflect on the
 $TV_{7j}(162)$
past, review the
 $TV_{7j}(162)$
patch in
 $TO_{2d}(156)$
patch up
 $TP_{2bi}(167); DI_{9}(126)$
patch up a quarrel
 $KA_{4caa}(103)$
pause
 $TU_{6'a}(133)$
pave the way (for)
 $KA_{2aa}(96)$
pay so. compliments
 $WT_{5d}(121)$
pay attention
 $EN_{9g}(83)$

pay attention to
 $EN_{9c}(83); KA_{4cdb}(105);$
 $EN_{9k}(84); WG_{1b}(124);$
 $NO_{2a}(111); DE_{2}(149)$
pay attention to, not
 $NO_{2}.(112)$
pay back
 $KA_{4bdb}(102)$
pay compliments
 $EN_{7aa}(79); WS_{bba}(123);$
 $DT_{1c}(128)$
pay heed to
 $EN_{9g}(83); WG_{1b}(124)$
pay heed to, not
 $NO_{2}.(112)$
pay homage
 $WT_{5d}(121)$
payment, demand
 $NO_{-2}(108)$
pay no attention
 $EN_{9c}(83)$
pay no heed to
 $EN_{9c}(83); WG_{1a}(123)$
pay off
 $KA_{4cad}(103); NO_{9b}.(117)$
pay one's respects
 $WT_{5d}(121)$
peace, leave in
 $KA_{3c}(99)$
peace with, make one's
 $KA_{4cac}(103);$
 $KA_{4caa}(103)$
peg, take so. down a
 $KA_{4ac}(100)$
penalty, inflict a
 $NO_{8a}(116)$
penance, do
 $NO_{8a}.(117)$
penetrate
 $KA_{4ae}(100); ET_{-1b}(134);$

penetrate (cont.)
 $IN_{2a*}(142)$
penetratingly,
 persevere in too
 $KA_{1ccc}(95)$
pension off
 $NO_{0dd}(110)$
perceive
 $TO_{2bb}(156); TO_{2bc}(156);$
 $ET_{-1a}(134); DE_{1}(149)$
perceive the reason
 $ET*_{-1a}(134)$
perfect
 $TV_{7c}(161);$
 $ET/TE_{a}.(139)$
perform a play
 $TE_{0aa}(140)$
perform a
 psychoanalysis
 $IN_{1ac}(142)$
permission to, give
 $NO_{0b}(108)$
permission to
 speak, beg
 $TU_{1}(131)$
permission to speak, give
 $TU_{2}(131); DI/TU(134)$
permission to speak, impart
 $TU_{2}(131)$
permit
 $EN_{9b\S}(83); NO_{0b}(108)$
persevere
 $KA_{4bab}(101);$
 $KA_{1ccb}(95);$
 $KA_{1cca}(95); TV_{7d}(161)$
persevere in
 (too penetratingly)
 $KA_{1ccc}(95)$
persiflage
 $IR_{2b}(130)$

persiflage, make
 IR_{1b}(130)
persist
 TV_{7d}(161)
persist in
 KA_{1ccc}(95); KA_{1dc}(96);
 KA_{1ccb}(95)
person, confer with a
 DT_{1a}(127); NO_{2ba}(111);
 NO_{6f}(115)
personify
 TP_{2ac}(164)
person, quiz some
 IN_{1ab}(142)
person, relieve another
 $TU_{3'''}$(132)
persuade
 KA_{2cab}(98); EN_{7ag}(80)
persuade so. of sth.
 KA_{-1c}(87)
peruse
 TE_{-1b}(140)
pervert
 TP_{2be}(166)
pessimistically, put
 TP_{2bba}(165)
peter out
 DI_{10}(127)
petition
 EN_{2b}(75); $EN_{2b\S}$(75);
 $NO_{-2\S}$(108)
pettifog
 DT_{3}(129)
philosophize
 DT_{3}(129)
phrase, use a hackneyed
 TP_{2be}(167)
pick holes (in)
 TV_{7b}(160); TE_{0bb}(141)

pick out
 DE_{6b}(150); IN_{3ba}(143);
 IN_{5ac}(144)
pick out (a word)
 ET_{1b}(137)
picture sth. to os.
 DE_{2}(149)
pieces, pluck into
 TV_{7b}(160)
pieces, pull into
 TV_{7b}(161); TE_{0bb}(141)
pieces, shred to
 WT_{4c}(120)
pieces, take to
 KA_{1aa}(91); KA_{4ac}(100);
 KA_{4ae}(101)
pieces, tear into
 TE_{0bb}(141); WT_{4c}(120)
piece together
 TP_{2bi}(167)
pigeonhole so.
 WT_{5a}(120)
pillory
 IR_{2cb}(131); IR_{1b}(130)
pillory, put in the
 NO_{8a}(116)
pillow, consult with one's
 DE_{4}(149)
pin down
 KA_{1cab}(94)
pissed off, be
 EM_{2ca*}(72)
pity
 EN_{7ca}(80)
pity so.
 EM_{2j}(73)
placate
 KA_{4cac}(103)
place above
 NO_{0dc}(109); DE_{8c}(152);

place above (cont.)
 DE_{8e}(152)
place at so.'s disposal
 EN_{2a}(75)
place differently
 TO_{3b}(157)
place in the forefront
 TO_{5a}(158)
place in the foreground
 TO_{5a}(158)
place one's trust in
 VE_{0}(147)
place one's trust in so.
 WT_{3}.(119)
place, teach so. his
 KA_{4ac}(100)
place together
 TO_{3b}(157); DE_{6f}(151)
plagiarize
 $VE_{1"a}$(148)
plan
 DE_{6f}(151); DE_{8d}(152);
 ET/TE_{c}(139)
plan (theme)
 TV_{3}(159)
plan to do sth.
 EN_{0ab}(74)
play an unfair trick on
 KA_{1aa}(91)
play a trick on
 KA_{4bdb}(102); KA_{4ac}(100)
play, bring into
 TV_{5}(159)
play down
 KA_{1bbc}(92); TO_{5c}(158)
play off against
 KA_{0j}(90)
play, perform a
 TE_{0aa}(140)

play practical jokes
  $IR_{2a}(130); IR_{1c}(130)$
play the fool
  $IR_{1c}(130); IR_{2a}(130)$
play the imbecile
  $IR_{2a}(130)$
play up
  $TP_{2bba}(165)$
plead
  $EN_{2b}(75)$
plead for
  $EN_{2c\S}(76); KA_{2cb}(98);$
  $NO_{6e}(115)$
plead for so.
  $WT_1(118)$
plead guilty
  $NO_{6b}(114); IN_{6c}(146)$
pleased, be
  $KA_{4a'}(101)$
pleasure in other's
  misfortune, take
  $KA_{4a'}(101)$
pleasure, show malicious
  $KA_{4a'}(101)$
pledge
  $EN_{6d}(79); NO_{0dd}(110)$
pledge one's word
  $NO_1(111)$
pledge, take in
  $EN_{3db}(77)$
plot
  $EN_{7cc}(81); WP_{0ac}(122);$
  $KA_{-1c}(88); DT_{1h}(128);$
  $KA_{0d}(89); DE_{8d}(152);$
  $VE_{-2}(147)$
plot secrets
  $VE_{-2}(147)$
plot sth.
  $NO_{2bb}(111)$

plot treason
  $VE_{-2}(147)$
pluck into pieces
  $TV_{7b}(160)$
pluck out
  $IN_{5ac}(144)$
plug at
  $KA_{1bcd}(94)$
plume os.
  $WS_{bc}(123)$
pluralistic position,
  take up a
  $KA_{1cb}(95)$
poem, reel off a
  $TP_{1a}(163)$
poeticize
  $TP_{2bba}(165)$
poetry, write
  $ET/TE_{ac}(138)$
point at
  $EN_{1ac}(74)$
point, belabor a
  $TP_{2b}(164)$
point, carry a
  $KA_{0c}(89)$
point, carry one's
  $KA_{-2a}(86); KA_{4aa}(99)$
point, clear up a
  $WT_{4b}(119)$
point, deepen the
  $TV_{7c}(161)$
point, miss the
  $TV_{6'b}(160)$
point of, make a
  $KA_{4cbc}(104)$
point out
  $AV_3(106); TO_{2bb}(156);$
  $ET_{0db}(136); EN_{6a}(78);$
  $KA_{2cab}(97)$

point, strengthen the
  $TV_{7b}(161)$
point, stretch a
  $TP_{2b}(165)$
point to
  $EN_{6a}(78)$
point to (an argument)
  $AV_3(106)$
point to sth.
  $EN_{1ac}(74)$
poison the atmosphere
  $KA_{0e}(89)$
poke fun (at)
  $IR_{2a}(130); DT_{1d}(128)$
polemize
  $KA_{1aa}(91)$
police, report (one's arrival,
  one's departure) to the
  $IN_{6b}(145)$
polish
  $ET/TE_{a'}(139)$
polite, be
  $TO_{5c}(158)$
pompously, speak
  $TP_{2b}(165)$
ponder
  $EN_{9c}(83); VV_g(155);$
  $EN_{9g}(83); EN_{9k}(84);$
  $DE_{8c}(152)$
ponder over old books
  $TE_{-1b}(140)$
ponder sth.
  $DE_4(149)$
pony, use a
  $VE_{1'''b}(148)$
poor English, speak
  $TE_{0ab}(141)$
popularize
  $TE_{-2a}(139)$

popular, make
  $TE_{-2a}(139)$
popular, make more
  $ET/TE_a(139)$
portray
  $DT_2(129); TP_{2aa}(164);$
  $TU_4(132); ET_{0a}(135)$
position, change one's
  $KA_{4bbb}(102)$
position clear, make one's
  $KA_{-1b}(87)$
position, consolidate
  $KA_{1ccb}(95)$
position, defend a
  $TV_{6b}(160)$
position, define one's
  $KA_{-1b}(87)$
position, determine the
  $VV_a(152)$
position, let so.
  take up a
  $KA_{1cab}(94)$
position, secure
  $KA_{1dc}(96)$
position, stabilize
  $KA_{1ccb}(95); KA_{1dc}(96)$
position, take up a
  $KA_{1bca}(93)$
position, take up a
  pluralistic
  $KA_{1cb}(95)$
possession of, take
  $KA_{-2a}(86)$
post
  $NO_{0a\S}(108); IN_{6b'}(145);$
  $IN_{6aa}(144)$
post bills
  $NO_{0a\S}(108); IN_{6b'}(145)$
postdate
  $NO_{0g}(111); VV_{bd}(154)$

postpone
  $KA_{1bba}(92); TV_{8b}(163);$
  $TU_{6'a}(133)$
postpone to another day
  $NO_{0g}(111)$
postulate
  $DE_5(150)$
pout
  $EM_{2f}(72); EM_{2k}(73)$
powers, invest with full
  $EN_{3b}(76); NO_{-4}(107)$
practical jokes, play
  $IR_{2a}(130); IR_{1c}(130)$
practice
  $ET_{0da}(136)$
praise
  $WT_{4e}(120); TE_{0bb}(141)$
praise extravagantly
  $EN_{7ad}(80); WS_{bbb}(123)$
praise, mention with
  $WT_{4e}(120)$
praise so. for sth.
  $WT_{5d}(121)$
praise to, give
  $WT_{4e}(120)$
prattle
  $TP_{2bj}(167); DT_{1bc}(128);$
  $TP_{1e}(163)$
pray
  $TP_{1a}(163)$
pray for sth.
  $EN_{2b}(75)$
preach
  $TP_{1d}(163); DT_2(129);$
  $ET_{0da}(136)$
preach at
  $KA_{1cca}(95)$
preach from the pulpit
  $NO_{0a\S}(108)$

precise, make more
  $TP_{2ac}(164)$
precise, making more
  $TV_{7c}(161)$
preclude
  $KA_{1ba}(91)$
predict
  $ET/TE_c(139)$
predestinate so.
  $ET/TE_c(139)$
predestine so.
  $ET/TE_c(139)$
predetermine
  $ET/TE_c(139)$
preface
  $TV_4(159); DI_6(125)$
prefer
  $EN_{0aa}(74); DE_{8c}(152);$
  $DE_{8e}(152)$
preference to, give
  $DE_{8c}(152); DE_{8e}(152)$
prejudge
  $WT_{3''}(119)$
prejudge a matter
  $TV_{8a}(162)$
prejudice
  $WT_{3''}(119)$
prejudices, show
  $WT_{3''}(119)$
preliminarily,
  discuss
  $DT_{1bb}(128); TV_1(158)$
preliminary remarks,
  make
  $TV_4(159)$
preliminarily, say
  $TV_4(159)$
preliminarily, treat
  $TV_1(158)$

prelude
  $DI_6(125); TV_4(159)$
prematurely, speak
  $TV_{8a}(162)$
premise
  $TV_4(159)$
prepare
  $KA_{2aa}(95)$
prepare a digest
  $ET_{0da}(136)$
prepare an abstract
  $ET_{0da}(136)$
prepare for an exam
  $ET_{0da}(136)$
prepare so.
  $EN_{3c}(76)$
prepare so. for an exam
  $ET_{0da}(136)$
preplan
  $ET/TE_c(139)$
prescribe
  $EN_{6b}(78)$
present
  $EN_{3da}(77); TV_1(158);$
  $TP_{2aa}(164); ET_{0db}(136);$
  $ET_{0de}(137)$
present (a subject)
  $TV_{6b}(160)$
present expansively
  $TP_{2bba}(165)$
present os.
  $VV_a.(153)$
present so. with sth.
  $EN_{3da}(77)$
present sth. in a
  brilliant manner
  $TP_{2ab}(164)$
presidency, run for
  $EN_{2c\S}(76)$

preside (over)
  $EN_{6c}(78)$
preside over
  $NO_{-3}(107); DI/TU(134)$
press
  $EN_{8aa}(81); KA_{1ccb}(95)$
press hard
  $KA_{0d}(89)$
presume
  $KA_{-2b}(87); KA_{4cbc}(104);$
  $WS_{bc}(123); DE_5(149)$
presuppose
  $DE_5(149)$
presuppositions, make
  $KA_{4cbc}(104)$
pretend
  $WS_{bc}(123)$
pretend to
  $WS_{bc}(123)$
pretend to fight
  $KA_{-3cb}(86)$
pretensions, have great
  $KA_{-2a}(86)$
pretensions to, have no
  $KA_{1bbb}(92)$
pretentiously, speak
  $TP_{2b}(165)$
prevail upon
  $EN_{2b}(75)$
prevaricate
  $KA_{4bba}(102)$
prevent
  $EN_{8ab}(82); KA_{1bcb}(93);$
  $NO_{0c}(109)$
prevent from continuing
  $TU_3.(132); TU_6(133)$
previously known,
  not to be
  $KA_{-3a}(85)$

previous remarks,
  supplement
  $TV_{7a}(160)$
priest, ordain so. as a
  $NO_{0da}(109)$
prime
  $EN_{7cc}(81)$
printing, make public by
  $TE_{-2b}(139)$
prisoner's cell,
  smuggle letters in a
  $VE_0(147)$
privilege
  $NO_{0b}..(109)$
probe with questions
  $EN_{5cc}(78)$
problem, master a
  $IN_{2a}.(143)$
problem, raise a
  $TV_5(159)$
proceedings against
  so., institute legal
  $NO_4.(113)$
proceedings against,
  take legal
  $NO_4.(113)$
proceed (with a topic)
  $TV_{7g}(162)$
process, make
  $ET_{1b}(137)$
proclaim
  $NO_{0a\S}(108); ET_{0a}(134);$
  $IN_{6ab}(145); IN_{6b}.(145)$
procrastinate
  $KA_{1bba}(92)$
procrastinate (rare)
  $TV_{8b}(163)$
produce an argument
  $AV_3(106)$

produce an example
   $AV_4(106)$
produce euphemismus
   $TP_{2bba}(165)$
produce (science) fiction
   $ET/TE_b(138)$
produce (texts)
   $ET/TE_{aa}(138)$
profile, sketch in
   $TO_{2a}(155); TV_3(159)$
prognoses, make
   $ET/TE_c(139)$
prognosticate
   $ET/TE_c(139)$
progress
   $TV_{7g}(162)$
progress, make
   $ET_{1b}(137)$
prohibit
   $NO_{0c}(109); EN_{8ab}(82);$
   $DI_{8b}(126)$
project
   $DE_{6f}(151); ET/TE_c(139)$
project, set up a
   $DE_{8d}(152)$
prolong
   $TU_5(132); DI_{10}"(127)$
prominence, bring into
   $TO_{5a}(158)$
promise
   $KA_{2cb}(98); EN_{6d}(79);$
   $NO_1(111); NO_{0dd}(110)$
promise (=accept to do)
   $WT_{4fa}(120)$
promise, keep a
   $NO_{2a}(111)$
promise, make so.
   $NO_{0a}(108)$
promises, make
   $KA_{1cb}(95)$

promises, make no
   $KA_{1cb}(95)$
promise solemnly
   $EN_{6d}(79); NO_{0dd}(110)$
promote
   $NO_{0dc}(109)$
prompt
   $KA_{2cab}(97)$
promulgate
   $IN_{6aa}(144); VE_{1a}(148)$
promulgate a law
   $NO_{-4§}(107); NO_{0a§}(108)$
promulgate ideas
   $TE_{-2a}(139)$
pronounce
   $ET_{0a}(135)$
pronounce a judgement
   $NO_7(115)$
pronounce for so.
   $ET_{0dc}(137)$
proof, bring forward
   $AV_3(106)$
proof of, show
   $AV_3(106); IN_{9b}(147)$
proofreading, do
   $ET/TE_{a'}(139)$
proofs, correct
   $ET/TE_{a'}(139)$
proof, show
   $NO_{6da}(115)$
propaganda for, make
   $EN_{2a}(75)$
propagandize
   $EN_{2a}(75)$
propagate
   $IN_{6aa}(144); TE_{-2a}(139)$
property, cede one's
   $EN_{3da}(77)$
prophesy
   $ET/TE_b(138); ET/TE_c(139)$

propose
   $EN_{2a}(75); EN_{2b§}(75);$
   $NO_{-2§}(108)$
propose a motion for
   $EN_{2b§}(75); NO_{-2§}(108)$
propose a toast to so.
   $WT_{5b}(120)$
propose so.
   $WT_1(118)$
propose (to a lady)
   $EN_{2b§}(75)$
prop up
   $KA_{2cab}(97)$
prorogue
   $TV_{8b}(163); TU_{9a}(133)$
prorogue (parliament)
   $DI_{10}(127)$
proscribe
   $NO_{8a}(116)$
prose, write purple
   $ET/TE_b(138)$
prospect of sth. to so.
   hold out
   $NO_{0f}(110); EN_{6d}(79)$
protection, give
   $KA_{2caa}(97)$
protest
   $KA_{2cab}(97); EN_{9f}(83);$
   $EN_{9h}(84); IN_{8b}(146);$
   $NO_{2bb}(111)$
protest against
   $KA_{0g'}(90); NO_{9aa}(117)$
protest, enter a
   $AV_1(106)$
protest, lodge a
   $KA_{0g'}(90)$
protest, raise a
   $AV_1(106)$
protract
   $TU_5(132); DI_{10}"(127)$

prorude
  $KA_{-1d}(88)$
prove
  $NO_{6da}(115); NO_{60}(113);$
  $AV_3(106); VV_c(154);$
  $TV*_{7b}(161); IN_{9b}(147)$
prove by exclusion
  $DE_{6d}(150)$
prove guilty
  $NO_{6c'}(114)$
prove true
  $IN_{9b}(147)$
provisionally, sign
  $VV_{bc}(154)$
provisos, limit by
  $TP_{2bbc}(165)$
provoke
  $KA_{0g}(90); EN_{7cc}(81);$
  $NO_{2'}(112)$
pry
  $KA_{0d}(89)$
psalms, read
  $ET/TE_b(138)$
pseudonym, write under a
  $IN_{6ac}(145)$
psychoanalysis, perform a
  $IN_{1ac}(142)$
public by printing, make
  $TE_{-2b}(139)$
public debate, have a
  $DT_{1ba}(127)$
public discussion, have a
  $DT_{1a}(127)$
public debate/discussion
  have a
  $DI_{7a}(126)$
publicize
  $ET_{0b}(135)$
publish
  $NO_{0a\S}(108); IN_{6aa}(144);$

publish (cont.)
  $IN_{6b}(145); IN_{6b'}(145);$
  $ET_{0a}(135); VE_{1a}(148);$
  $TE_{-2b}(139)$
publish from the pulpit
  $IN_{6b'}(145)$
puff up
  $TP_{2bba}(165)$
pull apart
  $KA_{4ac}(100); TV_{7b}(160);$
  $TE_{0bb}(141)$
pull into pieces
  $TV_{7b}(161); TE_{0bb}(141)$
pull out
  $IN_{5ac}(144)$
pull out of shape
  $TP_{2be}(166)$
pull passages from
  $TE_{-1b}(140)$
pulpit, preach from the
  $NO_{0a\S}(108)$
pulpit, publish from the
  $IN_{6b'}(145)$
pull (so.'s) leg
  $IR_{1a}(129)$
pump
  $NO_{6c}(114)$
pump so.
  $IN_{1ab}(142)$
pun, have a
  $IR_{2a}(130)$
punish
  $NO_{8a}(116)$
punishment, inflict a
  $NO_{8a}(116)$
punishment on,
  inflict disciplinary
  $WT_{4a}(119)$
punishment, remit a
  $NO_{9bb}(117)$

puns, make
  $IR_{1c}(130)$
pupil's lesson, hear a
  $EN_{5cd}(78); IN_{1ac}(142)$
purple prose, write
  $ET/TE_b(138)$
purport to be the original
  $TE_{0ab}(141)$
purpose, defeat a
  $EN_{8ab}(82)$
purse-proud, be
  $WS_{bc}(123)$
pursue
  $KA_{1ccb}(95); TU_{8a}(133);$
  $TV_{7g}(162)$
pursue an argument
  $AV_1(106)$
push into the background
  $KA_{3c}(99)$
put a law into effect
  $NO_{-4\S}(107)$
put an antithesis
  $AV_1(106)$
put so. out of temper
  $WP_{0ab}(121)$
put so. to a severe test
  $EN_{5cd}(78)$
put a question to so.
  $EN_{5cc}(78)$
put aside
  $KA_{3b}(99)$
put a signet
  $VV_{bc}(154)$
put a stop to
  $KA_{1bca}(93); DI_{10}(127)$
put a ticket on
  $VV_{ba}(153)$
put down
  $TE_{0bb}(141)$

put first
  $TO_{5a}(158)$
put in a bad temper
  $EN_{8d}(82)$
put in a favorable light
  $TP_{2bba}(165)$
put in a good word for
  $KA_{2cb}(98)$
put in a word
  $TO_{2bc}(156)$
put in bad order
  $IR_{2cb}(131)$
put information to
  $IN_{2a*}(142)$
put in ill repute
  $IR_{2cb}(131)$
put in limelight
  $TO_{5a}(158)$
put in order
  $TV_{7c}(161); IN_{3aa}(143)$
put in parentheses
  $TO_{5ad}(158)$
put in the know
  $VE_0(147)$
put in the pillory
  $NO_{8a}(116)$
put into metaphors
  $TP_{2bc}(166)$
put into words
  $TO_2(155); ET/TE_{ac}(138); ET/TE_{aa}(138)$
put mechanical
  $TP_{2be}(166)$
put off
  $KA_{1bba}(92); TV_{8b}(163)$
put on airs
  $WS_{bc}(123)$
put one over on
  $KA_{4bdb}(102); KA_{4ac}(101)$
put one's name to
  $VV_{bc}(154)$
put one's trust in
  $VE_0(147)$
put on hold
  $EN_{3ab}(76)$
put on layaway
  $EN_{3ab}(76)$
put on one side
  $KA_{3b}(99)$
put on reserve
  $EN_{3ab}(76)$
put on the list of speakers
  $DT/TU(134)$
put on the shelf, be
  $KA_{4baa}(101)$
put out feelers
  $DI_{1}.(124)$
put pessimistically
  $TP_{2bba}(165)$
put right
  $KA_{4cac}(103); KA_{4cad}(103); NO_{6b}(141); TV_{7c}(161)$
put so. back on his feet
  $KA_{2cab}(97)$
put so. off with
  $KA_{1cb}(95)$
put sth. on the ballot
  $WT_2.(119)$
put sth. into
  $TP_{2bc}(166)$
put stereotyped
  $TP_{2be}(166)$
put the audience to sleep
  $TP_{2b}(165)$
put the blame on so.
  $NO_{6a}(114)$
put the skids on
  $KA_{-1c}(88)$
put straight
  $KA_{4cad}(103); KA_{4cac}(103); TV_{7c}(161)$
put together
  $TO_4(157); DE_{6f}(151)$
put to fight
  $KA_{4ad}(100)$
put to rights
  $KA_{4cad}(103)$
put to the test
  $VV_c(154)$
put under an obligation
  $NO_{7a}(116)$
put under oath
  $NO_{0a}(108)$
put under tutelage
  $NO_{8a}(116); NO_{0dd}(110)$
put up a fight
  $KA_{1bca}(93)$
put up against
  $KA_{1bca}(93)$
put up with
  $KA_{4cda}(105); KA_{4bda}(102); KA_{0g}.(90)$
puzzle
  $KA_{1ab}(91)$

Q
quack
  $DT_{1bc}(128)$
qualify
  $TV_{7c}(161)$
qualify as
  $DE_{6c}(150)$
qualify so. sth. as something
  $VV_f(154)$

Lexicon Section II

quarrel
  $KA_{0d}(89); KA_{-1c}(87);$
  $KA_{-3ca}(86); KA_{-3c}(86);$
  $EM_{2f}(72); KA_{1da}(96)$
quarreling with, keep (on)
  $KA_{1aa}(91)$
quarrel, make up the
  $NO_{7a}(116)$
quarrel, patch up a
  $KA_{4caa}(103)$
quarrel, settle a
  $NO_{60}(114)$
quash
  $EN_{6e}(79)$
quash a judgement
  $NO_{9ba}(117); NO_{3bb}(112)$
query so.
  $IN_{1ab}(142)$
querulous, be
  $KA_{4bab}(101)$
question
  $IN_{1ab}(142); DE_{7}(151);$
  $NO_{6c}(114); EN_{5cc}(78)$
question, ask a
  $EN_{5cc}(78); TU_{2}(131)$
question, call into
  $DE_{7}(151)$
question closely
  $NO_{6c}(114)$
question, disregard the
  $EN_{9i}(84)$
question, evade the
  $EN_{9i}(84)$
question, ignore the
  $EN_{9i}(84)$
questioning, bring out by
  $EN_{5cd}(78)$
question, raise a
  $TV_{5}(159)$

questions, probe with
  $EN_{5cc}(78)$
question to so., put a
  $EN_{5cc}(78)$
quickly over, into; glance
  $TE_{-1b}(140)$
question witnesses
  $IN_{1ac}(142)$
quick-witted, be
  $KA_{1bcc}(93)$
quiet
  $EN_{7ca}(80)$
quieten
  $KA_{-1b}(87); KA_{4cac}(103)$
quit
  $KA_{4bac}(101); NO_{0dd}(109)$
quiz
  $EN_{5cc}(78)$
quiz some person
  $IN_{1ab}(142)$
quote authorities
  $AV_{3}(106)$

R

rack one's brain about
  $DE_{4}(149)$
rage, get into
  $EM_{2b}(71)$
raise
  $KA_{1bca}(93)$
raise an objection
  $TV_{6'a}(160)$
raise (a problem)
  $TV_{5}(159)$
raise a protest
  $AV_{1}(106)$
raise a question
  $TV_{5}(159)$
raise hopes
  $KA_{2cab}(97)$

raise objections
  $KA_{1bca}(93)$
raise one's hand
  $TU_{1}(131)$
raise one's voice
  $EM_{2aa}(71)$
rake
  $KA_{0c}(98)$
ramble (delirium)
  $ET/TE_{b}(138)$
rampage, (go on the)
  $KA_{0a}(88)$
rank
  $DE_{6b}(150); DE_{6f}(151)$
ranks, form into
  $DE_{6f}(151); TO_{3a}(157)$
rate
  $WT_{0}(118); VV_{g}(155)$
ratify
  $NO_{-4§}(107); NO_{0e§}(110);$
  $VV_{bc}(154); KA_{4cbd}(104)$
rationalize
  $DE_{6c}(150)$
rattle off
  $TP_{1a}(163)$
rave
  $TP_{2bj}(167); EM_{2i}(73);$
  $ET/TE_{b}(138)$
rave about
  $WT_{4e}(120); TP_{2bba}(165);$
  $TE_{0bb}(141)$
raving, be
  $TP_{2bj}(167)$
reach agreement
  $KA_{4cac}(103)$
reach back to
  $TV_{7i}(162)$
react bindly
  $KA_{0a}(88)$

react negatively
  $EN_{9c}(83)$
read
  $TE_{-1b}(140)$
read a paper
  $TE_{0aa}(141)$
readiness, ascertain
  $DI_{2}(124)$
readiness to converse,
  explore
  $DI_{1}.(124)$
readjust one's ideas
  $ET_{1d}(137)$
read off
  $TP_{1a}(163); TU_{4}$
read out
  $TU_{3}(132); TE_{0aa}(141)$
read over
  $TE_{-1b}(140)$
read psalms
  $ET/TE_{b}(138)$
read tarot cards
  $ET/TE_{b}(138)$
read through
  $TE_{-1b}(140)$
ready answer, give a
  $KA_{1bcc}(93)$
realize
  $ET^{*}_{-1a}(134)$
reappear
  $TV_{7i}(162)$
rearrange
  $TO_{3b}(157)$
reason, perceive the
  $ET_{-1a}(134)$
reasons, adduce
  $AV_{3}(106)$
reassure
  $EN_{7ca}(81); VV_{c}(154)$

reassure os.
  $KA_{1ba}(91)$
reasons for, give
  $KA_{1bcd}(94); AV_{3}(106);$
  $NO_{60}(113); TV^{*}_{7b}(161)$
reasons, transfer for
  disciplinary
  $NO_{8a}(116)$
reason why, give a
  $ET_{0df}(137)$
reassure (os.)
  $KA_{1ba}(91)$
rebel
  $NO_{2bb}(111); KA_{0g}.(90)$
rebel against
  $EN_{9h}(84); EN_{9k}(84)$
rebuff
  $KA_{0g}(90); DI_{3}.(125)$
rebuke
  $WT_{4a}(119)$
rebuke so.
  $NO_{8a}(116)$
rebut
  $AV_{1}(106); KA_{4ae}(101);$
  $KA_{1bcc}(93)$
recalcitrant, appear
  $KA_{1ccc}(95)$
recalcitrant, be
  $KA_{4bab}(101)$
recall
  $IN_{5aa}(144); IN_{5b}(144)$
recall the past
  $TV_{7j}(162)$
recall to memory
  $IN_{5aa}(144)$
recant
  $DI_{3}.(125); IN_{9a}(146)$
recapitulate
  $TV_{7j}(162); TE_{-1b}.(140);$
  $TV_{7f}(161)$

recapitulation, make a
  $TV_{7f}(161)$
receipt for, give a
  $WT_{4fg}(120)$
receipt, give a
  $VV_{bc}(154)$
receipt of, acknowledge
  $IN_{9b}(147)$
receipt (a bill)
  $VV_{bc}(154)$
receive
  $EN_{9a}.(85); DE_{1}(149)$
receive with exultation
  $WT_{5b}(120); EM_{2h}(73)$
rechristen
  $VV_{bb}(153)$
recite
  $TP_{1a}(163); TU_{4}(132);$
  $TE_{0aa}(141)$
recite in a sing-song
  manner
  $TP_{1a}(163)$
reckon up
  $KA_{1db}(96)$
reclaim
  $KA_{-2a}(86)$
recognize
  $DI_{3}(124); KA_{4cda}(105);$
  $WT_{4fa}(120); IN_{8a}(146)$
recognize identity
  $IN_{3ba}(143)$
recollect
  $IN_{5b}(144)$
recommence
  $TV_{7a}(160)$
recommend
  $WT_{4e}(120); WG_{0b}(123);$
  $EN_{2a}(75); WT_{1}(118);$
  $EN_{2c}(76)$

reconcile
  $KA_{-1b}(87); DI_9(126)$
reconcile conflicting ideas
  $NO_{7a}(116)$
reconciled, become
  $KA_{4caa}(103)$
reconstruct
  $TV_{7j}(162); TE_{0ac}(141)$
record
  $ET/TE_{ab}(138); VV_a(153);$
  $DE_1(149)$
record of, keep a
  $ET/TE_{ab}(138)$
recreate
  $TE_{0ac}(141)$
recruit
  $NO_{0da}(109); KA_{2aa}(96)$
rectify
  $NO_{6b}(114); TV_{7c}(161);$
  $TO_{2e}(156); ET/TE_a$
  (139)
recur
  $TV_{7i}(162)$
redefine
  $TE_{-1cd}(140)$
redeem
  $KA_{4cad}(103)$
red face, have a
  $EM_{2ab}(71)$
redress
  $KA_{4cad}(103)$
reduce (the severity)
  $TP_{2ac}(164); TO_{5c}(158)$
reduce to
  $DE_{6d}(150); DE_{6c}(150)$
reduce to silence
  $KA_{4ac}(100)$
reel off (a poem)
  $TP_{1a}(163)$

reenter into
  $TV_{7a}(160)$
refer a paradigm
  $AV_4(106)$
refer back to
  $TV_{7i}(162); EN_{1ad}(75)$
refer (back) to
  $KA_{1bcd}(94)$
referee, be counted out by
  $KA_{4bad}(102)$
refer one's money to so.
  $EN_{3da}(77)$
refer to
  $NO_{60}(114); TV_{7i}(162);$
  $IN_{10}(147); EN_{1ac}(74)$
refer to (an argument)
  $AV_3(106)$
refer to an example
  $AV_4(106)$
reflect (on)
  $DE_4(149)$
reflect on
  $IN_{5aa}(144)$
reflect on the past
  $TV_{7j}(162)$
retort
  $NO_{60}(114)$
refrain from
  $KA_{3b}(99)$
refresh so.'s memory
  $EN_{1ad}(75)$
refuse
  $KA_{1bcd}(94); IN_{8b}(146);$
  $EN_{9b}(82); EN_{9a}(82);$
  $NO_{0c}(109); EN_{9b\S}(84);$
  $EN_{9d}(83); EN_{9h}(84);$
  $KA_{1bcc}(94); EN_{9k}(84);$
  $DI_3.(125); DE_{8c}(152);$
  $WT_{4fb}(102); KA_{1bcb}(93);$
  $DE_{8e}(152)$

refuse to do
  $NO_2.(112)$
refuse to answer
  $EN_{9i}(84)$
refuse to have anything
  to do with
  $KA_{-3ca}(86)$
refuse to tolerate
  $KA_{0g}.(90)$
refute
  $KA_{4ae}(101); KA_{1bca}(93);$
  $KA_{1bcc}(94); NO_{60}(114);$
  $NO_{6e}(115); KA_{1bcd}(94);$
  $AV_1(106)$
regain
  $KA_{1bcc}(94)$
regard
  $VV_g(155)$
regard for, have
  $KA_{4cbd}(104)$
regard to, have
  $TO_{2bb}(156)$
register
  $ET/TE_{ab}(138); IN_{6b}$
  $(145); VV_a(153)$
regret
  $NO_{6b}(114)$
regularly, inform
  $IN_{6ad}(145)$
regularly, report to so.
  $IN_{6ad}(145)$
regulate
  $EN_{6c}(79); NO_{-3}(107)$
regulation, issue a
  $NO_{0a}(108); NO_{-4\S}(107)$
rehearing, enter a
  $NO_{9aa}(117)$
rehearse
  $TP_{1a}(163)$

reinterpret
  $TE_{-1cd}(140)$
reiterate
  $TV_{7d}(161); ET_{0da}(136)$
reject
  $VV_g(155); DE_{8e}(152);$
  $IN_{8b}(146); KA_{1bcd}(94);$
  $KA_{1bcc}(94); KA_{1bcb}$
  $(93); DE_{8c}(152); DI_3$
  $(125); EN_{9b}(82); EN_{9a}$
  $(82); EN_{9b§}(83); EN_{9d}$
  $(83); EN_{9h}(84); EN_{9i}$
  $(84); EN_{9j}(84); WT_{4fb}$
  $(120); TO_{2c}(156); WG_{1a}$
  $(123); EN_{9k}(84)$
reject so.
  $WP_{0aa}(121)$
rejoice
  $EM_{2e}(72); KA_{4a'}(101)$
rejoice at
  $EM_{2h}(73); WT_{5b}(121)$
rejoin at
  $KA_{1bca}(93)$
relate
  $DT_2.(129); TP_{2aa}(164);$
  $ET_{0a}(135)$
relations, enter into
  $KA_{2aa}(96)$
relativize
  $TP_{2bbc}(166); WG_{0a}(123);$
  $KA_{1bbc}(92)$
relax
  $KA_{1bbb}(92)$
release
  $NO_{3bd}(112); KA_{-1d}(88)$
release from an obligation
  $NO_{7a}(116)$
relegate
  $NO_{0dd}(110)$

relent
  $KA_{1bbb}(92); KA_{4cba}(104)$
relief, bring to
  $TO_{5e}(158)$
relief, throw into
  $TO_{5a}(158)$
relieve (another person)
  $TU_3...(132)$
relieve (of a guilt)
  $NO_{7c}(116)$
relinquish
  $KA_{3b}(99); KA_{4bc}(102);$
  $TU_3...(132); KA_{4bac}(101);$
  $EN_{9h}(84); KA_{-1d}(88)$
rely on
  $KA_{2cab}(97); IN_{10}(147)$
rely on so.
  $WT_3.(119)$
remain silent
  $TU_1.(131)$
remark
  $TO_{2bb}(156); TO_{2bc}(156);$
  $ET_{0a}(135)$
remark, make a brief
  $TU_5.(132)$
remark, say a
  $ET_{0a}(135)$
remarks, make
  $TO_{2bb}(156)$
remarks, make preliminary
  $TV_4(159)$
remarks, make witty
  $IR_{1c}(130); DT_{1d}(128)$
remarks, supplement previous
  $TV_{7a}(160)$
remedy
  $KA_{4cad}(103)$

remember
  $IN_{5b}(144); IN_{5aa}(144)$
remember, not
  $IN_{5ab}(144)$
remind
  $EN_{4a}(77)$
remind so.
  $EN_{1ad}(75)$
remit
  $EN_{3da}(77)$
remit a punishment
  $NO_{9bb}(117)$
remodel
  $TO_{2e}(156)$
remorse, show
  $NO_{6b}(114)$
remove
  $TO_{2c}(156); NO_{0dd}(110)$
remove a guilt
  $NO_{9bb}(117)$
remove (from office)
  $NO_{0dd}(110); NO_{8a}(116)$
remove objections
  $AV_1(106)$
remove one's support
  $KA_{2d}(98)$
rename
  $VV_{bb}(153)$
renew (a dispute)
  $TV_{7i}(162)$
renounce
  $KA_{-1d}(88); EN_{9h'}(84);$
  $KA_{1bbb}(92); KA_{3b}(99);$
  $KA_{4bac}(101)$
renounce one's turn to speak
  $TU_3...(132)$
reorder
  $TO_{3b}(157)$

reorganize
 ET/TE$_a$.(139);
 NO$_{3bc}$(112); TO$_{2c}$(156)
repair
 KA$_{4cad}$(103); TV$_{7c}$(161);
 KA$_{1bcc}$(94)
repair a paper
 ET/TE$_a$.(139)
repay
 KA$_{4bdb}$(102)
repeal
 NO$_{3bb}$(112); DI$_3$..(125);
 IN$_{9a}$(146)
repeat
 TV$_{7d}$(161); KA$_{1cca}$(95);
 TP$_{1a}$(163); IN$_{6aa}$(144)
repeat an order
 EN$_{3a}$(76)
repeat another's word
 ET$_{1c}$(137)
repeat mechanically
 ET$_{1c}$(137)
repeat over and over
 TV$_{7d}$(161)
repeat (too often)
 KA$_{1ccc}$(95)
repeat (what so. else
 has said)
 ET$_{0a}$(135)
repeat (what one has heard)
 ET$_{0a}$(135)
repeat (what one has heard
 before)
 TE$_{0aa}$(141)
repeat (what one has heard
 oneself)
 TP$_{2aa}$(164)
repeat (what one has said)
 TU$_4$(132); DT$_2$(129)

repeat (what so. else has said)
 TP$_{2aa}$(164); ET$_{0a}$(135)
repeating a formula
 TP$_{1a}$(163)
repel
 EN$_{9h}$(84); EN$_{9b}$(82);
 KA$_{1bcb}$(93)
repetitive, make
 TO$_{3a}$(157)
(replace a law), supersede
 NO$_{3bb}$(112)
reply
 NO$_{6e}$(115); NO$_{60}$(114);
 KA$_{1bca}$(93); AV$_1$(106);
 KA$_{1bcd}$(94)
report
 TV$_{7i}$(162); TP$_{2aa}$(164);
 ET$_{0a}$(135); VE$_{1b,c,d}$(148);
 ET$_{0b}$(135); NO$_4$(113);
 DT$_2$(129); TU$_4$(132);
 IN$_{6b}$(145); IN$_{6aa}$(144)
report on
 TU$_4$(132); DT$_2$(129)
report (what one has heard)
 TE$_{0aa}$(141)
report somebody
 IN$_{6ab}$(145)
report to (someone
 regularly)
 IN$_{6ad}$(145)
report (one's arrival, one's
 depature) to the police
 IN$_{6b}$(145)
report upon a matter
 TU$_4$(132); DT$_2$(129);
 ET$_{0a}$(135); TP$_{2aa}$(164);
 IN$_{6aa}$(144)
report of, draw up the
 official
 ET/TE$_{ab}$(138)

represent
 KA$_{2cb}$(98)
represent somebody/
 something as something
 VV$_g$(155)
reprimand
 WT$_{4a}$(119); NO$_{8a}$(116)
reprimand sharply
 WP$_{0ad}$(122)
reproach so. with
 WT$_1$(118)
reproach so. with a th.
 NO$_{6a}$(114)
reproduce
 ET$_{1c}$(137); TE$_{0aa}$(141)
reprove
 WT$_{4a}$(119)
reprove so.
 NO$_{8a}$(116)
repudiate
 KA$_{1bcb}$(93); IN$_{8b}$(146);
 KA$_{4ae}$(101); WT$_{4fb}$(120);
 KA$_{1bcc}$(94)
repulse
 EN$_{9b}$(82); EN$_{9a}$(82);
 EN$_{9h}$(84); KA$_{1bcd}$(93);
reputation, devalue so.'s
 NO$_{10}$(117); WT$_{5a}$(120)
repute, put in ill
 IR$_{2cb}$(131)
request
 EN$_{5a}$(77); KA$_{-2a}$;
 EN$_{2b}$(75); EN$_{2b§}$(75);
 DI$_{2\cdot a}$(124)
request, make a formal
 EN$_{2b§}$(75); NO$_{-2§}$(108)
request to keep secret
 VE$_{-1}$
require
 EN$_{2b}$; KA$_{-2a}$(86);

require (cont.)
  $EN_{5b}(77); NO_{-2}(108)$
requiring participation
  $DI_1(124)$
requisition
  $KA_{-2b}(87)$
requite
  $NO_{8a}(116); KA_{4bdb}(102);$
  $KA_{1bca}(93)$
rescind
  $EN_{6e}(79)$
resentful of, be
  $NO_{10}(117); WT_{5a}(120)$
reservations, make
  $KA_{4cbc}(104)$
reserve
  $KA_{4cbc}(104); EN_{3ab}(76)$
reserve a seat
  $EN_{3ab}(76)$
reserves, call up the
  $IN_{6b}\text{'}(145)$
reserve the right to
  $KA_{4cbc}(104)$
reshape
  $TE_{0ae}(141)$
resign
  $KA_{1bbb}(92); KA_{3b}(99);$
  $KA_{4bac}(101); IN_{6b}(145);$
  $EN_{9\text{'}c}(85); NO_{0db}(109);$
  $KA_{-1d}(88)$
resigned to, be
  $KA_{4bda}(102); KA_{4cda}(105)$
resignate
  $KA_{4bda}(102)$
resignation, announce one's
  $KA_{4bac}(101)$
resigned to, be
  $KA_{4bda}(102); KA_{4cda}(105)$
resign os. to
  $KA_{4bda}(102)$

resist
  $KA_{1bcb}(93); KA_{1bca}(93);$
  $KA_{0g}\text{'}(90); EN_{9f}(83)$
resist the judgement
  $NO_{9aa}(117)$
resolve (on)
  $DE_{8c}(152); DE_{8e}(152)$
respect
  $KA_{4cdb}(105); NO_{2a}(111);$
  $WT_{5d}(121)$
respect, command
  $KA_{1ab}(91)$
respects, pay one's
  $WT_{5d}(121)$
respond blindly
  $KA_{0a}(88)$
responsibility for, take
  $NO_1(111)$
rest on
  $IN_{10}(147)$
restore
  $ET/TE_a\text{'}(139); KA_{1bcc}(94)$
restrain
  $KA_{1bcb}(93); EN_{8ab}(82)$
restrain os.
  $KA_{3b}(99)$
restrict
  $KA_{4cbc}(104);$
  $KA_{1bcb}(93)$
restrict (rights)
  $NO_{0c}(109)$
resume
  $TV_{7i}(162); TV_{7g}(162);$
  $TV_{7a}(160)$
retail (texts)
  $TE_{-2b}(139)$
retaliate
  $KA_{4bdb}(102)$
retard
  $KA_{1bcb}(93);$

retard (cont.)
  $KA_{1bba}(92)$
retell
  $TE_{0aa}(141); TE_{0ac}(141)$
retire
  $DI_{10}\text{'}(127); KA_{4bac}(101)$
retire from
  $NO_{0db}(109); KA_{5bc}(102)$
retort
  $NO_{60}(114); AV_1(106);$
  $KA_{1bcd}(94); KA_{1bca}(93)$
retouch
  $ET/TE_a\text{'}(139)$
retract
  $DI_3\text{'}(125); EN_{6e}(79);$
  $NO_{3ba}(111); IN_{9a}(146)$
retract a judgement
  $NO_{9ba}(117)$
retranslate
  $TE_{0ae}(141)$
retreat
  $KA_{-1d}(88)$
retrospect
  $TV_6\text{'}_b(160)$
return
  $KA_{1bca}(93); TV_{7i}(162)$
return to
  $TV_{7i}(162)$
return to the subject
  $TV_{7g}(162)$
reveal
  $VE_{1a}(148); ET_{0c}(136)$
reveal (secrets)
  $VE_1(148)$
reveal something to so.
  $ET_{0dd}(137)$
revenge
  $NO_{8a}(116)$
revenge on, take
  $KA_{4bdb}(102)$

249

Lexicon Section II

revenge os. on
  $KA_{4bdb}(102)$
revere
  $WT_{5d}(121)$
reveries, indulge in
  $DE_9(152); ET/TE_b(138)$
review
  $TE_{-1b}(140); ET/TE_a.(139);$
  $TV_{6'b}(160); TV_{7b}(161);$
  $TE_{0bb}(141)$
review the past
  $TV_{7j}(162)$
revile
  $WP_{0ab}(121); KA_{0g}(90)$
revise
  $TV_{7c}(161); DI_3\cdot\cdot(125);$
  $IN_{9a}(146); NO_{9ba}(117);$
  $VV_c(154); ET/TE_a.(139)$
revise a judgement
  $NO_{3bb}(112)$
revoke
  $EN_{6e}(79); DI_3\cdot\cdot(125);$
  $IN_{9a}(146)$
revolt
  $NO_{2bb}(111); EN_{9f}(83)$
rework
  $ET/TE_a.(139)$
rewrite
  $ET/TE_a.(139)$
rhymes, make
  $ET/TE_{ac}(138)$
ride roughshod over
  $KA_{4ae}(101)$
riddle, solve a
  $IN_{2a}.(143)$
ridicule
  $WP_{0ab}(121); KA_{0g}(90);$
  $IR_{1b}(130); IR_{2b}(130);$
  $IR_{2cb}(131)$

(ridicule)
  $NO_2.(112)$
ridicule, expose to
  $IR_{2cb}(131); IR_{1a}(129)$
ridicule, hold to
  $IR_{2b}(130)$
ridiculous, make os.
  $WS_{ab}(122)$
ridicule sth.
  $IR_{1c}(130)$
ridicule sth. so.
  $DT_{1d}(128)$
right, put
  $KA_{4cac}(103); KA_{4cad}(103);$
  $NO_{6b}(114); TV_{7c}(161)$
righten
  $KA_{4cad}(103)$
rights, claim one's
  $KA_{0j}(90)$
rights, encroach on
  $NO_2(112)$
rights, put to
  $KA_{4cad}(103)$
rights, restrict
  $NO_{0c}(109)$
right to, reserve the
  $KA_{4cbc}(104)$
rip apart
  $TE_{0bb}(141)$
rise to, give
  $EN_{1ae}(75)$
risks, try to avoid
  $KA_{1ba}(91)$
romanticize
  $TP_{2bba}(165)$
rote, do by
  $ET_{1c}(137)$
round, get
  $KA_{2aa}(96)$

round, scrub
  $KA_{4aa}(99)$
rouse
  $EN_{1aa}(74); EN_{7cb}(81);$
  $KA_{-1c}(87)$
rousing speech, make a
  $TP_{2ab}(164)$
route open, keep an
  escape
  $KA_{1cb}(95)$
rubrify
  $VV_a(153)$
ruin
  $KA_{1aa}(91)$
rumble
  $EM_{2k}(73)$
rummage
  $KA_{0c}(89)$
rumors about so.,
  spread
  $WP_{0ac}(121)$
rumors, spread
  $IN_{6ac}(145);$
run around
  $DI_{8a}(126)$
run down
  $TV_{7b}(161); WT_{4c}(120);$
  $TE_{0bb}(141)$
run down the checklist
  $TV_{6a}(159)$
run for (presidency)
  $EN_{2c\S}(76)$
running, stop
  $DI_{8a}(126)$
run one's head against
  a brick wall
  $TV_6\cdot\cdot\cdot(160)$
run through
  $TE_{-1b}(140)$

rush ahead and start
  speaking
  $TU_3(131)$
rush over
  $TO_{2bc}(156)$
rusticate (a student)
  $NO_{0dd}(110)$

S

sabotage
  $KA_{0c}(89)$
sacrifice
  $KA_{1bbb}(92)$
sad, be
  $EM_{2ab}(71); EM_{2cb}(72)$
sad, get
  $EM_{2aa}(71)$
sad, I am
  $EM_{2cb*}(72)$
sad, turn
  $EM_{2aa}(71)$
safeguard
  $KA_{2b}(97)$
sails, take wind out of so.'s
  $KA_{1bbc}(92)$
sale, offer for
  $EN_{2a}(75)$
salient, make
  $TO_{5a}(158)$
salute
  $EM_{2h}(73)$
sanctify
  $EN_{3da}(77); WT_{5d}(121)$
sanction
  $KA_{4cbb}(104); NO_{0b}(108)$
sanctions, impose
  $NO_{8a}(116)$
sap
  $KA_{0c}(89)$

satirize
  $TE_{0ab}(141)$
satisfy
  $KA_{4cac}(103); KA_{4cad}(104)$
say
  $IN_{6aa}(144)$
say again
  $TV_{7d}(161)$
say (a remark)
  $ET_{0a}(135)$
say beforehand
  $TV_4(159)$
say goodbye
  $DI_{10}(127)$
say goodbye to
  $TU_{9a}(133)$
say grace
  $TP_{1a}(163)$
say in advance
  $TV_4(159)$
say in, have a
  $KA_{0g'}(90)$
say, let so. have his
  $TU_2(131)$
say obscenities
  $DT_{1e}(128)$
say over and over again
  $ET_{0da}(136)$
say preliminarily
  $TV_4(159)$
say sweet nothings
  $DT_{1c}(128); EN_{7aa}(79); WS_{bba}(123)$
say with conviction
  $ET_{0a}(135)$
say yes to
  $KA_{4cda}(105)$
scale down
  $KA_{-1d}(88); KA_{3b}(99); TO_{5c}(158)$

scandalized by, be
  $WT_0(118)$
scare
  $EN_{8b}(82); EN_{8d}(82)$
scare (away)
  $KA_{1ab}(91)$
scare off
  $KA_{4ad}(100)$
schedule
  $VV_a(153)$
schematize
  $TU_{2bbb}(165)$
scheme
  $DE_{8d}(152)$
school
  $EN_{3c}(76); EN_{8c}(82)$
science fiction, produce
  $ET/TE_b(138)$
scoff at
  $IR_{1a}(129); IR_{1b}(130); WP_{0ab}(121)$
scoff (at)
  $IR_{2cb}(131)$
scold
  $EM_{2l}(73); NO_{8a}(116); WT_{4a}(119)$
scolding, give a good
  $WP_{0ad}(122)$
scolding, give a thorough
  $WT_{4a}(119)$
scolding, give so. a severe
  $EM_{2l}(73)$
scorn
  $WP_{0aa}(121)$
scorn, laugh to
  $IR_{2cb}(131)$
scorn, treat with
  $IR_{1a}(129); IR_{2cb}(131)$
scrape acquaintance
  $KA_{2aa}(96)$

251

Lexicon Section II

scream
  $EM_{2b}(71)$
scream at
  $WP_{0ab}(121)$
screen
  $IN_{6d}(145); TO_{5ad}(158); TP_{2bc}(166)$
scrub around
  $KA_{4aa}(99)$
scrutinize
  $ET/TE_a.(139); TE_{-1b}(140); VV_c(154)$
seal
  $VV_{bc}(154)$
seal, affix a
  $VV_{bc}(154)$
search
  $IN_{1aa}(142)$
search out
  $IN_{1aa}(142)$
search through
  $IN_{1aa}(142)$
seat, reserve a
  $EN_{3ab}(76)$
seats, book
  $EN_{3a}(76)$
secede
  $KA_{4bac}(101)$
secede from
  $NO_{0db}(109)$
second to, be
  $KA_{-1d}(88)$
second to, come
  $KA_{3b}(99)$
secret, betray a
  $VE_1(148)$
secret, classify as
  $VE_{-1}(147)$
secret, divulge a
  $NO_{6db}(115)$

secret, keep a
  $VE_1.(147)$
secret, keep sth.
  $VE_1.(147)$
secret, let out
  $VE_1.(148)$
secret, let the matter go no further of a
  $VE_1.(147)$
secret, mark as
  $VE_{-1}(147)$
secret, request to keep
  $VE_{-1}(147)$
secret, stamp as
  $VE_{-1}(147)$
secrete
  $TP_{2bg}(167)$
secrets, disclose
  $NO_{6db}(115)$
secrets, keep
  $VE_1(148); TP_{2bg}(167); KA_{1bba}(92)$
secrets, plot
  $VE_{-2}(147)$
secrets, reveal
  $VE_1(148)$
secure
  $KA_{2b}(97)$
secure (position)
  $KA_{1dc}(96)$
seduce
  $KA_{0g}.(90); KA_{2aa}(96); EN_{7af}(80)$
see
  $ET_{-1a}.(134); ET*_{-1a}(134)$
see eye to eye
  $KA_{4cbb}(104)$
see off
  $KA_{4ad}(100)$

see over, manage to
  $TP_{2bf}(167)$
see sth. in a different light
  $KA_{-1b}(87)$
see trough
  $VV_c(154)$
see trough (the trick)
  $ET_{-1b}(134)$
segment
  $DE_{6c}(150); TO_{3a}(157)$
seize
  $EN_{3db}(77); NO_{-2}(108); NO_5.(113)$
seized, have so.
  $NO_5.(113)$
select
  $DE_{6b}(150); IN_{3ba}(143); TO_{3a}(157); VV_g(155)$
select so.
  $NO_{0b}".(109); WT_1(118)$
self-effacing, be
  $WS_{aa}(122); WS_{ab}(122)$
send
  $EN_{3aa}(76)$
send about one's business
  $KA_{4ac}(100); KA_{4ae}(101)$
send so.
  $EN_{6c}(79)$
send a p. to
  $NO_{-3}(107)$
send a stiff
  $VE_0(147)$
send away
  $EN_{8b}(82)$
send down
  $NO_{0dd}(110)$
send for so.
  $EN_{3a}(76)$

send one's money to so.
  $EN_{3da}(77)$
send packing
  $KA_{4ad}(100)$
send so.
  $EN_{3aa}(76)$
send in one's name/card
  $TU_1(131)$
sentence
  $NO_7(115); NO_{7b}(116)$
sentence on so., pass
  $NO_7(115)$
sentence, pass
  $NO_{7a}(116)$
separate
  $DE_{6b}(150); IN_{3ba}(143);$
  $VV_e(154); VV_g(155)$
separate from
  $KA_{2d}(98)$
sequence, change the
  $TO_{3b}(157)$
sequester
  $KA_{-2a}(86)$
series, making
  $TO_4(157)$
seriously, take
  $KA_{4cdb}(105); NO_{2a}(111)$
sermonize
  $ET_{0da}(136); TP_{1d}(163)$
services, offer one's
  $KA_{2ab}(97); EN_{2a}(75)$
session, close the
  $DI_{10}(127)$
session, have a
  $NO_{2ba}(111); NO_{0f}(110)$
session, open
  $DI/TU(134)$
set about
  $KA_{0h}(90); KA_{0i}(90)$

set about (a task)
  $TV_1(158)$
set about speaking
  $TU_3(131)$
set against
  $KA_{1bca}(93); KA_{1bcd}(94)$
set a limit
  $NO_{0g}(111)$
set an example
  $AV_4(106)$
set aside
  $IN_{3ba}(143); DE_{6b}(150)$
set aside, be
  $KA_{4baa}(101)$
set forth
  $ET_{0a}(135); ET_{0de}(137);$
  $TP_{2aa}(164)$
set in order
  $IN_{3aa}(143)$
set off
  $TO_{5a}(158); TO_{5e}(158)$
set one's cap at
  $KA_{-2b}(87); KA_{2aa}(96)$
set over
  $DE_{8c}(152); DE_{8e}(152)$
set right
  $KA_{4cac}(103); NO_{9b'}(117);$
  $TV_{7c}(161)$
set right again
  $KA_{4cad}(104)$
set so. off
  $KA_{-1c}(88)$
set so. off against so.
  $KA_{-1c}(88)$
set up a list
  $IN_{-1}(143)$
set up a project
  $DE_{8d}(152)$
settle
  $KA_{-1b}(87); KA_{1db}(96);$

settle (cont.)
  $KA_{2b}(97); KA_{4ac}(100);$
  $KA_{4cad}(104);$
  $KA_{4cbb}(104);$
  $KA_{4cbd}(104); NO_{7a}(116);$
  $NO_{9b'}(117)$
settle accounts with
  $KA_{4bdb}(102)$
settle (a difference)
  $DI_9(126)$
settle a quarrel
  $NO_{60}(114)$
settlement, make a
  $KA_{4cbd}(104)$
settle one's difference
  $KA_{1db}(96)$
severe scolding, give so. a
  $EM_{21}(73)$
severe test, put so. to a
  $EN_{5cd}(78)$
severity, diminish the
  $TO_{5c}(158)$
shade
  $TP_{2bbc}(166)$
shake
  $KA_{0g}(90)$
shake off
  $EN_{9h}(84); KA_{1bcb}(93)$
shallow, make
  $TP_{2bbb}(165)$
shape
  $TV_{6a}(159)$
shape, pull out of
  $TP_{2be}(166)$
share opinion, do not
  $WT_{4fb}(120)$
share the opinion
  $KA_{-3b}(85)$
share the same opinion
  $IN_{8a}(146); KA_{4cca}(105)$

253

sharpen
  $KA_{-1c}(87); TV_{7c}(161)$
sharply, reprimand
  $WP_{0ad}(122)$
shelf, be put on the
  $KA_{4baa}(101)$
shelve
  $KA_{3b}(99)$
shift
  $KA_{1bba}; TP_{2bf}$
shingle, hang out a
  $IN_{6b}`(145)$
shirk
  $KA_{1bba}(92); KA_{4aa}(99);$
  $TP_{2bf}(167)$
shock
  $EN_{7b}(80); WP_{0ab}(121)$
shocked, be
  $EM_{2ab}(71)$
shoot at
  $KA_{0g}(90)$
shoot down
  $KA_{0c}(89)$
shop, talk
  $DT_{3}(129)$
short, cut a conversation
  $TU_{3}`(132); TU_{6}(133)$
short, cut so.
  $TU_{6}(133)$
short, cut so.
  $TU_{3}`(132)$
short, keep
  $TU_{5}`(132)$
short, stop
  $TU_{6}(132); TU_{3}`(132)$
short, stop so.
  $TU_{6}(133)$
shorten
  $ET/TE_{a}`(139)$
shorten too much
  $TP_{2bi}(167)$
should ...
  $NO_{0}`(111)$
shout
  $EM_{2b}(71); EM_{2e}(72)$
shout at
  $EM_{2l}(73)$
shout down
  $DI_{8b}(126); EM_{2h}(73)$
shout for joy
  $EM_{2b}(71)$
shout to each other
  $DT_{1g}(128)$
shout to so.
  $EM_{2h}(73)$
shout with joy
  $EM_{2e}(72)$
show
  $AV_{3}(106); EN_{1ac}(74);$
  $EN_{6c}(79); IN_{9b}(79);$
  $NO_{-3}(107); NO_{60}(114);$
  $TP_{2ac}(164)$
show and tell
  $ET_{0da}(136)$
show bias
  $WT_{3}``(119)$
show distrust
  $WT_{3}`(119)$
show doubts about so.
  $WT_{3}`(119)$
show goodwill towards so.
  $WT_{5c}(121)$
show how to do
  $ET_{0db}(136)$
show interest
  $DI_{2}(124)$
show malicious pleasure
  $KA_{4a}`(101)$
show off
  $WS_{bc}(123)$
show one's colors
  $NO_{6b}(114)$
show prejudices
  $WT_{3}``(119)$
show proof of
  $AV_{3}(106); IN_{9b}(147)$
show proof
  $NO_{6da}(115)$
show remorse
  $NO_{6b}(114)$
show sympathy
  $EN_{7ca}(81)$
show the way
  $EN_{1ac}(74); EN_{6c}(79)$
show up
  $KA_{0g}(90)$
shred to pieces
  $WT_{4c}(120)$
shriek
  $EM_{2b}(71)$
shun
  $TP_{2bf}(167)$
shun so.
  $WP_{0aa}(121)$
shut so.'s mouth
  $KA_{4ac}(100)$
shut so. up
  $KA_{4ac}(100)$
sicken
  $EN_{7d}(81)$
side, put on one
  $KA_{3b}(99)$
side, take so.'s
  $KA_{2cb}(98)$
sides, change
  $KA_{4bbb}(102)$
sidestep
  $KA_{1bba}(92)$

side to side, jump from
  $KA_{1cb}(95)$
sidetrack
  $EN_{1b}(75)$
side with
  $KA_{2cb}(98); KA_{4cca}(105);$
  $NO_{6e}(115)$
side with so.
  $KA_{-3b}(85)$
sift
  $VV_a(153)$
sift through
  $IN_{1aa}(142)$
sight of, lose
  $KA_{3c}(99)$
sign
  $NO_{-4\S}(107)$
sign
  $VV_{ba}(153); VV_{bc}(154);$
  $WT_{4f\S}(120)$
sign (a contract)
  $EN_{6d}(79); NO_{0e\S}(110);$
  $NO_{0f}(110)$
signet, put a
  $VV_{bc}(154)$
sign provisionally
  $VV_{bc}(154)$
sign (with a flourish)
  $VV_{bc}(154)$
silence
  $KA_{-1b}(87); KA_{4ac}(100)$
silence, reduce to
  $KA_{4ac}(100)$
silence, pass over in
  $TP_{2bg}(167)$
silent, become
  $TU_{6'a}(133)$
silent, remain
  $TU_1.(131)$

silly, be
  $IR_{1c}(130)$
simplify
  $TP_{2ac}(164); TP_{2bbb}(165)$
simulate fighting
  $KA_{-3cb}(86)$
sing (like a canary)
  $VE_{1b}(148)$
single out
  $DE_{6b}(150); IN_{3ba}(143);$
  $VV_g(155)$
sing-song manner, deliver in a monotonous
  $TP_{1a}(163)$
sing-song manner, recite in a
  $TP_{1a}(163)$
sing small
  $KA_{4bac}(101)$
sink into oblivion, let sth.
  $KA_{4caa}(103)$
sins, take away
  $NO_{9bb}(117)$
sketch
  $DE_{8d}(152); DT_2(129);$
  $ET/TE_{ac}(138); TO_{2a}(155);$
  $TP_{2ac}(164); TV_3(159)$
sketch in profile
  $TO_{2a}(155); TV_3(159)$
skids on, put the
  $KA_{-1c}(87)$
skim through
  $TE_{-1b}(140)$
skip
  $EN_{9i}(84); TO_{2c}(156);$
  $TU_2.(131)$
skip
  $KA_{1bba}(92)$
skirmish
  $KA_{0d}(89); KA_{0g}(90);$
  $KA_{1da}(96)$

slander
  $KA_{0g}(90); NO_3.(113);$
  $WP_{0ac}(122)$
slant
  $IN_{6d}(145)$
sleep, lull to
  $EN_{7ca}(81)$
sleep on something
  $DE_4(149)$
sleep, put the audience to
  $TP_{2b}(165)$
slight
  $KA_{1bcc}(94)$
slightingly, treat
  $TV_{8b}(163)$
slip out from
  $VE_{1g}(149)$
slur on, cast a
  $IR_{2cb}(131)$
small, make so. feel
  $KA_{4ac}(100)$
small, sing
  $KA_{bac}(101)$
smooth over
  $TP_{2bba}(165); TP_{2bc}(166)$
smuggle letters in prisoner's cell
  $VE_0(147)$
smut, talk
  $DT_{1e}(128)$
smutty jokes, make
  $DT_{1e}(128)$
smutty jokes, talk
  $DE_{1e}(128)$
snatch up
  $DE_1(149)$
snap at
  $EM_{2l}(73)$
snarl at
  $EM_{2l}(73)$

sneer (at so.)
　$IR_{2ca}(130)$
sneer at
　$EM_{2l}(73); IR_{1a}(129)$
sneer (at)
　$IR_{2b}(130); IR_{2cb}(131)$
snob, be a
　$WS_{bc}(123)$
sob
　$EM_{2aa}(71)$
society, initiate so. into a
　$VE_0(147)$
soften
　$EN_{7ca}(81); KA_{-1b}(87);$
　$KA_{1bbb}(92);$
　$KA_{4cac}(103); TO_{5c}(158)$
soften down
　$TP_{2bbc}(165)$
solace
　$EN_{7ca}(81)$
solemnly, promise
　$EN_{6d}(79); NO_{0dd}(110)$
solicit
　$EN_{2b}(75); EN_{2b\S}(75);$
　$NO_{-2\S}(108)$
solidarity with, declare
　$KA_{2b}(97)$
solidify
　$TO_{2f}(157)$
soliloquize
　$DT_2(129); TU_4(132)$
(solve)
　$EN_{5ca}(78)$
solve (a riddle)
　$IN_{2a}.(143)$
soothe
　$EN_{7ca}(81); KA_{-1b}(87);$
　$KA_{4cac}(103)$
sore spot, hit on the
　$TO_{2g}(157)$

sore spot, touch on a
　$TO_{2g}(157)$
sorry for, be
　$EM_{2cb}(72)$
sorry, I am
　$EM_{2cb*}(72)$
sort
　$IN_{3aa}(143); VV_a(153);$
　$VV_g(155)$
sort out
　$DE_{6b}(150); IN_{3ba}(143)$
soundings, take first
　$KA_{2aa}(97)$
sound out
　$KA_{2aa}(96)$
sound out so. (as to his views)
　$IN_{1ab}(142)$
sound out sth. for so.
　$ET_{0dc}(137)$
spare
　$KA_{-1d}(88); NO_{9bb}(117);$
　$KA_{3b}(99)$
spare with words, be too
　$TP_{2bi}(167)$
sparingly, use words
　$TP_{2ad}(164)$
sparingly, use words too
　$TP_{2bi}(167)$
speak
　$TU_4(132)$
speak, allow so. to
　$DI/TU(134); TV_2(159)$
speak a memorial address
　$WT_{5d}(121)$
speak, begin to
　$TU_3(131)$
speak, beg permission to
　$TU_1(131)$

speak bombastically
　$TP_{2b}(165)$
speak concisely
　$TU_5.(132)$
speak distoted English
　$TE_{0ab}(141)$
speak drivel
　$TP_{1e}(163)$
speaker, introduce the
　$DI/TU(134)$
speakers, put on the list of
　$DI/TU(134)$
speak for
　$KA_{2cb}(98)$
speak, give permission to
　$TU_2(131); DI/TU(134)$
speak ill of os.
　$WS_{ab}(122)$
speak ill of so.
　$WP_{0ac}(122)$
speak impart permission to
　$TU_2(131)$
speak in a beastly way
　$DT_{1e}(128)$
speak in broken English
　$TP_{1b}(163)$
speaking, forego
　$TU_1.(131)$
speaking, rush ahead and start
　$TU_3(131)$
speaking, set about
　$TU_3(131)$
speaking time, extend
　$DI/TU(134)$
speaking time, limit
　$DI/TU(134)$
speak in tongues
　$ET/TE_b(138)$

speak in very high
  terms of so.
  WT$_{4e}$(120)
speak, no to give a
  chance to
  TU$_2$.(131)
speak one's mind
  DI$_{7b}$(126)
speak of
  DT$_2$(129)
speak (parliament),
  ask leave to
  TV$_1$(158)
speak pompously
  TP$_{2b}$(165)
speak poor English
  TE$_{0ab}$(141)
speak prematurely
  TV$_{8a}$(162)
speak pretentiously
  TP$_{2b}$(165)
speak, renounce one's
  turn to
  TU$_3$"(132)
speak to
  DI$_5$(125); KA$_{2aa}$(96)
speak together
  DT$_{1a}$(127); DT$_{1bc}$(128);
  DI$_{7a}$(126)
speak to so.
  DI$_1$(124)
special attention to, call
  TO$_{5a}$(158)
specify
  TV$_{7c}$(161)
specify in a list
  VV$_a$(153)
speculate
  DE$_5$(150)

speech, break down in a
  DI$_{8a}$(126); TU$_6$'$_b$(133)
speech, deliver a
  DI$_{7b}$(126); DT$_2$(129);
  TU$_4$(132)
speech, draft a
  ET/TE$_{ad}$(138)
speech, give a
  DI$_{7b}$(126); DT$_2$(129);
  TU$_4$(132)
speech, make a moving
  TP$_{2ab}$(164)
speech, make a rousing
  TP$_{2ab}$(164)
speech, make a stirring
  TP$_{2ab}$(164)
spell out something for so.
  ET$_{0dc}$(137)
spill in beans
  VE$_{1b}$(148)
spin out
  KA$_{1bba}$(92); TV$_{6a}$(159)
spin yarns
  DE$_9$(152); ET/TE$_b$(138);
  TP$_{2bj}$(167)
spit at
  EM$_{2l}$(73)
splice
  TO$_{3a}$(157)
split hairs
  DT$_3$(129); TP$_{2b}$(165);
  TP$_{2bh}$(167)
split up
  KA$_{-1c}$(87); TO$_{3a}$(157)
spoil
  TP$_{2be}$(167)
spoon-feed
  ET$_{0da}$(136)
sport of, make
  IR$_{1a}$(129)

spot, hit on a sore
  TO$_{2g}$(157)
spotlight
  TO$_{5a}$(158)
spot, touch on a sore
  TO$_{2g}$(157)
spread
  IN$_{6aa}$(144); TE$_{-2a}$(139)
spread about
  IN$_{6aa}$(144); TE$_{-2a}$(139)
spread rumors
  IN$_{6ac}$(145)
spread rumors about so.
  WP$_{0ac}$(122)
spread stories about so.
  WP$_{0ac}$(122)
spread the news
  KA$_{0c}$(89)
spur (on)
  EN$_{7cb}$(81); EN$_{7cc}$(81)
spurn
  IN$_{8b}$(146)
squabble
  EM$_{2f}$(72); KA$_{0d}$(89)
squash
  KA$_{4ac}$(100); TP$_{2bj}$(167)
squeeze out
  KA$_{4ad}$(100)
squirm
  KA$_{4bab}$(101)
stabilize (position)
  KA$_{1ccb}$(95); KA$_{1dc}$(96)
stage, boo so. off the
  EM$_{2h}$(73)
stage, hiss off the
  EM$_{2h}$(73)
stagger
  EN$_{7b}$(80)
stagnate
  DI$_{8a}$(126); TV$_6$"'(160)

Lexicon Section II

stake out
  $TO_{2a}(155)$
stammer
  $EM_{2aa}(71)$
stamp
  $IN_{3c}(144); VV_{ba}(153)$
stamp as secret
  $VE_{-1}(147)$
stand apart from
  $KA_{3b}(99)$
standardize
  $TV_{7c}(161); VV_a(153)$
stand by
  $KA_{-3b}(85)$
stand by (claim)
  $KA_{1ccc}(95)$
stand down
  $KA_{4bac}(103)$
stand for, not to
  $KA_{0g}(90)$
stand still
  $DI_{8a}(126); TV_6\text{'''}(160)$
standstill, come to a
  $DI_{8a}(126); TU_{6'b}(133)$
stand up for
  $KA_{1bca}(93); KA_{1ccb}(95); KA_{2cb}(98); NO_{6e}(115)$
start
  $DI_6(125); TV_5(159)$
start a conversation
  $EN_{7ac}(79)$
startle
  $EN_{7b}(80); EN_{9l}(84)$
start speaking, rush ahead and
  $TU_3(131)$
start to grumble about
  $EM_{2d}(72)$
state
  $ET_{0a}(135); TO_{2bb}(156)$

statement, make a
  $TO_{2bb}(156)$
state terms
  $KA_{4cbc}(104)$
status, make so. lose his
  $WT_{5a}(120); NO_{10}(117)$
stay flexible
  $KA_{1cb}(95)$
stay hard
  $KA_{1ccc}(95)$
steer the conversation upon a subject
  $TO_{5ac}(158)$
step back
  $KA_{4bac}(101)$
step down
  $KA_{4bac}(101)$
step in between
  $TU_3(132)$
step into the breach
  $KA_{2cab}(98); KA_{2cb}(98)$
step out
  $NO_{0db}(109)$
stereotype
  $TP_{2bbb}(165)$
stereotype so.
  $NO_{10}(117); WT_{5a}(120)$
stereotyped, put
  $TP_{2be}(166)$
stick at
  $KA_{1dc}(96)$
stick bills on
  $IN_{6b'}(145)$
stick obstinately to sth.
  $TV_{7d}(161)$
stick out from
  $KA_{-1d}(88)$
stick to
  $KA_{1cca}(95); KA_{1ccb}(95)$

stick together
  $KA_{4cca}(105); TO_4(157)$
stick to (too fiercely)
  $KA_{1ccc}(95)$
stick upon (a bulletin board)
  $IN_{6b'}(145)$
stiff, send a
  $VE_0(147)$
stifle
  $TP_{2bbc}(166)$
stigmatize
  $NO_{8a}(116)$
still
  $EN_{7ca}(81)$
(still) adhere to a viewpoint
  $TV_{7a}(160)$
still, be
  $TU_1(131)$
still cling to sth.
  $TV_{7a}(160)$
still maintain (a claim)
  $TV_{7a}(160)$
still, stand
  $DI_{8a}(126); TV_6\text{'''}(160)$
still undecided, leave everything
  $KA_{1cb}(95)$
stimulate
  $EN_{1ae}(75); EN_{7cb}(81); EN_{7cc}(81); KA_{2cab}(98)$
stipulate
  $KA_{4cbc}(104)$
stipulations, make
  $KA_{4cbc}(104)$
stir
  $KA_{0d}(89)$
stirring speech, make a
  $TP_{2ab}(164)$

stir up
  $EN_{1ae}(75); EN_{7cc}(81);$
  $KA_{-1c}(87); KA_{2cab}(98)$
stop
  $DI_{8b}(126); KA_{1bcb}(93);$
  $KA_{4ac}(100); TU_{6"b}(133)$
stop a person short
  $TU_{3}.(132)$
stop flowing
  $DI_{8a}(126); TV_{6""}(160)$
stop (intentionally)
  $TU_{6'a}(133)$
stop running
  $DI_{8a}(126)$
stop somebody short
  $TU_{6}(133)$
stop to, put a
  $KA_{1bca}(93); DI_{10}(127)$
stories about so., spread
  $WP_{0ac}(122)$
stories, tell
  $TP_{2bj}(167)$
stories, tell dirty
  $DT_{1e}(128)$
story, narrate a
  $ET_{0a}(135)$
straighten out
  $KA_{4cac}(103); KA_{4cad}(104)$
straight, put
  $KA_{4cad}(103); KA_{4cac}(103);$
  $TV_{7c}(161)$
strange, be
  $KA_{-3a}(85)$
straws, grasp at
  $EN_{7cb}(81)$
strengthen so.
  $EN_{7cb}(81); KA_{2cab}(98)$
strengthen (the point)
  $TV*_{7b}(161)$

stress
  $TO_{5bab}(158)$
stress on, lay
  $TO_{5ab}(158)$
stretch
  $TV_{6a}(159)$
stretch a point
  $TP_{2b}(165)$
stretch out
  $DI_{10"}(127); TU_{5}(132)$
strike
  $EN_{7b}(80)$
strike for
  $EN_{0ab}(74)$
strike one's mind
  $IN_{5b}(144)$
strike so.
  $ET_{0dd}(137)$
strive
  $EM_{2f}(72)$
strive after
  $EN_{2b}(75)$
strive for
  $DE_{8b}(151)$
strongly upon so, urge
  $EN_{8aa}(81)$
struck, be
  $DI_{8a}(151)$
struck dumb, be
  $TU_{6'b}(133)$
structure
  $TO_{3a}(157)$
struggle
  $KA_{-3c}(86); KA_{-3ca}(86);$
  $KA_{1da}(96)$
strut
  $KA_{4a}.(101)$
stubborn, be
  $KA_{4bab}(101)$

stuck, be
  $TU_{6'b}(133)$
stuck, get
  $DI_{8a}(126); TU_{6'b}(133)$
student, rusticate a
  $NO_{0dd}(110)$
study
  $TE_{-1b}(140)$
stuff and nonsense, talk
  $TP_{2bj}(167)$
stutter
  $EM_{2aa}(71)$
style
  $VV_{ba}(153)$
style (call) so./sth.
  as sth.
  $VV_{f}(154)$
stylize
  $TP_{2ad}(164)$
subdivide
  $TO_{3a}(157)$
subject
  $KA_{4ac}(100)$
subject, bring up a
  $TO_{2g}(157)$
subject, change the
  $DI_{10}.(127)$
subject, come around to a
  $DI_{10}.(127)$
subject, control the
  conversation upon a
  $TO_{5ac}(158)$
subject, get to the
  $TV_{5}(159)$
subject, guide the
  conversation upon a
  $TO_{5ac}(158)$
subject, leave off a
  $DI/TU(134)$

259

subject, offer an opinion on a
$NO_{60}(113)$
subject, present a
$TV_{6b}(160)$
subject, return to the
$TV_{7g}(162)$
subject, steer the conversation upon a
$TO_{5ac}(158)$
subject, take as
$TO_{2ba}(155)$
subject, talk around the
$TV_{6'b}(160)$
subject, talk round the
$TP_{2bf}(167)$
subject, turn the conversation upon a
$TO_{5ac}(158)$
subjoin
$TV_{7a}(160)$
subjugate
$KA_{4ac}(100)$
submit
$KA_{4bac}(101)$
submit to
$EN_{9'c}(85); NO_{2a}(111);$
$KA_{4bda}(102);$
$KA_{4cda}(105)$
subordinate
$NO_{0dc}(109); TO_{3a}(157)$
subordinate os. to
$NO_{2a}(111)$
subscribe
$VV_{bc}(154)$
subscribe to
$EN_{3a}(76)$
subsequently, order
$EN_{3a}(76)$

substantiate
$ET_{0a}(135); KA_{1bcd}(94);$
$TV*_{7b}(161)$
substantiate/support an argument
$AV_{3}(106)$
subsume
$DE_{6c}(150); TO_{2d}(156)$
subtle, be too
$TP_{2b}(165)$
subversively, act
$KA_{0c}(89)$
succeed
$KA_{4ac}(100)$
succeed in
$EN_{9'b}(85); KA_{4aa}(99)$
succession, alter the
$TO_{3b}(157)$
succinctly, formulate
$TP_{2ad}(164)$
succumb
$KA_{4baa}(101)$
suddenly, chill
$EM_{2aa}(71)$
sue
$NO_{4'}(113)$
sue so. for debt
$NO_{4'}(113)$
sue (for)
$EN_{2b\S}(75); NO_{-2\S}(108)$
sugar-coat
$ET_{0da}(136)$
suggest
$DE_{5}(149); EN_{1ae}(75);$
$EN_{2c}(76); TO_{2bc}(156)$
suggestion, influence by
$EN_{7af}(80)$
suggestions, make
$EN_{7aa}(79)$

suitable for so., be
$NO_{0'}(111)$
sulk
$EM_{2f}(72); EM_{2k}(73)$
sulky, be
$KA_{0e}(89)$
summarize
$DE_{6f}(151); DI/TU(134);$
$IN_{3ac}(143); TE_{-1b'}(140);$
$TO_{2f}(157); TV_{7f}(161)$
summary, conclude with a
$DI_{10}(127); TU_{9a}(133)$
summary, make a
$TV_{7f}(161)$
summon
$DI_{2'a}(124); DI_{2'b};$
$DI_{2'c}; EN_{2b}(75);$
$EN_{5a}(77); EN_{5b}(77);$
$NO_{5}(113)$
sum up
$TE_{-1b'}(140); TV_{7f}(161)$
superfluous things, leave out
$TP_{2ad}(164)$
superfluous things, omit
$TP_{2ad}(164)$
superior court, appeal to a
$NO_{9aa}(117)$
superficial, make
$TP_{2bbb}(165)$
superordinate
$TO_{3a}(157)$
superpose
$DE_{8e}(152)$
supersede (replace a law)
$NO_{3bb}(112)$
supervise
$VV_{c}(154)$
supplant
$KA_{4ac}(100)$

supplement a validation
  $AV_3(106)$
supplement (previous remarks)
  $TV_{7a}(160)$
supplicate
  $EN_{2b}(75)$
supply
  $KA_{-1b}(87)$
supply, order a fresh
  $EN_{3a}(76)$
supply with (marginal) notes
  $TE_{0bb}(141); TV_{7b}(161)$
support
  $AV_6(107); KA_{1bcd}(94);$
  $KA_{2cab}(98); KA_{-3b}(85);$
  $TV_{6b}(160); WG_{0b}(123);$
  $WT_1(118)$
support so.
  $EN_{7cb}(81)$
support a view
  $TV_{6b}(160)$
support, gain
  $KA_{2caa}(97)$
support, remove one's
  $KA_{2d}(98)$
suppose
  $DE_5(149); KA_{4cbc}(104)$
suppress
  $KA_{1bcb}(93); KA_{4ac}(100);$
  $TP_{2bg}(167)$
sure (of), make
  $VV_c(154); KA_{2b}(97)$
sure of sth., make
  $VV_c(154)$
sure of (the truth), make
  $IN_{9b}(147)$
surmise
  $DE_5(150); IN_{1ab}(142)$

surpass
  $KA_{1bcc}(94)$
surprise
  $EN_{7b}(80); KA_{0f}(89);$
  $KA_{0h}(90); KA_{0i}(90)$
surprise, take by
  $KA_{0f}(89); KA_{0h}(90);$
  $KA_{0i}(90)$
surrender
  $NO_{0b}(109); KA_{-1d}(88);$
  $KA_{3b}(99); KA_{4bac}(101);$
  $KA_{4bc}(102); TU_{8a}(133)$
suspect
  $DE_5(149); DE_7(151)$
suspect so. of
  $NO_3.(113)$
suspend
  $DI_3.(125); EN_{6e}(79);$
  $IN_{9a}(146); NO_{0dd}(110);$
  $NO_{3bb}(112); NO_{8a}(116)$
  $TU_6(133)$
suspicion on, cast
  $NO_3.(113)$
suspicion on (upon) throw
  $NO_3.(113)$
suspicious of, be
  $DE_7(151); NO_3.(113)$
suspicions upon, throw
  $EN_{8aa}(81); DE_7(151)$
sustain an argument
  $AV_3(106)$
swagger
  $WS_{bc}(123)$
swallow
  $KA_{4bda}(102)$
swear
  $ET_{0a}(135); EM_{2e}(72);$
  $EM_{2ga}(72); IN_{6c}(146)$
swear allegiance
  $WT_{5d}(121)$

swear at
  $KA_{1ab}(91)$
swear at so.
  $EM_{2j}(73)$
swear, curse and
  $EM_{2e}(72)$
swear in
  $NO_{0a}(108); NO_{0da}(109)$
swear on oath
  $NO_{6da}(115)$
swear to
  $IN_{9b}(147)$
sweep aside
  $KA_{4ac}(100)$
sweep of, make a clean
  $KA_{4caa}(103)$
sweet nothings, say
  $DT_{1c}(128); EN_{7aa}(79);$
  $WS_{bba}(123)$
swell
  $TP_{2bba}(165)$
swindle
  $WS_{ba}(122)$
swindle so. out of sth.
  $EN_{8aa}(81)$
switch the topic
  $DI_{10}.(127)$
sworn depositon, make a
  $VE_{1b}(148)$
symbolize
  $TP_{2ac}(164); TP_{2bc}(166)$
sympathy, express
  $EM_{2cb}(72)$
sympathize
  $EN_{7ca}(81)$
sympathize with
  $KA_{-3b}(85)$
sympathize with so.
  $WT_{5c}(121)$

sympathy with, express
  $KA_{-3b}(85)$
sympathy with, feel
  $KA_{-3b}(85)$
sympathy, show
  $EN_{7ca}(81)$
synopsis, make a
  $TV_{7f}(161)$
synthesize
  $DE_{6f}(151)$
systematize
  $DE_{6f}(151); TO_{3a}(157)$

T
taboo
  $NO_{0c}(109)$
tabulate
  $VV_a(153)$
tackle
  $TO_{2ba}(155)$
tactics, employ
  $KA_{1da}(96)$
tactics, employ clever
  $KA_{1aa}(91)$
tactics, employ good
  $KA_{0d}(89)$
take a lenient view of sth.
  $WT_3\text{'}(119); NO_7\text{'}(115)$
take amiss
  $WT_{5a}(120)$
take an inventory of
  $VV_a(153)$
take an oath
  $ET_{0a}(135)$
take a note of
  $ET/TE_{ab}(138)$
take apart
  $KA_{1aa}(91)$
take (ap.) in
  $IR_{2b}(130)$

take ap. into one's confidence
  $VE_0(147)$
take ap.'s part
  $NO_{0f}(110); EN_{6d}(79)$
take ap. to task
  $NO_5(113)$
take as subject
  $TO_{2ba}(155)$
take away (sins)
  $NO_{9bb}(117)$
take back
  $IN_{9a}(146); KA_{4cba}(104);$
  $KA_{3b}(99); DI_3\text{''}(125);$
  $KA_{-1d}(88)$
take by surprise
  $KA_{0f}(89); KA_{0h}(90);$
  $KA_{0i}(90)$
take counsel together
  $DT_{1ba}(127); DI_{7a}(126);$
  $NO_{2ba}(111); WT_2(118);$
  $NO_{6f}(115)$
take down (a deposition)
  $ET/TE_{ab}(138)$
take exception to
  $TV_6\text{'}_a(160); NO_{60}(114)$
take first soundings
  $KA_{2aa}(97)$
take for granted
  $KA_{4cbc}(104)$
take in
  $KA_{1bcc}(94)$
take in charge
  $NO_5\text{'}(113)$
take in pledge
  $EN_{3db}(77)$
take in so.
  $IR_{1a}(129)$
take into account
  $IN_{5aa}(144);$

take into account (cont.)
  $TO_{2bb}(156); TO_{1b}(124);$
  $DE_2(149)$
take into consideration
  $KA_{4cdb}(105);$
  $TO_{2bb}(156); DE_2(149)$
take into custody
  $NO_5\text{'}(113)$
take it out on
  $KA_{4bdb}(102)$
take it to be
  $TE_{-1cb}(140)$
take leave of
  $DI_{10}(127); TU_{9a}(133)$
take legal proceedings against
  $NO_4\text{'}(113)$
taken aback, be
  $KA_{0b}(88)$
taken down a peg, be
  $KA_{4bac}(101)$
take no notice of so.
  $WP_{0aa}(121)$
take notice of
  $KA_{4cdb}(105);$
  $ET_{-1a}(134); DE_1(149);$
  $DE_2(149)$
take offense
  $EM_{2ca}(71)$
take offense at
  $WT_0(118)$
take on (an employee)
  $NO_{0da}(109)$
take one's turn
  $TU_2\text{''}(131); TU_3\text{''}(132)$
take out of the context
  $TP_{2bh}(167)$
take part in a contest
  $KA_{-3cb}(86)$

take pleasure in others's
  misfortune
  $KA_{4a}(101)$
take possession of
  $KA_{-2a}(86)$
take responsibility for
  $NO_1(111)$
take revenge on
  $KA_{4bdb}(102)$
take seriously
  $KA_{4cdb}(105);$
  $NO_{2a}(111)$
take so. as
  $VV_g(155)$
take so. down a peg
  $KA_{4ac}(100)$
take so.'s side
  $KA_{2cb}(98)$
take sth. through
  $KA_{4cab}(103)$
take testimony
  $IN_{1ac}(142)$
take the liberty
  $KA_{-2b}(87)$
take the wind out of
  so.'s sails
  $KA_{1bbc}(92)$
take to flight
  $KA_{4bba}(102)$
take to heart
  $NO_{2a}(111); KA_{4cdb}(105);$
  $EN_{9g}(83); EN_{9k}(84);$
  $EN_{9c}(83); WG_{1b}(124)$
take to pieces
  $KA_{1aa}(91); KA_{4ac}(100);$
  $KA_{4ae}(101)$
take to task
  $WT_{4a}(119)$
take unawares
  $KA_{0i}(99); KA_{0h}(90);$

take unawares (cont.)
  $KA_{0f}(89)$
take up
  $TV_{7a}(160); DE_1(149)$
take up again
  $TV_{7i}(162)$
take up a pluralistic
  position
  $KA_{1cb}(95)$
take up a position
  $KA_{1cab}(93)$
take up a position, let so.
  $KA_{1cab}(94)$
tales, tell
  $NO_4(113);$
  $ET/TE_b(138)$
talk
  $DT_{1a}(127)$
talk so. into
  $EN_{7ag}(80)$
talk around the subject
  $TV_{6'b}(160)$
talk at so.
  $KA_{1da}(96)$
talk bawdy
  $DT_{1e}(128)$
talk big
  $WS_{bc}(123); TP_{1c}(163)$
talk balderdash
  $TP_{2bj}(167)$
talk bosh
  $TP_{1e}(163); TP_{2bj}(167)$
talk brilliantly
  $DI_{7b}(126)$
talk cleverly
  $DI_{7b}(126)$
talk, commence to
  $TU_3(131)$
talk disconnectedly
  $TP_{2bj}(167)$

talk filthy
  $DT_{1e}(128)$
talk gibberish
  $TP_{1e}(163); TP_{1b}(163)$
talk giftedly
  $DI_{7b}(126)$
talk, give a
  $TU_4(132); DT_2(129)$
talk idly
  $ET/TE_b(138)$
talk indecent
  $DT_{1e}(128)$
talk insistently
  $KA_{-1c}(88)$
talk lewd
  $DT_{1e}(128)$
talk longer than one
  wanted
  $DI_{10}(127)$
talk loudly
  $DT_{1g}(128)$
talk masterfully
  $DI_{7b}(126)$
talk nonsense
  $DT_{1bc}(128); TP_{1e}(163);$
  $TP_{2bj}(167)$
talk obscene
  $DT_{1e}(128)$
talk out
  $TV_9(163)$
talk over
  $DT_{1ba}(127); DT_{1bb}(128);$
  $DI_{7a}(126); WT_2(118);$
  $NO_{6f}(115); EN_{7ag}(80);$
  $NO_{2ba}(111)$
talk round the subject
  $TP_{2bf}(167)$
talk shop
  $DT_3(129)$

talk smut
 $DT_{1e}(128)$
talk smutty
 $DT_{1e}(128)$
talk sth. through
 $KA_{4acb}(103)$
talk stuff and nonsense
 $TP_{2bj}(167)$
talk too much
 $EN_{7ae}(80)$
talk twaddle
 $TP_{1e}(163); TP_{2bj}(167)$
talk with so.
 $ET_{0a}(135)$
talk wittily
 $IR_{1c}(130); DT_{1d}(128);$
 $DI_{7b}\cdot(126)$
tally
 $KA_{-3b}(85)$
tangle
 $TP_{2bd}(166)$
tap (the telephone, the wire)
 $VE_{1a}(148)$
taste
 $ET_{-1a}(134); ET^*_{-1a}(134)$
tarot cards, read
 $ET/TE_b(138)$
task, give a
 $EN_{3a}(76)$
task, set about a
 $TV_1(158)$
task, take so. to
 $NO_5(113); WT_{4a}(119)$
task to, give a
 $NO_{0a}(108)$
task, undertake a
 $TV_1(158)$

taunt
 $IR_{1a}(129); IR_{2ca}(130);$
 $IR_{1a}(129)$
teach
 $DI_{7b}(126); ET_{0da}(136);$
 $EN_{8c}(82); NO_{-3}(107);$
 $DT_2(129); EN_{3c}(76);$
 $EN_{6c}(79)$
teach so. manners
 $ET_{0da}(136)$
teach so. his place
 $KA_{4ac}(100)$
tea leaves, tell fortunes in
 $ET/TE_b(138)$
tear apart
 $TE_{0bb}(141)$
tear into pieces
 $TE_{0bb}(141); WT_{4c}(120)$
tease
 $IR_{2b}(130); IR_{2ca}(130);$
 $IR_{2a}(130); DT_{1c}(128);$
tease so.
 $IR_{1a}(129)$
teeth, grit one's
 $EM_{2b}\cdot(71)$
telegraph
 $ET_{0a}(135); IN_{6aa}(145)$
telephone
 $DI_{7a}(126); DT_{1bc}(128);$
 $DT_{1a}(127); ET_{0a}(135);$
 $IN_{6aa}(145)$
telephone, tap the
 $VE_{1"a}(148)$
tell
 $DT_2(129); IN_{6aa}(145);$
 $ET_{0a}(135)$
tell apart
 $VV_e(154)$
tell dirty stories
 $DT_{1e}(128)$

tell fish-stories (dial)
 $ET/TE_b(138)$
tell fortunes
 $ET/TE_b(138)$
tell fortunes in tea leaves
 $ET/TE_b(138)$
tell on (American)
 $VE_{1c}(148)$
tell (one's beads)
 $TP_{1a}(164)$
tell others
 $VE_1(148)$
tell, show and
 $ET_{0da}(136)$
tell something with the greatest of ease
 $TO_2(155)$
tell stories
 $TP_{2bj}(167)$
tell tales
 $NO_4(113);$
 $ET/TE_b(138)$
tell tales (in school, Eng.)
 $VE_{1c}(148)$
tell the younger, others
 $TE_{-2a}(139)$
tell untruths
 $ET/TE_b(138);$
 $TP_{2bj}(167)$
temper, lose one's
 $KA_{0g}(90); KA_{0i}(90);$
 $KA_{0h}(90); KA_{0g}(90);$
temper, put in a bad
 $EN_{8d}(82)$
temper, put so. out of
 $WP_{0ab}(121)$
tempt
 EN_{7af}

term
  $VV_{ba}(153)$
terminate
  $DI_{10}(127); TV_{7e}(161);$
  $TU_{9a}(133)$
terminate in
  $TU_{9a}(133); DI_{10}(127)$
terms, come to
  $KA_{2b}(97); KA_{4cbb}(104)$
terms, couch in concise
  $ET/TE_{ad}(138)$
terms, make
  $KA_{-1b}(87)$
terms, not to come to
  $KA_{-3c}(86)$
terms of so., speak in very high
  $WT_{4e}(120)$
terms with, come to
  $KA_{4bda}(102);$
  $KA_{4cda}(105); NO_{60}(114)$
terrorize
  $KA_{1ab}(91); KA_{1cca}(95);$
  $KA_{1aa}(91)$
test
  $EN_{5cd}(78); TE_{-1b}(140)$
testify
  $ET_{0a}(135); NO_{6da}(115)$
testify (to)
  $IN_{6c}(145)$
test so. on
  $IN_{1ab}(142)$
testimony, take
  $IN_{1ac}(142)$
testimony to, give
  $ET_{0a}(135); NO_{6da}(115)$
tether, be at the end of one's
  $KA_{4baa}(101)$

test, put on the
  $VV_c(154)$
test, put so. to a severe
  $EN_{5cd}(78)$
texts, produce
  $ET/TE_{aa}(138)$
texts, retail
  $TE_{-2b}(139)$
texts, write
  $ET/TE_{aa}(138)$
text, turn sth. into a bad
  $TE_{0ab}(141)$
that, leave at
  $KA_{3c}(99); KA_{3b}(99)$
theme, get to the
  $TV_5(159)$
theme, plan
  $TV_3(159)$
theologize
  $DT_3(129)$
theoretize
  $DT_3(129)$
they are at loggerheads
  KA_{-1c}
things, leave our superfluous
  TP_{2ad}
thing to another, jump from one
  $TV_6\text{'}_b(160)$
think
  $DE_5(149); DE_4(149)$
think back (on)
  $IN_{5aa}(144)$
think of
  IN_{5aa}
think out
  $DE_{8d}(152)$
think over carefully
  $DE_4(149)$

think the matter over
  $DE_4(149)$
thoroughly, chew
  $TV_{6a}(159)$
thoroughly, discuss
  $TV_9(163)$
thoroughly, examine
  $IN_{1aa}(142)$
thorough scolding, give a
  $WT_{4a}(119)$
thoughts, be lost in
  $DE_4(149)$
thoughts, divert a man's
  $EN_{1b}(75)$
thread, lose the
  $TV_6\text{'''}(160)$
threaten
  $KA_{0g}(90)$
threatening gestures, make
  $EN_{4c}(77)$
threaten (so. with sth.)
  $EN_{4c}(77)$
throttle
  $TU_6(133)$
through, muddle one's way
  $KA_{4aa}(99)$
through, talk sth.
  $KA_{4cab}(103)$
throw in one's hand
  $KA_{4bac}(102)$
throw in one's lot with
  $KA_{2b}(97)$
throw into confusion
  $KA_{1ab}(91)$
throw into relief
  $TO_{5a}(158)$
throw out
  $EN_{8b}(82); KA_{4ad}(100);$

throw out (cont.)
  $KA_{1bcd}(94)$
throw sth. in so.'s face
  $WT_1(118)$
throw suspicion on
  $NO_3.(113)$
throw suspicion(s) upon
  $DE_7(151); EN_{8aa}(81)$
throw together
  $TP_{2bd}(166)$
thrust
  $KA_{1ccb}(95)$
thrust sth. upon so.
  $EN_{8aa}(81)$
thunder at
  $EM_{2l}(73)$
thunderstruck, be
  $KA_{0b}(88)$
thwart
  $KA_{0c}(89); KA_{-1c}(87);$
  $EN_{8ab}(82); KA_{1aa}(91);$
  $KA_{1bcb}(93)$
ticket on, put a
  $VV_{ba}(153)$
tie down
  $KA_{1cab}(94)$
tied up in one's own words, get
  $TV_6...(160)$
tie together
  $TO_4(157)$
tighten
  $TP_{2ad}(164)$
tighten up
  $TV_{7c}(161)$
time, extend speaking
  DI/TU(134)
time gossiping, waste
  $DI_{10}.(127)$

time in chattering, pass
  $DT_{1bc}(128); DI_{10}.(127)$
time, limit speaking
  DI/TU(134)
tint
  $TP_{2bbc}(166)$
tip off
  $KA_{2cab}(98)$
tip off the authorities
  $VE_{1b,c,d}(148)$
tired of, be
  $KA_{3a}(98)$
title, give a heading
  $VV_{ba}(153)$
title to, give a
  $TV_2(159)$
toast, bring out a
  $EM_{2h}(72)$
toast, make a
  $EM_{2h}(73)$
toast to so., propose a
  $WT_{5b}(120)$
toes, tread on so.'s
  $KA_{0b}(88)$
together, bind
  $TO_4(157)$
together, bring
  $KA_{4cac}(103)$
together, call
  $DI_{2'b}(124)$
together, chain
  $TO_4(157)$
together, confer
  $NO_{2ba}(111); NO_{6f}(115);$
  $WT_2(118)$
together, gather
  $DE_{6a}(150)$
together, get on well
  $KA_{-3b}(85)$

together, link
  $TO_4(157)$
tolerate
  $NO_{0b}(108)$
tolerate, refuse to
  $KA_{0g}(90)$
tone down
  $KA_{3b}(99); TO_{5c}(158)$
tongue, hold one's
  $TU_1.(131)$
tongues, speak in
  $ET/TE_b(138)$
too spare with words, be
  $TP_{2bi}(167)$
too subtle, be
  $TP_{2b}(164)$
topic, change the
  $TV_7.(162)$
topic, exhaust a
  $TV_9(163)$
topic, get to the
  $TV_5(159)$
topic, go ahead with a
  $TV_{7g}(162)$
topic, leave off a
  DI/TU(134)
topic, switch the
  $DI_{10}.(127)$
topic to another, turn from one
  $DI_{10}.(127)$
topic, vary the
  $TV_7.(162)$
torment
  $KA_{4ac}(100)$
torpedo
  $KA_{0c}(89)$
torpedo so. with arguments
  $AV_1(106)$

touch, get in
 $DI_1.(124)$
touch lightly
 $TO_{2bc}(156)$
touch on
 $TO_{2bc}(156)$
touch on a sore spot
 $TO_{2g}(157)$
touch so.
 $EN_{7d}.(81)$
touch up
 $ET/TE_a.(139)$
touch upon
 $TO_{2bc}(156); TV_5(159)$
touch with, get in
 $KA_{4caa}(102)$
towards, contribute
 $TV_{6b}(159)$
trace
 $IN_{1aa}(142); TO_{2a}(155)$
trace back
 $TV_{7j}(162)$
trace back to
 $DE_{6c}(150)$
track, lose the
 $TV_6...(160)$
track of, lose
 $KA_{3c}(99)$
trade information
 $ET_{0b}(135)$
train
 $EN_{3c}(76); NO_{-3}(107);$
 $EN_{8c}(82); ET_{0da}(136)$
train
 $EN_{6c}(79)$
transact business
 $NO_{0e}\S(110)$
transcend
 $TP_{2bf}(167)$

transcribe
 $TE_{0ad}(141)$
transfer
 $EN_{3da}(77)$
transfer for disciplinary
 reasons
 $NO_{8a}(116)$
transfer (to)
 $TU_{9b}(133)$
transfigure
 $TP_{2bba}(165)$
transform
 $TO_{2e}(156)$
transgress against (law)
 $NO_2(112)$
transition, form a
 $TV_{7h}(162)$
translate
 $TE_{0ad}(141)$
translate back
 $TE_{0ae}(141)$
transmit in morse code
 $IN_{6aa}(145)$
transmit to someone in
 morse code (a message)
 $ET_{0a}(135)$
transmit to someone in
 morse code that
 $ET_{0a}(135)$
transpose
 $TO_{3b}(157)$
trap
 $KA_{-2b}(87)$
trashy, make
 $TP_{2bba}(165)$
travesty
 $TE_{0ab}(141); IR_{1b}(130);$
 $IR_{2b}(130)$

tread on so.'s toes
 $KA_{0b}(88)$
treason, plot
 $VE_{-2}(147)$
treat
 $KA_{4cac}(103);$
 $TV_{6a}(159); TO_{2ba}(155);$
 $KA_{-1b}(87)$
treat bluntly
 $KA_{0g}(90)$
treaties, write
 $ET/TE_{ad}(138)$
treat preliminarily
 $TV_1(158)$
treat so. with indiffe-
 rence
 $WP_{0aa}(121)$
treat with
 $KA_{1db}(96)$
treat with distinction
 $NO_{0b}..(109)$
treat with ignorance
 $TP_{2bf}(167)$
treat with indifference
 $TP_{2bf}(167)$
treat with irony
 $IR_{2ca}(131)$
treat with scorn
 $IR_{1a}(129); IR_{2cb}(131)$
treaty, enter into a
 $EN_{6d}(79); NO_{0f}(110)$
treaty, make a
 $NO_{0e}(110)$
tremble
 $EM_{2ab}(71)$
trick
 $KA_{4ac}(100)$
trick on, play a
 $KA_{4bdb}(102);$

267

Lexicon Section II

trick on, play a (cont.)
    $KA_{4ac}(100)$
trick on, play an unfair
    $KA_{1aa}(91)$
trick, see through the
    $ET_{-1b}(134)$
tricks, learn new
    $ET_{1d}(137)$
trifle
    $TP_{2bbb}(165)$
trim
    $ET/TE_a{}^\cdot(139)$
triumph
    $KA_{4a}{}^\cdot(101)$
triumphant, be
    $KA_{4a}{}^\cdot(101)$
trivialize
    $KA_{1bbc}(92)$; $TP_{2bbb}(165)$
troops, disband
    $NO_{0dd}(110)$
trouble
    $DI_{8a}(126)$; $EN_{7d}{}^\cdot(81)$
true colors, force so. to show his
    $KA_{1cab}(94)$
trump
    $KA_{1bca}(93)$; $KA_{1ba}(94)$
trumpet
    $VE_1(148)$
trumps, turn up
    $KA_{4a}{}^\cdot(101)$
trust in, place one's
    $VE_0(147)$
trust in, put one's
    $VE_0(147)$
trust into so., place one's
    $WT_3{}^\cdot(119)$
trust so.
    $WT_3{}^\cdot(119)$

truth, insure the
    $IN_{9b}(147)$
truth, make sure of the
    $IN_{9b}(147)$
truth out, get the
    $IN_{2a}{}^\cdot(143)$
try
    $VV_c(154)$
try so.
    $EN_{5cd}(78)$
try to avoid risks
    $KA_{1ba}(91)$
try to get into so.'s favor
    $KA_{-2b}(87)$
try to get something
    $DE_{8b}(151)$
try to make out
    $IN_{1aa}(142)$
tune, be in
    $KA_{2b}(97)$
turn
    $KA_{4bab}(101)$
turn away attention
    $EN_{1b}(75)$
turn, being at one's
    $TU_3{}^{\cdot\cdot\cdot}(132)$
turn, cancel one's
    $TU_3{}^{\cdot\cdot\cdot}(132)$
turn down
    $KA_{1bcb}(93)$; $KA_{1bcc}(94)$; $KA_{1bcd}(94)$
turn (Queen's, King's, State's) evidence
    $VE_{1b}(148)$
turn, forego one's
    $TU_3{}^{\cdot\cdot\cdot}(132)$
turn from one topic to another
    $DI_{10}{}^\cdot(127)$

turn, give so. a
    $TU_2(131)$
turn, having the
    $TV_3{}^{\cdot\cdot\cdot}(132)$
turn, it's my
    $TU_2{}^{\cdot\cdot}(131)$
turn one's coat
    $KA_{4bbb}(102)$
turn out well
    $EN_{9'a}(82)$
turn pale
    $EM_{2aa}(71)$
turn sad
    $EM_{2aa}(71)$
turn something into a bad text
    $TE_{0ab}(141)$
turn, take one's
    $TU_2{}^{\cdot\cdot}(131)$; $TU_3{}^{\cdot\cdot\cdot}(132)$
turn the conversation upon a subject
    $TO_{5ac}(158)$
turn to
    $DI_{10}{}^\cdot(127)$
turn to speak, renounce one's
    $TU_3{}^{\cdot\cdot}(132)$
turn up
    $KA_{0c}(89)$
turn up trumps
    $KA_{4a}{}^\cdot(101)$
turn, withdraw one's
    $TU_3{}^{\cdot\cdot}(132)$
tutelage, put under
    $NO_{8a}(116)$; $NO_{0dd}(110)$
twaddle, talk
    $TP_{1e}(163)$; $TP_{2bj}(167)$
twist
    $TP_{2be}(167)$; $KA_{4bab}(101)$

typify
  $VV_a(153); TP_{2ac}(164)$

U

unacquainted with, be
  $KA_{-3a}(85)$
unawares, take
  $KA_{0i}(90); KA_{0h}(90);$
  $KA_{0f}(89)$
unbosom
  $VE_0(147)$
unbosom os. to so.
  $VE_0(147)$
uncomfortable, be
  $EM_{2cb}(72)$
uncover
  $NO_3(113); VE_{1a}(148);$
  $ET_{0c}(136)$
undecided, leave
  $TV_{8b}(163)$
undecided, leave everything still
  $KA_{1cb}(95)$
undecided, leave sth.
  $NO_{60}(114)$
under an obligation, be
  $NO_{0'}(111)$
undermine
  $KA_{0c}(89); AV_1(106);$
  $KA_{1bcd}(94)$
underpin
  $NO_{60}(114); AV_3(106)$
undersign
  $VV_{bc}(154)$
understand
  $ET_{-1b}(134); TE_{-1cb}(140);$
  $DE_1(149)$
understand, cause so. to
  $ET_{0dd}(137)$

understanding, come to an
  $ET*_{-1a}(134)$
understand from
  $TE_{-1cb}(140)$
understand, give so. to
  $TP_{2bc}(166)$
understand one another
  $KA_{4cca}(105);$
  $KA_{-3b}(85)$
understate
  $WS_{aa}(122)$
undertake (a task)
  $TV_1(158)$
undervalue so.
  $WP_{0aa}(121); WT_3.(119)$
underwrite
  $VV_{bc}(154)$
unearth
  $VE_{1a}(148)$
undo
  $KA_{3b}(99)$
unfair trick on, play an
  $KA_{1aa}(91)$
unify
  $TV_{7c}(161); KA_{-3b}(85);$
  $KA_{4cca}(105);$
  $KA_{4cac}(103)$
unintentionally, offend
  $KA_{0b}(88)$
unite
  $TO_4(157); KA_{-3b}(85);$
  $KA_{4cac}(103);$
  $NO_{2ba}(111); NO_{6f}(115);$
  $KA_{4cca}(105)$
  $DI_{5a}(125)$
united, be
  $KA_{-3b}(85);$
  $KA_{4cca}(105)$
unknown, be
  $KA_{-3a}(85)$

unmask
  $WP_{0ab}(122); VE_{1a}(148)$
(unravel)
  $EN_{5ca}(78)$
unravel
  $IN_{2a}(143)$
unsettled, leave
  $KA_{1cb}(95)$
untie
  $KA_{3b}(99)$
untruths, tell
  $ET/TE_b(138);$
  $TP_{2bj}(167)$
unveil
  $VE_{1a}(148); ET_{0c}(136)$
upbraid
  $WP_{0ad}(122); WT_{4a}(119)$
upgrade
  $NO_{0dc}(109);$
  $TP_{2bba}(165)$
upset
  $KA_{0c}(89); EN_{8d}(82);$
  $EN_{7d}.(81); DI_{8a}(126);$
  $KA_{4ac}(100); KA_{1aa}(91)$
upset, be
  $KA_{4bac}(102)$
urge
  $EN_{4a}(77); EN_{7cc}(81);$
  $KA_{2cab}(98);$
  $KA_{1cca}(95)$
urge os.
  $EN_{7ae}(80)$
urge participation
  $DI_1(124)$
urge strongly upon so.
  $EN_{8aa}(81)$
use a cribshead
  $VE_{1"b}(148)$
use a hackneyed phrase
  $TP_{2be}(166)$

use a paradigm
　AV$_4$(106)
use a pony
　VE$_1$"$_b$(148)
use four-letter words
　DT$_{1e}$(128)
use words sparingly
　TP$_{2ad}$(164)
use words too sparingly
　TP$_{2bi}$(167)
usher in
　TV$_5$(159); DI$_6$(125)
usurp
　WS$_{bc}$(123)
utter
　ET$_{0a}$(135)
utter maledictions
　(in general)
　EM$_{2ga}$(72)

V
vacate one's office
　KA$_{4bac}$(102)
vaguely, express os.
　TP$_{2bd}$(166)
validate
　WT$_{4f\S}$(120); AV$_3$(106);
　IN$_{9b}$(147); ET$_{0a}$(135)
validation, deliver a
　AV$_3$(106)
validation, furnish a
　AV$_3$(106)
validation, supplement a
　AV$_3$(106)
valuate (infrequent)
　IN$_{3bb}$(143)
value
　WT$_0$(118); VV$_g$(155);
　NO$_{-1}$(108)

value to so., be of
　KA$_{-3b}$(85)
value highly
　WT$_0$(118); WT$_3$·(119)
value sth. highly
　NO$_7$·(115)
varnish over
　TP$_{2bf}$(167); TP$_{2bba}$(165)
vary the topic
　TV$_7$·(163)
vehemently, fight for too
　KA$_{1ccc}$(95)
veil
　TP$_{2bc}$(166)
ventilate
　TV$_5$(159)
vent to anger, give
　EM$_{2aa}$(71)
vent to, give
　KA$_{0a}$(88); KA$_{0g}$·(90)
venture
　KA$_{-2b}$(87)
verbalize
　TO$_2$(155)
verify
　WT$_{4f\S}$(120); NO$_{6da}$(115);
　VV$_c$(154); IN$_{9b}$(147);
　ET$_{0a}$(135)
verify an argument
　KA$_{1bcd}$(94)
very high terms of so.,
　speak in
　WT$_{4e}$(120)
vex
　WP$_{0ab}$(122); KA$_{1aa}$(91)
vexed, get
　EM$_{2ca}$(71)
view, change one's
　ET$_{1d}$(137)

view, have in
　DE$_{8b}$(151)
view, hold a
　KA$_{1bca}$(93)
view of sth., take
　a lenient
　WT$_3$·(119); NO$_7$·(115)
viewpoint, (still)
　adhere to a
　TV$_{7a}$(160)
views, agree to so.'s
　AV$_6$(107)
views, exchange
　KA$_{4cab}$(103)
view, support a
　TV$_{6b}$(160)
vilify
　WP$_{0ab}$(122)
vindicate
　KA$_{2cb}$(98); KA$_{1bcc}$(94);
　KA$_{1bca}$(93); KA$_{1bba}$(92);
　NO$_{6b}$(114)
vindicate os.
　NO$_{6e}$(115)
violate
　NO$_2$(112); EN$_{9i}$(84)
voice, lower one's
　EM$_{2aa}$(71)
voice, raise one's
　EM$_{2aa}$(71)
voice to, give
　ET$_{0a}$(135)
void, declare
　EN$_{6e}$(79); NO$_{3bb}$(112)
void, declare an argument
　null and
　NO$_{3bb}$(112)
vote for so.
　WT$_2$·(119)

vouch
  $EN_{6d}(79); NO_{0f}(110)$
vouch for
  $WT_{4fg}(120); NO_1(111);$
  $IN_{9b}(147); KA_{2cb}(98);$
  $IN_{6c}(146)$
vow
  $NO_{0f}(110)$
vulgarize
  $TP_{2bbb}(165)$

W
wait
  $EN_{0ba}(74)$
wait for
  $EN_{0bb}(74); DE_{8a}(151)$
wait in the antechambers
  $KA_{2aa}(97)$
waive
  $KA_{-1d}(88); TU_3\text{"}(132);$
  $EN_{9h}\text{"}(84)$
waken so.
  $EN_{1aa}(74)$
wake (up) so.
  $EN_{1aa}(74)$
walk up to so.
  $EN_{7ab}(79)$
wall, run one's head against a brick
  $TV_6\text{'''}(160)$
wangle
  $KA_{4aa}(99)$
want
  $DE_{8b}(151); EN_{0ab}(74)$
want to contribute
  $DI_1(124)$
want to have
  $EN_{0ba}(74)$
want to have sth.
  $EN_{0ab}(74)$

want to participate
  $DI_1(124)$
war, declare
  $KA_{0g}(90)$
ward off
  $KA_{1bcb}(93);$
  $EN_{8ab}(82)$
warn
  $EN_{4b}(77); WT_{4a}(119)$
warning, give
  $NO_{0dd}(110); NO_{3ba}(111)$
warp
  $TP_{2be}(166)$
warrant
  $NO_1(111); NO_{0f}(110);$
  $EN_{6d}(79)$
war with one another, be at
  $KA_{-3c}(86); KA_{-3ca}(86)$
wash one's hands of
  $KA_{2d}(98)$
waste time gossiping
  $DI_{10}\text{"}(127)$
waste (words)
  $TP_{2ae}(164)$
watch for
  $EN_{0bb}(74)$
way, feel the
  $KA_{2aa}(96)$
way for, pave the
  $KA_{2aa}(96)$
way forward, feel one's
  $DI_1\text{.}(124)$
way, get one's own
  $KA_{0c}(89)$
way, give
  $KA_{1bbb}(92);$
  $KA_{3b}(99); KA_{-1d}(88)$
way into, worm one's
  $KA_{2aa}(97)$

way, let so have his own
  $NO_{0b}(108)$
way, lose one's
  $TV_6\text{'}_b(160)$
way, make one's
  $KA_{4ac}(100)$
way, show the
  $EN_{1ac}(74); EN_{6c}(79)$
way, speak in a beastly
  $DT_{1e}(128)$
way through, find one's
  $IN_{2a}\text{.}(143)$
way through, muddle one's
  $KA_{4ae}(101)$
way towards, feel one's
  $DI_1\text{.}(124)$
weaken
  $KA_{1bcd}(94);$
  $TO_{5c}(158)$
weaken an argument
  $NO_{6o}(114)$
wear away
  $AV_1(106)$
wear down
  $KA_{1aa}(91)$
wear out
  $KA_{4ac}(100)$
wear out an old horse
  $TP_{2be}(167)$
wear out (with, by)
  $KA_{1aa}(91)$
weather, forecast
  $ET/TE_c(138)$
weigh
  $DE_4(149); DE_{8c}(152);$

weigh (cont.)
  $KA_{4cdb}(105)$
weigh the factors
  $WT_3.(119)$
well, consider
  $EN_{9c}(83); EN_{9g}(83);$
  $NO_{2a}(111)$
well-disposed towards, be
  $KA_{4cca}(95)$
well, get on
  $KA_{4cca}(105);$
  $KA_{4caa}(102)$
well, hit it off
  $KA_{4caa}(103);$
  $KA_{-3b}(85)$
well together, get on
  $KA_{-3b}(85)$
well, turn out
  $EN_{9`a}(85)$
wheedle
  $EN_{7aa}(79); KA_{-2b}(87);$
  $WS_{bba}(123); KA_{2aa}(97)$
wheedle so. out of sth.
  $EN_{7ag}(80)$
whimper
  $EM_{2b}(71)$
whine
  $EM_{2k}(73); KA_{1caa}(94)$
whisper
  $VE_{1f}(148)$
whistle on, blow the
  $VE_{1b,c,d}(148)$
widen
  $TO_{2a}(155)$
will to
  $EN_{0ab}(74)$
win
  $KA_{4ac}(100)$

win back
  $KA_{1bcc}(94)$
wind out of so.'s sails, take the
  $KA_{1bbc}(92)$
wind up
  $TV_{7e}(161)$
wire, tap the
  $VE_{1``a}(148)$
wish
  $EN_{0ab}(74); DE_{8a}(151)$
wish so. evil
  $EM_{2ga}(72); EM_{2h}(73)$
wish sth. to happen to so.
  $NO_{8a}(116)$
wish that sth. happens
  $EN_{0aa}(74)$
wish to attack
  $KA_{-3c}(86); KA_{-3ca}(86)$
wish to do sth.
  $EN_{0aa}(74)$
wish to harm
  $KA_{-3c}(86); KA_{-3ca}(86)$
withdraw
  $KA_{3b}(99); KA_{4cba}(104);$
  $DI_3.(125); KA_{4bba}(102);$
  $EN_{6e}(79); IN_{9a}(146)$
withdraw from
  $KA_{4bac}(102);$
  $DI_{10}.(127);$
  $NO_{0db}(109)$
withdraw (from an engagement)
  $NO_{3ba}(111)$
withdraw one's aid
  $KA_{2d}(98)$
withdraw one's turn
  $TU_3.(132)$
withhold
  $TP_{2bg}(167)$

witness, confront
  $IN_{1ac}(142)$
witnesses, question
  $IN_{1ac}(142)$
witness to, bear
  $NO_{6da}(114)$
wittily, talk
  $IR_{1c}(130); DT_{1d}(128);$
  $DI_{7b}.(126)$
witty at another's expense, be
  $DT_{1d}(128)$
witty remarks, make
  $IR_{1c}(130); DT_{1d}(128)$
wonder (at)
  $DE_3(149)$
woo
  $NO_{-2§}(108); EN_{2b§}(75)$
wool, gather
  $DE_9(152)$
woolly manner, express os. in a
  $TP_{2bd}(166)$
word
  $ET/TE_{ac}(138)$
word, catch a
  $VE_{1``a}(147)$
word for, put in a good
  $KA_{2cb}(98)$
word in edgewise, not allow so. to get a
  $TU_2.(131)$
word, not break a
  $VE_1.(147)$
word of honor, give one's
  $NO_1(111); NO_{0f}(110);$
  $EN_{6d}(79)$

word, pick up a
  ET$_{1b}$(137)
word, pledge one's
  NO$_1$(111)
word, put in a
  TO$_{2bc}$(156)
word, repeat another's
  ET$_{1c}$(137)
words, be too spare
  with
  TP$_{2bi}$(167)
words, burst out
  with
  TU$_3$.(131)
words, coin
  ET/TE$_{ac}$(138)
words, economize
  TP$_{2ad}$(164)
words, get tied up in
  one's own
  TV$_6$...(160)
words, indulge in
  TP$_{2b}$(165)
words, lavish
  TP$_{2ae}$(164)
words, luxuriate in
  TP$_{2b}$(165)
words, overburden
  with big
  TP$_{2b}$(165)
words, overload with big
  TP$_{2b}$(165)
words, put into
  TO$_2$(155); ET/TE$_{ac}$(138);
  ET/TE$_{aa}$(138)
words sparingly, use
  TP$_{2ad}$(164)
words too sparingly, use
  TP$_{2bi}$(167)

words, use four-letter
  DT$_{1e}$(128)
words, waste
  TP$_{2ae}$(164)
words with, have
  KA$_{1da}$(96); KA$_{0g}$(89)
words with so., have
  KA$_{-1c}$(87); KA$_{-3c}$(86)
work at
  TO$_{2ba}$(155)
work backwards
  DE$_{6d}$(150)
workmen, lock out
  NO$_{8a}$(116)
work on so.
  KA$_{0c}$(89)
work out
  KA$_{2b}$(97); KA$_{1db}$(96);
  KA$_{4cac}$(103);
  KA$_{4cbc}$(104); TV$_{6a}$(159)
work through
  TV$_{6a}$(159)
worried, be
  EM$_{2cb}$(72)
worry
  EN$_{7d}$.(81)
worry so.
  KA$_{1aa}$(91)
worm one's way into
  KA$_{2aa}$(97)
worse instead of better,
  make
  ET/TE$_a$.(139)
worse, make
  ET/TE$_a$.(139)
worship
  WT$_{5d}$(121)
wrangle
  KA$_{1da}$(96); EM$_{2k}$(73);
  KA$_{0d}$(89)

wrap up
  KA$_{1bba}$(92)
wrest
  KA$_{4ab}$(99)
write
  ET/TE$_{ac}$(138)
write abstracts
  TE$_{-1b}$.(140)
write an essay,
  treaties
  ET/TE$_{ad}$(138)
write anonymously
  IN$_{6ac}$(145)
write down
  ET/TE$_{aa}$(138);
  ET/TE$_{ab}$(138)
write down
  experiences
  ET/TE$_{ad}$(138)
write off
  KA$_{2d}$(98)
write out
  ET/TE$_{aa}$(138)
write out sth. for so.
  ET$_{0dc}$(137)
write poetry
  ET/TE$_{ac}$(138)
write purple prose
  ET/TE$_b$(138)
write (text)
  ET/TE$_{aa}$(138)
write under a pseudonym
  IN$_{6ac}$(145)
writing, confirm in
  NO$_{0f}$(110); NO$_1$(111)
wrong, get so
  KA$_{-1c}$(87)

Y
yarns, spin
  $DE_9(152)$;
  $ET/TE_b(138)$;
  $TP_{2bj}(167)$
yell
  $DT_{1g}(128)$
yell at
  $WP_{0ad}(122)$

yell at so.
  $EM_{2j}(73); EM_{2e}(72)$
yes to, say
  $KA_{4cda}(105)$
yield
  $KA_{1bbb}(92)$;
  $KA_{2d}(98); KA_{-1d}(88)$
yielding, be
  $KA_{1cb}(95)$

younger, tell the
  $TE_{-2a}(139)$

Z
zoom in
  $TO_{5a}(158)$

G. Herdan

The Advanced Theory of Language as Choice and Chance

1966. 30 figures. XVI, 459 pages
(Kommunikation und Kybernetik in
Einzeldarstellungen, Band 4)
ISBN 3-540-03584-2

Contents: Introduction. – Language as Chance I – Statistical Linguistics. – Language as Choice I – Stylostatistics. – Language as Chance II – Optimal Systems of Language Structure. – Language as Choice II – Linguistic Duality. – Statistics for the Language Seminary. – Author Index. – Subject Index.

G. Hammarström

Linguistic Units and Items

1976. 17 figures. IX, 131 pages
(Communication and Cybernetics,
Volume 9)
ISBN 3-540-07241-1

Contents: Introduction. – Spoken Language. – Written Language. – Written Language in Relation to Spoken Language. – Spoken Language in Relation to Written Language. – The Tasks of Linguistics. – Bibliography. – Author Index. – Subject Index.

Springer-Verlag
Berlin
Heidelberg
New York

H. Hörmann
Psycholinguistics
An Introduction to Research and Theory
Translated from the German by H. H. Stern, P. Leppmann
2nd revised edition. 1979. 60 figures, 21 tables.
IX, 342 pages
ISBN 3-540-90417-4

„...provides a comprehensive introduction to the psychology of language by concentrating on the behaviourist conception...
the translation is written in a clear, concise and compact English...
The substance of this book, which has become a standard textbook in German as well as the brilliancy of its translation will certainly secure its position in the English speaking world as well." *IRAL (Deutschland)*

B. Malmberg
Structural Linguistics and Human Communication
An Introduction into the Mechanism of Language and the Methodology of Linguistics
Reprint of the 2nd revised edition
1976. 88 figures. VIII, 213 pages
(Kommunikation und Kybernetik in Einzeldarstellungen, Band 2)
ISBN 3-540-03888-4

Contents: Introduction. – Signs and Symbols. The Linguistic Sign. – The Communication Process. – Preliminary Expression Analysis. Acoustic and Physiological Variables. Information. – Segmentation. Forms of Expression. Oppositions and Distinctions. – Paradigmatic Structures. – Redundancy and Relevancy. Levels of Abstraction. – The Distinctive Feature Concept. The Binary Choice. – Syntagmatic Structures. Distribution and Probability. – Content Analysis. – The Functions of Language. – Perception and Linguistic Interpretation. – Primitive Structures and Defective Language. – Linguistic Change. – Bibliographical Notes. – Author Index. – Subject Index.

Springer-Verlag
Berlin
Heidelberg
NewYork

"A general survey of modern structural linguistics by B. Malmberg...
The book is essentially intended for the advanced student, but others will also find it useful, since the author manages to deal lucidly and intelligibly with a difficult subject." *The Years Work in English Studies*

OHIO UNIVERSITY LIBRARY

Please return this book as soon as you have finished with it. In order to avoid a fine it must be returned by the latest date stamped below.

QTR. LOAN
FEB 4 1983
MAR 3 0 1983

QTR. LOAN
MAY 23 1983

JUN 1 3 1983

QTR. LOAN
NOV 6 1983

DEC 2 9 1983

QTR. LOAN
JAN 2 0 1984

FEB 1 7 1984
QTR. LOAN
MAR 6 1984
MAR 2 7 1984

QTR. LOAN
APR 1 1 1984
JUN 2 5 1984

QTR. LOAN
NOV 2 3 1984
JAN 7 1985

QTR. LOAN
SEP 9 1986
AUG 2 5 1986
MAR 3 0 1987
MAR 3 1 1987

QUARTER LOAN
JAN 3 1989

JAN 3 1990

QUARTER LOAN
JUN 1 1 1984
MAR 2 1 1989

JUN 12 1994
QUARTER LOAN
JUN 1 2 1994

QUARTER LOAN
APR 0 6 1999

CF